VICTORIA HALL, HANLEY

THURSDAY, 19th FEBRUARY, '81
at 7.30 p.m.

M.C.P. presents

SLADE

PLUS SUPPORT

THIS PORTION TO BE RETAINED
BY THE STEWARD

Ticket Unreserved

£3.00 IN ADVANCE **£3.50** AT THE DOOR
(including V.A.T.)

№ 845

Official Merchandise is only on sale inside the Hall.

Cameras, Tape Recorders and Alcohol of any sort will not be allowed into the venue.

The Management reserve the right to refuse admission.

NO PASSOUTS

MIKE LLOYD (MUSIC) LTD.
15, Percy Street, Hanley 24641
23, High Street, Newcastle 610940
109, High Street, Tunstall 84660

New Victoria Theatre
WILTON ROAD, S.W.1
Telephone No. 834 0671
Manager: E. C. CARTER

MEL BUSH presents
SLADE + Support
E
SA
AF
S
£2·00

Y31

No ticket exchanged nor money refunded
This portion to be retained [P.T.O.

CITY HALL
Northumberland Road, Newcastle upon Tyne 1

Sunday, 8th May, 1977, at 7.30 p.m.

MEL BUSH ORGANIZATION
presents

SLADE
IN
CONCERT

AREA £1.00 SEAT EE 39

Booking Agents: City Hall Box Office
Northumberland Road, Newcastle upon Tyne (Tel. 20007)
This Portion to be retained.

SMITH PRINT GROUP

SUNDERLAND POLYTECHNIC STUDENTS' UNION

SLADE

in Concert at Wearmouth Hall
Saturday, 21st February. 1981

No Admission-Re-admission after 10.30 p.m.

Tickets Members £2.50
Non-Members £3.00
№ 811

WILD! WILD! WILD!

A PEOPLE'S HISTORY OF SLADE

Malcolm Wyatt

Spenwood Books
Manchester, UK

First published in Great Britain 2023
Spenwood Books Ltd, 2 College Street,
Higham Ferrers, NN10 8DZ

spenwoodbooks.com

A CIP record for this book is available from the
British Library

ISBN 978-1-915858-07-8

Printed in the Czech Republic via Akcent Media Limited

Design by Bruce Graham, The Night Owl

Front cover image: Getty/Gijsbert Hanekroot
Rear cover images: Steve Woodward, Richard Gomersall, John Barker,
Gwen Dale, Tom Saunders
End paper images: Steve Woodward, Stu Rutter, Bill Briceland, Nick
Latham, Simon Harvey, Peter Smith, Dylan White, Richard Gomersall,
Alun Perkins, Colin Grant

All other image copyrights: As captioned.

ACKNOWLEDGEMENTS

From the loyal fans who shared tales about seeing Slade numerous times, those who reported on key shows and those who attended more unlikely venues, I'm truly grateful for your contributions. The same goes for those who never got to see the band but still conveyed love for this amazing Black Country outfit – friends and new friends alike.

In particular, praise be to Slade historian Chris Selby for his hard graft down the years, digging out evidence of dates back to 1962, and answering my queries via phone and email. There's plenty online, and much of the credit needs to go his way.*

I've wallowed lately in my many Slade CDs and DVDs, including another *Slade in Flame* viewing (it gets better every time). But this is *A People's History* and I'm grateful for Dave Graham's Slade in England online content and his stories, and the fact that Stuart Rutter phoned in when I was on air at BBC Radio Lancashire as John Gillmore's guest, opening another invaluable communication channel. Thanks also to all on my contacts list who put pen to paper or phone to ear to talk Slade, and fellow fan turned publisher/editor Richard Houghton for having the faith to let me take control as this train kept-a-rollin' towards and beyond its deadline.

The North-East's own Dave Hill was integral on the Lindisfarne and Status Quo front, Matt Ingham and Maria Philippou approached several more interviewees and correspondents – including the wonderful Suzi Quatro and fellow legend Andy Scott – and Mark Baxter, Nick Clift, Carl Delahunty, Rob Kerford, Ferg and Gerry Ranson, and James Wallace need take a bow too.

As for Slade poet laureate Paul Cookson, Haircut One Hundred guitar supremo Graham Jones, master photographer Gered Mankowitz ('I don't take snaps, I paint with light!') and The South/Sunbirds' Phil Barton and Dave Hemingway, I thank you, as I do former *Lancashire Post* buddies Jude Dornan, Mike Hill and Dave Hurst. Thanks also to: Michael Parker for permission to quote from his blog sladestory.blogspot.com/1973/03/Wembley-empire-pool; Lenny Hartley aka Dug Timo; Andy Lindsay, Mod Shoes And 66 Clothing; Tony Beesley, Author/Publisher, Days Like Tomorrow Books; Ian Edmundson, Author: *The*

Noize – The Slade Discography & Slade: Six Years On The Road; Stuart Deabill, co-author, *Every Ticket Tells A Story, Thick As Thieves: Personal Situations With The Jam*; Mike Philpott, author, *Time's Gonna Make Me A Man Someday*; David Stark, author, *It's All Too Much: Adventures Of A Teenage Beatles Fan In The '60s And Beyond.*

And I know Richard Houghton would like to thank designer Bruce Graham and web wizard Bruce Koziarski. And his wife, Kate Sullivan. Everyday.

Putting so many hours in had a knock-on effect, so a huge grovelling thank you and much love to my better half, Jayne, taking on extra foster child-wrangling/domestic duties while I spent too many hours in front of my computer, descending rabbit holes and ironing out queries. Walking our Millie, the rescue lab-cross, helped my sanity, but in return she saw far too much of my back at times, and I've missed my gorgeous girls, Molly and Lottie, on the run-in.

Finally, love to sisters Sue, Jackie, Tracy and brother Mark for providing my essential early years soundtrack, our much-missed Mum and Dad for bringing us up proper, and Dave, Don, Jim and Noddy, the Black Country's finest, their down-to-earth charm shining through on these pages. What's more, while Don remains busy, he still agreed to a late chat – I'm truly not worthy! Keep on rockin', one and all.

All band quotes from the author's interviews with Dave Hill (December 2015, December 2018), Jim Lea (July 2018) and Don Powell (December 2017, December 2020, December 2022, May 2023) for www.writewyattuk.com, and Jude Dornan's *Lancashire Evening Post* interview with Noddy Holder from May 2013 (with permission).

* Incidentally, the afternoon I was born in late October 1967, The 'N Betweens were off to The Greenway pub on the Miners' Estate, Baddeley Green, Stoke-on-Trent, not so far far away from their own roots but a world away from mine. And that's just one example of the amazing detail out there these days, courtesy of Chris Selby.

ABOUT THE AUTHOR

Surrey-born Malcolm Wyatt is a music writer, editor and Slade fan who lives in Leyland, Lancashire with his partner, Jayne. A foster carer with two grown-up daughters, he is the author of *This Day in Music's Guide to The Clash (2018)* and regularly publishes feature interviews on his website at www.writewyatt.com.

When not walking his beloved rescue Labrador-cross Millie, his spare time is spent catching up with family and friends, supporting Woking FC and planning the next big move to Cornwall. He can be contacted at thedayiwasthere@gmail.com.

Photo: Gered Mankowitz © Iconic Images Ltd 2023

Slade captured by Gered Mankowitz for 1976's *Nobody's Fools* album, but EMI overruled his choice of image

Slade were the complete package. Not only did they write the material, they looked the business and outperformed anybody else on the bill. They weren't trendy. They were just there, and they were in your face. They were sort of unique.

Gered Mankowitz, photographer

In The Stranglers we did do a Slade song a few times, when we had to learn cover versions in the early days. I don't know what song it was… They were a gritty rock 'n' roll band, they wrote some good songs and they were from around Wolverhampton, which was where my mother came from.

Hugh Cornwell

I've always been attracted to music that has loads of energy in it. And no one can take that away from Slade. They were like a bolt of lightning.

Pauline Black, The Selecter

FOREWORD

Most of us musicians who started having hits in the Seventies were learning how to play in the Sixties, which was the golden era for acquiring your 'chops', playing shows in every bar, on every gymnasium floor, every seedy club, anywhere and everywhere gigging was a possibility. There is no substitute for learning your craft this way, it's the only way. By the time the hits started rolling in, we were ready for it. Boy oh boy were we ready for it.

I was discovered in 1971, in Detroit by Mickie Most, who had come to record at Motown Studios with Jeff Beck and Cozy Powell. My brother had gotten wind of this and convinced all three of them to come down and see the band I was in, the second wave of The Pleasure Seekers, called Cradle. Mickie offered me a solo contract and I relocated to the UK in October of that year. I have been here ever since.

I spent around 15 months kicking my heels, living in a tiny room in a hotel on Cromwell Road, recording, recording, and recording, but nothing was happening. Finally, I told Mickie I needed a band. I was going stir crazy. So, I found my musicians and we started to do all my own compositions and toured the college circuit.

Mickie asked his friend Chas Chandler, the bass player from The Animals, who he had produced many hits for and was now producing Slade, if he could add me to the programme on their first international UK tour. I had 15 minutes at the start of the show, followed by Thin Lizzy and headliners Slade.

I watched the venues erupt every night as they played their numerous hits. Coming from Detroit I have an uncompromising opinion of what a good rock 'n' roll band should sound and look like. Slade fit the bill.

The flamboyant Dave Hill (who broke his ankle during the tour and had to finish it sitting on a throne, which I am sure he secretly liked), multi-talented musician, bass player Jimmy Lea with his melodic lines, Noddy, front man supremo, and my buddy to this day, Don Powell. The entire tour was a joy to be on and I treasure the memories. Love you guys.

This was November or December 1972, and by May 1973, I had my first No.1 with 'Can The Can'. Also, Don Powell, Andy Scott (lead guitarist from Sweet) and myself actually made an album together in 2017 called Quatro, Scott and Powell, which got to No.16 in Australia.

God bless rock 'n' roll and all of us who sail in her.

SUZI QUATRO

Photo: Dick Barnatt

I first encountered Slade on a Caribbean Island in 1967. I was with The Elastic Band and they were called The 'N Betweens. There were two nightclubs on Grand Bahama. We played in one and they were in the other. So I guess that makes Don Powell my oldest musician friend, beating Mick Box (of Uriah Heep) by a few months.

Flash forward to 1971 and now I'm the guitarist with Sweet and the same four guys are now Slade. Imagine arriving at *Top of the Pops* and then to look across from our stage to theirs. I thought, 'Didn't we do well!'

During that period in the 1970s, Slade and Sweet (and T.Rex) were never off the box, and here we are more than 50 years on, true legends, with our music still relevant today.

Lads, I salute you!

ANDY SCOTT, SWEET

INTRODUCTION

So you think we had a lazy time, well you should know better…

It all started in suburban Surrey for me, 150 miles and a world away from The Trumpet in Bilston, in the small bedroom of a council house in the idyllic rural setting of Shalford, near Guildford. I was barely four when 'Coz I Luv You' became Slade's first UK chart-topper, I turned five as 'Mama Weer All Crazee Now' had its ninth week in the Top 40, and I was six when 'Merry Xmas Everybody' became their third 45 to go straight in at No.1, but Slade were already my band by then, albeit shared with brother Mark, seven years older.

He was a fortnight off his teens when 'Cum On Feel The Noize' did the same earlier that year. And while I wasn't on the field with his mates at Tillingbourne School as Johnnie Walker announced that momentous feat, I felt I was in later years, Mark's tale increasingly spectacular with every re-telling.

All 17 Slade Top 20 hits from 1971 through to 1976 will forever be steeped in nostalgia for this fan-boy, and it's hard to convey my sense of wonder at getting to interview Dave, Don and Jim in recent years. Slade forever Take Me Bak 'Ome to idyllic days when the youngest of five kids dipped between David Essex, Hot Chocolate, Bay City Rollers, Pilot and ABBA in my sisters' bedroom and The Beatles and Slade in ours. And while Dad had no time for all that racket (he preferred massed military bands quick marching at Wembley tattoos), Mum appreciated those Holder/Lea ballads, and we caught most of those iconic *Top of the Pops* appearances, this lad sold on the Glam pop/rock dream. So imagine my delight at Suzi Quatro and Sweet's Andy Scott contributing forewords here.

In time, punk and new wave rocked my brother's world and mine, but as the Walker Brothers put it in late '65 – while the 'N Betweens toiled away in Dortmund and Witten – 'You were my first love, and first love never ever dies.' What's more, many of those who came through afterwards later acknowledged a debt to Slade, even if Bowie, Bolan, Mott and Roxy got more kudos.

Mark was there with schoolmate Alan as Slade played Surrey Uni on my 11th birthday in '78 (telling me he caught H – his hair growing back under a bandana – with a flying bog roll) and again in early '81, and I joined them on 18th December '82 for my first London gig.

Heading up by train, Hammersmith bound, that night is sketchy and vivid in equal measures. Barely 15, I shouldn't have touched the ale, but the occasion commanded it, the Britannia across the road, a motley mix of hippies, rockers, skins, punks and new wavers creating a cracking pre-gig vibe. The first series of *The Young Ones* had just aired, and it seemed I was living it. A ginger-haired guy led the choir, his voice strong enough to secure the gig if Noddy rung in sick; a biker on the balcony poured beer on a stranger's head below (getting little more aggro than a few swear-words); and a Vyvyan-like skinhead commanded, 'Oi, hippie, buy me a pint!' and his brazen request was granted.

At the Odeon, the absolute power certainly registered, as did the sight of Santa-suited Nod and his scantily-clad elves for the inevitable 'MXE' encore. My evening caught up with me on a packed Tube jolting back towards Waterloo, but what a night. And thankfully there are more in-depth recollections for that show and many more within this publication.

Memories play tricks and it didn't always quite happen the way we recall it, a few entries here differing from others. But who's to say what's right. Besides, we've all slept a few times since, our versions evolving over time. The point is that most of these accounts nail Slade's phenomenal live splendour and spirit. Those hours put in since the early Sixties clearly paid off.

As for the band, there were major ups and downs, but it's about how you ride them when the whole world's going crazee. In the UK in the 1970s, there was no bigger band, yet six No.1 singles, three consecutive No.1 albums, 17 straight Top 20 singles and eight Top 20 LPs don't tell the whole story. And from Nod's wondrous voice and showmanship to Jim's studio/stagecraft and genius, H's guitar mastery, unique style and glitz, and Don's dependable drumming and utter cool, they were the full package and deserve all the praise coming their way across these pages.

Malcolm Wyatt
Leyland, Lancashire
June 2023

4 APRIL 1946

David John Hill (Dave) born in Holbeton, Devon.

15 JUNE 1946

Neville John Holder (Noddy) born in Walsall, Staffordshire.

10 SEPTEMBER 1946

Donald George Powell (Don) born in Bilston, Staffordshire.

14 JUNE 1949

James Whild Lea (Jim) born in Wolverhampton, Staffordshire.

1953

Neville Holder makes his performing debut, aged seven, at Walsall Labour Club, singing Frankie Laine's 'I Believe', the year a boy in his class gave him the nickname that stuck, 'Noddy'.

1958

At Christmas, Noddy – saving up for a while, his window-cleaning round money mostly spent on records – receives his first guitar from his parents, Walsall jazz guitarist Freddie Degville soon giving him lessons.

1960

Having learned to play drums with the Boy Scouts, Don is recruited by vocalist Johnny Howells and guitarist Mick Marson to The Vendors, playing popular hits on the Black Country youth/social club and party circuit.

I was a member of this youth club, and Johnny and Mick from The Vendors came down, asking me to join. I hadn't a clue about anything, but borrowed some drums off a schoolmate, Dave Bowdley. I don't think he had them back for about five years! Come to think of it, I don't know what happened to those. **Don Powell**

Dave buys his first guitar, going halves with his dad, his money earned from a paper-round. Arriving in a cardboard box, the left-hander plays it upside down. After his first lessons, he forms The Young Ones with schoolfriends, making their live debut at the Victory Club in Lower Penn, south Staffordshire.

I found a cheap guitar out of a Kay's catalogue… when I wasn't very good at school. (Science teacher Brian Close) told me it was dreadful, and I needed something better. He was a jazz guitarist. I'd go around his house and sit there with a sheet of music. One of the first pieces I learned was 'Tell Laura I Love Her'… I was left-handed and had my guitar upside down. He told me, 'You can't have it that way! You'll have to play it right-handed. You'll get used to it.' **Dave Hill**

1961

Jim, having passed his violin exams with distinction a year before, joins the Staffordshire Youth Orchestra.

I was born a month late – I must have been gripping on the womb walls. I was reluctant even then! My mum said when I was about nine, 'Your grandmother and I have been wondering if you might want to play violin.' I wasn't bothered, really, but went along for lessons and kind of picked it up. But I always felt a bit out of place there, listening to John Mayall and the Bluesbreakers, and The Yardbirds – a bit of Clapton – thinking, 'How does he get his guitar to sound like a violin? He was really the first in Britain who was able to bend strings to play the blues. I didn't know anything about that. **Jim Lea**

1962

Noddy plays his first dates in schoolboy rock 'n' roll covers quintet The Phantoms, in Bloxwich, Walsall, while Dave's band have become The Sundowners (with several variations) and Don is increasingly busy with The Vendors.

We were just miming along to three or four songs (at Saturday morning matinees at a local cinema). Then John came to us and said, 'I've got us a gig, we're playing this wedding reception… and we're gonna get paid!' I looked at him, said, 'We're gonna get paid for this?' We were getting £6 – £2 each. That was incredible. We could have a bag of chips each! Then we were just sort of gigging, local pubs and clubs. One of the kids in another part of the factory (where I worked) saw us the night before in a local battle of the bands, telling my boss. But he just said, 'You never told me you were in a band.' He was great and if need be, he'd let me finish early, the van picking me up outside the factory. **Don Powell**

JUNE 1963

Dave joins Don in The Vendors, playing Eddie Cochran, Buddy Holly and Gene Vincent covers.

SEPTEMBER 1963

Noddy's band, now The Rockin' Phantoms, become regulars on the Black Country circuit.

THREE MEN IN A BOAT

JANUARY 1964, BLOXWICH, UK

Dave and Don's first gig together.

MAY 1964

Noddy's band become the Memphis Cut-Outs, but he is recruited to Steve Brett's backing band, The Mavericks, by early September.

SHIP & RAINBOW

8 NOVEMBER 1964, WOLVERHAMPTON, UK

The Vendors appear as The 'N Betweens for the first time.

I wasn't fully grown, looking like a child, with rosy cheeks and a bass as big as me and in the Sixties you couldn't go into pubs if you were a child... But I went to see a concert where the 'N Betweens were playing. They were really fantastic. And the backing sounded like The Undertones. I always felt when 'Teenage Kicks' came on the radio, it sounded like the early 'N Betweens. **Jim Lea**

WILLENHALL YOUTH CLUB

3 JANUARY 1966, WILLENHALL, UK

I WAS THERE: ROG WARD

I used to go to a youth club in Willenhall in the West Midlands. They would cover over the swimming pool when they put on concerts. Cream, the Spencer Davis Group and the Hollies all played there. And the 'N Betweens, who later became Slade, rehearsed at the club and did concerts for us. They had the original line-up, before Noddy Holder and Jimmy Lea joined. Only Dave Hill and Don Powell carried on, renaming the band Ambrose Slade, dropping Ambrose later.

Rog Ward saw The 'N Betweens at his local youth club

BLUE FLAME CLUB

12 FEBRUARY 1966, WOLVERHAMPTON, UK

Having turned pro in March '65, with their first overseas dates the following autumn, when Dave and Don meet Noddy en route to separate dates in Germany, The 'N Betweens advertise in the Wolverhampton *Express & Star* for a new bass player after Cass Jones decides to leave. Jim Lea auditions.

I went along with no equipment, my bass in a polythene bag, and was the last to be auditioned. I walked into the Blue Flame club and they were on stage, and there was a guy who looked like a blond Mick Jagger playing, and singing 'My Girl'. It sounded fantastic. I was thinking, 'Oh my God!' He went home, but unbeknown to me they told him he'd got the job. Then I walked up there. Don told me later, 'We looked out there and said, 'Is there anybody else out there?'' When you've got the lights on stage, all you can see is that and anyone right down the front. He was told, 'There's a little kid out there with a bass as big as him, in a polythene bag. And they agreed, 'We'll get him up and let him play a song, then we'll send him home.' Of course, they didn't reckon with what they were going to get!

Dave broke a string and Don said, 'Hey mate, come over here.' He's got this quick wit and he said, 'It says here you play the violin, is that right?' I said 'yeah' and he said, 'Do you play anything else?' I said, 'Well, a bit of piano and err...' and I just lied and said, 'Oh, and the cello', which I'd never even played. He said, 'Ooh, cello as well?' and I said, 'Well, I didn't get very far with that.' And he said, 'Did the spike keep sticking in your neck?'

Then Dave said, 'Hey mate, we're just going to check out this string, and it'll be you and me playing – quiet, no band. I wanna see if you're bluffing, 'cos you play really fast. But then, I think I was auditioning Dave rather than the other way around. **Jim Lea**

BEATTIE'S COFFEE BAR
WOLVERHAMPTON, UK

Having announced that he was quitting The Mavericks at Christmas, Noddy meets Dave and Don and is told about their new bass guitarist.

THREE MEN IN A BOAT
MARCH 1966, WOLVERHAMPTON, UK

Nod rehearses with the 'N Betweens.

They said, 'We want to form a brand-new band doing different sorts of material, would you be interested?' I said, 'Yeah, I'll have a rehearsal and see how it goes.' I wouldn't say it was fantastic right from the off. We put a lot of work in. But you know there's a certain magic and even a certain sound there that you seem to be creating for the first time. And I think it was in the style we played, because we all came from very different backgrounds. **Noddy Holder**

We'd already recruited Jim Lea but had this rehearsal in the pub opposite, where Nod lived with his mum and dad, the Three Men and a Boat… The first song we played was something we knew and (which) Nod was playing with his band, 'Mr Pitiful' by Otis Redding. And it worked straight away. We just looked at each other, started laughing, and just went into other things the four of us knew. It worked so well, and we thought, 'This is it, this is the one!' **Don Powell**

TOWN HALL

19 MARCH 1966, WALSALL, UK

With Mick Marson gone, Noddy joins the 'N Betweens.

LOCARNO BALLROOM

25 JUNE 1966, SWINDON, UK

Johnny Howells leaves the 'N Betweens.

When he left we were going to ask Robert (Plant) to join us. I haven't seen him for a while, but we used to bump into one another all the time, especially in America. The last time I saw Zeppelin play, it was at Earl's Court, and he said, 'I'm going to do a song now for my ex-roadie, Noddy Holder,' and he did 'Kashmir', knowing I love that song.' **Noddy Holder**

It was very sad when Dave and myself decided to make the break. It was very hard, because I'd started with Johnny and Mick. But while I haven't seen Johnny for a few years, me and Mick often see each other and have a laugh. **Don Powell**

SILVER BLADES

26 JUNE 1966, BIRMINGHAM, UK

The classic Holder, Lea, Hill and Powell four-piece step out for the first time.

STAR PALAST

7, 8 & 11-16 JULY 1966, KIEL, GERMANY

The 'N Betweens share a bill with Paul Raven, later known as Gary Glitter.

We were playing eight hours a night – 45 minutes on, 15 off, starting about eight o'clock, going on 'til four in the morning. But that's the way it was in those days. **Don Powell**

ABBEY ROAD STUDIOS

1967, LONDON, UK

After a local hit with a cover of 'You Better Run', The 'N Betweens make a demo at Abbey Road Studios while The Beatles are in residence working on *Sgt Pepper's Lonely Hearts Club* Band. The demo comes to nothing, but the band remain determined to build on their live reputation with shows in Scotland and locally, helped by dates with Cream, Graham Bond, Jimmy Cliff, The Mindbenders, John Mayall and Zoot Money.

TROPICANA CLUB

MAY 1968, FREEPORT, GRAND BAHAMA

A month-long residency at the Tropicana Club in the Bahamas proves to be far from the paradise expected and is extended to three months due to an unpaid hotel bill. The band part company with their agents on their return, going to Jack Baverstock, head of A&R at Philips.

That really brought us together – our four personalities. We were stuck with an incredible hotel bill, which we didn't realise we were going to pay for, and no money. All we had were our return flights, and our equipment as excess baggage. We were still paying for it. We couldn't leave that. It was on HP. We had to get that back. **Don Powell**

BEGINNINGS RELEASED 9 MAY 1969

The debut album by Ambrose Slade, as they are now known, features a photo of the band on Pouk Hill in Walsall, close to Noddy Holder's home. The LP sinks without trace, but former Animals bassist and Jimi Hendrix manager Chas Chandler sees the band at Rasputin's in New Bond Street, London and offers to manage them, rebranding them with their skinhead look.

I WAS THERE: IAN ASHLEIGH

A growing reputation in the Wolverhampton area led to Ambrose Slade's 1969 debut LP, *Beginnings* (in the USA, *Ballzy*, with Slade's trademark deliberate misspelling). As a first album, with four original compositions and eight covers, it didn't set the world alight, with too many different styles on show. It did, however, point towards the potential the future held, highlights including that fine cover of 'Born To Be Wild' with which they closed their live shows, while I commend the Holder and Lea-penned 'Pity The Mother' as an early example of the duo's songwriting skills. Looking at the plight of a mother widowed by war, there's possibly an element of Holder and/or Lea's own childhood in it. It's quite unlike what was to follow. 'Mad Dog Cole', credited to the whole band, is a stomper of an instrumental.

I WAS THERE: GERED MANKOWITZ, PHOTOGRAPHER

I was doing work for Rik and John Gunnell. They managed bands and I'm sure Chas was involved in some way. He asked me to photograph Hendrix, and we remained in touch. I photographed other artists for him, and then he approached me to photograph Ambrose Slade, in, I guess, '69. They were quite independent in their thinking, even then. And Dave was very opinionated, very full of himself.

Gered Mankowitz got to know Slade famously

Chas rang and said, after I'd done either the first or second Ambrose Slade session, 'You better get back here… quick,' so I did and we did the skinhead session. The thing is, they were so sweet looking… Don was possibly the hardest looking, but they just looked sweet. And Dave, he looked like a baby. They certainly didn't look hard, but I guess with the music and the boots and stomping around on stage, it tapped into that skinhead vibe. With the beat, the raucousness, and the quality of the band, they were something to watch.

GEORGE HOTEL
20 OCTOBER 1969, WALSALL, UK

I WAS THERE: PETER BIRKETT

I used to go see them before they were famous in the George Hotel, Walsall. I worked at Albert Jagger's in Walsall. He worked in export and I worked home trade. I know we chatted a few times, but I can't remember what about.

'WILD WINDS ARE BLOWING' RELEASED
24 OCTOBER 1969

The band's new single is credited to 'The Slade'.

MOSSLEY YOUTH CLUB/ BLOXWICH BATHS
NOVEMBER 1969, WALSALL, UK

I WAS THERE: BRIAN WAIN

I saw them first when they played Mossley Youth Club, and later Bloxwich

Swimming Baths. I started going to the youth club in Bloxwich when I was 13 or 14. I lived in Short Heath, Willenhall, and it was quite a trek to get there. I went with a guy called Micky Carter who went to my school and who lived in that direction. We'd meet a couple of lads off the Mossley estate there. I loved it. There were discos most nights, and in the club you had pinball machines. Every Friday was band night, with a different group each week. One Friday, this band turned up and filled the floor to the ceiling with speakers, and boy, were they loud. We loved them, although I lost my hearing. The place rocked, and I just fell in love with them. I think they were Ambrose Slade then. A couple of months later, we saw them at Bloxwich Baths, where they used to cover the swimming pool over with wooden boards. They were that loud that the boards bounced! I think I saw them at Willenhall Baths too. Same deal – they covered the pool over. I followed them through their skinhead phase on to the glam rock days, and in all fairness the music never changed – just a great mixture of rock 'n' roll with fab lyrics. As an add-on, Dave Hill lived where my wife lived, on the Warstones Estate in Wolverhampton.

CHELSEA COLLEGE

15 NOVEMBER 1969, LONDON, UK

The gig is cancelled due to the fear of violence as a result of Slade's skinhead following.

The Skinhead cult is alive and well and flourishing throughout the country. Perhaps nowhere can the cult be seen to better advantage and displaying all the true cultural heritage it has bought to these shores than at The Shed in Chelsea football ground. And this Saturday should mark something of an occasion in the Skinhead calendar. For not only are Chelsea at home to Everton, but the Skinhead pop group 'Slade' will be at the Chelsea College in Manresa Road in the evening. So once more, as the plaintive cry of 'Aggro' rings throughout Chelsea football ground, 'Slade' will know they are amongst friends. The Gods will have at last found a resting place… and the police will have found they have another busy night. **Kensington Post**

ALDRIDGE COMMUNITY CENTRE
11 JANUARY 1970, WALSALL, UK

I WAS THERE: CHRIS SELBY

In September 1969 I transferred from Junior School to big school. Frank F Harrison Comprehensive was almost exactly midway between the estate I lived on, Dudley's Fields, and, as I would find out later, Noddy Holder's estate, Beechdale. Bloxwich was a small village, so to any eleven-year-old, Walsall was the place to go to. To get there, the No.33 bus was used. It went via Beechdale.

One day a gang of us decided to go to Walsall, and as we got close to the Three Men in a Boat pub, I saw a group of skinheads. My memory says there were four of them, but it could have been two. Someone on the bus said they were a pop group called Slade and one of them was named Noddy Holder, which caused a certain amount of sniggering. I thought no more of it other than remembering that there were skinheads local to me.

In January 1970, one of my friends said that the skinhead group were playing at Aldridge Community Centre and did we fancy going. With all the bravura of a twelve-year-old, I said yes. I didn't really know where Aldridge was or how to get to it, but the decision was taken to go.

So our intrepid band set off. We walked. I have no idea which way we went or how long it took to get there... too long, I think. Everyone was older than us and we stood at the back of the hall. I can't remember what songs they played but they were extraordinarily loud, not school disco loud but slam-against-the-wall loud. One of the group played the violin and the singer sang louder than anyone else. Incredible. A life-changing moment. I know we didn't stay until the end because we were at school the next morning.

Over the next few months, I saw them as many times as possible. Records were obtained and any mention in the local newspapers was a bonus. I lost them in 1971 when they became national property.

LAMLASH HALL
27 SEPTEMBER 1970, ISLE OF ARRAN, UK

I WAS THERE: DUG TIMO

September weekend was the third weekend of September and a public holiday in Glasgow and most of west central Scotland. Arran was very popular with the Glasgow crowd and the island would be overflowing with a mass of humanity. After September Weekend, the island went into hibernation until Easter weekend, when the crowds in those pre-package holiday days would return. Arran saw many top bands play in the late Sixties and early Seventies, such as the Kinks, the Foundations, the Sensational Alex Harvey Band, Nazareth, Thin Lizzy – and Slade.

Ambrose Slade played Brodick Hall in 1969 and came with a reputation as worth seeing, although we were not prepared for the skinheads that appeared on stage. I just remember being blown away by them. For the 1970 September Weekend, Slade were playing the three main villages on the island; Friday in Brodick, Saturday Whiting Bay and Lamlash on the Sunday night, supporting the supergroup Blodwyn Pig. A local film director, Mike Alexander, who did work for the BBC, produced a documentary on the September Weekend called *Friday, Saturday, Sunday.* They filmed in Lamlash Hall but only got a short segment before the camera packed up due to humidity. A guy I knew who worked on the gate that night says they took fifteen hundred pounds, not bad for a £1 a ticket and a hall capacity of around 500! I just remember it being so cramped you could not move and being very hot. Oh, and a bird getting her tits out on the stage with Blodwyn Pig. Quite a thing when you were fifteen!

PLAY IT LOUD RELEASED
28 NOVEMBER 1970

Don and Jim are the main songwriters, credited for the nine originals of the twelve tracks on *Play It Loud.*

Me and Jim basically wrote that album, but when Nod and Jim came up with 'Coz I Luv You', we realised they could do it. And it just worked out they could do it quicker and better, so soon enough I handed over to them. **Don Powell**

GREAT HALL, COLLEGE OF ART & TECHNOLOGY

4 DECEMBER 1970, DERBY, UK

I WAS THERE: RICHARD COX

I first met Slade in early December 1970 at a Derby College of Art & Technology gig. We became friends pretty much immediately. Jim Lea told Dave Kemp he remembers me because I was one of the few journos on a local music page who wrote about the music rather than the outfits. You'll find my name on the sleeve of the *Slade Alive!* album. The band came back to my flat afterwards and we sat on the floor and chatted. I was invited to the Great Western Festival at Bardney and went to the Slade caravan, where actress Julie Ege was drinking heavily. We stood in the press area and watched Slade take control of that prog rock crowd within two or three bars.

Earlier that year, Slade played Lanchester College, where Chuck Berry recorded the live 'My Ding-a-Ling'. Apart from the band and Chas Chandler (an absolute gent – but I was press and would never cross him!), the key person was Swinn, who always looked after me and made sure I was able to take up the band's invite to join them backstage pre-gigs. Heady days.

GALA BALLROOM

13 MARCH 1971, NORWICH, UK

I WAS THERE: JOHN CONLIN

I saw them a few times at the Gala in Norwich. They were skinheads then; the Gala was a great skinhead venue. I remember they came on stage and took the piss, because their team (Wolves) had beaten us

(Norwich City) at football. They then had to run off stage as they had beer mugs thrown at them. They came back on, only for the same thing to happen again. One beer mug hit the drum and came back into the crowd and smacked into someone's face. It was a right mess. They played Norwich a lot, even when they became more famous and were no longer dressed as skinheads, playing bigger venues like the Melody Rooms.

TEMPLE CLUB

19 MARCH 1971, TEMPLE, LONDON, UK

I WAS THERE: MARTIN O'REGAN

I saw them in the Temple Club near Temple tube station in London, an all-night club opening at midnight and closing at 6am. It was in a basement, and loads of people took drugs down there. I never touched them myself, although I had a funny experience being offered speed by a couple of girls there. They told me it would keep me awake through the night. The last I saw of them, they were asleep on the floor. I was still dancing.

BASILDON ARTS CENTRE

14 MAY 1971, BASILDON, UK

I WAS THERE: BOB RAIKES

I was living near Brentwood in Essex and went to see Barclay James Harvest in Basildon. When we got to the gig, we heard that the singer was ill. The substitute band was Slade. I'd heard the name. They had been associated with the skinhead movement, and I wasn't keen on them. We weren't sure about watching them, but we'd made the journey, it was a bit late to find another event and it was Saturday night, so we thought we'd go in. I think they played their first big hit, 'Get Down And Get With It', but I can't be absolutely sure. They were just transitioning from skinheads to rockers. They were very loud, but very tight as a band, and played mainly what was then called R&B. It was obvious that Noddy

Holder had a real presence on stage, and Dave Hill could play a mean guitar. Their dress was not the full Glam Rock set up that they later adopted. They were a very, very fine live band!

'GET DOWN AND GET WITH IT'
RELEASED 21 MAY 1971

Slade's first chart single reaches No. 16.

I WAS THERE: CLAIRE MELHADO

1971 was a pivotal year for music and momentous for me, as it was the year I turned 13. I was experimenting with and developing my own sense of style, and music was a large part of that. My brothers and I had been brought up listening to all kinds of music, and as I approached my teenage years, I was searching for sounds that captured who I was. Not the music of the 1960s, or the prog rock my older brother was into, but something I could call my own.

The year 1971 was a momentous one for Claire Templeton, as she was then, and Slade

The thumping, stomping sound of 'Get Down And Get With It', with Noddy Holder's raucous call demanding a response, caught my mood exactly. And it was short, sweet and straight to the point, in direct contrast to the long ramblings of my brother's music, which made it all the more exciting. So much was happening that year. So many different styles and sounds – it felt anything was possible. I'd never heard anything quite like Slade, and this song with its links back to the era of rock 'n' roll but with an exciting 1970s vibe opened up such a huge sense of possibility and opportunity. It demanded attention and I absolutely loved it.

When they followed it up with 'Coz I Luv You', with Jimmy Lea playing violin, it cemented their individual and exciting sound. A violin on a pop song seemed unreal, especially to my brother, who was learning to play one! How cool this sound was compared to the screeching sounds that came from his bedroom door every evening.

As Slade's sound developed, along with their trademark title misspellings, my tastes moved to Bowie and Bolan. Slade at that time appealed to the skinheads and the following on the streets of Kenton in Newcastle, where I grew up, was huge; but I was too timid and too much of a loner to adopt the uniform. The lads with their eight-hole, highly polished, ox-blood Dr Martens symbolised the anti-establishment vibe of Slade.

I preferred the individuality of Glam, so I was always interested in what Dave Hill wore, and *Top of the Pops* was essential viewing, not just for the music. His outlandish looks and enormous platforms were more aligned with the Glam style, and this gave Slade a foot in both camps, not least because they didn't like the association with the bovver boys of the time. As they continued releasing hit after hit, it seemed they couldn't put a foot wrong. They were joyful and fun. Those deliberate misspellings were playful. Their Christmas 1973 hit was fantastic and still, 50 years later, sends a familiar shiver whenever I hear those famous opening bars.

WHITING BAY

29 – 31 JULY 1971, ISLE OF ARRAN, UK

I WAS THERE: ALISTAIR MUTCH, AGE 15

In the summer of 1971, I was working for my father. We lived at Brodick on the Isle of Arran, which had a thriving live music scene in those days. Three villages close together on the east side of the island each had a village hall, and bands would play each in turn across a weekend, with a ready-made audience thanks to the large number of young people who came for summer work in the many hotels, plus those who came across on holidays. A particular favourite of mine was Glasgow band Tear Gas, who played *very* loud. They had a couple of albums out of their own material, one of which, *Piggy Go Getter*, I got on Virgin mail order. One extraordinary gig was when they were joined halfway through their set by a much older, frankly rather scary-looking Glaswegian singer. He proceeded to sing in a fairly menacing fashion about seedy goings on in the docks. This was Alex Harvey, trying out Tear Gas as his new band, who in due course became the Sensational Alex Harvey Band and went on to much bigger things.

Another firm Arran favourite was Slade. My memories of their Arran gig, just before they too really hit the big time, was actually of their support band, the Dundee-based Sleaz Band. A fairly standard blues rock outfit, what sticks in my mind is that the bass player was out of his head on something and clearly unable to hold a tune, even though he continued to try. I recall him being carried off upright, still with bass in hand, and being replaced by Jim Lea who played on at least one song, their cover of 'Crossroads'. Jim, of course, made a fantastic difference to the performance. Slade I just recall as being full of energy – and very loud!

I missed them when they played a mini-festival in the next village with Thin Lizzy and Nazareth. I was too young to be allowed to go. But I did see Thin Lizzy.

I WAS THERE: BARBARA READ

They played on Arran not long before they became famous, staying at my mum and dad's B&B. My claim to fame is that they babysat me and my cousin.

I WAS THERE: BILL BRICELAND

Slade played Arran and Ayrshire quite a lot under the names 'N Betweens and Ambrose Slade, and then eventually Slade.

'COZ I LUV YOU' RELEASED 8 OCTOBER 1971

Slade's second charting single reaches No.1 and begins a run of 12 successive Top Ten singles. 'Coz I Luv You' is knocked off in half an hour by Nod and Jim, inspiring a writing partnership that continues throughout Slade's career, the added

Bill Briceland recalls Slade playing on Arran several times

clapping, boot-stomping and misspelled title becoming trademarks. A Top of the Pops *performance propels it to No.1 by early November, staying there for four weeks, spending eight weeks in the top ten.*

There was an awful lot going on. We'd already been in the ballpark a long time, but by the time we started to score a goal – as in our first hit with 'Get Down And Get With It', and with 'Coz I Luv You' reaching No.1 – we were everywhere. **Dave Hill**

I WAS THERE: ADRIAN BOWD

I was hooked on Slade as soon as I heard their first No.1, 'Coz I Luv You', with that great heavy bass beat, Noddy's unusual but fantastic voice, and then they put a violin into the mix. What a stroke of genius that was! When I was working as a mechanic in a Royal Mail motor transport workshop in Canterbury in the early Seventies, the radio was always on, and when a Slade number came on, nearly everyone used to sing along. They were so joyful and catchy, songs such as 'Cum On Feel The Noize', 'Mama Weer All Crazee Now', and much later, 'My Oh My'. They just had that ability to get everyone going. Remembering those songs now puts a smile on my face. They've stood the test of time. Slip the odd Slade song into a present-day radio show, and it always goes down well. And come the end of the year, it's never Christmas until Noddy says it is!

Adrian Bowd channels his inner Don Powell on 'drums' as an apprentice at a garage in Canterbury in the late Sixties, as the 'N Betweens were learning their trade

I WAS THERE: GINI COMYNS

I remember Slade in late 1971 when I was eleven or twelve. We used to love it when they were on *Top of the Pops* as the music was so good!

Gini Comyns in a 1973 portrait by her stepfather, Chris Barham, a *Daily Mail* photographer whose coronation shot of the Queen and Prince Philip made his name

Every so often we'd have discos in the local village hall, in Hurst Green on the Kent/Sussex border, and Slade were guaranteed to get everyone hastily assembled in a line, where we all did this curious dance, completely uniform, everyone doing the same thing – a line of kids stood opposite us and did a mirror image of what we were doing. This was hugely exciting!

Nobody at school fancied anyone in Slade. Noddy Holder looked like someone's dad with his bushy sideburns. Come 1972, we preferred Donny Osmond or David Cassidy; much prettier and somehow cleaner. But when Noddy opened his mouth and sang with that rasp, that power, we forgave him his middle-aged looks and rushed to the dance floor in a riot of teenage hormones and wild abandon. Brilliant.

I WAS THERE: MARTIN LING, SERIOUS DRINKING

Greater London's suburbs in the early 1970s could be pretty rough at times for the youth of the day. In my hometown of Romford, there were several tribes – skinheads becoming suedeheads, the big four London teams to support and row about – West Ham, Arsenal, Chelsea and Spurs, grammar and secondary school rivalries which could result in mass pupil turf wars played out in leafy avenues, and a new shopping centre where numerous bored teenagers could hang out and get into all manner of petty crime.

The band I most associate with that era is Slade, and during that glorious run of singles beginning with 'Coz I Luv You' in October 1971 through to 'Everyday' in the spring of 1974, they were the band who captured the imagination and adoration of the kids of Romford and beyond. How could they fail? Romford was full of yobs and Slade had a Super Yob. The walls of the town were daubed with misspelt graffiti – Slade's songs used misspelt yob words like 'coz', 'dun', 'bak', 'crazee' and 'gudbuy' – their language was our language. They were ex-skinheads, and Romford was full of ex-skinheads who spent their weekends on the North Bank (s), the Shelf or the Shed, bunking the fares on British Rail to go to the football on Saturday afternoons.

Everybody's favourite TV show in the early 1970s was *Top of the Pops*, and the whole town tuned in on Thursday nights to check out the 'hits' and 'smashes' which would then be discussed in great detail the following morning in the playground. This would be followed by the weekly pilgrimage to Woolworths, WH Smith, Wells Music or Downtown Records to get the latest 45rpms. Every one of those Slade singles made its way into our house during that period.

The 1970s also saw the emergence of the school and youth club discos where fledgling club DJs would take over the twin decks and play to packed dancefloors of suburban teenagers seeking their first kiss, showing off their new clobber and participating in whatever the new dance craze was. Slade were big at the school disco and guaranteed to fill the floor every time.

The cooler kids were getting into Bowie or Roxy, leaving Slade to those of a less pretentious bent. Romford's leading Slade fanatic was a guy called Lenny. He went to one of the Romford's even rougher schools, was a bit older and dated a girl in our class called Janice, who to quote Jarvis Cocker was 'the first girl at school to get breasts'. Lenny crashed our school disco, bouncing around the hall in a homemade mirror disc top hat to 'Mama Weer All Crazee Now'. He took the lovely Janice to see Slade at their legendary 1973 show at Earl's Court and she recounted her great night out over double geography the following Monday morning. Lenny was the suburbia/Slade love affair personified.

It all faded very fast after 1974, Slade made more grown-up songs, we all grew up too, and within a few months their glorious yob rock was fading from the memory as we moved on to the other great adopted suburban musical genres of the mid-1970s, disco, soul and prog rock.

I WAS THERE: DAMIAN O'NEILL, THE UNDERTONES & THAT PETROL EMOTION

I first came across Slade when I heard 'Get Down And Get With It' on 'wonderful' Radio 1 in the summer of '71. I was only ten years old but I distinctly remember being impressed with Noddy's rasping vocals. However, it was the follow-up single, 'Coz I Luv You', which made me really take notice. There was something weirdly exotic about it, and it wasn't until I watched them on *Top of the Pops* that I realised what it was – Jim Lea's electric violin! That and the lovely intricate interplay with Dave Hill's guitar hooks really impressed me, and I still love how the song starts slowly and builds and builds until it reaches the familiar Slade stomp at the end.

After that, Slade could do no wrong. They were ubiquitous on the radio, having hit after hit, and definitely were a big influence on The Undertones, especially with Billy Doherty, who would emulate Don Powell's incredible drumming finesse. Apparently, Noddy and Jim wrote 'Coz I Luv You' in 30 minutes. I'll bet it took longer than that for The Undertones to learn it, but once we did, 'Coz I Luv You' and 'Cum On Feel The Noize' became regular crowd pleasers when we played the Casbah in Derry.

I SAW THEM ON TOP OF THE POPS: COLIN CUNNINGHAM

By the time I had reached the age of seven in October 1971, I was already (thanks mainly to having three older siblings) a regular face and precocious voice amongst the group of kids who would gather in the school playground on a Friday morning to enthusiastically pick over the highlights of the previous evening's *Top of the Pops*. Although many of the most memorable Glam rock *TOTP* moments would come around six months later, the signs were already there in late '71, with Marc Bolan and T.Rex leading the way. But it was an appearance by Slade, performing their second chart hit, 'Coz I Luv You', that set the tone for the few wild years ahead.

Us kids of the 1970s now take completely for granted the ability to check at a couple of taps on a touch screen the accuracy of these foggy memories, using technology that even the mighty *Tomorrow's World* – which we would have sat impatiently through in anticipation of our Thursday fix of *Top of the Pops* – would not have considered possible. The performance of 'Coz I Luv You' has been available to view, albeit from that year's Christmas special, and I am pleased to say it is pretty much how I remember it first time around. The visuals were as important as the music, especially for impressionable seven-year-olds, and Slade certainly made an impact with their appearance, in particular Noddy, who even as a young man in his twenties looked like a much older, wiser and mysteriously mischievous character, plucked from the pages of Enid Blyton, Tolkien or Dickens.

Plus you had Dave with his unique, fringeless long hair style (one very subtle hybrid nod to the skinhead look they had briefly adopted at the request of their manager a year earlier), his permanent toothy grin and flamboyant stage clothing. Even with Don and Jim having the far more conventional early 1970s rock/pop star look, Slade's image was both unique and unmistakeable.

The visual impact of the band aside, 'Coz I Luv You' was and still is a striking piece of pop music; insistent, dramatic and with an air of melancholy in the melody. This is largely due to Jim Lea's show-stealing performance, including a solo on violin. In fact, it was most likely the unconventional sight of a man in a rock 'n' roll band playing a violin that immortalised this as one of the first great *Top of the Pops* performances that I had the pleasure to watch and hear, and then discuss amongst my fellow knowing seven-year-olds in the playground the next day.

When I look back now on those few short years of my childhood, where Slade, more than any other popular band or artist of that unique era, dominated the pop charts and were ever present on our weekly fix of *Top of the Pops*, all of those subsequent and huge No.1s – even 'that' Christmas song – are bookended by my two favourites of their singles; and for the run of hits between 'Coz I Luv You' and 'How Does It Feel?' I am as grateful to Slade in my late fifties as I was in my pre-teens.

BRISLINGTON
1971, BRISTOL, UK

I WAS BAK 'OME: JULIE S

My brother had quite a few Slade singles. He was eight years older, so as a nine-year-old I was quite familiar with their songs, 'Coz I Luv You' topping the charts just three weeks after my birthday, the first of their six No.1s in barely two years. He'd play them loud and often, my mum always shouting out, 'Turn it down!' She always said she may not recognise a lot of the bands she heard on the radio, but she always knew Slade because of Noddy's voice and The Undertones because of Feargal Sharkey's voice. I liked Marc Bolan and T.Rex at the time, but definitely enjoyed listening to Slade… although what I wanted most was Dave Hill's haircut! I had long hair with a long fringe and thought that, if I wasn't allowed to have my haircut, maybe I could just have my fringe cut. But after showing them a picture, no, my parents were not keen. Looking back, I would probably have had more success asking my mum if I could have a perm like Marc.

I still remember those red Polydor sleeves with the red labels, and I now have my brother's records. But in case anyone wondered, I still don't have a Dave Hill haircut!

I WAS THERE: BRUCE JENKINS

Pop music, or 'that ghastly noise' as it was known in our house, was not tolerated. At all. Access to the handsome polished radiogram with its three-speed platter and automatic record changer was granted only to Gilbert and Sullivan LPs and a small range of light classics. The gift of a transistor radio – a birthday present from a more progressive auntie – was a major step forward in my musical education. In addition to a state-of-the-art three-inch speaker, my new audio device came with a little white earpiece on the end of a yard of plastic-covered wire. This accessory was a major bonus. Privacy! Radio! Pop music!

From late November 1971, I spent every spare moment with that little hearing aid jammed into my ear, devouring new sounds. It didn't take long to work out that Melbourne's home of all things musically 'Now!' was AM radio station 3XY. The Top 40 chart appearing in the weekly *TV and Radio Guide* became required reading for my mid-teen self. It helped track what was happening on the radio while starting the process of working out what I did and didn't like. The song that most caught my ear as the Australian summer hotted up in January 1972 was a single by a band I'd never heard of, Slade. Were they connected to famous Melbourne soft drink manufacturer Slades? Probably not. That lemonade was as sweet as an icy pole and these guys sounded as rough as guts.

It was in those sleepy summer days between Christmas and New Year that I first heard it. Keeping an eye on the weekly chart I was delighted to see 'Cos I Love You' (sic) appear in the middle reaches in late January. By the following week it had leapt into the top 10 and was now listed as 'Cos I Luv You'. By mid-February the single had snuck a little further up the charts. Or at least I figured it was the same song. Now at No.7, 'Coz I Luv You' had, after weeks of confounding proof-readers, reached its 3XY chart peak under its 'correctly' misspelt title. By that stage, the song was burned into my teenage brain.

Two bars of an echoing drum-stomp open proceedings before a jangle-guitar crunches out the beat, setting the pace and tone of the rest of the song. It is simple, direct, and irresistible. The cover notes to the track on the compilation *Sladest* are revealing. 'This was the first time we deliberately sat down to write a commercial song. We hadn't had to worry about follow-ups before… we hadn't had bloody hit singles,' Jimmy Lea recalled. 'We wrote it in about half-an-hour. We just got the feel right early on, we seemed to have found the right formula, simplicity and atmosphere.'

Indeed, the song's lyrics seem to suggest a simple love song, encapsulated in the what-it-says-on-the-label title. And we all sang along, too, making up words when Noddy's diction lacked a little clarity. 'I won't laugh at you if you boo hoo hoo, coz I luv you…'. If you care about someone you don't mock them when they are upset. Sounds reasonable. 'I can turn my back on the things you lack, coz I luv you…' This is trickier. Cataloguing your beloved's faults is a given, it seems, but then magnanimously ignoring them represents true love. Might want to get a second opinion on that one. 'I just like the things you do, mmm; Don't you change the things you do, mmm…'.

At the tender age of 16, I knew nothing of 'lurve'. Still, appreciating someone's behaviour sounded like a good place to start. Similarly, not demanding they change their habits seemed quite liberating. My own model was more along the lines of 'polish your school shoes', 'do your piano practice' and 'when are those lawns getting mowed?'.

It was all seeming a bit bossy, until I deciphered the line, 'You make me out a clown and you put me down, I still luv you…'. His beloved is pushing back, but it scarcely seems a picture of relationship bliss. Maybe blokes with gravelly voices did things differently. Certainly in

1972 relationships between men and women were done differently. But in three-and-a-half minutes you don't get much time to ponder the finer points of love. Especially when there is lots of exciting stuff barrelling into your ear. The fuzz violin solo, for instance, is a rollicking treat. With a strong folk leaning and plenty of jazz bounce, it reflects both Jimmy Lea's skill on violin and his appreciation of the Django Rheinhardt/Stéphane Grappelli Quintette du Hot Club de France sound. It really dances, leading into a longish coda that eventually morphs into a tribal stomp taking us to the fade.

'Coz I Luv You' drifted back down the 3XY chart, as all singles eventually must, but it did not fade from memory and remains a key point in my earliest rock explorations. It's a stomping single that helped earn Slade a special place in my musical landscape for several years.

LOCARNO BALLROOM
18 OCTOBER 1971, SUNDERLAND, UK

I WAS THERE: PETER SMITH

Slade were, no question, one of the best live acts out on the road in the early 1970s. They had played Sunderland Top Rank for the Sunderland Poly Students' Union freshers' ball a few weeks earlier, when 'Get Down And Get With It' was in the charts. A few of my mates went and were raving about how great this band was. I saw them twice or maybe three times at Sunderland Locarno, in October/November 1971 and January 1972. The first time was just as they released their No.1 smash hit 'Coz I Luv You'. The ballroom was packed for these guys.

Support was Steamhammer, perhaps best known for 'Junior's Wailing', as covered by Status Quo. We all sat cross-legged on the floor, as you did back then, but when Slade came on, Noddy wasn't having any of this sitting on the dancefloor. Slade were a loud rock band. 'Come on, up on your feet, everybody.' The crowd jumped up and crushed to the front of the stage. The opening number was their cover of Ten Years After's 'Hear Me Calling' (it always was in those early days) and it was amazing. It started quietly and slowly, Noddy singing in (for him) quite a low voice, then after a few bars the pace picking up, Dave Hill's guitar, Jim Lea's bass and Don Powell's drums crashing in at an amazingly loud volume, so loud that I thought my ears would go. By then Noddy's voice was his normal raucous scream. And the crowd went Crazee; completely bananas. Slade were a force to be reckoned with. They played wild, fast and very, very loud. The set was short, probably around an hour, but furious, and by the end we were all wringing in sweat and totally whacked.

Slade were just coming out of their skinhead phase; their hair was starting to grow, but you could still see signs of crew-cuts. Except for Dave, whose hair was already growing right the way down his back. Nod was wearing a cap, a check-shirt, braces and jeans. The set included all the tracks from *Slade Alive!* and included a few covers; favourites of mine were 'In Like A Shot From My Gun', their excellent cover of John Sebastian's 'Darling Be Home Soon', which took the mood and the pace down a notch, the rocking 'Get Down And Get With It', during which we all had to follow Nod's instructions and 'stamp our feet' (as long as we had our boots on), their new single 'Coz I Luv You', Jim soloing on his violin, their cover of Janis' 'Move Over', and they closed with 'Born To Be Wild', an ear-piercingly loud take on Steppenwolf's classic. It was all over too soon, but it was amazing.

I saw them again a few months later. By then they had released 'Look Wot You Dun' and were becoming chart heroes. But the live set remained as wild, raucous and loud as before. After one gig, I think it was early 1972, The Groundhogs were playing the Rink (Top Rank) on the same night as Slade at the Mecca (Locarno). We went to see Slade, who were excellent as usual, earlier that night and came into the Rink just as The Groundhogs took to the stage, having missed support act, Ashton, Gardner and Dyke. I managed to make my way right to the front, stood right in front of Tony McPhee as he soloed on 'Amazing Grace' and 'Split II'. Seeing Slade and The Groundhogs on the same night, when both acts were on top form, happy days indeed.

SLADE ALIVE! RECORDING COMMAND STUDIOS

19 - 21 OCTOBER 1971, PICCADILLY, LONDON, UK

I WAS THERE: DAVID GRAHAM, AGE 14

The first time I saw them live was for the recording of *Slade Alive!* I'd sent off for fan club membership. I think it cost 65p. I sent my postal order and a stamped addressed envelope, as you used to do then. My fan club membership number was 00762. It was a red card with a black-and-white photograph of them on it, and in the newsletter there was an invitation to come along to the recording studio in October. My father was a non-commissioned officer in the Army, and he had a driver who was a kid of 19, although he was a man to me as I was only 14. My dad said, 'You can go if you go with this private.' So I went with him on the first day of the recording, on the Monday. I was just in awe of it all. It was a fantastic thing to see.

I remember it being quite tacky. It was a studio with bits of carpet and gaffer tape, and they'd just had their first No.1 record, 'Coz I Luv You'. I felt really quite special, but didn't get to see them again for a year or more because we moved to Northern Ireland, where they never toured or visited. My mum came back to England in '73, and I got to see them in Manchester and Liverpool in '74 because we were stationed up there in Cheshire and they were always my band. In terms of the audience, everybody was older than me when I first saw them. They were all students and people of the street. There were probably 300 or 400 people in the studio. They all seemed to be bigger than me. When I started to see them from '73 onwards, the girls and blokes were around about the same age.

I WAS THERE: NIALL BRANNIGAN

Chas Chandler was a frustrated manager. Slade were a hugely popular live band, who had been careering up and down the motorways and side-roads of Britain for five years, wowing audiences everywhere they went. Yet, two albums into their recording career, they had failed to trouble the chart compilers, especially with their singles. Chas was frustrated with himself as much as anything. He was constantly standing at the back of halls, watching his act tear the roof off the places, as their audience went wild. Slade were a sensational live band and, in Noddy Holder, were blessed with one of the best frontmen that Chas had ever seen. So he decided to record their next single as a live performance. The Little Richard version of a Bobby Marchan B-side had been a live favourite for months, so it was agreed that 'Get Down And Get With It' would be Slade's next single.

Niall Brannigan's shots of Piccadilly's Command Studios

The band arrived at Olympic Studios and the instructions from Chas were simple, 'Just play it like you do on stage. Blast it out like it's live, and pretend there's an audience in there with you.' What you hear is one take. They added extra stomps and hand-claps and it was done, in less than an hour. Polydor released the single on 21st May 1971, and then again a few weeks later. The band had always believed the song was a Little Richard original, so the credit on the single was 'Hill, Powell, Lea, Holder, Penniman'. However, as the single began to sell, publishers for Bobby Marchan got involved. The single was hurriedly reissued as 'Get Down And Get With It' and the writing credit went solely to 'Marchan'. The songwriting royalties from the first copies were redirected to Marchan's publishers, much to the annoyance of Little

Richard, I would imagine. The single went into the UK charts at No.45 and took nine weeks to peak at No.16. Finally, Slade had a hit record. And they performed the song at every live performance for the rest of their career.

Chas demanded they write a follow-up, quickly, to capitalise on their new-found success. Jim Lea turned up, unexpectedly, at Noddy's house with his violin, the pair having not written much of anything before and, 30 minutes later, they had 'Coz I Luv You'. They played it to Chas on acoustic guitars, and he grinned from ear to ear, declaring that it would be a No.1 record. He booked Olympic Studios for the next day and, after two days, they had their next single. Once again, they had overdubbed some 'Slade stomps' to give the sound a harder edge. It was Noddy who suggested spelling the title as if spoken in their Black Country dialect and Chas loved the gimmicky idea.

With characteristic understatement, Jimmy described the writing session, some years later, 'One afternoon I went over to Nod's, on the council estate where he lived with his mum and dad, and I said, 'Hey Nod, why don't we write a song?' I took my violin with me and said, 'Why don't we do a Stephan Grappelli thing.' 'Hot Love' was in the charts at the time, (by) Marc Bolan, and I said, 'Something like that, dead simple,' and we wrote the song in half an hour. We got the structure of the tune and Nod just filled in the gaps. That's the only song we've ever written like that.'

Polydor rushed the single into the shops on 8th October 1971. It made the chart at No.26 on 30th October. By 13th November, it was No.1, staying there for four weeks, remaining at No.3 for a further three weeks after that. In November, the *NME* reported that the band had turned down a 'multi-million dollar campaign, including a TV show and heavily-promoted American tour,' with Noddy saying, 'It would have meant the cancellation of many commitments here – and the last thing we want to do is mess around the people who have put us where we are.'

The next album had been planned since 'Get Down And Get With It', and Chas knew exactly what he wanted. He had been keeping an eye on the fit-out of the new Command Studios on Piccadilly, in London. The studio was being built inside what had until recently been the BBC's Piccadilly Theatre. The new studio had kept the stage and the place looked ideal to Chas as a place to record a live album. He got the fan club to alert every member, telling them that if they turned up outside 201 Piccadilly on Tuesday, Wednesday and Thursday, the 19th, 20th and 21st October 1971, they could be a part of the recording.

Noddy remembers the gigs. 'Our manager, Chas Chandler, had come up with the idea of us doing a live album, because he'd been Jimi Hendrix's manager and he'd seen how some of Hendrix's live performances had been turning points in his career. So we booked a little studio-cum-theatre on Piccadilly for three nights: the Tuesday, Wednesday and Thursday. The bulk of the album was from the Wednesday night, which was mayhem. 'Coz I Luv You' was No.1, and we'd come straight from doing *Top of the Pops*. We were still wearing our clobber from the telly, and we went pretty much straight onstage… Our aim onstage was to hit the crowd between the eyes and grab them by the balls.'

When the live album was mixed, Chas sat in the studio listening to a playback. He wasn't happy. Command's engineers had mixed it with the band and Chas felt that it didn't capture enough of the excitement of the recordings. He took the tapes and re-mixed it himself. When he played his mix to the band, they rejected it, insisting that their mix should be released. For once, Chas gave in. Prior to the album's release, a promotional single was released – just 500 copies – with 'Hear Me Calling' on the A-side and 'Get Down And Get With It' as the B-side.

Slade Alive! was released on 24th March 1972 and reached No.2 in the UK, and No.1 in Australia, where it was the biggest-selling album since The Beatles' *Sgt. Pepper's Lonely Hearts Club Band*.

To this day, *Slade Alive!* is one of the great live albums. So, next time you're in London, walking along the right-hand side of Piccadilly, towards Piccadilly Circus, just pause. You've passed Fortnum & Masons, with its wonderful windows, and crossed the side-road, Church Place. Ahead of you is a large bus stop, and just before what is currently a branch of Waterstones, is a pair of large brown doors. Stop for a few moments and imagine a queue of excited teenagers, all out on a school night, talking, singing and laughing, outside those very doors.

In a few moments, the doors will swing open and the kids will be ushered in, running, shouting, yelling to their friends, down to the front of the old theatre, crowding at the stage. And then, their four heroes arrive and Don starts to pound his bass drum, with Noddy, Dave and Jimmy, hands above their heads, clapping to Don's beat and encouraging every single kid to do the same. Jim and Noddy start to play their guitars, bent over as they tease the crowd, and Dave is stomping around in circles, playing that opening lick to 'Hear Me Calling', the air electric, thick with excitement and anticipation and joy and fun and togetherness. Slade are doing their thing. All of that happened behind those big, brown doors on Piccadilly.

I WAS THERE: STEVE BROOKES, CO-FOUNDER, THE JAM

We liked them as one of the contemporary bands at the time. In as much as we weren't really into any of the contemporary music at that time. We were looking backwards. There was Slade, Sweet, Mud, and all those Chinn and Chapman bands. But I remember Paul (Weller) bought the *Slade Alive!* album and was really impressed by the energy of the playing. Because they were a proper band, they weren't a manufactured band, they were a band that had been out gigging. As a musician, that's the sort of thing you tend to look up to, people who can actually do it, people that go out and are actually a band.

Steve Brookes, pictured live by David Coombs, recalls listening to *Slade Alive!* with The Jam co-founder Paul Weller

UNCLE TOM'S CABIN

31 OCTOBER 1971, DARWEN, UK

I WAS THERE: PAT FLECK

I saw Slade in the northern English town where I used to live, Darwen. They were appearing at a nightclub called Uncle Tom's. 'Coz I Luv You' had just hit the charts and Jim was playing his violin. Noddy announced that the manager had told him to stop swearing or else he would cut the power to the stage. Of course, Noddy did not stop swearing, and the power was duly cut… It came back on after Noddy promised to be a good boy!

CHRISTCHURCH COLLEGE
5 NOVEMBER 1971, CANTERBURY, UK

I WAS THERE: ROBERT HAYWARD

I saw them twice. The first time, they were playing at a college in Canterbury. I was due to go with a girl called Jane Flanders, but she stood me up, so I wasn't in a great frame of mind when I arrived at the gig. But Slade were great. I was a prog rock fan, so a little snooty about their music and wouldn't normally have gone had Jane not suggested it. Towards the end of the gig, I spied Jane with someone else near the back of the hall, but by this time I didn't really care – I'd enjoyed myself.

The second time was at the University of Kent in the early 1980s. They had been booked to play at Rutherford College by the Afro-Caribbean Society as a tongue-in-cheek gesture. Slade by this time were not so popular and regarded by many as has-beens (it was the time of the Clash, Jam, etc). The Afro-Caribbean Society had booked reggae acts and a reggae disco as the top billing and only added Slade as a bit of a joke. Big mistake. Slade were phenomenal and probably one of the heaviest bands I'd ever seen. Even the dreadlocked hardcore of Afro-Caribs could be seen rocking out to them, and the reggae acts just scuttled off – they couldn't compete with such slick professionalism. They played some of their hits but also some extended songs with improvisation. Dave Hill may have looked ridiculous but he gained massive respect that night.

SWANMORE MIDDLE SCHOOL
DECEMBER 1971, RYDE, ISLE OF WIGHT, UK

I WAS BAK 'OME: ANDY STRICKLAND, THE LOFT

When 'Coz I Luv You' came out in October 1971, I was twelve years old. I'd been having guitar lessons for a year and my teacher had recently kicked me out for playing T.Rex songs instead of set scales, while administering to her disabled daughter, who would routinely gate-crash my lesson on a Saturday morning, literally shouting the house down. I was relieved.

Andy Strickland's career in music started way back in a school assembly at Christmas 1971

Now I could focus on working out – by ear – my favourite songs from the charts. In the run up to Christmas 1971, my school decided it would be a good idea to hand over one assembly a week to something out of the ordinary (ie. not hymns, prayers and life lessons). Alongside the ubiquitous groups of disco dancing girls, I decided to round up a few mates and mime in assembly to 'Coz I Luv You'. Like you do.

We borrowed a school violin (Danny Gall) and rubbish drum kit (Ray Coyne) and I proudly brought in my terrible guitar. Mums' wardrobes were raided for flowery blouses, and I had an old fox fur stole on my head to approximate Dave Hill's incredible barnet.

We were all set, the seven-inch vinyl single cued up on the school stereogram, a hall full of kids and incredulous teachers, waiting for the headmaster, Mr Hague. In he came, did a double take and, 'You can take the sunglasses off for a start, boys.' It didn't matter. The needle dropped, those stabby opening chords rang out, we leapt about, Danny bashed the violin – and we were Slade.

SOUTH BRISTOL TECHNICAL COLLEGE
16 DECEMBER 1971, BRISTOL, UK

MY DAD WAS THERE: GARETH EVANS
Somewhat unbelievably, Slade played South Bristol Tech's 1971 Christmas party. That's where my dad worked. 'Coz I Luv You' had just gone to No.1. No more technical colleges after that.

ALEXANDRA ROOMS
18 DECEMBER 1971, SALISBURY, UK

I WAS THERE: IAN STACEY
The first time I saw Slade was at the Alex Rooms in Salisbury, along with my school friends. We were all aged 13 to 15, and skinheads. One of our mates had heard about them in the *NME* and raved to us about them. Slade's music was just what we wanted to hear – raw and with crowd or audience participation. Noddy Holder had such great stage presence and just captivated the room. As you might expect, there were occasional scuffles between the rival skinhead factions, but for an impressionable teenager like me it just added to the atmosphere. I didn't realise it at the time but 'Wild Winds Are Blowing' was going to become one of my favourite songs of all time. 'Get Down And Get With It' was probably the highlight of the evening, with a hundred or so Doc Martens-clad youngsters making themselves heard.

The next time I saw them was on *Top of the Pops*, where seeing Jimmy Lea playing the violin was awesome. Although they adopted the Glam rock image, Slade's music was still on the rock side to my ears. I saw them a few times at various venues in the early Seventies in that period. I never followed that dress sense, standing out like a sore thumb in my Sta-Prest and Harrington, but Slade always had that raw edge to their songs, with 'Take Me Bak 'Ome' and 'Cum On Feel The Noize' prime examples.

Other issues in my life sadly stopped me from attending other Slade concerts, but I still listened out for them on Radio 1 and Luxembourg 208 whenever possible. I was slightly disappointed when I saw them next in the early Eighties, as they seemed to have attracted a heavy metal following. I definitely didn't feel comfortable amongst that crowd, dressed as I was in my best Ben Sherman, tonic trousers and loafers! Slade have always been a completely underrated band for their contribution to music, but 'Merry Xmas Everybody' certainly put them amongst the most popular.

TOWN HALL

20 DECEMBER 1971, DEWSBURY, UK

I WAS THERE: CHRIS TOMLINSON, AGE 15

I became a Slade fan after they appeared at Dewsbury Town Hall in West Yorkshire, not the most renowned music venue. They had just got a first No.1 with 'Coz I Luv You'. I remember a great night, and us having to take the laces out of our Doc Marten boots – odd, as I was only five feet tall at the time. Sadly, that was the only time I saw them live, but I bought all their records thereafter and still listen to the classic songs now.

PIER PAVILION

22 DECEMBER 1971, WORTHING, UK

I WAS THERE: JOHN PARSONS

I took over from Freddie Bannister when he gave up promoting shows at Worthing to concentrate on other things. I did bands like KC and the Sunshine Band, Roy Wood and Wizzard. Slade were an absolute winner. What a night that was. I booked them for £250 or 60 per cent of the receipts. When I went down there about 4pm, there was a queue all the way along the seafront. It was a sell-out and the audience was full of screaming girls. They were brilliant. After the gig, Noddy said to me, 'This is it. This is the first time I realise we've got a following.' He was chuffed to bits, as were the rest of the band. It was a really good night, and we had a drink in the bar afterwards. He was quite elated. He said, 'I'd love to come back again.' But they went mega after that and with a capacity of 1,000 the Pier Pavilion wasn't really big enough for them.

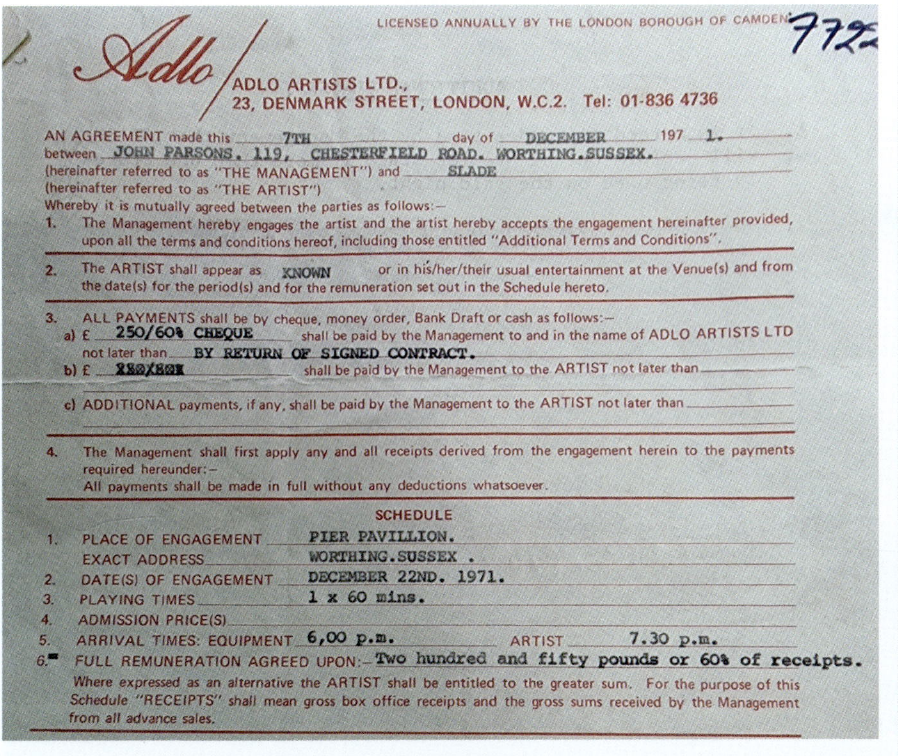

LICENSED ANNUALLY BY THE LONDON BOROUGH OF CAMDEN 772

Adlo

ADLO ARTISTS LTD.,
23, DENMARK STREET, LONDON, W.C.2. Tel: 01-836 4736

AN AGREEMENT made this 7TH day of DECEMBER 1971.
between JOHN PARSONS. 119, CHESTERFIELD ROAD. WORTHING.SUSSEX.
(hereinafter referred to as "THE MANAGEMENT") and SLADE
(hereinafter referred to as "THE ARTIST")
Whereby it is mutually agreed between the parties as follows:–

1. The Management hereby engages the artist and the artist hereby accepts the engagement hereinafter provided, upon all the terms and conditions hereof, including those entitled "Additional Terms and Conditions".

2. The ARTIST shall appear as KNOWN or in his/her/their usual entertainment at the Venue(s) and from the date(s) for the period(s) and for the remuneration set out in the Schedule hereto.

3. ALL PAYMENTS shall be by cheque, money order, Bank Draft or cash as follows:–
   a) £ 250/60% CHEQUE shall be paid by the Management to and in the name of ADLO ARTISTS LTD not later than BY RETURN OF SIGNED CONTRACT.
   b) £ XXXXXXX shall be paid by the Management to the ARTIST not later than
   c) ADDITIONAL payments, if any, shall be paid by the Management to the ARTIST not later than

4. The Management shall first apply any and all receipts derived from the engagement herein to the payments required hereunder:–
All payments shall be made in full without any deductions whatsoever.

SCHEDULE

1. PLACE OF ENGAGEMENT PIER PAVILLION.
   EXACT ADDRESS WORTHING.SUSSEX .
2. DATE(S) OF ENGAGEMENT DECEMBER 22ND. 1971.
3. PLAYING TIMES 1 x 60 mins.
4. ADMISSION PRICE(S)
5. ARRIVAL TIMES: EQUIPMENT 6,00 p.m. ARTIST 7.30 p.m.
6.* FULL REMUNERATION AGREED UPON:– Two hundred and fifty pounds or 60% of receipts.
   Where expressed as an alternative the ARTIST shall be entitled to the greater sum. For the purpose of this Schedule "RECEIPTS" shall mean gross box office receipts and the gross sums received by the Management from all advance sales.

John Parsons promoted the Slade gig in Worthing in 1971

PERCY GEE BUILDING

15 JANUARY 1972, LEICESTER, UK

I WAS THERE: RICHARD BENT

I remember them having really long guitar leads and coming off the stage into the audience, dancing with everyone as they were playing.

TOP RANK

19 JANUARY 1972, BRIGHTON, UK

I WAS THERE: DAVID HOLMES, AGE 17

I was heading to A-levels. I'd passed my driving test first time, six weeks after my birthday, and my mother was kind enough to let me borrow her car more-or-less whenever I asked for it. My then girlfriend Fiona (now grandma to our nine grandchildren) and I noticed that upcoming was a gig in Brighton by this shiny, lairy, loud band called Slade. Should we give them a go? We lived in, respectively, Wittering and Chichester then, so it was about 30 miles each way. Why not?

David and Fiona caught Slade twice in Brighton in '72, at the Top Rank and then The Dome

We duly turned up at Brighton's Top Rank. The support was Hello – the New York Groovers. The nearest we'd got to a Glam rock gig to this point was Hot Chocolate in Bognor Regis. This was very different. Hello were reasonably entertaining, but weren't in the same league as the headliners. Slade brought energy, rock (very much of the Glam variety), surprising musical competence, loud, foot-stomping songs and, above all, they were fun. What started effectively as an experiment turned into a memorable night out.

'LOOK WOT YOU DUN' RELEASED
28 JANUARY 1972

Slade's third chart entry spends ten weeks in the chart and reaches No.4. It also sparks protests from teachers who feel the phonetic spellings are confusing school pupils.

ESSEX UNIVERSITY
29 JANUARY 1972, COLCHESTER, UK

I WASN'T THERE: MAL WRIGHT

I didn't go to see Slade for various reasons. Picketing with and supporting 150 striking miners who stayed on our campus – power cuts were days away. Ipswich vs West Ham on the afternoon of the gig, a too-close-for-comfort brush with a football special full of skinheads. Not having a telly. And weren't Slade still skinheads? The day after the gig, 14 people were killed by the British Army while attending a Civil Rights march in Derry. Sharpeville in the UK. Perhaps the revolution was not just around the corner.

LANCHESTER ARTS FESTIVAL

3 FEBRUARY 1972, COVENTRY, UK

Chuck Berry was top of the bill, and there was also the Roy Young Band, his backing band. He'd turn up about ten minutes before and say, 'When I want you to start, I'll raise my arm, and when I want you to stop, I'll stamp my foot.' Everybody knew his songs anyway. We opened the show. If I remember right, we were all still skinheads. Then came Roy Young, then Chuck Berry, and he hardly sang, just let the audience sing. When that finished, they cleared the stage, and an hour or so later Pink Floyd were on, doing Dark Side of the Moon. *I'd never seen anything like that. What a bill that was, eh! But of all those incredible songs he's written, and everybody's recorded, he gets to No.1 with bloody 'Ding-a-Ling'!* **Don Powell**

PARR HALL

3 MARCH 1972, WARRINGTON, UK

I WAS THERE: CLIFF BOND

I saw them twice in 1972, just before their transition to silly pop band. The first time was at Parr Hall in Warrington, my first ever gig and the day after my 17th birthday. The support, Blind Eye, apparently split up weeks later, Mick Bolton going on to join Mott the Hoople. Slade really rocked and were very loud. I was in the balcony and it swayed up and down. I had a very stiff neck the next day. I don't remember who I went with.

Cliff Bond saw Slade twice

I WAS THERE: JOHN GILLMORE, BBC RADIO PRESENTER

John 'Gilly' Gillmore, on air on BBC Radio Lancashire, caught Slade at Warrington's Parr Hall in '72

I was 16 at the time, and I think it was about 75p to get in, which is going to sound daft now – 75 pence to see Slade! At that time, public transport was brilliant; you could get the Crosville H8 bus from where I lived in Prescot to Warrington and get the last bus home after the concert. I remember the Parr Hall being absolutely packed out, and what a fabulous concert it was. I was about seven or eight rows back, with a couple of mates. I think the person doing a lot of the talking and addressing the audience wasn't Noddy, but Dave Hill.

That following year is seen as Slade's golden era, and they've clearly stood the test of time, for now here we are, 50 years on, still talking about them! One of my favourite Slade songs is 'Everyday'. It's a lovely ballad, that. And in those days, when you flipped over those 45s, you got some great B-sides too. That's when you had to work at it to sell records. And while the voice of Noddy Holder sits brilliantly on 'Merry Xmas Everybody', it also sits brilliantly on B-sides like 'She Did It To Me' as well. Fabulous.

KINETIC CLUB
5 MARCH 1972, CHESFORD GRANGE, KENILWORTH, UK

I WAS THERE: DAVID FEARN

David Fearn heard 'Get Down And Get With It' being played at the fairground

My first recollection of Slade is of walking into the next village because the fair was there. As a twelve-year-old (nearly 13), it was a scary thing to do. This wasn't any old village – this one was full of rockers on bikes, who I'd heard would beat you up for just looking at them. But there was a fair with dodgems, ping-pong balls in goldfish bowls, and hook-a-duck, so my mate Dibble and I walked over the hill. In the distance, we could hear something I had never experienced in my limited life, an extraordinary sound, somebody belting out the words 'Get Down And Get With It' over and over, accompanied by a foot-stomping crescendo. By the time I got to the fair, I had picked up enough courage to ask what this was. I was told it was a band called Slade. I have been a disciple for them ever since.

My first Slade gig was at Chesford Grange, near Kenilworth, with my dad's work colleagues. How they got me in I don't know. 'Coz I Luv You' had come out and I loved it – the sound, the energy, the passion, the Noize. It wasn't the first gig I had been to. I'd been to the County Ground in Northampton with my school friend, Stuart, to see a band called Stray. We walked in and everyone was sat on the floor apart from this beautiful young lady dressed in a kaftan and smelling divine. She swayed and wafted in a rhythmical way, and I was in love.

CIVIC HALL
6 MARCH 1972, WOLVERHAMPTON, UK

I WAS THERE: ANDY SMITH, AGE 15

I lived in Willenhall, a Black Country town midway between Wolverhampton and Walsall. Noddy Holder lived on the Beechdale estate in Walsall, about a mile away, and the other guys also came from very close to where I lived, so they were very much local heroes. This was my first ever concert. Support acts on the night were Suzi Quatro and Thin Lizzy, who I had never heard of, and they were brilliant. But it was my local band, Slade, who I had come to see, and they blew the audience away!

Andy Smith (right) was blown away by Slade and has met the bloke Noddy used to act as chauffeur for

I worked in a Willenhall supermarket as a schoolboy. Don Powell came in once and I was too nervous to speak to him. Noddy Holder's parents lived in the same house on the Beechdale estate until they passed away. Noddy's dad was a window cleaner and, as a young guy, his son borrowed his dad's van to drive Robert Plant to gigs.

TECHNICAL COLLEGE
17 MARCH 1972, LUTON, UK

I WAS THERE: STEVE WOODWARD

I was there at Luton Technical College, and still have the ticket. They played almost the same set as *Slade Alive!* and were excellent. It was a strange audience though. Usually, it was music fans at those gigs, but this one included a large number of 'chart fan' types, and they didn't get a lot of the stuff Slade did outside the hits. It was a great gig and as a 15-year-old guitar-learning rock fan, it confirmed to me that Slade were much more than a chart singles band, as they proved over the next few years. The support acts were even more puzzling to a large number of the punters. Gothic Horizon were a local-based electric folk band and Flash were very heavy but very prog, and not at all pop-song style. I enjoyed all three acts though, despite Flash getting a bit of abuse from one particular group of moronic imbeciles!

Steve Woodward paid 70p to see Slade

SLADE ALIVE! RELEASED 24 MARCH 1972

Slade Alive! *is the first Slade album to chart, reaching No.2 in the UK and No.158 on the* Billboard 200.

I WAS THERE: MICK JONES

In 1972, I was 13 and fully immersed in the hormonal turmoils of school; homework, bullies, girls (ugggh, run away!), and trying to look cool in your school uniform. Music – as with most of us – was the way of getting some level of macho individuality amongst the complete bland uniformity of Birmingham and going to school in Saltley in the early 1970s. I grabbed that with both hands!

There were three major music cliques at our school – the colourful oddballs who followed Bowie and Roxy Music (who'd have known?), the poppy lot who followed the charts, and us; the intellectuals constantly trying to find the weirdest, anti-normal and far-flung music that nobody else would listen to (that made it very cool). You know, the normal division that existed in most schools in whatever decade. So, at the time my music listening consisted of conversations around whether Tangerine Dream were the new Beatles; what the words to Genesis' *Selling England by the Pound* really meant; were we allowed to listen to Mike Oldfield's *Tubular Bells* or was it pop crap; was Jan Akkerman the 'best guitarist in the world', as claimed by *Melody Maker*; and when would the next Steely Dan album be released?

We all watched *Top of the Pops* on Thursdays, but actually listening to a 'pop' music record was still deemed a crime punishable by excommunication and the forceful removal of the turn-ups on your Oxford Bags. Despite that, someone from the 'other side' nervously introduced me to *Slade Alive!* – probably at chess club, which was a cover for our music club because the room had a record player. They said I should listen to it 'coz they speak like uz…'. Imagine the scene, similar to the handing over of the 'goods' in a drug deal, but this was the *Slade Alive!* album in a brown paper bag.

My music was played on an ancient Ferguson portable record player, so anything loud just came out as a fuzzy mess, but the sheer emotion of the occasion, the raw power and brilliant musicianship on this record cut through all of that. I bought the album in secret immediately, and it's probably still my favourite live album of all time! It's certainly my favourite live 'burp' of all time! And it set me on a wonderful road of watching as many bands live as I possibly could, rather than simply listen to the album… And from that point I loved Slade (in secret), 'Coz they speak like uz.'

STUDIO 4 RECORDS

MAY 1972, RYDE, ISLE OF WIGHT, UK

I WAS THERE: ANDY STRICKLAND

I'm standing outside Studio 4 in Union Street, staring at the window display. One record sleeve in particular catches my eye. It's red and black and impossible to decipher. In the top right corner it says 'SLADE ALIVE!' and at the bottom on that same side is a Polydor logo. I can see a bloke wearing Noddy Holder's flat hat, so I'm fairly sure that's him. There's what looks like a microphone in front of him and some sort of

Andy Strickland struggled to work out what was happening on the cover of Slade Alive!

brick chimney rising past his face. But what's baffling me is a large blob in the foreground. It can't be Noddy's leg (one early theory), because it's too thick and has a fat bit on the end with a weird face wearing a burglar's mask. The next week I take my big brother (a 14-year-old T.Rex fan) into town with me, and he stares in through the window, just as bewildered as me. Nope.

Some weeks later, he buys this record and brings it home. Miraculously, he opens the sleeve into a double-size gatefold image and Don and Dave appear on the left, faces twisted in rock 'n' roll ecstasy, staring at the blob. Then I see what they're staring at – it's bloody Jim Lea! The blob is a horizontal Jim, left leg raised, leaning back at an impossible angle, staring skywards with a curly guitar lead between his legs. I can also see now that Noddy's chimney is actually his guitar, and it's frets, not bricks.

We don't yet have a record player in our house, so we have no idea what this record sounds like. I notice that it doesn't have 'Coz I Luv You' on the track listing and I am disappointed.

SLADE TOUR NATIONWIDE

Tour news from 1972

ST GEORGE'S HALL

10 MAY 1972, BRADFORD, UK

I WAS THERE: STEVEN LANGFIELD, AGE 21

Looking back, I don't really know why I went to this gig! The support band was Status Quo. I'd recently bought their *Dog of Two Head* album, which must've been a mad moment because I had no great love for that band. I wasn't a great fan of Slade either, but they had a growing reputation for live performances, so that must've been the reason I went. I saw them on my own as none of my mates at that time shared the same musical taste. The hall had a capacity of 3,500, and back in the day tickets could only be bought from the booking office.

Steven Langfield doesn't know why he went to the gig

It was seated only, although once the bands came on there was usually a rush to leave seats and stand by the stage. My favourite spot was the front row of the dress circle, as near to the band as I could get, overlooking them. Back then, to see a top band cost the same as the price of an album, £1.50. As usual, it looked pretty full on the day. By this time in their career Slade were beginning to take off, having found their sound. The album *Slade Alive!* and their singles were riding high in the charts. I can't recall any specific moments about the appearance, but I do remember I went home happy. Slade were amazing, blowing Quo away.

LIVERPOOL STADIUM

13 MAY 1972, LIVERPOOL, UK

I WAS THERE: TONY NEWBURY, AGE 19

This was the first time I saw Slade and one of my first gigs. I went with a bunch of friends. Liverpool Stadium was an old wrestling venue which became a rock venue. We went to see Status Quo, who were about to break and were promoting the *Dog of Two Head* album. Slade were really loud, but not the Glam band quite yet. I really liked them.

I WAS THERE: JOHN RADFORD

The *Liverpool Echo* reported on this concert the night after, basically saying it was the loudest, but also that the stadium seats were wrecked, fans standing up on the seats doing the Quo thing, then doing the Slade stomp.

I WAS THERE: DENNIS BERRY

I first saw them aged 13, watching *Top of the Pops* on a black and white TV, singing 'Coz I Luv You'. I missed who the band was then, because someone walked across the screen and yelling took place. But the sound just got hold of me. Skinheads were mentioned though, so the next day in school I went up to the skinhead hangout and asked if they knew anything about it, I got my answer – Slade. That single got to No.1, so I knew they would definitely be on again, and I sat up in the corner closest to the TV so my family wouldn't be able to wind me up by walking in front of me on purpose. I was only a short kid and those skinheads took me under their wing, so I never had any trouble in school. I saw them around 30 times. I soon had a copy of *Slade Alive!* I bought it at a Liverpool show. But I only had it for three minutes – a bunch of skinheads robbed it off me, teased me for a while, handing me the cover but no record. One of them saw my tears. He must have had a heart. He had a hard time getting it back off his mates. I've still got it. The best album ever.

'TAKE ME BAK 'OME' RELEASED
19 MAY 1972

'Take Me Bak 'Ome' is Slade's second No.1 UK single. It reaches No.97 on the Billboard *100.*

I WAS THERE: JOHN WINSTANLEY

I had it down as 'Coz I Luv You', but the first ever single I bought was 'Take Me Bak 'Ome', which I realised when I discovered the actual single

The freewheelin' John Winstanley's first 45 was 'Take Me Bak 'Ome'

whilst recently decluttering our house, and I now value the B-side, 'Wonderin' Y' to be a lost gem of theirs compared to the hits they are better known for. I built up my money to buy this single in two ways – keeping the bus fare money by walking to school (2p a day when not raining) and the 5p I got as weekly pocket money (if 'good and all chores done'). However, Mother's disapproval at the extravagance of wasting money on vinyl was loudly vocal and I had to plead with her to let me go to a record shop to buy it one day while in Wigan.

It was a memorable moment, clutching the copy in a paper bag all the way home on the bus. So, as an act of 'anarchy' as I approached the age of ten, I chose that single. I think it cost 35p and was a huge commitment both financially and morally for the child I was then. Slade (initially) were the bad boys – skinheads who looked as if they had just finished working a shift on a building site. Then they embraced the decadent fashion of Glam and became the kings amongst those bands, as their longevity has proven – far exceeding Sweet, Wizzard et al.

Seeing them on *Top of the Pops* was, like all TV appearances in those days, playground fodder on Fridays and until next Thursday's show. They pushed the Glam label to the full, Dave Hill being the most prominent member of the band. From his severely-cut front-and-long-back haircut, excessively glittered make-up and outlandish clothes to his truly iconic platform shoes, he led the way as one of the Seventies' much underrated axemen. Yes, I felt my purchase was an act of rebelliousness long before Punk. Did I feel moved to follow them, buy more of their material, or watch them live? No! But I never did with any other band or musician until I discovered The Jam – absurdly on Marc Bolan's TV show, the Glam prophet himself.

CAIRD HALL
20 MAY 1972, DUNDEE, UK

I WAS THERE: GWEN DALE (NEE HILL), AGE 14

I'm originally from Dundee, Scotland, and my friend Helen – who was a year older and lived next door to me – and I both loved Slade. Our bedroom walls were covered in posters of the band. The first time I saw them was at Dundee's Caird Hall. I was still at school. My next Slade shows were just a day apart, in May and June the following year. For the Glasgow show, at Green's Playhouse, Helen's aunt and uncle put us up for the night and drove us to the gig. And the following day we travelled 60 miles to see them again at Edinburgh's Empire Theatre. We managed to save just enough money to get there, and had to hitch back after the gig. We were fortunate to get picked up by a lorry driver, and very luckily for us our parents never knew! I told my mum I was staying at Helen's, and she told her mum she was staying at mine.

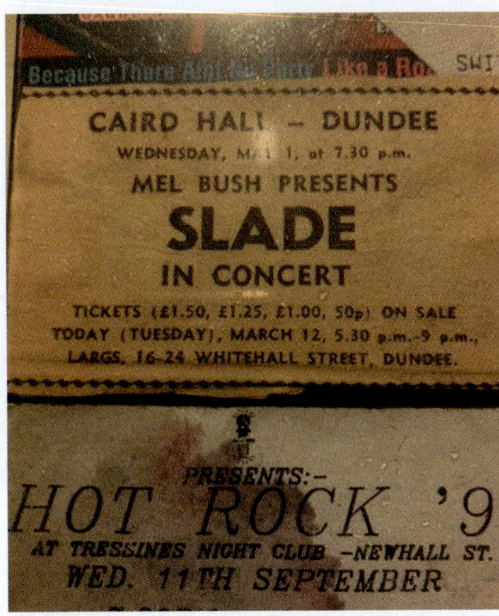

Gwen Dale with 'H', the Slade legend who shared her maiden name, and her ticket collection

Back in Dundee, we decided we were going to go to Walsall to see Noddy, as we had found his address, so we got on a train to Wolverhampton. When we got to Noddy's mum's house, it took us an hour to pluck up the courage to knock on the door but she was very timid and so lovely. She was mortified that we had come all the way from Scotland. (We had told our parents that I had gone to stay with Helen's work family, as she was a nanny in Montrose.) Noddy's mum said that Slade had gone off to America. We were gutted, and off we went back to Scotland.

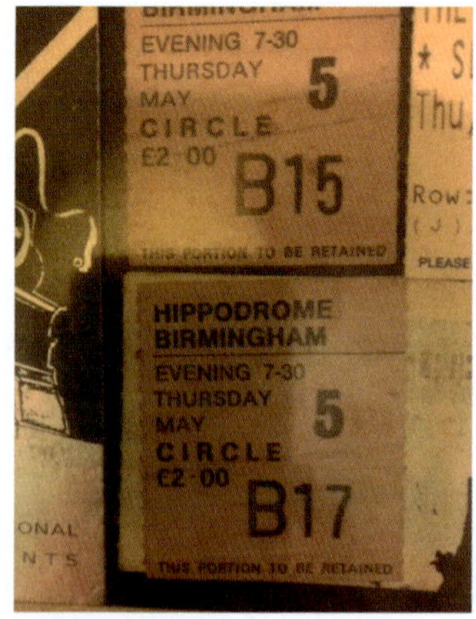

ORCHID BALLROOM

25 MAY 1972, PURLEY, CROYDON, LONDON, UK

I WAS THERE: COLIN BAKER

It's strange to think that sometimes you can't remember what you did yesterday, but still can picture what happened over 50 years ago! On a warm evening alongside my two best mates, Rob King and Andy Lunn, we boarded a 234A bus from Wallington to Purley, our destination the Orchid Ballroom. As the venue's title suggests, it was more a dance venue from the 1950s to the early 1960s and featured early performances from the likes of The Hollies, Small Faces, The Animals, The Yardbirds, The Who and Jimi Hendrix, the venue under Mecca's ownership as they tried to modernise. And as the 1970s hit us, more famous named bands played there, including Deep Purple, Sweet, Family, and the Faces, while The Who reappeared.

On this particular evening, the main attraction was support group, Status Quo, who previously appeared there in 1968. We'd seen the Quo two or three times at The Greyhound in Croydon and the album *Dog of Two Head* was one of the early purchases in my collection. The listed main event though was the band Slade, who'd already had UK No.1 success at the back end of 1971 with 'Coz I Luv You', a song I really liked – there's always been something about a violin on a record that appealed since I saw my first ever act, Curved Air, in 1970.

What we didn't realise or perhaps overlooked was the different audience appeal both Quo and Slade had. Whilst Quo at that time had a hard rock boogie sound appealing to the shoulder-length hair-clad, like myself, Slade were a Glam rock band that in their infancy appealed very much to the skinhead elements, this crowd a mixture of both factions. Fortunately, from memory, there was no undercurrent in the audience.

Quo did a shortened set to the previous gigs we attended, but what we were to experience was – and is to this day – a sound that far exceeded the decibel level I have experienced at any gig. Boy, did Slade play it loud.

Noddy Holder's presence was big and bold, the curly ginger hair and top hat along with that booming voice; Dave Hill, with big boots and glitter clothing, again had a personality that dragged your eyes towards him; Jim Lea more in the background but of course playing violin on 'Coz I Luv 'You'; then there was Don Powell on drums, the heartbeat of the band but rarely in the limelight.

Slade would give us a great night, including singles 'Look Wot You Dun' and 'Get Down And Get With It'. We also got a taste of new single, 'Take Me Bak 'Ome', which became their second UK No.1. But for a more rock-minded guy, the key song that sticks in the memory was their version of the Steppenwolf classic 'Born To Be Wild', a song I love to this day, stoking up memories of the film *Easy Rider.* Noddy's voice was perfect for the song.

A few days away from my 16th birthday, it was the audience mix that scared me somewhat and meant this would be my one and only experience of seeing Slade. A few months later, attending a gig by my friend Andy's band, a similar audience mix left me the victim of a skinhead's toe-capped boot, the impact still a feature on the bridge of my nose. If questioned, I guess I'd say 'Cum On Feel The Bump' if evidence was ever requested.

Slade's chart music always appealed to me though, and they produced some great songs, including ballads 'Everyday' and 'Wonderin' Y', B-side to 'Take Me Bak 'Ome'.

And it was an experience from the Noize level I will never forget from a band that had immense stage presence and 'pop songs' that certainly appealed to a guy more on a rock trip at the time, as shown by my love for Quo disappearing by 1978, an unappealing 'commercial side' seeing key members depart in time.

As for The Orchid in Purley, a year later it closed, reopening as Tiffany's nightclub around 1975.

GREAT WESTERN EXPRESS FESTIVAL
26 - 29 MAY 1972, BARDNEY, LINCOLN, UK

I WAS THERE: PETER SMITH, AGE 15

I was so excited to be going to a real pop festival. My dad drove me and a couple of mates down on Friday night, after we'd been to the local Mecca ballroom. We arrived in the early hours of Saturday morning, missing Friday's bill, sleeping in a big crash tent for a few hours. We soon ran into a group of other lads who had also come down from Sunderland, and between us we built a cabin out of bales of hay and planks of wood lying around in the fields. I swear there were around 20 of us sleeping in there. We were quite close to the stage, and I pretty much stayed in that cabin all weekend. We could also stand on the roof and watch the bands. There was a massive (and very empty) press enclosure which divided the crowd from the stage, so no one could get that close, which was bad planning. The weather was wet, raining for most of the weekend. But I didn't care; this was a real pop festival, and I was determined to enjoy every minute. The line-up for the remaining three days of the event was really strong.

Lindisfarne were first to get the crowd going, a big hit of the weekend. We were on the roof of our cabin singing along to 'Fog On The Tyne'. But the big hit of the day was Slade, who just tore the place apart. They started out with a lot to prove to a 'hippie' crowd who viewed them as a pop act. By the end everyone was singing along and converted.

This was a sort of 'coming-of-age' performance by Slade. All the crowd warmed to the band, encouraged by Noddy's loud voice and sheer charisma. They started the set as a flimsy pop act in the eyes of much of the crowd, and finished a loud, proper rock 'n' roll band. All the music papers carried headlines the next week proclaiming Slade as the breakthrough heroes of the event. I will never forget their performance. They were followed by Monty Python's Flying Circus, the entire cast doing all their famous sketches, including 'Dead Parrot', 'Lumberjack Song' and 'Argument'. All good fun. The Beach Boys closed the evening and were wonderful, singing their classic hits. A great end to a great day. But Slade remained the heroes of the day, everyone talking about them, my friends amazed how good they were.

I was very proud that my idols had, in one short hour, turned around their career.

I WAS THERE: PETER ROBINSON, AGE 20

It was awful weather, and people were not in a good mood. When Slade came on, everyone was waiting for Rory Gallagher and didn't want to see this 'pop', so spent the first few minutes booing loudly. But it soon became clear that they were pretty good. I think they did about 20 minutes, but by then the crowd were bowled over and wanted more. They had to do another 15 minutes and got at least a five-minute standing ovation. It was awful weather, but a fantastic experience.

Peter Robinson (left) was at the Lincoln Festival

I WAS THERE: JOE MURPHY, AGE 16

I saw Slade on a number of occasions. I'm sure they played Bellshill YMCA in Lanarkshire, Scotland as a sort of skinhead band, then later in their new format before they became famous! I wasn't a big Slade fan and didn't have any of their albums, but I was aware of what they could do live. They never let you down. I also saw them at the Great Western Festival in Lincoln in 1972. I won two tickets from *Sounds* magazine. We hitchhiked there. The line-up was fabulous, with so many great bands and artists playing. Slade played on the Sunday in the early evening to a long-haired hippy audience and went down a bomb. They had to do an encore.

Joe Murphy saw Slade earn an encore at the Great Western Festival

I WAS THERE: CLIFF BOND

My second Slade sighting was at the Great Western Festival, near Lincoln, late May. My mum had a new lover who was a creepy bastard and he introduced me to these hippie types who liked Cream and Free, who I'd never heard of. They were two years older than me, and I thought they were very worldly. We drove there, about six of us, in an old Morris Oxford estate, in which I slept at night. When Slade came on that Sunday, they got bottled and booed, but by the second song the crowd were all dancing along. I thought that was very funny. Having seen them two months previously, I knew they rocked. That weekend was a revelation and a disappointment for me – the Faces, The Beach Boys, Roxy Music and Joe Cocker were awful, but Slade, Humble Pie, Sha Na Na, Rory Gallagher and Status Quo were just brilliant.

FREE TRADE HALL

30 MAY 1972, MANCHESTER, UK

I WAS THERE: TONY PYE, AGE 15

Tony Pye saw Slade 89 times

I saw the original group 89 times, the first time in May 1972 at the Free Trade Hall in Manchester. Status Quo were the support (the first of 90 times I saw them). The first record I ever bought was 'Look Wot You Dun', earlier that year. This led me to buy *Slade Alive!* which remains one of my favourite albums of all time. I think 'Take Me Bak 'Ome' had just been released. I don't remember much about the gig except them opening with Hear Me Calling' and my hearing 'Move Over' for the first time. I'd never heard the Janis Joplin version and presumed it was a Slade original. It was also the first time I'd heard 'Look Wot You Dun' and 'Take Me Back 'Ome' live. The next time I saw them was also at the Free Trade Hall, in November 1972, with Thin Lizzy and Suzi Quatro as support.

I WAS THERE: COLIN GRIMSHAW

Colin Grimshaw first saw Slade in 1972

When I was about nine, a mate of mine came to my house to see if I had heard of this band called Slade. Me? No, never. His dad had just got him a new record player and this LP called *Slade Alive!* Did I want to go to his house and listen to it? I'd never seen an LP before. He put it on, and what can I say…? I still play that record. I first saw Slade at the Free Trade Hall in Manchester. It blew my mind. I came out of the hall deaf, missed my bus home and had to walk home 14 miles – it was about 1.30 in the morning when I got back, and my dad kicked shit out of me. Well, he was a twat. I was also at Belle Vue.

DREAMLAND BALLROOM

3 JUNE 1972, MARGATE, UK

I WAS THERE: ROY TAPPENDEN

When I left school in 1971, I kept up friends with some of my mates. One particular friend, Phil, rang me and said he was moving to Margate with his mum and dad. They'd bought a guest house, the Burlington, a couple of minutes from the station. We got talking on the phone and he said I should come down to see him and we could see the nightlife down there. I agreed, but a year went by and I hadn't heard from him so I decided to ring him. We got chatting and he said they had some good groups appearing at the Rondi club very shortly, and he mentioned Slade, asking if I wanted to go and see them. It didn't take me long to say yes. He got the tickets, six weeks ahead, and the Thursday before the Saturday they were appearing at Margate they were on *Top of the Pops*, having just bought out 'Take Me Bak 'Ome'. By the beginning of July, it was at No.1.

What a night it was, girls throwing items of underwear at Noddy and the rest of the group. They played all their singles and some of their earlier stuff. I stayed at Phil's mum and dad's guest house that night and they wouldn't take anything from me. I went home the following day and couldn't wait to tell my other mates.

The second time I went to see this great group was in 1973, at Earl's Court, with the Sensational Alex Harvey Band as support. They were mad, especially Alex, smashing his guitar up on stage. Then, after the break, Earl's Court exploded. The Noize, wow, everybody going mental as Slade came on. If I remember right, 'Hear Me Calling' came blasting out first, all their brilliant singles were played, and again girls threw their undergarments, the crowd jumping up and down, another great concert. They were certainly the best group around at the time and still going strong, with hit after hit.

My last Slade concert was at the London Palladium, with the support group Geordie. Then the great Slade came on, the Noize and excitement from all the fans electric, dancing in the aisles. Another brilliant concert.

UNIVERSITY OF EXETER

9 JUNE 1972, EXETER, UK

I WAS THERE: MIKE WATTS

I booked them for a Rag Hop when they'd just had a hit with 'Coz I Luv You', but not many turned out to see them in the Dining Hall, as was the case for then unknown support band Roxy Music. A year later they were one of the biggest acts in the country and headlined the Summer Ball. My girlfriend at the time lent Dave Hill some make-up in the Green Room, and he returned the compliment by painting a sparkly star on her cheek.

PIER PAVILION

12 AUGUST 1972, FELIXSTOWE, UK

I WAS THERE: WILLIAM MARTIN

I will never forget this concert. Slade were at the top of their game and the hits kept coming – 'Mama Weer All Crazee Now', and so on. There was a long wait to get in, three or four allowed in at a time. Inside, it was packed. They played all the hits and most of the *Slade Alive!* LP, with tickets £1. It was a great concert with all the glam rock, top hats and glitter. I saw them again on 17th January 1981 at Ipswich Gaumont. Admission by then had increased to £3.25!

'MAMA WEER ALL CRAZEE NOW' RELEASED 25 AUGUST 1972

Slade's third single reaches No.1 in the UK and stays in the charts for ten weeks. It reaches No.76 in the US.

I WAS THERE: ANDY KERSHAW, BROADCASTER & AUTHOR

It's still a good loutish record… and by God we could do with some loutishness in rock 'n' roll now. It's all so bloody polite.

Slade embark upon their first American tour.

MEMORIAL HALL

2 SEPTEMBER 1972, SACRAMENTO, CALIFORNIA

I WAS THERE: JOHN MARTIN

I was over from the UK for a month in California visiting relatives. Slade were opening for Humble Pie, with Boz Scaggs providing the 'meat in the sandwich'. I had seen Slade once before in their previous existence as Ambrose Slade, at Leicester University. Their gig in Sacramento was faultless, although the critic from local newspaper *The Sacramento Bee* slated them. It prompted me to write a letter to the editor criticising the review, which was published. Some vindication at least!

DEUTSCHLANDHALLE

26 OCTOBER 1972, BERLIN, GERMANY

I WAS THERE: HEATHER BLANDFORD

My father was with the armed forces and stationed in Berlin. I read somewhere that this venue held just under 9,000. A group of us queued for a few hours prior to the doors opening, in order to get a good spot. When they did, our teenage legs sprinted towards the front of the stage, where we stayed for the duration of the concert. We were literally leaning on the stage. If memory serves me right, there was no security keeping us away. They got to No.1 the previous month with 'Mama Weer All Crazee Now', and the whole place went wild as soon as they came on. From that day I was hooked on their music, they were fantastic live and always put on a great show. I went on to see them a further five times, all with the original line-up, always coming away with ringing in my ears but with memories of a great concert.

Heather Blandford's dad was stationed in Germany so she saw Slade there

FLAMINGO BALLROOM

POOL, REDRUTH, UK

I WAS THERE: KEVIN LEAN

That night they played all their hits and more. Tartan was the rage then, and skinhead was the rage, and us youngsters followed suit, with Doc Martens, braces, the lot – to think we used to dress like that! I was courting a girl when I had my hair exactly like Noddy's (permed). At the same time my girlfriend sent a photo into a *Women's Own* competition – 'Copy A Star', and lo and behold, I won it and was matched with Noddy! Good days!

In '76, Troon FC toured and went to Wood Green FC in London, and the only cassette played up and back was *Slade Alive!* I remember having that LP, reading a report in the record sleeve where Noddy was described as 'a gentleman with a voice like a cut-throat razor'. And Noddy and Slade will go to my grave with me – forever a part of me. And to meet 'the boys' would make me complete.

A Flamingo gig scheduled for 10 September 1972 was cancelled due to US touring commitments. It's uncertain when it was finally played, but apparently Flamingo owner Joy Hone told Slade to turn the volume down 'or I'll pull the plug, my lovelies'.

SLAYED? RELEASED 1 DECEMBER 1972

Slayed? *was Slade's third studio album. It reached No.1 in the charts and remained on the chart for 34 weeks.*

I WAS THERE: ANDY LINDSAY

Slade entered my world in 1975 or 1976, when I was six or seven. It was a Saturday and my dad had worked that morning and was spending the afternoon having some 'him time', in the front room, cigar in one hand, the *Daily Mirror* next to him on the sofa. On the hi-fi – a Garrard deck with a separate amp and two-way speakers he built himself, with a proper crossover so the bass was solid – was *Slade Alive!*

He hadn't got it all the way up to eleven, but it was really loud when I came in the room. I think Mum was staying well out of the way, and after five minutes of me staring and listening, she came and found me and told me to leave my dad alone.

Soon after, I had my own deck, also a Garrard (an SP25, for the nerds out there). I had loads of singles from my grandad, and in there was 'Merry Xmas Everybody'. As a kid, any record would be played over and over, even if it wasn't Christmas. Fast forward to 1979, when The Specials and The Jam entered my life… and so did guitars. It wasn't long after that I had that Slade LP upstairs, desperately trying to play along.

What struck me was the quiet and loud. They played really well, really tight, quiet when needed and loud as hell when needed. It's good stuff to play along to. Fast forward to 1991, and I had the *Play It Loud* LP on CD. I was busy trying to be the next Paul Weller, and I so badly wanted my band to be as good as them. On the insert of our single for Detour Records, we did a collage of our influences, and there in the corner was the *Slayed?* LP.

Photo Simon Parr

Andy Lindsay, still on the decks all these years on

We got to play with a few bands round that time, and they all mentioned Slade. It was like a generation of future indie guitar bands loved The Jam, the Pistols, The Smiths, etc., but they also wanted that Slade power. And, as we all know, Noel Gallagher made no secret of his love of the band. So, I am pleased someone took their torch and did something good with it. Nowadays Slade get played at Mod Shoes when I am on my own and have got pictures to do. And, of course, I have it up nice and loud.

I always thought Nirvana must have been fans. They did that quiet loud thing so well. And I have often pondered, 'Did they nick that from Slade?' I can't think of anyone else that did it before them. 'Pouk Hill' and 'Look At Last Nite' are my faves. Both could have been big hits. But they get eclipsed by the mega-singles.

CITY HALL

3 NOVEMBER 1972, NEWCASTLE-UPON-TYNE, UK

I WAS THERE: COLIN PETERSEN, AGE 13

I was 13 when I went to see Free at Newcastle City Hall in 1972, my first concert, and the next month I saw Led Zeppelin, also at the City Hall. So my street cred was pretty good as far as musical taste went, if not my choice of clothes, and it was with some trepidation that I attended the City Hall to see Slade. I agreed to go with a school mate, presumably on the promise there'd be plenty of girls in attendance. I seem to recall he liked Thin Lizzy, who were the support band.

Colin Petersen saw Slade at City Hall

I wasn't particularly a Slade fan – they were at that time very much a chart band – but they were very good, a tight band and very entertaining. I did have *Slade Alive!* but that was a different set from what we saw that night, incorporating lots of their hits up to then. I don't think I told my other mates I was going, as they were of a Free, Zep, Sabbath and Wishbone Ash persuasion.

There was a pleasant surprise in seeing the Suzi Quatro Band too. They were very good, the days before her pop stuff. I think it might have been their first UK gig, or first significant gig. They played a short but rocking set, including an excellent version of 'Free Electric Band'. Thin Lizzy were disappointing, a tight band but their material was a bit dull and limited. I saw them again in 1976, again at the City Hall, that time as headliners, in their pomp.

Slade were very impressive; a band who'd honed their live performances over a few year, musically very proficient, and the material really rocked. They played their hits of the time, 'Take Me Bak 'Ome', 'Get Down And Get With It' and so on, plus things like 'Hear Me Calling' and 'In Like A Shot From My Gun'. The City Hall was absolutely bouncing. Fast forward 47 years and I saw them again, albeit with only Dave Hill from the original line-up. A friend asked if I fancied going to see their 2019 Christmas gig in Newcastle, so off we went with our better halves on 23rd December. As you'd expect, a party atmosphere and a run through all the hits. Neither of the guys sharing lead vocals sounded as good as Noddy Holder, but they made a decent fist of it and a good night was had by all.

PUBLIC HALL

4 NOVEMBER 1972, PRESTON, UK

I WAS THERE: NICK HOLME

Slade played the Public Hall in Preston, Lancashire, twice in 1972, on 1st March and 4th November. I'm not sure which I went to, but I suspect it was the later one. They were very popular and lots of my mates had the *Slade Alive!* album. The Public Hall was Preston's main entertainment venue then, built originally as the Corn Exchange around 1822 and remodelled as a meeting hall and dance hall/entertainment venue around 1882. It was famous for its sprung dance floor, designed to flex a little and help absorb shock, giving dancers a more pleasant experience. All the big bands played there until the end of 1972, when the Guild Hall opened and the Public Hall shut down. This was done so a major road ('the Ring Road', although it goes through the centre of Preston!) could be built. It was finally partly demolished during the Eighties, the remaining front section now a pub.

Incidentally, the first rock gig at the Guild Hall was Emerson, Lake and Palmer (ELP), on 18th November that year, which I was lucky to attend on the front row, so Slade must have been pretty much the last band to play the Public Hall, which played host to many major bands, including The Beatles and the Rolling Stones.

The Public Hall was laid out with a stage at one end with the dance floor in front and a first-floor level of seating all the way round. There were no seats on the dance floor – everyone just piled in a big crowd in front of the stage. I remember the crowd filling about half of the floor area, even when they were all crushed together. If you went in the first-floor seating area, where the seats extended to the side of the stage, you could get pretty close to the band, and we spent some time there. Noddy Holder had his extremely large sideburns and his top hat with mirrors. When the band played 'Coz I Luv You', Jim took up his classic stance, one foot up on the bass drum, leaning back playing the violin – rock magic.

We decided to go down and join the crowd on the dance floor. Approaching from the back we could see audience heads going up and down together. As we walked forward, we could feel the floor coming up to meet our feet as we walked. The crowd were jumping together, causing the sprung dancefloor to flex up and down. It was like walking on a boat in a stormy sea.

I can't tell you much more about the gig apart from the fact that our ears were still ringing the next day. We used to say you could tell how good a gig had been by how long your ears were ringing for afterwards. Unfortunately, this came back to haunt me – many years watching and playing in rock bands leaving me with tinnitus, so I've got the ringing for the rest of my life. Good gig though.

CIVIC HALL

6 NOVEMBER 1972, WOLVERHAMPTON, UK

I WAS THERE: STEVE MURTAGH

I was asked to go to a concert with a mate, It was Slade, so I jumped at the chance, but had no idea who was supporting them. I was new to concerts, so no arriving after the warm-ups or going straight to the bar. It was directly to our seats, waiting for the fun to begin. We were looking forward to a good show!

First of all, this little woman came on with her band. She had a massive bass guitar that seemed bigger than her. It was Suzi Quatro! They only had a short slot, but they were very good. I think they did 'Can The Can', but my memory may be playing tricks about that. She then introduced another band, at which point lots of obvious regulars came in from the bar, as this band was obviously popular. It was Thin Lizzy. They were a three-piece, and from the start had something about them. Their single 'Whiskey In The Jar' had just been released and the place erupted when they started that. I was well impressed! They rattled off a couple of real rockers, and I was hooked immediately. The Irish drawl of Phil was mesmerising, and he knew how to get the audience going. It really was a great set. They did well and left to rapturous applause, which was rare for a Slade support band! Slade then came on and did an amazing show. What a night.

I WAS THERE: CHRIS HILL, ACE PROMOTIONS

My Slade journey started as a Black Country lad into music at an early age and anything that was in the Top 20. Then along came Slade, from basically up the road, and that was it. I was hooked, I had every single and LP released and every possible publication where there was a feature on them, mainly to get their pictures on my bedroom wall. My first actual interaction with Slade was by way of getting their autographs in the departure lounge at Birmingham Airport when they were en route to Amsterdam. I just happened to be in the right place at the right time with my parents.

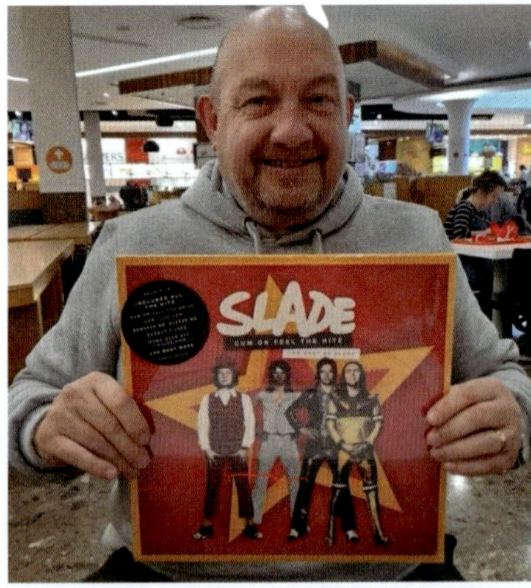

Chris Hill with the Cum On Feel The Hitz box set, and Noddy signing it

As a teenager, I saw Slade live at Wolverhampton Civic Hall in both 1972, supported by Suzi Quatro and Thin Lizzy, and 1973, when they were supported by The Sensational Alex Harvey Band. After their departure to America in 1975, I remained an avid fan but knew I wouldn't see them live again for some time to come, and never did as the original four.

I went on to work for Guest Motors, a main Ford dealer in West Bromwich. About a year into his employment with us, a young salesman named Ian Powell said to me, 'I have a sale coming up on 1st August with my uncle, who was part of a famous rock band. You might have heard of him. He's named Don Powell, from Slade, and he's coming up from Devon to collect the car, a gleaming 2.8 Ford Granada Estate.' I had spoken with Ian every day, not knowing he was Don's nephew.

I made sure I was there at the handover stage on the front row.

Not long after, Allan Atkins, who also worked at Guest Motors (and who was a founder member of Judas Priest), said to me, 'If you come to the Coach and Horses, West Bromwich, this Thursday, I will be there with big Archie and Noddy Holder. Nod's coming down to see Trevor Burton from The Move and his band.' And true to his word, when I got there, all three of them were standing by the bar. It was like a dream come true – an evening on the lash with my teenage pop idol.

Chris Hill's treasured Slade Alive! eight-track cartridge, as a schoolboy around 13, and his bedroom wall around then

After my Ford days, I started contracting to a local music promoter who dealt with loads of retro bands and artists, including Martha Reeves and the Vandellas, Ben E King, The Real Thing. And then the big one came up, Don and Dave as Slade II on their Christmas tour. I did a few shows with them, almost pinching myself to see if this was real. Don's stories are legendary, and he even remembered me from picking the Granada Estate up all those years ago.

I attended Don's autobiography signing at

Waterstones in Wolverhampton in October 2013, followed by afternoon tea and a few stories in aid of his chosen charity, the National Autistic Society, at the Connaught Hotel.

I helped arrange two Slade conventions at the Robin 2 in Bilston with Slade's fifth man, the late Dave Kemp, and the venue's proprietor, Mike Hamblett. And I attended both of Jim Lea's solo shows at the same venue in 2002 and 2017, the first being a charity gig in aid of Jim's late father, where he sang a right old mash-up of songs from Slade to the Sex Pistols, with The Beatles and The Who in between, while the second was a Q & A session ('for one night only – an audience with Jim Lea') that very unexpectedly turned into a music show at the end. Grown men were seen with tears in their eyes when Jim appeared on stage with a guitar and started belting a few Slade tunes out.

WINTER GARDENS

8 NOVEMBER 1972, BOURNEMOUTH, UK

I WAS THERE: DAVID MCINTYRE

I was working at Bournemouth's Winter Gardens installing air conditioning on and around the stage area, and amongst the artists were Slade. They were amazing. Come the show they were so loud, Noddy at his best! Thin Lizzy were support.

RAINBOW THEATRE

10 & 11 NOVEMBER 1972, LONDON, UK

I WAS THERE: DON BUTTON

I first saw Slade in 1972 at the Rainbow, Finsbury Park. I was in awe when I walked into the foyer and saw the *Sladest* LP cover pinned around the walls. The evening was electric, with Thin Lizzy, Suzi Quatro, and then Slade. At the time, I worked as a tape room boy for the *Evening News* and went with a friend, John Branch. Slade came in for an interview with John Blake, which was exciting. Unfortunately, I didn't meet them, but I was given a lot of photos of Slade live in concert. I wish I still had them; I don't know what happened to them.

I also saw them at the opening night of the Sundown, Mile End, East London. They came back part-way through a US tour for that. It was ram-packed and hot, a good gig. Then there was the London Palladium, with support act Geordie, who had Brian Johnson on vocals, now with AC/DC. Me and my mate Stephen Durbridge had front row seats, right up against the PA speakers. It was absolutely fantastic, although I couldn't hear properly for about a week afterwards. Noddy did his usual thing – a spotlight on the mirrors of his top hat projecting it out to the audience.

And then it was the big one, Earl's Court in 1973, supported by the Sensational Alex Harvey Band. Again, I went with Stephen. The PA system was absolutely amazing, the stage was huge and there were close-ups of the band projected onto screens. Unfortunately, it wasn't recorded to make any proper film or sound recording and Noddy won't release what recordings there are because the sound and film quality is very poor, but I'm sure it could be remastered.

It wasn't a long set – only about an hour, with an encore. I thought at the time, 'Fancy booking a big venue like that with thousands of fans and only doing an hour.' A lot were moaning about that coming out of the gig. But it was a good gig nonetheless.

I saw them in 1980 too – quite a big gap – at The Marquee on Wardour Street, Soho, a small gig but the boys were very good. I also once met Jim Lea coming out of Air Recording Studios in Oxford Street at about two in the morning. I was working in the building at the time. He was just about to get into his car. Such a nice bloke.

I WAS THERE: TERRY MASKELL

The first song I heard them do was 'Get Down And Get With It'. I thought Noddy's voice was incredible. The first Slade record I bought was *Slade Alive!* I saw them at the Rainbow in Finsbury Park in about 1972. I went with my sister, Shirley, some of her school friends, my cousin John, and another friend, also called John. Hawkwind were the warm-up. They had only

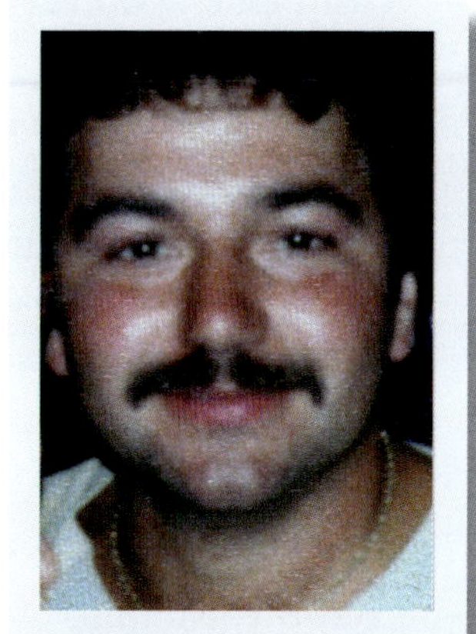

Terry Maskell saw Slade at the Rainbow

done 'Silver Machine', so they made the one song last half an hour, although they did throw paper plates out into the audience! It was the one and only time I saw Slade, but I did have the Noddy Holder trousers and the massive platform shoes, in beige. Oh, what it is to be a slave to fashion...

I WAS THERE: KRIS JOZAJTIS, FOLK DEVILS

Slade were the first. The first band I ever got into properly. The first I went to see live. The first I wanted to identify with as a fan, and the first that I, myself, chose to incorporate into my own story. My tastes might have developed and moved on, but, like a first love, the impression they made on me was indelible and the thought of those days still makes me tingle.

Grammar school kid turned Cumbernauld high school teacher Kris Jozajtis, seen in action with davesnewbike, wanted to be part of a Slade gang

Don't get me wrong; there had been a lot of music priming my 13-year-old ears prior to my first hearing of 'Take Me Bak 'Ome' in the spring of 1972. My dad had a lifelong interest in music, and from an early age I was exposed to a wide range of stuff; Elvis, The Beatles, Sinatra, Tom Jones, popular classics, music from Poland (where my family came from), some jazz, songs from the musicals, etc., as well as all the pop hits of the day via *Top of the Pops* and the other light entertainment shows on the telly.

I even knew a real-life musician. In the low-rise block council block we were living in at the time in Feltham, Middlesex, one of the rougher south-western fringes of Greater London, we had a neighbour called Iain Hines who kept a Hammond Organ in his living room. Iain had hung out and played with Tony Sheridan and The Beatles in Hamburg. At the time he was in a band called Icarus. Iain introduced me to more rocky stuff like the early Stones and 'Layla' by Derek and the Dominos. But my listening moved from passive acceptance of what was around to an active interest one sunny Sunday afternoon. I daresay my hormones had something to do with it.

Around half a dozen of us, including a girl called Lyn that I had a huge crush on, were hanging out at the entrance to one of the blocks with a portable transistor radio blaring. Suddenly, I was transfixed by the raunchy opening twin guitar riffs of the new single from Slade. And then that voice, singing a song that, to this young naif, spoke of something dark, dangerous, thrilling, and utterly irresistible.

After three minutes of stomping rhythm and raunch, I realised I needed plenty more of where this came from. Unfortunately, Lyn wasn't that interested in me, but my discovery of Slade more than made up for her oversight. I quickly found out that the band had already made a sizeable dent in the national consciousness with several previous chart hits.

As a grammar school kid, I was amused by the deliberately misspelt titles. Their performances on *Top of the Pops* were joyous and exciting. My first purchase of any music paper was prompted by my need to read reports of Slade stealing the show at the Great Western Festival near Lincoln that same spring. And to a young wannabe football hooligan (I was and remain a Chelsea supporter), their image of glammed-up former bovver boys was nigh on perfect. I wanted a hair style like Dave Hill. I wanted to be part of the Slade gang.

One problem was the lack of a record player in the house, as my father used reel-to-reel tape recorders to play music recorded from the radio. But this was a time of near Slademania; they seemed to be everywhere on the TV and the radio. And regular airplay was supplemented by hanging out with pals who had one or more of the singles or, crucially, a copy of *Slade Alive!* My youth cultural capital was considerably enhanced though, when, after much pleading, I convinced my dad to record a BBC Radio 1 *In Concert* featuring the band playing live in Golders Green.

I'm not sure my parents approved of the music but my mum was accepting of the pals that now had a reason to come round to our ground floor flat. By the autumn, all the reports of how great a live act Slade were had convinced me the only way to show that I was a true fan was to go see them live. I duly used some saved up pocket and 14th birthday money to send off a postal order with an SAE, and on Saturday 11th November 1972 and wearing some glitter on my face, I took a bus (on my own) to Hounslow East and thence on the Piccadilly line to Finsbury Park to see Slade at the Rainbow Theatre, my first proper gig.

From my seat in the circle, I got to see a hitherto unknown Suzi Quatro open the show and then Thin Lizzy (with Eric Bell on guitar), both on the cusp of chart success. I thought they were both pretty good. But I was there for my favourites, and Slade did not disappoint. I can still recall the swirling lights, Noddy's mirrored hat, and how loud, brash, exciting and totally in charge of proceedings they were. There was a lot of foot-stomping and hand-clapping as I looked down on a scene of crazy, wild abandon in the stalls. They set a high benchmark for all the great live rock 'n' roll I would come to witness over the next half-century or so.

Slade weren't the only thing forging my musical tastes in 1972. Bolan and T.Rex were already massive and getting bigger; Bowie's epochal performance of 'Starman' on *Top of the Pops* and 'School's Out' by Alice Cooper ensured there was plenty to talk about as the summer term wound down at school. And then Roxy Music released 'Virginia Plain'. Yet Slade were more than able to cope with all the competition, and released 'Cum On Feel The Noize', probably my favourite single of theirs, at the beginning of 1973.

By then though, I had a record player, and the exploration and discussion of music with friends, and even some tentative attempts to play guitar, had led me to broaden my listening, and Slade became just one of many bands that held my attention, particularly after I discovered The Who, just in time to have my teenage mind blown by *Quadrophenia*, an album I was given for Christmas 1973, just as 'Merry Xmas Everybody' topped the single charts.

From obsession to merely keeping a soft spot is probably a journey most music fans make over and over. Beyond a muttered 'great' and turning the volume up when one of their classic singles happens to be played on the radio, I don't really seek out Slade's music anymore. But their influence abides. For a start, by fusing the entertainment traditions of the music hall (including learning your craft by paying your dues) with the visceral thrill of a primal, hard rock 'n' roll sound, Slade taught the self-conscious, serious-minded, angsty teenager that I once was, that there is nothing wrong with smiling and having fun; that having a good time happens in the here and now.

FREE TRADE HALL
15 NOVEMBER 1972, MANCHESTER, UK

I WAS THERE: PHIL BRENNAN

The first gig I ever went to was Slade at the Free Trade Hall in Manchester. I had been given a ticket by my mate Jimmy Campbell for my 14th birthday. Having spent several months at home listening to the radio whilst recovering from a badly broken leg, ending any potential football career, I was really getting into music. I loved T.Rex and David Bowie and had been listening to the first 'live' music I ever heard – a cassette of *Slade Alive!*

Slade were Phil Brennan's first gig

When Jimmy told me he had tickets for us to go and see Slade in town, I was beside myself with excitement. We went to his house in Fallowfield straight from school in Whalley Range, had tea and got changed before catching a bus into Manchester. One thing I had learnt about Slade was that earlier in their career they had been a skinhead band, and as such still had a skinhead following among their fans.

I saw two other bands before the main act, Suzi Quatro and her band playing a set, followed by Thin Lizzy. I remember several skinheads in the audience heckling Suzi regarding her skin-tight leather catsuit. And they were more abusive towards Thin Lizzy, particularly front man Phil Lynott. Those who witnessed Lizzy in concert will no doubt be aware of Lynott's favourite saying, 'Is there anybody here with any Irish in them?' followed very quickly by, 'Is there any of the girls that want a little more Irish in them?' Most people saw the funny side of it, but not many of the shaven-headed bigoted youths near the front, and before you knew it there was mayhem.

As much as I enjoyed the support bands, I had come to witness the main act, and the boys from the Midlands didn't disappoint. I prepared for the concert by listening to a cassette of *Slade Alive!* repeatedly. I thought I was ready but found myself in complete awe at the sound Slade made. The Noize was almost unbearable, albeit a sound I absolutely loved. Having started with 'Hear Me Calling', they ran through an impressive set, including some hit singles and a few songs new to me.

A packed crowd sang along to the likes of 'Look Wot You Dun', 'Coz I Luv You', 'Take Me Bak 'Ome', 'Mama Weer All Crazee Now' and 'Get Down And Get With It' before they finished with a Little Richard song, 'Good Golly Miss Molly'.

After the concert, there were slight skirmishes outside between a few skinheads and the lads that stood up to them earlier in the evening, but we just stepped away and made our way to the bus stop in Piccadilly Gardens. I stayed the night at Jimmy's, and we caught the bus to school the following morning, chattering about the previous evening's gig all the way. I don't think I paid attention to a single lesson all day, such was my excitement at the prospect of going to more and more gigs.

'GUDBUY T' JANE' RELEASED 17 NOVEMBER 1972

'Gudbuy T' Jane' spends eight weeks in the UK Top Ten, peaking on 16 December at No.2.

I WAS THERE: DAVID LANCE CALLAHAN, THE WOLFHOUNDS

Slade wiv yor sweeties

Dropped off by dad in a blue minivan
clutching 10p in scrounged coppers that filled his palm

the sweet shop was pretentious
a tobacconist–confectioners
outside blaring traffic
glaring sunlight made it too dark and muffled inside

emerging from the sepia
army and navys
flying saucers
cola bottles chewy and consumable
or glass and returnable for a few extra pennies (or fractions thereof)
superman cigarettes, matches
(he collected the labels from gritty roadsides)
players fag numbers 6 to 10
(according to the age you started on them)
a rack of new english library paperbacks and pans and panthers
buy one magazine and you have to buy the lot
until you have an unexplained set of the unexplained
(minus the one that the postman lost)
minstrels in interchangeable pastels
on front and back covers
animals, fishing, air guns and shotguns
eagerly subscribed to make sure you got 'em

5p for a dc tales from the crypt
a humanoid in black pizza-cheese quicksand
inexplicable distant pain in its eyes
a trick ending with a grim surprise

5p left and up to the counter
a wood brown ale crate seven inches wide
the carpenters, hawkwind in pic sleeves inside
pretty boy gangs in clothes you'd get a kicking in

in the middle of the box
magic spelling you could afford
in plain black ink and polydor red
Slade wiv yor sweeties: gudbuy t' jane it said

I WAS BAK 'OME: STEVE HILL

My first bought single was 1972's 'Gudbuy T' Jane', having agonised whether to spend my pocket money on Slade or Lynsey De Paul's 'Sugar

Me'. My first album was *Slayed?* Happy days indeed. I only regret never having a chance to see them live back then. And they were a cracking rock 'n' roll band in '72, looking at You Tube footage nowadays.

LIVERPOOL STADIUM

18 NOVEMBER 1972, LIVERPOOL, UK

I WAS THERE: JOHN RADFORD

The next time I went to see Slade at the Stadium, they didn't do themselves any favours, at the end mocking 'You'll Never Walk Alone'. A section of the crowd then tried to rush the stage, resulting in Dave Hill going over on his ankle, trying to run off the stage. Some say he broke it.

I WAS THERE: TONY NEWBURY, AGE 19

I went back to Liverpool Stadium in November that year to see Thin Lizzy supporting them. Noddy knew how to engage the audience, which was filled with teenage screaming girls wearing red knickers and short skirts. I remember Noddy shouting, 'Anyone wearing black knickers?' The screams were deafening. I was 19 and felt old. There must have been 3,000 people there.

They opened with a cover, 'Hear Me Calling', by another band I liked, Ten Years After, but Nod was no Alvin Lee. They also did a version of Liverpool FC's anthem 'You'll Never Walk Alone'. It was hot and sweaty, and the chairs got ripped out. I remember 'Mama Weer All Crazee Now' – the fans went wild. These were still relatively small gigs, but things would change quickly with the birth of Glam.

TOWN HALL

19 NOVEMBER 1972, BIRMINGHAM, UK

I WAS THERE: JEFF COLLINS

When I went to see Slade at Birmingham Town Hall, Thin Lizzy were the support. The thing I remember most was Phil's long legs. His bass looked like a little banjo! That was when 'Whiskey In The Jar' was out.

THE DOME

20 NOVEMBER 1972, BRIGHTON, UK

I WAS THERE: DAVID HOLMES

Fast forward to November. Slade have jumped up a couple of levels and are due in at the Brighton Dome, supported, almost incredibly, by Suzi Quatro *and* Thin Lizzy! I don't remember how we secured tickets. We probably had to make a special trip to Brighton just to visit the box office.

Then, just a few days before the gig, in Dave Hill's own words:

I managed to break my ankle. Crack! It was just like a gun being fired. My Glam-tastic high-heeled boots may have looked great then, but I'm sure nowadays health and safety might just have something to say. The thing is, although Slade were a massive chart-topping band then, and we were a live band touring non-stop, playing well over 150 gigs a year in 1972, there was only one thing for it... the show must go on! It's amazing the results you can get with some silver paint and a roll of tin foil. I must have had the only Glam-rock plaster cast, and performed those shows on a massive silver throne, having been rolled out on stage.

I remember this probably more than the music as it was so unusual – we'd been convinced the show would be cancelled. Hill seemed to revel in the extra attention and, ensconced on his throne, smashed out his riffs and licks absolutely as normal. Noddy had his top hat with silver discs, while Suzi Quatro (head-to-toe in leather) and Thin Lizzy comprised a fabulous undercard and contributed to a very memorable night.

We subsequently saw other Glam acts – including Sweet, Mud, Mott the Hoople and (whisper it softly) Gary Glitter twice – and they led us in time to the Faces and Elton John, but none could ever capture the nuclear energy and sheer fun, for them and us, of Slade live. We've been to a very large number of concerts since 1972, but Slade still have a tight grip on a spot in the top five live acts I've ever seen.

GREEN'S PLAYHOUSE

23 NOVEMBER 1972, GLASGOW, UK

I WAS THERE: JOHN HENRY, AGE 14

I am old enough to have seen most of the great bands, including Slade in 1972 and 1973. It probably started with 'Coz I Luv You' and then *Slade Alive!* A crowd of us, all boys, went to each other's houses armed with the latest single. This was my first concert; it was my 15th birthday the day after. Although the concerts were brilliant, my main memories are about the support bands. It cost me 75p, and no booking fee, and we got three bands for that, although neither Suzi Quatro nor Thin Lizzy had become famous at that stage. Slade were always great, but they always had brilliant support bands, also including Status Quo. And the next time I saw them they had the Sensational Alex Harvey Band supporting.

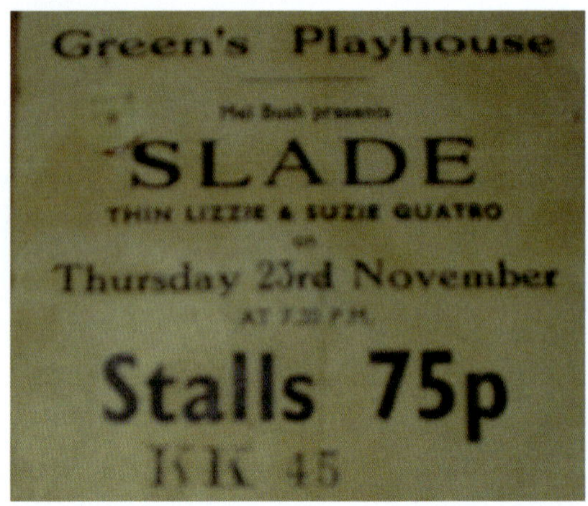

John Henry saw Slade just before his 15th birthday

GUILDHALL

2 DECEMBER 1972, PLYMOUTH, UK

I WAS THERE: PAUL GREGORY

I saw the original three-piece Thin Lizzy supporting Slade – Phil Lynott, Eric Bell and Brian Downey. Tickets were £1. Suzi Quatro was also supporting and came on first. Lizzy's 'Whiskey In The Jar' had just been released. The Guildhall was packed to capacity for Slade, and they were brilliant, Noddy wearing his mirror hat and Dave Hill with his Super Yob guitar.

LONDON PALLADIUM

7 JANUARY 1973, LONDON, UK

I WAS THERE: DYLAN WHITE

I was 14 in 1973. For us school kids, the radio was on, *Top of the Pops*, that was our life. T.Rex were there with 'Ride A White Swan', 'Hot Love', 'Get It On', and then 'Get Down And Get With It' came out, *Slade Alive!* and 'Look Wot You Dun'. The hits were coming. They were doing something to my teenage body. It's hard to explain really. My dad was an amateur classical pianist, so he was into music and I was getting into music, but it was different to his music. It was a big hoo-hah when I started buying singles and that. 'Do you want to play them on the gramophone?' 'Yes, get your classical records out of here!'

So here I am, this teenager, getting into the music you hear on the radio. I just loved listening to music, and *Top of the Pops* was the most golden moment of the week. A few of us at school had transistor radios in our pockets. You made a hole in your blazer and you'd run the wire for the earpiece up into your ear so you could sit at the back of the class with your hand over it and listen to Johnnie Walker do the chart rundown on a Tuesday lunchtime. I wrote the chart down religiously every week. It was the same thing with The Jam and Oasis in later

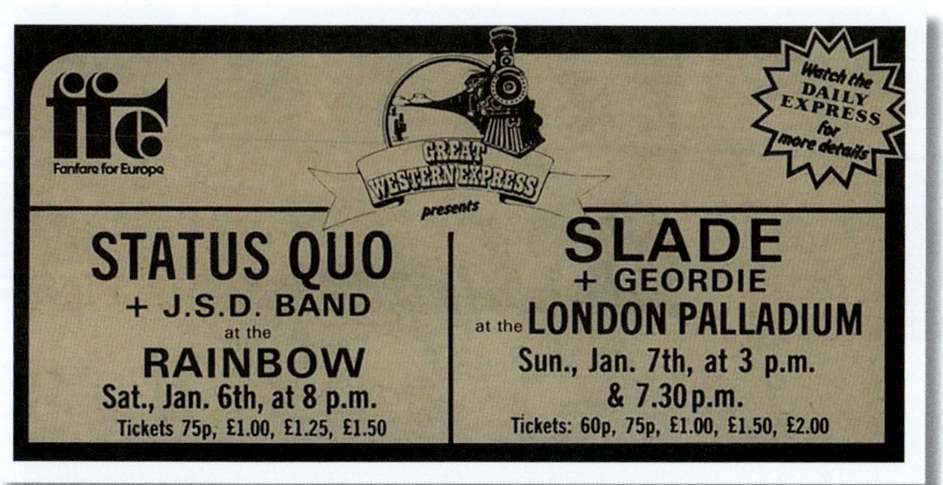

Slade played a high profile show at London Palladium in January 1973

generations. You've got to get your favourite artist to No.1. Listening to the charts with the earpiece became your life.

I had a mate, Terry, who went to see T.Rex. I still kick myself that I never went with him. Terry said, 'Slade are playing at the Palladium, do you want to go?' That was the first gig I went to, and it was a big gig for them. There hadn't really been any loud bands at the Palladium before. We were all stomping up there, the whole balcony shaking. I just couldn't believe it. I couldn't believe how the audience looked, all the girls dressed up in hot pants and the rest of it. I didn't see girls dressed like that at school. They wore bloody school uniforms. All of a sudden, everyone's glittered up. I was trying to look smart. I had whatever on at the time, platform shoes and all that. It was just this extravaganza. And it was so loud, phenomenal volume, and the four of them looked like they did on *Top of the Pops*, but in colour of course, because we had a black and white TV at home. It just blew my mind. Geordie were the support band, with Brian Johnson on vocals. It was a monumental night.

With Slayed? *topping the album charts after the showpiece gig at London Palladium as part of the Government's* Fanfare For Europe *celebrations signalling the UK joining the Common Market, Slade head to New Zealand and Australia for a tour alongside Status Quo, Lindisfarne and Caravan, arriving Down Under to wild scenes of Slademania, and by mid-February* Slayed? *is No.1 there, remaining at the top for four weeks.*

RANDWICK RACECOURSE

28 JANUARY 1973, SYDNEY, AUSTRALIA

I WAS THERE: DAVE FREE

Randwick Racecourse was a huge outdoor event area, right in the city. Several local top bands took part, plus four overseas acts. Slade were riding high with the recently released *Slayed?* and several top ten singles. They were likened to the Rolling Stones on that album. The assaults were on several levels – the glam as an obvious visual, the strong rock sound, Jim Lea's unique (for that era) violin, the rebellious poor spelling (gosh, weren't they naughty?) and Noddy's amazing guttural melodic voice.

Dave Free was at Randwick Racecourse

I was a boy from regional New South Wales, 200 kilometres away. The local radio station (2BS) sold tickets and ran a bus for the day. For most of us it was our first big outside concert experience. Most boys where I lived had Slade written on their knuckles in blue biro. The other main act was Status Quo, a double bill that's hard to beat even now!

It rained for much of the day. The music didn't start on time and the crowd got bored. Eventually, all the local acts were canned. This included reigning local heroes, Sherbet. The first of the four overseas bands to make the stage were Caravan. They were probably quite good (certainly good enough to come all this way) but the crowd wasn't in the mood by then and they weren't treated well.

Lindisfarne were fabulous. It was impossible to dislike their boyish folk rock. I have a fondness for them that extends through to today. Slade were next! Noddy dominated the stage and the crowd with a fabulous rough voice and made every effort to involve the audience in a great late afternoon show. I cannot recall before or since so many thousands clapping with arms held high with such precision. It was all there for us locals to see and experience – the glitter, the over-the-top brilliance of Dave, the rock chops and the cutting violin. It was a great show and won many hearts when it could've been a wet disaster.

I got a job and moved away from my country hometown (although I'm now back) and I confess I drifted away from Slade until the wonders of the internet brought me back to them again. Slade are now in a fairly exclusive rock band club. The four band members are still alive and (I hope) well. Sadly, the same can't be said for Quo or Lindisfarne. This of course means, should they wish, these gentlemen can reform, however briefly and for whatever project takes their fancy. I urge them to do so.

I WAS THERE: DONALD HARKNESS, AGE 13

Way back in 1973, I had long hair and was chasing the girls. A lot of my mates were into David Bowie, Led Zeppelin and those sorts. I liked a lot of music, but I was mainly into voices, people who actually had great singing voices. As an Australian, I liked Johnny Farnham, Marcia Hines, David Essex and so on. I was hanging around this goofy kid at the time, Peter. He had really curly hair and coke-bottom glasses and he had the gift of the gab. We went to the beaches of Sydney on the weekends, and amazingly this kid could pick up the chicks, so I hung with him for quite a while, being a bit of a looker myself with really long hair. The chicks loved it. We were going to school dances, having a great time, AC/DC were just starting out, and I'd seen them for $2 back in the day. There was some really good bands progressing, including INXS and Ted Mulry Gang, and one day Peter came up to me at school, asking if I would go and see Slade with him. Not knowing who they were, only that they were English, all I pictured was music and chicks. Trying to stay cool, I said yes. They were coming over in six months. I heard a few of their songs, including 'Gudbuy T' Jane' and 'Mama Weer All Crazee Now', purchased my ticket at $5.50 – paying it in 50 cent pieces, it took me three months to save – and the big day finally came.

Peter and I caught the train to Sydney from the western suburbs and made our way to Randwick Racecourse in amongst thousands, eager for the concert to start. I was completely overwhelmed by the crowd, with people everywhere, and when the music started my heart was pumping in anticipation when three blokes with hair down to their arses and playing guitars came out on stage. I was bewildered, I didn't realise a back-up band came out first. They started playing and people went berserk, dancing on the Pavilion rooftops. I didn't know who they were, and a big bloke next to me clipped me on the ear, saying, 'That's Status Quo, you fuckhead!' I settled in, and then the main event, Slade, came out, Noddy Holder addressing the crowd. It was awesome, and from the first note that came out of Noddy's mouth I was hooked. The power of the man's voice was nothing but phenomenal and the band were incredible. I feel very privileged to have been so young to have had that opportunity to go and see them. I haven't seen Peter for 45 years and I don't know what ever happened to him, but I thank him, and we still have one thing in common; the day we saw Slade.

ROYAL MELBOURNE SHOWGROUNDS
4 FEBRUARY 1973, MELBOURNE, AUSTRALIA

I WAS THERE: JANET BROOM

My boyfriend back then used to play Slade on his record player. I'd never heard of them before. But they were the best band I've ever seen, and wonderfully entertaining. My boyfriend's brother came with us. I spent the concert alternating between each brother's shoulders. It rained towards the end of the concert and we were drowned rats and had to catch the train home wet through. What a great band though. Years ago, a man came into my son's computer shop while I was helping out. I noticed a tattoo on his leg, 'Slade'. I went 'wow'. Turned out he was Noddy's cousin.

I WAS THERE: JANICE M-TALENT

I always loved Slade's music and they were really good when they came to Melbourne Showgrounds. A lot of bands just sing their music and that's it, but Slade really got the crowd into the concert and into totally enjoying their music and singing along with the band.

I WAS THERE: RAY LAIDLAW, LINDISFARNE

It was the first time we'd been (to Australia), and the first time Slade had been… It was like 1963 in Australia, getting to grips with big shows, with a sense of wonder for all the Australian kids. They'd never seen anything like it. We'd been on the same bill as Quo before, at festivals and things, but we'd never met the Slade lads. But we got on like a house on fire. We were blown away at how good they were. Obviously, there was a lot of machismo in it, they enjoyed the fun and having a good time. But underneath that was a sound bloody band that could really play.

They weren't one-hit wonders. It was hit after hit after hit, and they were such a powerful band. It's not the sort of music I would have bought, but you really could appreciate how good they were at what they did. And they were very affable lads, good fun to be around. And we were never concerned about going on a bill with other bands that were great, because that made the whole show better. But while the bands got on like a house on fire, the managers didn't, so if we looked like we were gonna go down too well, when we got to our last number, soon as the last chord was ringing out, Chas (Chandler) would have Slade's roadies on, getting our gear off so we couldn't do anymore!

When we were coming back from New Zealand… they were very big on what you could bring out of the country… and with three or four bands coming through customs at the same time, they had a bloody field day. We didn't have much luggage so they're going through everyone's hand luggage, while we're signing all these forms promising you hadn't been in any livery stable or whatever. They're looking at what you've written and going through your stuff. Everybody else had toothpaste and pairs of socks. And they get to Dave Hill and his bag's just full of tinsel.

Ray Laidlaw, right, with Lindisfarne bandmate and singer-songwriter, Alan Hull back in the day

---

We did our first tour of Australia and were trying to find out what we meant to people down there, which was more difficult to find out in those days, without the internet and all that. When we landed in Sydney, all these cameras and photographers were waiting, and we were looking behind us wondering who was on the plane with us – who were they waiting for? But it was because of the success of Slade Alive!, *and it was non-stop from there – a great tour. There was us, Status Quo, Lindisfarne, Caravan…* Slade Alive! *actually outsold* Sgt. Pepper *there. It was incredible. We were travelling on the same tour bus and (the radio) was playing Slade all the time, all the other bands saying, 'Oh no, not you lot again!' But it was a great tour and us and Quo have been mates ever since.* **Don Powell**

'CUM ON FEEL THE NOIZE' RELEASED 23 FEBRUARY 1973

'Cum On Feel The Noize' goes straight in at No.1, the first single to do so since 'Get Back' by The Beatles.

BEECHDALE ESTATE

1973, WALSALL, UK

I WAS THERE: CHRIS SELBY

When Slade ruled the charts, the sighting of any of their vehicles going to Nod's parents' house on the Beechdale estate spread around the school like wildfire. Dave's Jensen was the easiest to spot. It became a regular thing to go down to Mr and Mrs Holder's house at lunchtime in the hope that Noddy or one of the others or… the Holy Grail… all four of them would be there.

Occasionally we would get lucky, but most of the time we would be greeted by Mrs Holder telling us he wasn't there, but we could have a piece of signed paper he had left. These were gratefully received and soon became a form of currency at school. Mrs Holder didn't seem keen on us asking for Noddy though… 'His name is Neville!' 'Sorry, Mrs Holder.'

One of the other rituals was listening to the BBC chart on Tuesday. My parents' house was a ten to 15-minute walk away from school. A few of us would collect a bag of chips, go to my house and listen with intent as the countdown had begun. Once we knew where Slade were, we knew we could get back to school in time. Happy days.

THE HARDROCK

27 FEBRUARY 1973, STRETFORD, MANCHESTER, UK

I WAS THERE: ALAN WHITNEY

I first saw Slade on the day 'Cum On Feel The Noize' went into the charts at No.1. I used to go to my nan and grandad's for dinner

Alan Whitney remembers 'Cum On Feel The Noize' getting to No.1

and listen to the chart rundown. It was the first time since The Beatles that anyone had gone straight in at the top! I caught the bus home at 5pm, having treated my sister to the concert as she was still at school. We got dressed up. It was cold, so I wore a purple suit with a green and black satin lining, plus a leather coat. You can guess how hot it was later.

We were five rows from the front, and The Hardrock was unusual as the left side was seated and the right-side standing, the stage being quite high. Suzi Quatro was support and wearing a pink satin jumpsuit (pre-black leather, more Glam rock!). She had a tough time playing covers. There were no hits then. 'Can The Can' came later. I remember a group of skinheads getting thrown out before Slade came on. It was mayhem, and we had to stand on the seats from the start.

Slade looked like they did on the telly. Nod, Jim, Dave and Don, our heroes. Fifth song in, Nod said, 'We had a bit of news today…' and they played 'Cum On Feel The Noize'. The place went mad. I had never been so hot, so excited or heard anything so loud! The gig ended too soon, and we missed the last bus so had to walk back home (about three miles). My ears were ringing for days after!

I was lucky enough to see the original Slade twelve times, on the '74, '75 and '77 tours, and then in '78 and '79 on the chips-in-a-basket venues. December 1980 (after Reading) was fantastic, as were the '81 and '82 tours. I also had tickets for the 1985 *Rogues Gallery* tour that never was. I saw a few bands, including Sweet, Mud, Suzi Q, Quo, Queen, ELO, and T.Rex in '75. They were all good, but Slade were the best for me.

I collected most of the singles and albums on vinyl, then again on CD. The 1983 and '84 success in USA was well deserved, and they probably would have had more if Jim Lea had not been taken ill after one gig, supporting Ozzy Osbourne. Nod decided he did not want to tour, and Slade became a studio band for the last two albums.

They never got the recognition they deserve, except perhaps at Christmas! This became a double-edged sword really, as some folk think Slade had just one hit. Of course, Dave and Don carried on in various line-ups as Slade II then Slade, and Nod did his radio/acting/celebrity stuff, while Jim studied therapy and looked after his ailing father and brother, but still recorded songs, playing that one-off gig as Jim Jam at the Robin 2 in Bilston in 2002, playing lead guitar with drum and bass backing. And *Therapy* and its added live show package proved Jim remains a great songwriter and performer.

I WAS THERE: ALAN G HAWES

I first became aware of Slade in a five-minute clip on *Granada Reports*, a mid-evening news show for North West England. They were dressed as skinheads, unusual in itself. It was recorded at Granada Studios, the original *Top of the Pops* studio. It didn't really compliment any band, so I'm not really sure it was a great deal of benefit, but after their first hit single, Glam rock was at its height.

About ten of us went to the Hardrock, a former Top Rank bowling alley that was quite wide and whose low roof created a vacuum of noise – perfect for a band like Slade, who unlike many Glam rock bands always had a good support. Suzi Quatro was no exception on this evening. As soon as Slade hit the stage, Noddy Holder was in command. The audience was as Glam as the guys on stage, in homemade stove-pipe hats and tons of glitter, adding to the atmosphere.

We knew the hits word for word, with *Slade Alive!* and *Slayed?* well established albums by then. But it wasn't just about the noise – they could really play, years of gigging up and down the country making them a real tight band. And it wasn't just about Noddy's rasping voice. Jimmy Lea, Dave Hill and Don Powell were accomplished musicians and had a sound unique to them. Several bands tried to copy it. I recall Geordie for example, with Brian Johnson on vocals, coming on the scene, but Slade ruled supreme. They were from working class backgrounds, and we loved them for that.

Over the years I've seen hundreds of gigs. Noddy Holder is up there with the best as a frontman. I still see a couple of friends I went to the Hardrock with all these years later, and I saw many bands there but never any better than Slade. And they influenced so many bands.

I WAS THERE: SUE SHEARD

When I think of Slade, it's not the 'C' word that first comes to mind (that's never mentioned in this house outside the months of December and January – years in retail does that to you) or Noddy's sideburns and trousers louder than his singing, or even the crazy spellings of the songs (crazier than Dave Hill's crazy fringe and his amazing glittery cat-suits we all aspired to wear one day).

A 'Cum On Feel The Noize' singalong got Sue Morton (as she was then) and her classmates in trouble. Sue is pictured with Dash, who 'followed me home from a bus stop one day and refused to leave'

In June 1973, we were in our last year at junior school. All the exams were done, and we were waiting to find out which schools we would be moving on to. We were the big kids now, the ones with the radios and clackers and hot pants and beanie hats and no worries now the exams were done. It was a gorgeous sunny day and all the windows were open. We had just had lunch and heard Slade playing on the radio while we were in the playground. Miss Bolton, my favourite teacher ever until that point, had just nipped out, supposedly to pick up some extra craft materials for our art session that afternoon, but in hindsight it was more likely she nipped out for a crafty smoke.

I'm not sure whose idea it was to write 'Cum On Feel The Noize' on the blackboard, or for the 30 of us to try to sing it as loudly was humanly possible. I suspect it was Gwenda Abrams, because she was usually the troublemaker, and she's a primary school teacher herself now so enough said. We were over halfway through the second chorus when we were, surprisingly, surprised as a scarlet-faced Miss Bolton launched herself back in the room explaining that everyone had been able to hear us in the building next door, in the headmaster's office, and all the way back up the corridor. Then she saw the writing on the blackboard and, in a voice that would have made Noddy proud, explained that we would no longer be spending the afternoon crafting happily, we would be doing spellings and long division, and there would be no more noize.

NATIONAL STADIUM

24 MARCH 1973, DUBLIN, IRELAND

I WAS THERE: KEIRAN FLANAGAN

I first heard Slade as a child, sitting in front of my parents' TV in the front room. *Top of the Pops* came on and Noddy yelled out the start of 'Get Down And Get With It'. My dad's face was priceless. I was hooked. I bought all their records. I saw them in Dublin. They were loud. Very loud, but great...

EMPIRE POOL

25 MARCH 1973, WEMBLEY, LONDON, UK

I WAS THERE: GEOF GALE

The late Sixties and early Seventies were drab, music-wise. The Stones were in a lull, The Beatles had broken up, there was a guy singing about riding a white swan (good grief, RIP), and Major Tom was floating in space. Then there were these four guys playing heavy, but commercial tracks. The first time I saw Slade was at

Geof Gale thought the Seventies were drab until Slade came along

Wembley in 1973, just after 'Cum On Feel The Noize' went straight to No.1. The crowd were so hyped up by the end that they somehow had to calm them down by piping out the original 'Singing In The Rain', which seemed to have that effect. They were brilliant live, also being the loudest I ever witnessed.

I WAS THERE: DAVID FEARN

The second Slade gig I saw was a very different experience. They were now massive, Stuart and I off to London by train to see them at the Empire Pool, Wembley. We had on our Doc Martens, sprayed silver to match the hair under our mirror top hats. If only I had a picture. The place went mental for Slade.

I WAS THERE: GARY SMITH

I was only about ten. I was pulled onto the edge of the stage, so I wasn't hurt. It was loud, loud, loud!

Slade played two shows at Wembley's Empire Pool

I WAS THERE: IAN SMITH, AGE 15

Slade was the first gig I ever went to. Back in 1973, music was having a growing impression on me and I was into the glam rock scene in a big way. Marc Bolan and David Bowie were megastars and were leading the way at the time, along with a Black Country band from Wolverhampton called Slade.

I was a regular reader of the *NME* and they announced the winners and line-up for the concert celebrating their Poll Winners' awards. Slade were voted best group and would be doing an afternoon matinee performance and another in the evening. Something in my head urged me to buy a ticket for the evening show, priced at £1 and £1.50 (it's rather more expensive these days!).

It was a big thing for me and my schoolmate Rob Dunkley to catch a train to London from Hinckley, Leicestershire, at the age of 15 – scary and exciting at the same time. My sister, who lived in London, drove us to the arena, and it was a real eye-opener to see thousands of teenagers milling around, all glammed up in tinsel and Noddy Holder-style top hats. This was a different world, and I was literally buzzing with anticipation.

Rod Stewart, Maggie Bell and a band called Home were the other award winners and support acts on the night, but I couldn't wait for Slade to make their appearance. And when they did, wow! The atmosphere was unlike anything I'd ever experienced. Even writing this now, I have a shiver going down my spine. They were absolutely superb and Noddy was so loud I don't think he really needed a microphone. I was shouting and screaming and had never felt such excitement in my life.

I saw T.Rex a few months later, followed by Bowie and Roxy Music, and since that first gig I've never stopped. I went to every Bowie tour and have seen most of the top artists in more than 300 gigs, including Bruce Springsteen six times and Fleetwood Mac in Melbourne, Australia in 2015. I am 65 this year and still gigging, with Slade a lightbulb moment for me. I came out of the Empire Pool (now Wembley Arena) thinking, 'I want more of this.' I still do.

I WAS THERE: JOHN BUTLER

I was lucky enough to see Slade eight times, starting in 1973 at Wembley. I couldn't believe how fantastically loud they were – I thought the building was going to fall down! I was hooked. Noddy Holder had a voice like a razor blade and had the rampant audience in the palm of his hand all night. I also saw them twice each in Hammersmith, Watford and Dunstable, and once at the Lyceum. And I was lucky enough to meet Noddy in Stevenage. They say never meet your idols, because you will be

John Butler got his guitar signed by Noddy

disappointed, but that couldn't be further from the truth. I told him I had a guitar at home and he said, 'Go home and get it, and I'll sign it for you,' which he did. He then started to play 'Far Far Away' on my guitar – fantastic. I was in rock heaven! Slade were my band and always will be.

I WAS THERE: MICHAEL PARKER, AGE 13

I saw Slade twice in London in 1973, the first time at Wembley at the *NME* Poll Winners concert in March, and again at Earl's Court on July 1st. These were my first Slade gigs. Despite Earl's Court being considered the highest point of their career, the Wembley show took place just a month after 'Cum On Feel The Noize' had smashed its way straight to the top of the charts. The song was still No.1 on the day of the gig. I was a couple of months short of my 14th birthday and had to harass my parent into letting me attend the concert. I was too late for the evening gig but managed to get tickets for the afternoon show.

Michael Parker thought Wembley eclipsed Earl's Court as the zenith of Slade's career

The *NME* concert was really an awards ceremony. Votes were cast before they were totally consumed by the teeny-bopper frenzy, as was the performance. I don't remember the poll mentioning Slade. I'm fairly sure they started with 'Hear Me Calling' and the set list probably consisted of 'Take Me Bak 'Ome', 'Move Over', 'Gudbuy T' Jane', 'Darling Be Home Soon', 'Coz I Luv You', 'Let The Good Times Roll', 'Get Down And Get With It', 'Cum On Feel The Noize', and 'Mama Weer All Crazee Now'.

I know the experience made me feel like an adult. I remember being ripped off outside the venue for a poster and a programme, neither of which were official. I went with a couple of friends. My dad drove us, 25 miles around the North Circular (there was no M25 back then), and I assume the poor bugger waited somewhere nearby. When we got inside, I felt like a child amongst many adults. A walkway full of concessions seemed to go all around the venue. Of course, this was not the football stadium, but it felt like a circuit under the terraces. The general air was very much a football match, and the alcohol was awash, although I didn't manage to get any.

This was the concert that epitomised Slade for me. I don't have to remember it to know how good it was. Pure rock 'n' roll raunch that went straight for the wobbly bits and hung on like a terrier. Oddly, I have yet to find another fan that attended this afternoon concert.

A ten date European tour started on 27 March 1973 at Saint Ouen in Paris, France.

GRUGAHALLE

6 APRIL 1973, ESSEN, GERMANY

I WAS THERE: OLIVER BINNENBÖSE

I was a young boy, nine years, together with my mom. She was sitting and because I was so small, the security, the Hot Wheels biker group, lifted me over the barrier and I stood together with a few of them right in front of the stage! It was an amazing moment in my young life and I still can't keep my feet still when I hear the music of Slade. Around one month before, I had seen T.Rex at the Grugahalle, my first gig.

In April, Slade embark upon another North American tour.

Oliver Binnenbose was just nine years old when he saw Slade

WINTERLAND ARENA

5 MAY 1973, SAN FRANCISCO, CALIFORNIA

I WAS THERE: RON SANCHEZ

Ron Sanchez saw Slade at Winterland

I fell into radio in 1968. Local underground station KSJO was mostly staffed by guys who had gone to 'radio school' with the intention of doing top 40 commercial radio. That meant music wasn't the primary reason they were on radio. Hard to believe. Some of the DJs were clued in, but none were music collectors, like I was. I heard a guy talking about The Yardbirds or something, and it was clear he didn't know. I called him up and corrected something. He said, 'Why don't you come up and bring some of your records.' I was welcome to hang out after that. I finally got an hour to do a produced show. A feature about a band. I did one about Yes, when *Fragile* came out. Atlantic heard it and paid me for it. I continued at KSJO then moved across town to KOME. I'd met Phil Charles, a DJ who did like music. We hit it off and he said come over. The big step was in 1975 when, along with Sean Donahue we all moved up to KSAN in San Francisco.

I was reading *Melody Maker*, so I guess that's when I first learned about Slade. I got *Play It Loud* when it came out, probably a promo copy from the station. That was 1970. I know I pushed them to play 'Get Down And Get With It' and 'Coz I Luv You' in 1971. I still have my promo copies.

I still like *Play It Loud* a lot and suspect I found the Ambrose Slade album soon after. So it seemed like I was hearing them as they were happening. I think there were plenty of guys on the radio around the country like me who were pushing Slade, T.Rex and Bowie before they were mainstream. That meant there was an audience for them when they came over.

I saw them twice. The first time was on their first US tour, with Humble Pie and Steely Dan, where they got a good reaction. They didn't know if their act would be understood in America. They thought they could replace the football references with something about baseball. That was silly, and I told them. They were also reluctant to play the hit singles, because they didn't think anyone here knew them. Again, just silly.

My radio boss set up an interview at KSJO. That's a blur. I know I got to hang out backstage at the Winterland shows. I was hoping to meet Steve Marriott, but they never came down to Slade's dressing room. It was that tour where I got taken out to dinner with some media people, and I met Chas Chandler. He was imposing. I wanted to ask him about Hendrix, but just couldn't think of what to say. He noticed I had an ELO t-shirt on, leaned over, pulled my jacket aside and just said, 'Hurrmp!'

I must have hung out with them on the next tour too. I know Noddy told me about Don's accident. I remember Back Door opening. There was a huge party at an old synagogue near Winterland after the show. There was a rope tied to the ceiling and people were swinging off the balcony. Don had a go with a girl on his shoulders. The song 'Miles Out To Sea' was written about that night.

I still have my records, and I play them on the radio as much as all the other old faves. I don't forget the bands that were important to me in my life. I like all that rocking Glam stuff, still. And it still has an audience with the young DJs at the station I work at now, KGLT-FM.

CAPITOL THEATRE

25 MAY 1973, PASSAIC, NEW JERSEY

I WAS THERE: RUSSELL CAREY

Right off the bat, they were loud! I liked them because they were a good time band. 'Clap your hands and stamp your feet!' I don't remember how I found out about them, but WNEW FM NY 102.7 had a show on Fridays at 6pm, *Things from Britain*, featuring top bands from England, also including T.Rex, Supertramp and ELO, bands that didn't get much US airplay. There was also *The King Biscuit Flower Hour* and on TV, *In Concert* and *Midnight Special*, which I also saw Slade on. I came home from my second Slade concert and they were on TV – double whammy. My dad went to bed!

My first album was *Slayed?* Then *Slade Alive!* and *Sladest*, and on and on. They were also the first live rock 'n' roll concert I attended. I've got the ticket stubs. This was 1973 and I was 16 or 17. And what can be said about Noddy's voice? I loved it! 'Get Down And Get With It'! I read they were the first band in England to break The Beatles' record sales, and Ozzy Osbourne considered Noddy's voice the best in the business.

Russell saw Slade in 1973

The second Slade concert I went to, on 21st September 1973, the backup band was ZZ Top. When Slade came on, my friends left me. I didn't care, I was there for Slade. Am I beginning to sound like a fanatic?

ELMDON AIRPORT
SPRING 1973, BIRMINGHAM, UK

I WAS THERE: JOHN PAGE
Working in the Met Office at Birmingham Airport back in the days when it was a small airport, Elmdon, and not the monster it is now, I popped down to the little airport shop to get a Mars bar or similar one day, and found myself standing between Noddy Holder and Roy Wood. It was only very briefly, as they both went their separate ways a few seconds later, after they were separately served. Roy Wood was in a pinstripe suit and had a briefcase but it was the hair and beard that gave him away.

GREEN'S PLAYHOUSE
31 MAY 1973, GLASGOW, UK

I WAS THERE: TOMMY ADAMS

I saw Slade at Green's Playhouse in Glasgow, before it was renamed the Apollo, when they were absolutely at the top of their game. But my biggest memory from this concert is of the support band, the Sensational Alex Harvey Band. I guess Harvey must have thought he was going to get an easy ride, especially playing in his hometown. Nothing could have been further from the truth. This was a 99.9 per cent Slade crowd. During his set, the band were getting drowned out with chants of 'WE WANT SLADE!' by the entire crowd. Eventually he got so pissed off that he stormed off and came back on with a big searchlight. He shone it into the crowd. It went something like this, 'Right, you cunts, fuckin' keep quiet and listen to us. When we're fuckin' done, then you'll get to hear fuckin' Slade!' Everybody sat down and he finished his set. I bet he never got over getting flak from a Glasgow crowd. Slade? They were immense.

I WAS THERE: CON BOYLE, AGE 9

I was nine years old for my first gig ever, with the support act the Sensational Alex Harvey Band. Alex was in some form. As the crowd shouted, 'WE WANT SLADE!' he shone a big spotlight into the audience and responded, 'You're no fuckin' Slade till I'm finished!' Just before Slade, a guy with Noddy-style mirrored hat was gonna be thrown out for something. The bouncers did a deal with him that if he gave me his hat, then he could stay in, which he agreed to. And I was delighted with my new hat. Ha! I was mesmerised when Slade came on. It was a magical set for a wee Glesga Boy, and I couldn't believe how noisy they were and how the circle seemed to sway as people rocked along. A great first gig!

I WAS THERE: GORDON MCWATTIE

I was there the night the front three rows in the stalls collapsed. I seem to remember they were on my knees, and I was terrified. That was Slade with Alex Harvey as support. The crowd were going crazy and Harvey came out and shouted, 'Right, cunts! Sit on your fucking arses or there will be no show!' I think if the stage hadn't been so high, he would've got lynched.

CIVIC HALL

3 & 5 JUNE 1973, WOLVERHAMPTON, UK

I WAS THERE: CHRIS SELBY

I was a Slade veteran at the ripe old age of 15, having seen them at town halls, public baths, community centres, and anywhere I knew I could get into without too much hassle and which could be got to by bus from my parents' house in Bloxwich. I had bought their records before they were fashionable, and had bathed in the reflected glory of their huge UK chart success. To be a Slade fan in 1973 was to be the king or queen of the playground. And when your school was less than a mile away from Noddy Holder's house and sightings of the group were a regular occurrence, your playground was the centre of Slade fandom.

As soon as the Civic Hall gig was announced in the national press, I knew what I would be doing on that day. Tickets were £1.25 and were either available from the Civic or the Lafayette Club in Wolverhampton. I was going to go with my best mate Mick and so, on a Saturday morning, we set off to Wolverhampton with cash in hand. Tickets were purchased and the long wait began. (Slade were going to appear at the Civic on Sunday the 3rd and on Tuesday the 5th, a school night, so that had been ruled out straight away.)

As the day got closer, excitement rose. The local boys made good were back where they belonged, and the chance to see them was fantastic. That Sunday, the phone rang at home. It was Mick. He couldn't go to the concert. He had been grounded for some reason. He didn't owe me money so I said I would tell him what happened at school on Monday.

I had worked out what bus to get and, within an hour, I was in Wolverhampton. Not being too sure of how to get from the bus station to the Civic, I followed the river of scarves and top hats that seemed to have invaded the town centre. I was on my own and feeling a bit nervous, but I soon spotted a few faces I knew from the estate and school. As I went through the columned entrance of the Civic, I bought a programme, a basic thing which informed me that the support group were called the Sensational Alex Harvey Band.I went to my seat and realised I had a choice. Mick's seat was empty. Luxury.

The SAHB came on stage. An old bloke in a stripey t-shirt, a clown and a bloke in a blue jockstrap thingy. They didn't stand a chance with the Slade audience but I made a note to look for their latest LP. As the SAHB trooped off stage, a sense of anticipation began to fill the Civic. After what seemed an age, the lights dimmed and the stage went black. The noise from the crowd rose. Tiny red lights twinkled and the thud of a drum and a bass guitar were heard.

The stage lights went on and there they were, in all their pomp and majesty. Slade. Noddy, Dave, Jim and Don. The Civic Hall erupted. Seating was ignored as I pushed my way to the left side of the stage – Jim Lea's side. If you wanted to Feel The Noize you had to be on the left. The combination of Jim's bass and Dons drums hit you in the chest.

Dave Hill pranced around the stage, putting out riff after riff, and stage centre was Noddy Holder in mirrored top hat with that voice. Slade at their finest. I can't remember the set list but I do remember what they didn't play. In a classic Noddy Holder moment, he calmed the crowd down to make an announcement. 'We have a new single coming out in a couple of weeks…' Cheers from the crowd. 'It's called 'Skweeze Me, Pleeze Me…' More cheers. 'But we ain't gonna fucking play it!' Two-second pause, then even louder cheers.

I came home deaf. You could tell the kids at school who had been to the gig. They couldn't hear. Slade in Wolverhampton in 1973. Unbeatable. I went on to see them another dozen or so times and they never disappointed, but 1973 was my gig.

I WAS THERE: WILL MORGAN

I first got into Slade when they played at a youth club where I live in Willenhall, St Giles Youth Club (Sammies). They were called the 'N Betweens then, and then Ambrose Slade and then Slade. In 1973, a bloke who owned a newsagent's in Willenhall told us he knew Dave Hill and he could get us tickets for a concert at Wolverhampton Civic Hall. We didn't take much notice because back then Slade were famous, and everyone had an aunt or uncle related to Noddy. We couldn't believe it when he actually got us two tickets in the front row.

Off we went to Wolverhampton, took up our seats and waited. When Slade came on, it was bedlam. Everyone rushed to the front of the stage and we went with them. I got split up from my mate and it was a bit scary. Slade were so loud and Noddy was telling the sound engineer, Charlie, to turn it up. It was deafening. But it was a great concert. I didn't see my mate until the next morning on our way to school. He had been treated for a neck injury but was okay. He missed the last bus to Willenhall and had run back home because he had to be in by a certain time or his dad would go mad. We still laugh about it. That night was the start of my love affair with Slade. I went to see them many times after.

TOWN HALL
8 JUNE 1973, BIRMINGHAM, UK

I WAS THERE: NICK CLIFT, FOLK DEVILS

Like any other kid who grew up in the West Midlands during the early Seventies with feathered haircuts, Crombies, bottles of Cresta and stolen No.6 cigarettes smoked behind the bike sheds at school, Slade exemplified for me the dynamic, unifying principle of working class youth culture of the times – football terrace chants, community centre discos, painful shoes, underage drinking. They were a colourful explosion of garish pantomime Glam rock amid the glum post-war political reality of labour unions, strikes, and power cuts.

I was 14, and my brothers and I were big fans of Trojan Reggae compilations, Tamla Motown, Radio 1 chart songs, and the post-skinhead appropriation of black musical styles. Into this mix came the cultural jolt of T.Rex, Bowie and Roxy Music, but perhaps more appealing to us Walsall kids were Slade. They talked like us, they walked like us, and, in a genius marketing move, they even deliberately misspelt their songs like some of us.

My first concert was Slade at Birmingham Town Hall in 1973, and I remember seeing the Sensational Alex Harvey Band too. I'm reminded that the show was cut short as Don Powell collapsed onstage from exhaustion. I'd forgotten that. The poor guy has had his troubles over the years. What I do remember is that hundreds of would-be hooligans in penny collar shirts and platform shoes did the stutter-step 'ker-clunk' clog dance in unison, creating a sound almost as loud as the band themselves. The floor shook, and it was a joyous release of pubescent energy.

I WAS THERE: STEVE HORNE, AGE 16

I attended this concert with my Slade-mad pal, Paul (RIP). I had my trusty Kodak Instamatic camera and collection of flash-cubes ready to capture the band in all their glory. First on stage was a middle-aged man wearing an overcoat with slick-backed hair and glasses to introduce support act the Sensational Alex Harvey Band. He spoke with a thick Scottish accent, but I could just make out the odd swear word and disparaging comment about the Brummie audience. The crowd gave it back big time and the wave of distain rolled from the stalls onto the stage. He just smiled, introduced the band onstage, threw off his overcoat and glasses, ruffled his hair and there stood Alex Harvey. Who knew? I hadn't a clue who he was. However, for the next 40 minutes they played a great set and eventually won the crowd over. They left the stage to applause and cheers. Great start.

Slade followed 30 minutes later, the place erupting. They were loud. Noddy's voice boomed through the hall. On the front of the stage was a silver cast taking pride of place. Dave Hill had just got over a broken ankle,the cast displayed like a trophy. The band got louder and the hall hotter as the crowd danced and went crazy. Time for a few photos. I attached the flash cube to my state-of-the-art camera and then someone knocked me, the camera going flying, along with my collection of flash bulbs. I recovered them but alas not one flash bulb worked. I wasn't that bothered at the time but now I would love to have had a few shots of the band. Regardless, Slade played at a relentless pace, one of the few bands at the time who could reproduce their records live. They got to the last song of the main set, and midway through there was a massive crash as Don Powell fainted over his drum kit. The stage lights came on and poor Don was carried off by the roadies. Noddy apologised but Don was in no state to carry on. I think he missed a couple of shows after due to illness. That was my introduction to the crazy world of Slade. I had never heard or witnessed anything like it. We got outside and I struggled to hear due to the whooshing sound in my ears, like the ocean was using my eardrums as rocks.

TOP RANK
10 JUNE 1973, CARDIFF, UK

I WAS THERE: CHRIS HARRIS, AGE 15

Chris Harris, photographed in Amsterdam, had a shock when the Sensational Alex Harvey Band warmed up for Slade at his first ever gig

Slade, my very first live concert. Here I was, 15 years old and all alone, about to see my favourite band. I couldn't quite believe it. Imagine my shock when on came the support band. Pretty scary or what? I'd never even heard of The Sensational Alex Harvey Band, and they were a little intimidating at first, but I soon got into their music. All in all, they were very good.

Then the main event. On came Slade, greeted by enthusiastic teenagers like myself. The place went wild, and Noddy's voice sounded just as it was on my vinyl at home. It was a fantastic concert, and everything I could have wished for. Finally seeing Noddy, Jim, Dave and Don in person was amazing. And, at the end, Dad's taxi was there waiting to Take Me Bak 'Ome. Ears ringing and feeling ten feet tall, what a night that was. I couldn't wait for school the following morning and being able to tell my classmates all about the concert. I don't think I slept much that night, and my ears were still ringing well into mid-week. Not that I minded.

I also remember school days where we would huddle around someone's old radio every Tuesday to listen to Johnnie Walker's Top 40 chart show, with the announcement of the top spot eagerly awaited at one o'clock and hoping Slade had beaten T.Rex, David Cassidy, The Osmonds, or whoever else to that prized No.1 spot.

Girls in my class would bring in copies of *Jackie* magazine, which mainly featured gossip and stories for girls plus up to date info and photos of the latest chart acts. Slade featured most weeks and the girls would usually let me have the Slade pictures or articles, unless the reverse featured David Cassidy, David Essex or The Osmonds. Annoyingly, it often did.

CITY HALL

12 JUNE 1973, SHEFFIELD, UK

I WAS THERE: MAGGIE BOURNE, AGE 12

I first heard Slade on the radio with their first hit, 'Get Down And Get With It'. I thought it was okay, but I was very young and only really got interested when 'Take Me Bak 'Ome' hit the charts and I started to notice Noddy Holder. I've managed to see Slade a number of times, and I got in trouble at school because I left early so that I could go to my first gig, at Sheffield. And bless them, my mum and dad took me. Boy, did they have a shock! That's the only time they took me.

Maggie (left) was 12 years old when she first saw Slade

I always saved my money so I could buy a 45 single, and *Slade Alive!* was my first Slade album. After playing this to my cousins, they ended up buying it too. One of my sisters is a drummer and really appreciates Don Powell's drumming on that record, especially liking the helicopter sound on 'Born To Be Wild'. I remember being very upset about Don Powell's accident. I tried phoning various hospitals to find out how he was… yep, I got in trouble again.

I moved a lot, but you could guarantee my bedrooms walls were filled with Slade posters, including the ceiling, much to my sister's dismay as we shared a room. I played my music as often as I could very loudly, Slade my music of choice, blaring out of the bedroom windows. Most neighbours thought there was a party going on, when actually it was me playing Slade.

I managed to see them live again at Belle Vue, Manchester, where I was at the front, dancing away, something I always managed to do. It was a great experience again, although I managed to get in trouble again – while dancing I grabbed a wire on the stage, this bloke on stage proper telling me off. I now know this roadie was Noddy's mate, Swinn.

When they moved to the States, I was very disappointed in them leaving England, so didn't see them live for a while. But I still listened to any music they released. When they came home, I was 17 or 18 and they were doing gigs at the universities. I went to see them and they were great – some students were about to discover what a rock gig was about!

KING GEORGE'S HALL

13 JUNE 1973, BLACKBURN, UK

MY HUSBAND WAS THERE: HELEN ROBINSON

I don't think there was a single kid in school who didn't try to emulate Noddy Holder throughout the festive season. It was always the final song at the school disco. It's potentially the sum total of some people's knowledge of Slade. Alternatively, it could well have been the reason they dug deeper and became proper fans! Either way, I suspect that Slade have formed an integral part of many personal stories throughout the 1970s and 1980s, with the invariable raucous shouts of 'It's Christmas!' still filling the air, every... single... year!

My own connection to the band isn't really as a fan – although I have been known to blast out 'Coz I Luv You' and 'Far Far Away' from my ultimate favourite songs mixtapes! My husband is a huge Slade fan, and this is where the tale becomes relevant, albeit at a tangent.

Many years ago, I received a call one afternoon from some guy who had bumped into a mutual friend in a supermarket in Glasgow. He'd been telling our friend about a project he needed help with, and my name and number had subsequently been handed over. I remember

SAHB drummer Ted McKenna was great pals with Don Powell

being really busy when that call came in and, unable to chat, I made a note of his name and said I'd ring him back as soon as I had time. When Graham, my husband, came home that day, I happened to mention that 'someone called Ted McKenna phoned me today about a new project', at which point my husband stood open-mouthed and was quite perturbed by the fact I seemed unfazed by this.

'You mean Ted McKenna, The Sensational Alex Harvey Band's drummer?' he exclaimed, slightly feverish. 'Yeah...,' says I. 'Bloody hell! They were the first band I ever saw! They supported Slade at Blackburn King George's Hall!' Ted laughed about this a lot. He remembered the tour fondly, and I should have quizzed him more when I had the chance. I wish he was still here to extract tales of rock 'n' roll debauchery from, but sadly he passed away in 2019, and there is a lovely tribute to him from Don Powell on his website.

Unsurprisingly, his fellow SAHB compadres can't remember much, although I did manage an unpublishable anecdote from Chris' sister Catherine. Ted would have loved sharing his version of events. My husband and his peers still vividly remember the gig, which (bizarrely) took place exactly five years before I was born! It's stayed with them, as songs and live performances often do.

Slade Alive! is cited as one of the best live albums ever, and I don't doubt it. For any fan, of any band, seeing them live or hearing the music in a bar or club is a collective escape, a collective opportunity to engage, dance and shout to the songs which shape our lives. Although, I have to be perfectly honest, with regards to Slade – there have been times where I've sworn I'd stuff the next person who shouts, 'IT'S CHRISTMAS!'

VICTORIA HALL
14 JUNE 1973, HANLEY, STOKE-ON-TRENT

I WAS THERE: MARK MILLICENT

You always remember your first time, and mine was at the Victoria Hall, Hanley, a pottery town of oat cakes and Wrights pies in Stoke-on-Trent, barely two weeks before 'Skweeze Me, Pleeze Me' went straight in at No.1 in the UK singles charts. The whole world was going crazy for Slade. I was a little young as a concertgoer, aged eleven, but we all need to start somewhere and I couldn't believe my luck. A Slade gig. Fuckin' great!

Mark Millicent remembers the first time... and has since worked with Don Powell as an illustrator

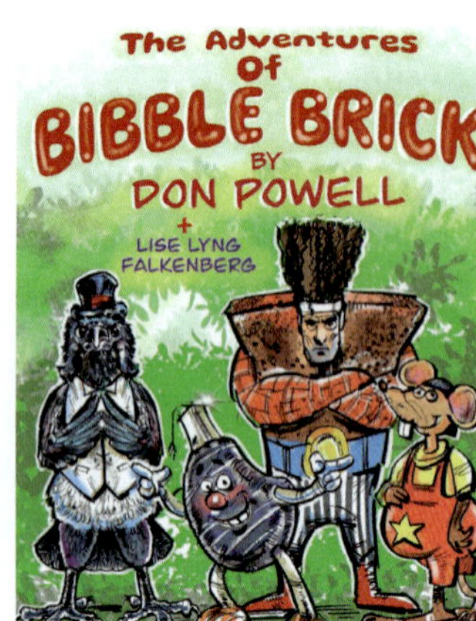

I'd been a fan ever since I was lucky enough to attend this show with equally young pals Mick and Phil. I was wowed by the glam of it all, crushed down at the front, sweating and screaming, watching a young Noddy Holder looking like he'd stepped straight off *Top of the Pops*. He was bedecked in mirrored top hat, red shirt, yellow braces, red-and-yellow stacked heels, plaid pants hitched high over red and white hooped socks, bellowing those immortal lyrics at a thousand decibels. Jim was in a shiny red reflective suit, Dave in knee-length silver coat and pants – and Don? Well, I don't remember what Don wore as he was at the back, drumming!

It was fantastic. 4,000 teenaged northern screaming pop-pickers who, like me, had paid £1.50 for a seat they would just stand on, singing along and clapping and stomping to every word. I have Noddy's framed autograph, along with those of the rest of the band, on my bathroom toilet wall in Los Angeles, where sadly few have heard of one of the best and most successful bands ever to emerge from UK shores.

'Run Runaway' made a slight hiccup stateside in '83, but that was about it. Steve Jones of Sex Pistols fame has a radio show, *Jonesy's Jukebox*, on 95.5 KLOS, and he sometimes plays Slade tracks on the US airwaves. My autograph – 'To Mil – Keep on Rockin'' written in biro on an old Roto-sound string packet, is pretty bloody cool!

Growing up in the Seventies, Thursday nights at 7.30 in the UK was good, but not as good as the real thing, a concert I somehow got a ticket for. *Top of the Pops* gave us our weekly dose of Slade. Sweet, Mud, Bowie and Glitter were good, as were Cooper and Hoople, et al, but to my young and music-discerning mind they weren't great. Slade were great! Nod, Jim, Dave, and Don were Glam and in their prime were great. When the charts were posted on the window of the local record shop – the Top 100 single charts, then if they were in the Top 20 there was a good chance they'd be on *Top of the Pops*, and between '71 and '76 they were always in that chart.

That night they took the stage at the absolute top of their game, for just over an hour of organised pandemonium, and looking like they'd just stepped out of the studios at Shepherd's Bush after a top recording session. It was a magic time, when we all had a massive future ahead of ourselves – when fashion was at its most dubious and TV shows were great – Tommy Cooper, Dick Emery, Morecambe and Wise – and they still had seats at concerts. And to paraphrase, 'They're jumping up and dancing on the seats.' We were, and we did. While the Sensational Alex Harvey Band were the support, the crowd was there for Slade. The SAHB did their best and tried hard to chants of 'WE WANT SLADE!' So bloody loud, but fantastic. That first proper rock concert stays with you.

UNIVERSITY OF LEEDS

15 JUNE 1973, LEEDS, UK

I WAS THERE: JANET BECKETT

I discovered Slade when 'Coz I Luv You' was released. It was the very first single I bought apart from 'Lily The Pink'. From then on, I was competely hooked, going on to purchase my first album, *Slade Alive!* After listening to that, I was totally addicted. My first Slade gig was my first ever gig. I was totally overwhelmed to see them so close, looking like their poster photographs. I was in love with Jimmy Lea, but apart from how they looked it was how they sounded. I was deaf for three days afterwards, but the word awesome didn't cut it! We sprayed our clothes gold and silver, sewed tartan turn-ups on our 'skinners' (skinhead wide jeans), and I sprayed my monkey boots gold.

What a night. We hung around chatting to the roadies, and one gave me a Coke can that Don had drunk from, which I added to a Slade shrine in my bedroom. A few weeks later, disaster struck. My gran, sleeping over after going to the bingo, tidied my room and chucked it away. I was devastated, sulking for weeks. How could my family not understand how disastrous this was? I don't think I've forgiven my gran, 50 years later.

I worked Saturdays in the local hairdresser's. The day after the gig, I overslept and arrived at work where, to my manager's horror, she saw my hair and scalp were bright green from the leftover gold spray. I had to wash it six or seven times before she allowed me into the salon front!

Another time, two mates and I heard Noddy and Don were at Mallory Park racing circuit in Leicestershire. We lived in Wakefield, West Yorkshire, so bought train tickets to Leicestershire and took a taxi from the train station to the circuit, having no clue how far, far away it was. We had a great day, got to chat to Nod and Don, and I got their autographs on my Double Diamond notepad. Nod even borrowed my pen to sign other people's autographs. We were absolutely buzzing. But then everyone started to leave. We had no money and no clue how to get back to the train station. Aged 14, we were going to be in real big trouble – our parents thought we were shopping in Leeds!

We started to walk, trying to hitch a ride, and after a few dodgy offers from lads in cars and vans (which we were clever enough to refuse), a gorgeous Opel Manta car stopped and one of the racing guys asked what the fuck we were doing. We explained our love for Slade (which didn't impress him, I don't know why) and he gave us a lift to the station. We got home safe, still glowing and in a daze from meeting Nod and Don, mum none the wiser.

I'm still a big fan. I have all their albums on vinyl and the artwork displayed all around my little house. I keep up with what the lads are up to, and I'm still in love with Jim.

'SKWEEZE ME, PLEEZE ME' RELEASED 22 JUNE 1973

Mirroring the achievement of 'Cum On Feel The Noize', 'Skweeze Me, Pleeze Me' also enters the UK singles chart at No.1, spending three weeks at the top.

I still wear colourful clothes. I invented the haircut, the boots and costumes, and I'm proud of it. And I know people tuned into Top of the Pops *to see what I'd wear next. I have great memories of everything I wore, and the 'Metal Nun' is always around – ha! I think the guitar was something of an extension to the stage clothes, wearing the silver and glitter and high boots, all very spacey, very big shoulders. My designer felt it would be great to have a guitar to go with all that. Everyone else was just using a Gibson. The fashion designer sketched out a guitar which looked like a cosmic raygun, and the Yob thing came from my car registration, deciding to call this guitar the Super Yob. We had it made by John Birch, a guitar-maker who designed for Tony Iommi of Black Sabbath, made by John Diggins. And we chose silver, Chas' idea.*

When I went on Top of the Pops *with it, little did I know that a young Marco Pirroni, later in Adam and the Ants, was watching and decided, 'I want that guitar!' He said it was like nothing he'd ever seen, and he was right. And Marco ended up getting the original. I sold it and he bought it, but he loans it out now and again. I had one remade too, and the one I use now also has lights up the neck. But I didn't get it made because it was a great guitar to play, but to use for a couple of songs then put to one side – as I do now. And to this day that's all part of the imagery of what we do.* **Dave Hill**

Now, if I said to you he was colour-blind, would that make more sense to you? **Don Powell**

EARL'S COURT
1 JULY 1973, LONDON, UK

I WAS THERE: DAVID FEARN

The next gig was the big one – Earl's Court – everyone again dressed up in all their Slade finery. Again, the place went crackers – Noddy preaching, Dave prancing around the stage in high heels, Jim playing like the rock god he is, and Don keeping it all together.

I WAS THERE: STEPHEN DIX, AGE 14

It was the first concert I was allowed to go to. I went with a school friend. We were both blown away by the volume, by Noddy's voice, and by how crazy the audience were. There were loads of fights between the security and the Wolverhampton Droogs, but what a night! I saw them many times after, and managed to convert many friends who weren't that keen on them over to the right side. The best place was Hammersmith Odeon, right at the front with me wearing a bowler hat with mirrors on, subsequently nicked by a large nasty looking bloke post-concert (bastard).

They were so good live and so tight as a band, and Noddy was such a great front man. He's one star I would still love to meet, to shake his hand and say thank you. My favourite songs are 'Dapple Rose' and 'Gudbuy T' Jane'. My wife's is 'Everyday'. I now cover 'Coz I Luv You' at open mic nights, and it always goes down well with my generation (old) and younger folk alike. I would love to cover more, but you can sing a lot of a Slade song and then you hit a note Noddy sang and realise you sound like Tiny Tim on helium. He had such a range.

I WAS THERE: CLIVE PARKER, AGE 16

Two of my school friends and I went. We were 16 and in the middle of O-level exams. We were from Aylesbury, Bucks (home of the famous Friars Music Club) and big Slade fans. It was the time of Glam rock! The previous year saw the rise of Ziggy Stardust, accompanied by the glam of T.Rex, Roxy Music and (dare I say it) Gary Glitter, amongst others. I guess we were all hooked by the working-class mantra of the Slade boys and being football fans the fashionable skinhead/suedehead origins of the band; the big driving rhythms, gritty lyrics and those misspellings!

And the band's costumes; Noddy's mirrored top hat, check trousers and waistcoat, and Dave Hill's outlandish dress sense, with the big platformed soles, were fascinating.

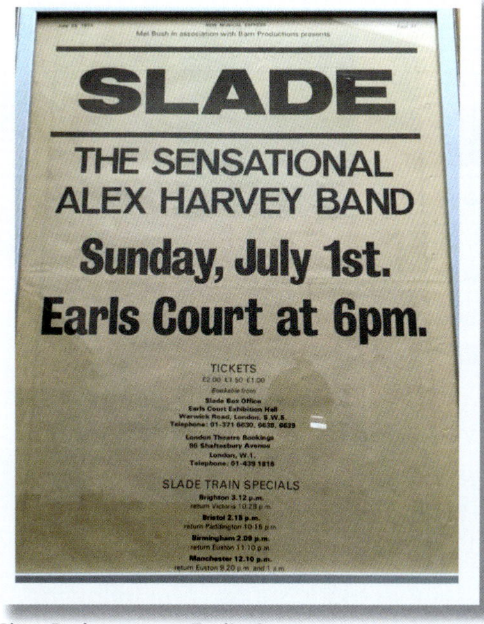

Clive Parker was at Earl's Court

I remember the Earl's Court gig like it was yesterday. It was my first big gig as a relatively young and naive lad. We travelled up by train. When we got out at the Tube station, the place was awash with Noddy and Dave lookalikes, girls and boys. There was glitz and glam everywhere! Vendors were selling programmes, scarves and all sorts of memorabilia and I bought a silver scarf with Slade printed on it.

Inside the arena, we had good seats, the stage to our right, 20 yards or so from us. The place was buzzing with anticipation and expectation. I hadn't heard of the Sensational Alex Harvey Band, the support. But they did their bit and were greeted with polite applause. Slade came on, introduced by the Emperor Rosko. The place went wild! Girls screaming constantly, us lads too cool to scream. The music was loud – really loud. I read that the PA was 11,500 watts that night.

The boys were dressed as we expected, Noddy in his check waistcoat and trousers over a red shirt with black mirrored hat, Jim Lea in a red lurex outfit, Don Powell in a white jumpsuit with blue pinstripes, and Dave Hill stealing the show in some sort of Pharoah's costume alongside his big platform-soled silver boots.

At about an hour the set was relatively short, but being a Sunday night and finishing at just after 10pm allowed us to get back home on the train to Aylesbury without too much difficulty. The band ran through their big hits; 'Skweeze Me, Pleeze Me' had just gone straight in at No.1. It was a fantastic night's entertainment. We were blown away by it. My ears rang for hours.

I WAS THERE: PETER HAWKINS

For Peter Hawkins, Slade were it in 1973. Slade and dungarees...

The atmosphere began to build on the train to London. The noise in Earl's Court was loud, loud, loud, and that was just the crowd. The Sensational Alex Harvey Band did not get a good reception – no one wanted to watch them (I now quite like his music). When Slade finally came on, the noise went up and up and they played an amazing set. When the concert ended, our train journey home was a continuation of the concert. Somebody was playing a tape and everyone was singing along to Slade songs. The following day I started my first job as an apprentice chef. The head chef was not impressed when the glitter fell out of my hair into the chopped parsley!

I WAS THERE: STEVE EDWARDS

Steve Edwards felt that watching Slade was like 'watching your mates'

I saw them at Earl's Court supported by the Sensational Alex Harvey Band, and in Brussels. I was also at the filming for *Slade in Flame* scenes at Hammersmith Palais and at the Rainbow, Finsbury Park. Great times. I loved the Seventies. All the bands coming through had a great sound and a unique look. But there was something about Slade that grabbed me, their music was raw and so upbeat and just made you feel part of this band. They had this togetherness that came across with their music, and their interaction with their fans made it feel like you were watching your mates.

I WAS THERE: STUART WILSON

I went out for cigarettes from the local off licence and met two friends, asking what they were doing. They said they were going to London to watch the Earl's Court concert and had a spare ticket, so I said I'd go with them. I got home three days later. My wife wasn't happy. Ha ha!

My son was recently travelling to London on the train and rang to say he was sat opposite Dave Hill who asked what concert I attended. When he told Dave, he said Earl's Court was the best concert they ever did.

I WAS THERE: DYLAN WHITE

I used to read the *Record Mirror*, the slightly more pop one of the music press. *Melody Maker* and *NME* seemed a bit more serious. You could take part in all these polls – your favourite band, favourite single, favourite album, and all the rest of it. The next gig I went to was the *NME* Poll Winners' Party in March 1973. I don't remember that show particularly, I wasn't right at the front. But I acquired a silver top hat at that concert which someone had made.

Then the next one was the big one at Earl's Court. The support band was none other than the Sensational Alex Harvey Band. I remember Alex Harvey and Zal Cleminson, the guitarist. He was quite a character with what he wore, the make-up and all the rest of it. At the time, Slade were the undisputed biggest band in Britain. It was a Sunday night, and the ticket was £1.50. Many years later, I took Noddy Holder's daughter to see Oasis at Earl's Court and said, 'I saw your dad here.'

Then they had the tragedy of Don Powell's accident. For them, it was coming crashing down from the top of the mountain. But the records kept coming, and I remained a fan.

COMPTON ROAD

4 JULY 1973, WOLVERHAMPTON, UK

DON'S CAR ACCIDENT

Three days after Earl's Court, Don is left critically ill and in a coma after his white Bentley S3 crashes in Wolverhampton. Angela Morris, his 20-year-old fiancee dies. Don has a stay in intensive care, finally coming round to major short-term memory and sensory issues, which remain with him to this day.

That concert (Earl's Court) means nothing to me. It was filmed, and I still want to see it if I can get a copy… just so I can see what it was like. I still have to keep a diary. That'll be for the rest of my life, I'm afraid. But it's part of my life now. It's like my bible. **Don Powell**

His dad called me at 4am and said, 'Don's been in a car crash.' I just thought he'd been in some little bump, but he dropped the bombshell that he'd only got 24 hours to live. I raced up to the hospital with his brother and he was lying in this big intensive care tent with all pipes coming out of him, his head was shaved, he'd got a massive gash down his skull where he'd gone through the windscreen, his girlfriend had been killed… and as far as we knew he wasn't going to last 24 hours. We'd had five No.1 records and we were sitting at the top of the charts with 'Skweeze Me, Pleeze Me'. Everything was going absolutely incredibly well. We were at our pinnacle. And here I was looking at Don in this oxygen tent. He had no memory, no taste or smell, we didn't know if he was going to live or die. We didn't know whether the band would survive or crumble. It was a very traumatic time. **Noddy Holder**

Jim's brother, plumber's mate Frank Lea, covers for two shows that month at the Isle of Man Festival.

PALACE LIDO

8 JULY 1973, DOUGLAS, ISLE OF MAN, UK

I WAS THERE: TONY PYE

I can't remember where I saw them next, but the most famous was probably at the Palace Lido in Douglas on the Isle of Man. I'd just finished my O-levels and had recently started work as a photographer. 'Skweeze Me, Pleeze Me' was No.1 in the charts so Slade were on top of the world. My mate and I had been in the Isle of Man for a week, and missed the Earl's Court gig the previous Saturday as we were on the ferry from Liverpool. After Don Powell's serious car accident, it looked like the gig would be cancelled. To say we were gutted was an understatement. But Jim's brother, Frank Lea, stood in for him. It was a great gig but I was disappointed they didn't play 'Move Over'.

I WAS THERE: TONY BEESLEY

I guess I was blessed by the fact that my next brother up was 16 in 1970. As a result, I got to hear all the seven-inch records he brought home every Saturday. He would religiously come home with a bunch of new singles every week, following his football match forays. His purchases would mostly be chart releases, but among them we had the likes of David Bowie, Mott the Hoople, T.Rex, The Sweet, Moody Blues, and one of my favourites at the time, 'The Theme from *The Persuaders*' by John Barry. I enjoyed all those records and would either listen in or sneak my own plays when my brother wasn't around. I would later claim the whole lot as my own at no extra costs but a few Mars Bars on me each time I paid a visit to the sweet shop down the road. Then there was Slade!

Top of the Pops was a Thursday evening ritual for so many of us back then, and we were no exception. I recall Bowie performing 'Starman', Sweet's 'Blockbuster' video, regular outings from T.Rex, Queen with 'Killer Queen', Suzi Quatro with 'Devil Gate Drive', and all the rest; plus the great, the laughable and the plain boring that were spoon-fed to us every week. However, being a pre-teen, one particular band also grabbed my attention, and that was Noddy Holder and his gang of Bovver Boys. Following their *Pops* appearances, watching Noddy in his glammed-up top hat and accompanying mutton whiskers, virtually all their singles were snapped up between us. From 'Coz I Luv You', 'Gudbuy T' Jane', 'Mama Weer All Crazee Now' and 'Cum On Feel The Noize' to 'The Bangin' Man' and 'Far Far Away', they all ended up on our Philips stereo record player… a thing of modern science to us in 1973. Only one long-playing Slade LP was bought though, 1974's *Old New Borrowed and Blue*.

From a late-fifties age perspective, it's hard to fathom exactly what ensured Slade would become my declared favourite band from around 1973 to maybe mid-1975. Perhaps it was their rowdy loud sound, that gritty Noddy growl, and the anthem-like addictive appeal of their singles that refused to be deleted from my impressionable young mind. They had tunes to die for and ones that would stick around long after the glam-styled trimmings had ebbed away. No Seventies band's songs sounded as exciting and appropriate – from the out-of-tune schoolkid playground chants to the grey Bovril-stained, crisp packet littered football terraces to our own front room. When Christmas 1973 arrived, Slade's evergreen festive classic, 'Merry Xmas Everybody' seemed to completely take over and that Christmas, and many others, will always be synonymous with that record. I got my first guitar that Christmas, a crappy kids-dedicated acoustic, and even though I couldn't play a single chord on the damned thing, I could effectively mime in our front room, guitar in hand, to the sound of Slade's never-to-be forgotten declaration of, 'It's Christmas!'

I WAS THERE: BOB BLACKMAN

At the start, I didn't like Slade. I was nine years old and lived in rural Cornwall with a very long bus ride home from school, during which we listened to the radio. I was fascinated by *Top of The Pops* but thought Glam rock was silly and pretentious. The rougher, bigger boys liked Slade. The ruder, older girls whom I found strangely attractive, liked Slade even more. Slade were competition for the affections of teeny boppers even before I was touched by the teenage rampage. School friends who liked them seemed insincere to me. It was like supporting a successful football club from Leeds or Manchester.

They liked Slade to get a reputation, and not a good one, these would-be football hooligans. They couldn't yet grow mutton-chop whiskers, but they might be able to pester their mum for a new pair of flares. Jonathan Oates particularly admired shrinking-violet and super yob, Dave Hill. However, when Don Powell was hurt in a car crash, Jon's concern was genuine. Unlike Bolan or The Sweet, Slade couldn't spell their songs properly. This was outrageous to someone with the reading age of a 14-year-old. Yet one of them could play a violin. And then – well, there it was, 'Merry Christmas, everybody's having fun…'. I began to feel the noize.

I tuned into their other rabble-rousing anthems. Slade appeared on *Blue Peter* – such was their standing – but then they disappeared, and

Punk happened, glorious Punk that sounded a bit like Slade. When Slade re-emerged in the hit parade in the Eighties, I revisited their back catalogue and gawped at their early photos as skinheads. The riffs and energy were better than I remembered, and nobody has a voice like Noddy Holder.

Slade return to the US for more shows.

CAPITOL THEATRE
21 SEPTEMBER 1973, PASSAIC, NEW JERSEY

I WAS THERE: DAVID HUGHES

I saw Slade with Blue Öyster Cult in Passaic, New Jersey, my second concert. There may have been a third band. Slade were known as they were on the radio and had two songs on the air, 'Cum On Feel The Noize' and 'Mama Weer All Crazee Now'. They did well and got the crowd rocking. I remember the guitarist climbing up on his Marshall stack and playing 'Cum On Feel The Noize'. I never saw that again in all my years. It was a good show. I came away pretty happy. They did all right.

In later years Quiet Riot were more associated with 'Noize' here than Slade. I never saw them again, but they made the rounds for some time afterward.

SLADEST RELEASED
28 SEPTEMBER 1973

Sladest, *a greatest hits compilation, reached No.1 in the UK album charts and No.129 in the US Billboard 200.*

'MY FRIEND STAN' RELEASED
28 SEPTEMBER 1973

'My Friend Stan' peaks at No.2 in the UK and No.1 in Ireland. Don has to be lifted onto his kit during the recording.

I WAS THERE: SIMON WILLIAMS

It's 1974 and I've spent the first four years of my life in Kingston, Jamaica, where my father was music teacher and choirmaster at the university. Life was bright and colourful, warm and magic. Long days in the sunshine, chasing lizards and eating tamarinds, our house filled with classical music and a hint of the middle of the road pop chart end of Jamaican Reggae and Calypso. It's all I knew.

Slade on Top of the Pops in 1974 blew Simon Williams' young mind

But it's 1974 and my mum is pregnant, and she wants to have her baby – my brother – in England. We stay with my grandparents and on a Thursday evening we watch *Top of the Pops*. My four-year-old mind is blown by the noise, the screams, the mirrors, the tartan, the excitement, the tunes. I use a walking stick as a microphone, and I put on my mother's boots. They come up to my waist and they're not altogether comfortable. But I am a pop star, and my parents and grandparents find it immensely amusing to watch me strut up and down the front room.

I am Noddy Holder. And so my mum buys me the *Sladest* compilation LP and the 'My Friend Stan' seven-inch. Forget kids' songs and stories, these are the first records I own, and I love them. At the end of the year, we return to the hard sun and cool breeze of Jamaica and life goes on. Only now I have a little something of my own that nobody else knows about. It's like my own little Punk rock movement in my tiny head.

Now it's 1978 and we have returned to England to start school in the middle of Shropshire. There's a school disco and I take *Sladest* with me to see if the DJ will play it. But everyone thinks they have moved on from the Glam of five years before. They don't seem to think Slade are cool. But they're all I can hear in everything. From the chart Punk that's now all over *Top of the Pops*, to the New Wave of British Heavy Metal that is emerging, I can hear my beloved Slade everywhere.

And now it's 2023 and I am in my mid-fifties. I still have my battered and bruised copy of *Sladest*, though the middle pages of the gatefold have long since disappeared. I have been in indie bands, managed Pere Ubu and Laibach, worn a little twee anorak and swayed to Talulah Gosh. I have visited different countries and learned different languages, had children and relationships. And Slade are always there. Not always on the turntable. But in every song I listen to I can hear them. Their joy. Their excitement. Their lust for life. It's been a 50-year love affair that keeps on giving. Slade are the story of my life.

ACADEMY OF MUSIC

6 OCTOBER 1973, NEW YORK, NEW YORK

I WAS THERE: STEVE WISNER

I remember first hearing about Slade on the radio, around Christmas 1972. I was 15, living in my childhood home in Mount Vernon, a suburb of New York City. I was really into music and my mind was open to new sounds. I went to Woodstock when I was twelve. My summer sleepaway camp was up in Winterdale, Pennsylvania, just outside Hancock, New York. In 1969, the counsellors said, 'Pack up your tents, we're going to a craft fair!' That was my first real concert and it was life changing. My dad, Harry, would drive my friends and I down to Madison Square Garden and I saw the likes of Crosby, Stills and Nash, and Jethro Tull. Now my appetite for music was huge. I loved music, especially live music.

In December 1972, 'Mama Weer All Crazee Now' from the *Slayed?* album came on the radio. I'd never heard a sound like this. I was hooked! I think what really did it was the live crowd effect, or the echo effect they used. Anyway, I was in, and needed to hear more. Shortly after, 'Gudbuy T' Jane' hit the air and again it was amazing. Noddy's raspy voice and the glam sound had me wanting more.

When I read in *Village Voice* the announcement that Slade were coming to New York, I was ready. There was no way I would miss that. By this time, my friends knew I was the biggest Slade fan. I went to school with the word Slade written on my fingers, as on the album cover, and my book covers made from paper bags (yes, we did that in the mid-Seventies) were covered with the writings of Slade songs.

In April 1973, Slade came to the US and announced a show at the old Academy of Music on 14th Street in Manhattan, a great place to see a concert. It was a smaller venue, maybe four or 5,000 seats. My pals were happy to join me and we were able to buy cheap Boones Farm wine. We stood in line drinking from paper bags and waited. The energy was incredible. There were people in line decked out in full glam gear, some with Dave Hill-type boots. It was 1973, and it was New York City! As we approached the entrance, I recall the sign that mentioned that Slade performed their music at high decibels and were not responsible for loss of hearing. That may have bothered some but I was excited by it.

There were two warm up bands. The opening act was Blue Öyster Cult (who I saw at the Canyon Club in Agoura Hills, California, 45 years later!), but there was no doubt everyone was there for Slade and were becoming impatient. After Blue Öyster Cult left the stage, the lights went dim again, the energy incredible. Being an outgoing fan, I started my friends yelling, 'WE WANT SLADE!' I recall this so vividly because shortly after the entire venue was chanting along with us!

When Slade came on, I was running up and down the aisles of the small theatre, raising my fists in the air, which absolutely increased the energy of those around me. We were all in utmost excitement. They did a set that was over one hour of non-stop Slade. The outfits Dave, Noddy and the rest of them were wearing were something I hadn't seen before. To this day, I haven't felt the energy I felt at my first Slade concert. This was exciting. There I was with Noddy, Dave and the band, hearing this amazing energy right before my eyes.

I went on to become an outgoing Slade fan and got into the Glam scene for a while. There were times that my girlfriend put blue mascara on my eyes as we headed out to the clubs and bars in New York.

THE SUNSHINE IN

8 OCTOBER 1973, ASBURY PARK, NEW JERSEY

I WAS THERE: DAVID JURMAN

David Jurman fell in love with 'Gudbuy T' Jane'

I discovered Slade's music in 1973 from a friend who turned me on to the *Slayed?* LP. The first track that caught my attention was 'Gudbuy T' Jane', which peaked at No.68 on the *Billboard* Hot 100. I started buying albums that year instead of singles. My first two LP purchases were The Allman Brothers Band's *Brothers And Sisters* and Pink Floyd's *Dark Side Of The Moon*. Until I discovered Slade, I was a huge fan of The Beatles, the first two Chicago LPs, The Beach Boys and The Rascals, and other groups that debuted in the 1960s. But that year I discovered heavier sounds. I liked the blend of driving rock by Slade, yet their material was melodic.

The first time I saw Slade was with two friends on Columbus Day. The Sunshine In was a converted bus garage in Asbury Park, New Jersey, the city made famous by Bruce Springsteen, 56 miles south of New York City. Many famous acts played the Sunshine In, including The Allman Brothers Band with opening act Bruce Springsteen, Black Sabbath, Mott the Hoople, Joe Walsh, Johnny Winter, Leon Russell, Argent, Procol Harum, and Yes.

I remember it being quite loud. It was an enthusiastic crowd and their performance was really energetic. I would go on to see them three more times. Regrettably, they would never tour North America after 1976, despite finally breaking through in 1984 with 'Run Runaway', which went to No.1 on the US Album Rock Tracks Chart.

AUDITORIUM THEATER
16 OCTOBER 1973, CHICAGO, ILLINOIS

I WAS THERE: BORIS BODEN

I saw Slade twice at the Auditorium Theater, with front row seats both times. The Climax Blues Band opened the first time I saw them, and 'Rubber Bullets'-era 10cc the second (21st June 1974). Slade were the loudest band I have ever seen, bar none, in a venue that was always billed as 'acoustically perfect'.

I WAS THERE: DON HEDEKER

I saw Slade three times in Chicago – in 1973, 1974 and 1975. The first two times they were headliners at the Auditorium Theatre, the Climax Blues Band and 10cc opening respectively. The third time I saw them, they opened for Black Sabbath at the International Amphitheater. I was a teenager when I saw Slade on a US music show on TV. I had their live LP first, and then I got *Slayed?* and then *Sladest*. They were a great live band with some excellent songs. In Chicago, they weren't that well known, so the shows that they headlined at the Auditorium Theater were only about half full. Because of that, they invited everyone to get closer to the stage, which was great since my ticket was in the balcony. Dave Hill had the Super Yob outfit on, which was cool, but I didn't know what a 'yob' was at the time. I found out later!

HEATHROW AIRPORT
23 OCTOBER 1973, LONDON, UK

I WAS THERE: DYLAN WHITE

Every teenager was a fan of one band or another, and you had all these newsletters that the artists of the day were doing. Somehow you found out there was a fan club. It must've been advertised in *Disco 45* or *Record Mirror* or something, and you joined. It cost a pound. You wrote in and they sent you a letter. I've still got all the fan club letters, and the stickers.

I was a teenybop kid, a Glam kid, so I wasn't listening to John Peel.

At the end of '73, listening to the radio all the time, it was Stuart Henry in the evenings, and he said that Slade were flying back into the country. I had kept awake in geography lessons so I knew where America was, and I knew they would be flying back and therefore they must arrive in the morning. We were on half term, so I rang up a mate and said, 'Slade are going to come into Heathrow; let's go and meet them.' He said, 'Alright then.' My mother thought I was nuts.

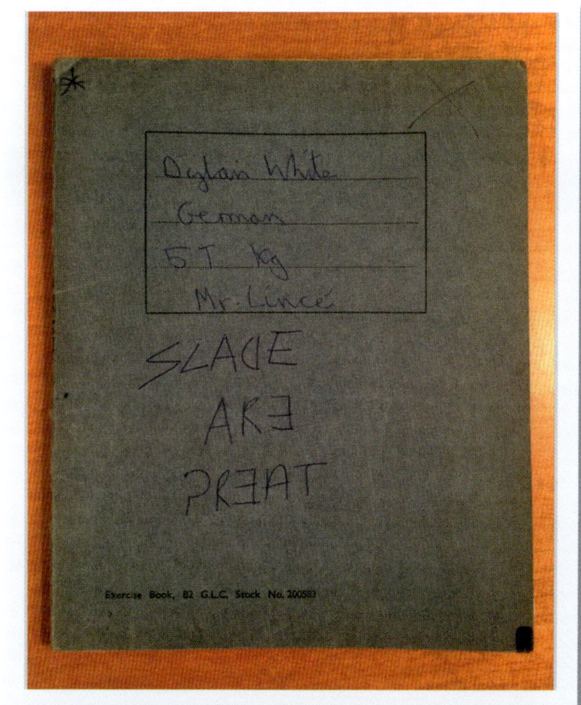

Dylan White was a huge fan whilst still at school

I said I was going to get up at five in the morning and go to Heathrow Airport. I lived in Merton Park. You had to get the Tube from Wimbledon up to Hammersmith and go on the Piccadilly line to Heathrow. Two teenage kids at five o'clock in the morning. We got to Heathrow and worked out the terminal for American flights coming in. There were two girls there in Slade gear and we said 'hello' to them. But after a while we worked out that we had the wrong day. We were a day early. So we had to do it all again the next day. I went home and said I was going to get up at five o'clock the next day.

Dylan's signed Slade pic

Slade at Heathrow in October 1973, fresh off the plane

My mother thought I was completely nuts.

So the next day we were standing there by the gate and – bang – the four of them came through the gate. They had just got off the flight from Chicago or wherever and they must've been absolutely knackered. But us five fans were stood there, and they gave us all the time in the world. They signed everything. I got a picture signed, and they signed my autograph book. None of us had cameras but there was a professional photographer there and she lined them up as they were leaving and took a photo of them. My girlfriend spotted the photo in *It's Here!* magazine in December 1973. I know it's the same occasion because I remember Dave had a 'We Try Harder' badge on.

I got back to Wimbledon, told my girlfriend and she couldn't believe I had actually met them. She was most miffed that she hadn't come with me. I was saying, 'I done it, I done it, I done it!' I had the trophy, the signed picture, the lot. I had pulled it off.

That moment has lived with me forever. They were pop stars. They'd been on *Top of the Pops*. They'd been on the stage at London Palladium and Earl's Court, and they were there, stood next to me, talking. That moment really crystallised my life. It made me think, 'I've got to be in music.'

'MERRY XMAS EVERYBODY' RELEASED 7 NOVEMBER 1973

Recorded during a New York City heatwave, 'Merry Xmas Everybody' becomes Slade's third single to debut at No.1, a UK chart first, selling 310,000 copies on the day of release. Also No.1 in Denmark, it becomes their best-selling single, charting many times.

The chorus and middle eight was the first song I ever wrote, way back in 1967. It was called originally 'Buy Me A Rocking Chair'. It was the same melody but a different song, very psychedelic. I played it to the band and they didn't like it at all, so it got thrown in the bin! Then about six years later I think it was Jim's auntie said, 'Why don't you do a song that will come out every year, like a Christmas or a birthday song?' Jim at first didn't want to do it but he'd got a verse melody that he'd had hanging around for a while and he was looking for a chorus to put with it and he remembered the chorus of this song I'd done all those years before, so we met up and put the two together. I went away and wrote all new lyrics to it as a Christmas song. **Noddy Holder**

That's what we call it – 'that song'. It's amazing, y'know. We've had something like 24 hits, but people only remember that one! Don't get me wrong. I'm not putting it down. It's just so funny. When we recorded that, we were on a world tour, in New York in a heatwave, around 100 degrees. Yet there we were, recording that song. Chas said, 'Do you have anything? If you have, we can go in the studio, do something.' I remember Nod and Jim saying, 'We've got this Christmas song.' They played it to us, and Chas said, 'We've got to do this!' So we booked the Record Plant in New York City, 100 degrees outside, and there we were, singing that record. And would you believe that when we finished it, we didn't want to release it? Chas thankfully said, 'I don't care what you lot say, this is coming out!' I don't reckon it's been out of the top 100 at this time of year since. It's phenomenal! Everybody must have this bloody record, but it keeps on selling. When I'm in a supermarket when it's playing and I'm getting my groceries, all the attendants are singing it at the top of their voices. **Don Powell**

I WAS THERE: ARTHUR MAGEE

Arthur Magee passed on his love of Slade and 'that song' to his son, Stephen

We'd never get the chance to see them live because we were too young, and even if we had been old enough, Slade wouldn't have been coming to Belfast in 1973 when 'The Troubles' was in the middle of its bloodiest period and North Belfast was particularly bloody. In the early Seventies in Belfast, Christmases weren't white, they were grey, and they were wet. Christmas time was a fight against the gloom with fairy lights, colourful paper streamers and luminous, vibrant balloons promising fun and cheer in a world that was far from cheerful. A few streets away, people were killed but somehow, we remained outside that, more concerned with endless street games of football – 'ten half time, 20 the winner' and George Best's endless fall from grace. Imagine choosing a Swedish Miss World over playing the beautiful game? To ten-year-old me, he was insane.

Whilst football was what we lived and breathed, pop music began making its way into our consciousness on tinny transistors and the 'happening sound' of Wonderful Radio 1. Not for us the stylistic musings or earnest prog, we loved stomp-along terrace chants that you'd hear once and know. T.Rex, The Sweet, Gary Glitter delivered, and then there was Slade. They looked like people you'd pass in the street. The big boys, with long hair, insane kipper ties, horrendous clothes sense and a raucousness that was never threatening but invited you to the party. They were up for a good time and didn't take themselves too seriously, but you knew they could handle themselves in a fight. They were the antisepsis of The Osmonds and David Cassidy, whom the girls on our street swooned over and whom we hated.

Christmas began early in our house with a Christmas club that started in spring and into which my mother would religiously pay each week. Generally, I'd get something football-related but the year previously recognising my growing interest in pop music, 'Santa' had delivered a Pickwick *Top of the Pops* compilation. These were LPs comprised of versions of the hit parade played by session men. The record was graced by covers featuring girls in bikini tops and a list of the songs on the record. The records themselves were dreadful. Versions were knocked off with little attention to sound quality or feel. You could almost hear the yawns as they ploughed through track after track; pale imitations of the originals.

Nowhere were their limitations more apparent than with Slade, because Slade kicked it and kicked it big style. There was no session singer in the world who could ever get close to Noddy Holder's voice, no drummer who could hit with the power of Don Powell, and no collection of studio musicians who could replicate the pure energy and joy that Slade brought. They'd also an attitude, Dave Hill's ridiculous pudding fringe and his six-inch platforms inviting you to laugh but never sneer, and Don Powell at the back, chewing gum with an attitude that screamed, 'I don't give two fucks!' He's still the coolest man in rock.

Even on our black and white TV, Slade seemed to exist in technicolour. They weren't exactly pretty boys, but any band that ugly has to be good, and Slade were bloody fantastic. Me and my mates loved them. They were laddish and that was just fine by us because we weren't interested in girls yet. At that time most didn't like football, and the one girl who did was harder than most of the boys in the area and definitely not to be messed with.

The run into Christmas began with *Blue Peter* and the making of their Advent candle holder, something constructed from wire coat-hangers and wrapped in silver tinsel which would probably break all sorts of rules today. When the coat-hangers came out, so did Christmas. By the time it was completed, we were in a state of hysterical excitement. On Christmas Eve, my uncle Pat would appear with a turkey that he 'got' from someone who knew someone. He was a Ted who loved Elvis, looked like Paul Newman, and played the piano and guitar. He brought joy and fun and wasn't like the other adults, frowning and muttering about The Troubles and when was it all going to end. He was on our side, as were Slade.

I can't remember when I first heard 'Merry Xmas Everybody' but I loved it and we knew it was going to be No.1. We even bought a copy, which we played on our blue Dansette record player, willing the time to pass until it was Christmas Eve. Our friends, Paul and Mickey Carolan, played football with us and for Christmas in 1973, Paul Carolan got the latest in hi-tech, a portable cassette player with its own microphone that you could record your own voice and speak into. This was unbelievable. He immediately set to recording songs off the radio, editing off the DJ's babble from the start and end.

On one dismal holiday day, the idea struck us that we could karaoke along to 'Merry Xmas Everybody' by playing the song in the background whilst holding the microphone and singing over the top of it. Given that we engaged in our own commentaries on our street football games, this wasn't a big step. All attempts were to be judged by the defining moment in the song, Noddy's 'it's Christmas!' scream on the run-out. At ten or eleven you'll not match him, but we tried, careful not to be seen to enjoying it too much for fear of ridicule. To be honest, I don't think we even bothered singing the song, all energy saved for the finale. The more 'over the top' the attempt, the more theatrical, the better. We laughed, made fun of each other, pretended it didn't matter when it did.

I can still remember this as clear as day. Music does that, doesn't it? It can transport you back to an instant 50 years ago that seems as fresh as last week. Lives remembered are often defined by small instances, a word or a phrase, the smell of a coal fire on a winter's day, or Noddy Holder screaming 'it's Christmas!' at the top of his voice. Slade were never hip, but they were loved. I stood outside a hall at Manchester University Students' Union sometime in the early Eighties when they played, and they blew it apart. For a band with their history, it seemed a fall from grace. I met Noddy once in a cafe. I had to go over. I told him how we'd all tried to sing his part. He was lovely and kind and gracious, but you could tell he'd heard it a thousand times before.

I hear he makes a fortune on royalties from it. It's played constantly on the approach to Christmas, a quick escalator to joy that shops and products want to latch onto. If he's making money from it, good. No one can begrudge him that. Every time I hear it, I think of us screaming along and I'm reminded that there are some who are no longer here. Christmas is a family time, it's meant to be joyful, but it can be desperately lonely for those who have lost.

When my son was three or four, 'Merry Xmas Everybody' came on the radio. He immediately latched on to the end and started to wait for it so he could 'Noddy' along. He's Cerebral Palsy, which affects his speech, and he has always been self-conscious about it. But not with his Noddy moment. To be able to lift anybody from a world that isn't always kind or fun is a wonderful gift. It's part of the furniture now is 'Merry Xmas Everybody', like old Morecambe and Wise re-runs and *The Sound of Music*, but it has never become stale or boring.

It translates the excitement I felt as a ten-year-old and makes me remember the pure euphoria and joy for life you have at that age. Noddy's voice is a siren call to a reminder of better days and the promise of better days to come when hurt and loss have subsided and new, old memories are made. I've another memory of 'Merry Xmas Everybody', and this is more recent, my son and I screaming along to Noddy's 'it's Christmas!' on the car radio. So, thanks Slade, thanks Noddy, thanks for the joy, thanks for 'Merry Xmas Everybody'. It's a part of a lot of people's lives and memories. If a song can have colours, 'Merry Xmas Everybody' is in primary shades, illuminating the damp and grey like the twinkling of Woolworth's fairy lights against a wood chip wall.

POLYDOR RECORDS

DECEMBER 1973, LONDON, UK

I WAS THERE: PAUL BRUHIN PRICE

I wasn't really a Slade fan, but I loved the revenue they earned for Polydor. When the third of their 'straight to No.1 on advance order singles' was released, I recall a case of champagne coming into the office, with thanks from their management! It was a nice gesture, considering their singles sold themselves then. A few of my colleagues caught them live and really rated them, and film of them in concert that I saw back then suggested they might be right.

THAT'S CHRISTMAS SEZ LES! 26 DECEMBER 1973

I WATCHED IT: MARTIN BLENCO

I can't remember when Slade entered my consciousness. I remember T.Rex performing 'Ride A White Swan' and then 'Hot Love' on *Top of the Pops* in 1970, and I remember Marc Bolan having glitter on his face, my ten-year-old self not entirely sure this was a good thing. Unlike every other teenager on the planet, I don't remember David Bowie performing 'Starman' on *Top of the Pops*. But Glam happened, Slade did enter my consciousness and I became a fan, albeit I didn't rush out and buy loads of their singles. When it was announced that Slade were going to be performing 'Merry Xmas Everybody' on television over Christmas, I had to watch it. There was only one problem. We didn't watch ITV in my house. My dad thought the three biggest evils of the modern world were Harold Wilson, Mick Jagger and commercial television, and the theme music of *Coronation Street* never sullied our ears. But I'd been given a secondhand reel-to-reel tape recorder for Christmas and persuaded Dad that, although it was on 'the other side', the Christmas edition of the Les Dawson show was a must see.

My dad relented, the family called to order (or shooed out of the room) as I set up my mic in front of the big black and white television. VCRs were many years away and for our family, colour television was only going to arrive when Cliff Pack, the local TV repair man, finally said our trusty 20-inch black-and-white had finally given up the ghost.

I still have the tape with Noddy's dismissive response to the host's jokey introduction. 'Ta for that introduction, Fatty. Don't call us, we'll call you.' History tells me Slade were actually miming to a backing track and weren't live at all, having pre-recorded the song at Yorkshire Television in September or October before an audience composed on Slade Fan Club members. Never mind. It was Christmas. Slade were on telly, and all was right with the world.

January 1974 sees Slade's bid to crack America gathering pace, with the first of two more tours there (sharing bills with Iggy and the Stooges, The James Gang, Golden Earring, Aerosmith, 10cc, and The New York Dolls during the year.

CENTENNIAL HALL
20 JANUARY 1974, ONTARIO, CANADA

I WAS THERE: TOD MCDONALD

I'm going to guess that it was late '72 or early '73 when I first heard Slade. A neighbourhood friend had bought the album *Slayed?* and I loved the cover, listening to 'Gudbuy T' Jane' over and over. Other songs would begin to be favourites. Then I stumbled on to *Slade Alive!* I took that LP to art class in high school to listen to. I got strange looks but my music taste was far from Top 40. They played in my hometown of London, Ontario in April 1973, opening for Johnny Winter, but I was in Florida with my family and missed out. They finally rolled into town again in January 1974. The show was amazing, my buddy and I pushing to the front of the stage and cheering every song. To this day, we say the ringing in our ears is from that show.

Tod McDonald missed the April 1973 show but caught Slade the following year

There's a picture where we can be seen front row, leaning on the stage. We became high school celebrities overnight. Dave Hill had shiny dots pasted to his face. A few fell off and I pocketed them, attaching them to my copy of *Sladest*.

The next show I caught was May 1976. By now they had strayed from the Glam look. The show was enjoyable nonetheless. And 20 years later, I was still spinning some of their tunes while working in the garage. My son came in while 'Mama Weer All Crazee Now' was playing and asked, 'What's wrong with your stereo?' He'd only heard the Quiet Riot version. I had a good laugh telling him how they became famous covering Slade.

OLD NEW BORROWED AND BLUE RELEASED 15 FEBRUARY 1974

Old New Borrowed And Blue *reaches No.1 on the UK album charts and 168 on the Billboard 200.*

I WAS THERE: CHRIS LEWIS

Old New Borrowed And Blue was the very first album I ever bought. It cost me 10p at Rowbarton Methodist Church Christmas Jumble Sale in 1975. A bloody bargain, and I still have it. Well, to come clean, the jumble sale was run by my mum and dad (who were both very religious, not something I've inherited), and the record was left over at the end of the day, so they made me buy it to increase the money raised.

In February 1974, Slade return to Australia. They also play shows in Hong Kong and Japan.

HORDERN PAVILION

21 FEBRUARY 1974, SYDNEY, AUSTRALIA

I WAS THERE: ALEX KAY

I think my first hearing of *Slade Alive!* was the catalyst for my discovering them in 1972. I would have been 24 years old. I don't think anything they did was released or played in Australia before this album. The first song I heard of theirs was 'Coz I Luv You' in late 1971. I was immediately hooked – Noddy's unique voice was so powerful, while being filled with emotion in many of his songs. I bought *Slade Alive!* on the first day of its release in Australia and drove all my mates mad, playing it incessantly, particularly at parties, when I'd take my very large speakers and hammer the album all night. They still speak about those 'Slade parties' on the site of the company I worked for at the time.

The concert I attended was at Hordern Pavilion. I went with a friend (my future wife was away at the time or she would certainly have been there) and we were fortunate enough to get seats three rows from the stage. It was an incredible concert, their stomping music enveloping the venue. I vividly

Alex Kay (second left, next to the coach) drove the football team mad playing *Slade Alive!* incessantly

recall the boys in their huge boots playing their instruments while standing on top of very tall speakers, particularly Jim who, if my memory serves me correctly, fell off a speaker and injured himself at some later concert. I couldn't believe that, apart from Noddy and the great harmonies, how they were such amazingly competent musicians. It was such a great night – my friend and I relive it whenever we catch up. The concert was so loud, with us being so close, it was also the start of my tinnitus – I had very loud ringing in my ears for four days after the night and really couldn't hear anything in that period. At least I have some great memories to 'thank' for the tinnitus!

I continue to follow Slade, buying all their Australian releases. I also liked some of their later US work, even though I found it a little overproduced. I would have loved to have seen them in concert while on my own visits to London and other parts of the UK.

FESTIVAL HALL

22 FEBRUARY 1974, BRISBANE, AUSTRALIA

I WAS THERE: DAWN WOOLNOUGH

I had their posters all over my bedroom wall. Don was my favourite. I went to this concert with three school friends and I remember standing right down the front near the speakers. It was so loud that our ears were ringing for days after.

Dawn Woolnough had Slade posters all over her wall

'EVERYDAY' RELEASED
29 MARCH 1974

Slade's first ballad reaches No.3 in the UK charts.

Slade embark upon a full UK tour before heading off to North America again.

OPERA HOUSE
20 APRIL 1974, BLACKPOOL, UK

I WAS THERE: GRANT ASHTON, AGE 7

I saw Slade twice, once aged seven in 1974 at Blackpool Opera House, the other aged 14 at Lancaster University. They were a great group then and remain as popular as ever. I found it very busy and loud at Blackpool, being so young. At Lancaster the place was bouncing, ears ringing long after a show which Noddy stole. 'We'll Bring The House Down' was their new song, I think.

KING'S HALL, BELLE VUE
21 APRIL 1974, MANCHESTER, UK

I WAS THERE: BARRIE GREGORY, AGE 11

I was still at school, with this my first ever gig. I remember how loud they were. Then the crowd went mad, smashing up the seating as it was getting in the way. It was absolute madness, but what an experience for an eleven-year-old. No one was attacked or beaten up, it was just fans having a blast. A neighbour took me as she had tickets and knew I liked Slade. I remember being very

Barrie Gregory (pictured right) thought Slade were very loud

excited and seeing them live was something I'd never experienced; it made my liking of rock music even stronger. I got into them through listening to them on the radio and seeing them on *Top of the Pops*, but being brought up around motorbikes and stock car racing, loud music appealed to me more. Their stage presence was great, especially Dave and his mad antics and outfits. I'd still love to meet him – I feel he's on my wavelength.

I WAS THERE: TONY KINDER, AGE 13

The gigs were at the long-gone King's Hall at Belle Vue, Manchester in '74 and '75. I went on my own. You can imagine what it was like for a 13-year-old going to see such a massive band. The '75 gig was on the back of the release of the *Slade In Flame* movie and they performed most of the tracks off that album alongside previous material. I love their cover of 'Move Over' on the *Slayed?* album, and still have a ticket stub somewhere from one of the gigs I went to.

WINTER GARDENS

23 APRIL 1974, BOURNEMOUTH, UK

I WAS THERE: DAVID ELKINS

I saw Slade several times at Bournemouth's Winter Gardens, once in the Seventies when I was still at school. The place was heaving, with girls screaming everywhere, chairs ripped up and general carnage. I next saw them in 1977. Those were lean years for Slade. Dave had shaved his head in an attempt to fit in with the punk movement but it didn't really work. The hall was about half-full, but Slade played as if it was full. They were very loud but with virtually the same set-list as '74.

My next gigs were in December '81 and '82. The last one seemed more polished, but they didn't seem to be enjoying it as much. Jim's solo spot dominated the show and I think Dave was miffed by this. Don was repeatedly holding his head, as if in pain. The banter was rehearsed and not spontaneous, which seemed a bit silly to me. Afterwards we waited at the stage door. Don had left straight away, with Jim moaning about the lack of light to sign autographs, while Nod wouldn't speak to anyone. He signed autographs but didn't look too happy. Dave was jovial and grinning though.

CAIRD HALL
1 MAY 1974, DUNDEE, UK

I WAS THERE: GWEN DALE (NÉE HILL)

I started work in the Timex factory in Dundee around April '74 and saw Slade back at the Caird Hall again soon after. I saved some money, and after seeing them at the Glasgow Apollo in May 1975, where we'd seen them two years earlier when it was Green's Playhouse, we decided to move to Walsall. We found a flat share in August '75 in a house in Glebe Street, later finding out it was just one street away from where Noddy was born in Newhall Street.

I met Steve in 1978 (S Dale – would you believe the anagram of his name!) and we married in 1981. I had many jobs to start with, mostly in factories, including one as a lock maker and another in a pub. Then I became a youth leader. My friend Helen went back home after a year, but I stayed on, my four children still living in and around Walsall, and having all met the band. I got to see Slade again at Birmingham Town Hall, Birmingham Odeon, *Monsters of Rock* at Donington Park, and at Aston University, and had to take the kids sometimes.

KING GEORGE'S HALL
8 MAY 1974, BLACKBURN, UK

I WAS THERE: GEOFF WEST, AGE 15

I first saw Slade on their *Crazee Nites* tour, and seeing them live after watching them on *Top of the Pops* was unbelievable. 'Everyday' had just slipped out of the Top 10 at that point. The atmosphere was electric, and the sound… well! I couldn't hear properly for days after. I lived in Chorley (and still do) and went with some mates from school. One of the dads took us in his car. I'd been a Slade fan since 1971, and the first song I bought was 'Coz I Luv You', that being the first song I liked and what attracted me to the band. I saw them many times after that, and they never disappointed. I also saw them at Southport Theatre (1978/79), Blackburn Bailey's aka the Cavendish Club (1978/79), Lancaster University (1981), and the King George's Hall in Blackburn again in 1981.

Their concerts were always full of energy, and when Noddy spoke to the audience, everyone listened. That was the respect people had for him. He was a bit crude at times with his banter with the audience, but nobody cared. There was no PC brigade in the Seventies and Eighties!

I know many people would have liked to have seen them reform for one last tour, but it wouldn't have been the same. I have great memories of seeing them live and will cherish them forever. For people that didn't see them live, that's their loss. I'm going to see Noddy this summer at the Lowry, appearing with Tom Seals. It should be a good evening. I saw him at Preston with Mark Radcliffe in 2013, and at Clitheroe in 2015. I was also at Bilston in 2017 when Jim did an afternoon Q&A and then played guitar and sang a few songs. That was an emotional afternoon.

'Keep on rockiiiinnnn'!'

CITY HALL

9 MAY 1974, SHEFFIELD, UK

I WAS THERE: CAROL HARWOOD, AGE 15

I first heard Slade on the radio in the early Seventies with 'Get Down And Get With It'. I loved the beat and, mainly, Noddy Holder's voice. His tone was appealing and John Lennon-ish (years later, I heard Noel Gallagher say the same). When I heard 'Coz I Luv You' I was hooked. I was 15 when I had a chance to see them live in Sheffield. Living in Doncaster, it wasn't far away but took a lot of persuasion to convince my parents to let me go.

I took a friend from school, Julie, the same age. Looking back, she was more into Jim Lea than the music. Slade at that time were at the top of their game. They'd had six No.1s and were the hottest ticket in town. We managed to get tickets in the third row from the front. We couldn't believe it. We spent the week leading up to the concert making a cardboard top hat with silver foil discs on and sorting out a tartan waistcoat and badges to look the part. Julie's parents were going to pick us up after the concert, so my parents felt a bit better about letting us go.

On the night, we were so happy. We were asked by a promoter if we would like to go on stage in a competition with five others and be

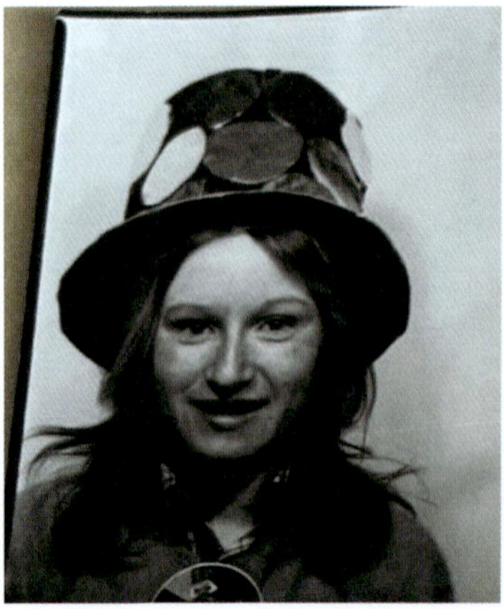

Carol Harwood in 1973, and with Nod in 1999 – 'it took me 25 years to track him down!'

judged as the best-dressed Slade fan. We had to go to the backstage door after the support act. We were so excited that we were going backstage, thinking we might see Nod, Don, Jim or Dave. I can't remember much about the support but I do remember turning around and seeing that the lad behind me had his back to the stage and was reading the newspaper!

We made it on stage but didn't win anything and didn't see Slade, but never mind. They still had quite a few skinheads following them from the early days, who mingled with a lot of young girls like ourselves. The lights went down, then I heard a rumble-like thunder and the bovver boot brigade started climbing over us. I got a boot in the side of my head and could feel my seat collapse to the floor. How I got up I don't know. I remember seeing a bright white light shining on Noddy Holder and the discs from his top hat shining bright, with him asking everyone to calm down.

I was fine, but Julie was screaming, 'Jimmy Lea!' at the top of her voice and crying… I didn't get that, I'm afraid – I just wanted to hear the music, the beat, Noddy's voice and the sound I had got to love in the last few years. But it was chaos. I fell off the seat I was standing on, and by this time all the seats at the front had been flattened and I had lost my glasses. I moved to the side and safety, but Julie was still in the middle, screaming over Jimmy. I stood at the side, squinting and trying to make out the songs.

I went out after about an hour and couldn't believe it. All round the corridor there were girls laid flat on the floor, St John's Ambulance staff trying to attend to everybody. At the end, I finally found my twisted glasses under my seat and my friend Julie in another world, in a state because she'd seen Jimmy Lea in the flesh!

We got outside to be confronted by police vans and dogs, but we finally found Julie's parents. It was not the night I expected, and I spent the journey home worrying about what my parents would say about my glasses. Next day at school we were heroes. Quite a few of our classmates had seen us on the stage. We were the talk of the school assembly.

Years later, I saw Slade a few more times and really got to hear them properly. They were a great live band, and Noddy was a powerful singer. I'm so glad the Reading Festival gave them another chance. I have all their albums and still play their music after almost 50 years. Till deaf do us part.

HAMMERSMITH ODEON

16 MAY 1974, LONDON, UK

I WAS THERE: MICK TALBOT, THE MERTON PARKAS, THE STYLE COUNCIL & DEXY'S MIDNIGHT RUNNERS

I saw them with my mate Paul, at Hammersmith Odeon. Slade just had their own thing. When 'Coz I Luv You' broke, that was really big. If you were a certain age, I suppose they seemed the acceptable face of long hair, because they were a bit yobbish, if you came from a background of football and other stuff. I suppose The Faces had a bit of that 'Jack the Lad' image as well. They're one of those bands that are taken more seriously in retrospect. Slade made some really good records, but at times the yobbish thing might have diminished people's seriousness about them. Because Noddy was a really good singer, and some of the ballads were really almost like… well, 'Everyday' is a bit like John Lennon, I think.

Slade return to North America for more gigs.

FELT FORUM

31 MAY 1974, NEW YORK CITY, NEW YORK

I WAS THERE: ELMO JOHN

The NYC Felt Forum was the annex of Madison Square Garden. It was my first concert. The opening act was Aerosmith! When Slade hit the stage, the 4,500 audience was on their feet for the whole show. When Noddy's voice split the dark and the spotlight hit his mirrored hat, I was hooked. The band was tight and loud. I had just started playing electric bass and that show made me make a lifelong commitment. And as I close in on being 64, I'm still playing music, so I thank Slade for getting me going. The band that night played all the hits. Thank God I saw that show.

I WAS THERE: STEVE WISNER

In May 1974, I went to see Slade for a second time. This time it was the Felt Forum, the smaller venue attached to Madison Square Garden. I was now 17 and my musical tastes were expanding. I bought every Slade vinyl record for several years, and then the band started to dissipate. They became a bit commercial, and their success obviously took a toll on them. I follow Slade on Facebook but only because I guess I've been hoping for a miracle. To me, Slade without Noddy is like Journey without Steve Perry. I hope to hear of a reunion, but I will have to keep these vivid memories alive in my mind.

THE AUDITORIUM

21 JUNE 1974, CHICAGO, ILLINOIS

I WAS THERE: MATT SHAUGHNESSY, AGE 15

I was there with my friend Tom for our first ever concert. And what a show it was! We headed off to the train station that would take us to downtown Chicago for the show. We were 15 years old, just finished with our sophomore year in high school, and quite innocent. We were a bit anxious about heading into the big city on our own, but after fiddling with a map we figured out a route we could walk the half-mile to the venue.

The Auditorium is a grand old theatre, with balconies and boxes, holding about 3,000 people and about three-quarters full. Upon arrival, we scoped the lobby for Slade memorabilia to no avail, which was disappointing as I wanted to upgrade my homemade t-shirt with a sewn-on mini-Slade fist patch. Oh well, them's the breaks.

Matt Shaughnessy with Nod in 1986

We headed to our seats: seventh row on JWL's side, settling in for a night to remember. But first we had to suffer 45 minutes of 10cc. If I had been more sensitive, I'd have felt bad for them as they were barraged with catcalls. Since I wasn't all that sensitive, I joined in. Once they finished, the place started getting rowdy. I can't remember how long it was until Slade began playing, but it was too long!

Finally, the moment came, 'Please welcome from England, Slade!' And with that, Nod shouted, 'Take Me Bak 'Ome' and we were off, out of our seats like a shot from a gun, shouting along from the get-go. Nod was decked out in plaid coat, vest and trousers, with iconic mirrored top hat, H was in his fish-scale outfit with dollar sign boots and the Super Yob guitar, Jim was in some type of yellow get up, and Don was in traditional striped pants and vest, chewing more gum than a playground full of kids.

The set included 'Good Time Gals', 'Gudbuy T' Jane', 'Move Over', 'When The Lights Are Out', 'Darling Be Home Soon', 'We're Really Gonna Raise The Roof', 'Just A Little Bit', 'Let The Good Times Roll', 'Cum On Feel The Noize', 'Get Down And Get With It', 'Mama Weer All Crazee Now' and 'Keep On Rockin''. Great show.

I much prefer Slade originals to covers and would have preferred 'Do We Still Do It', 'How D'You Ride' and more, but that's just quibbling. The band were in good form; Nod had the crowd going the entire evening, Dave Hill did his schtick, and Jim and Don laid down the foundation. And if there was one overall impression I took away from the show, it's that Slade were fucking loud! My ears rang for three days and Tom and I literally had to shout at each other to be heard as we headed back to the train station.

'THE BANGIN' MAN' RELEASED 28 JUNE 1974

'The Bangin' Man' reaches No.3 in the UK singles chart. It's written about the band's late road manager Swinn, whose job it was to wake each band member when it was time to move on.

RAINBOW THEATRE & HAMMERSMITH PALAIS

4 & 5 SEPTEMBER 1974, LONDON, UK

I WAS THERE: STEVE EDWARDS

I was part of the fan club and had started doing various jobs when I heard they were looking for fans to go to filming for *Slade in Flame*. I skipped work without hesitation. One filming was at the Hammersmith Palais, a dance club at the time. My memory from that day is the excitement of my fellow fans. We were asked to dance and have a good time. I think they did 'Them Kinda Monkeys Can't Swing' and possibly 'OK Yesterday Was Yesterday'. I'll always remember just rocking away, which I know we did more of in hope of being on film!

They also wanted fans for the filming of the finale concert, filmed at the Rainbow in Finsbury Park the day before. Fans were issued with white silk scarfs to wave, especially during 'Far Far Away'. That was a more controlled event. You were seated, as at a normal concert, whereas the Palais was a dance floor to throw yourself around. It was a special time and makes the film a special one for me. I've looked closely but never made the cut!

'FAR FAR AWAY' RELEASED
11 OCTOBER 1974

The lead single from the soundtrack to *Slade in Flame* reaches No.2 in the UK charts.

K B HALLEN

14 & 22 NOVEMBER 1974, COPENHAGEN, DENMARK

I WAS THERE: RENÉ ACUTE CHRISTENSEN, AGE 14

I first heard Slade on my 14th birthday in August 1974, when I was given a copy of *Sladest* on cassette. I was hooked. Later that year, they did two gigs in Copenhagen and my brother (three years older), a classmate and I got tickets for the second one. The day of the concert, I heard on the radio that 'Far Far Away' was No.1 on the Danish radio charts. In the middle of the concert, Noddy said to the audience that he'd been told that the next song they were about to play had just gone to No.1 in Denmark. Then they played it and the crowd went crazy. It was a seated concert but no one was sitting down at that moment!

SLADE IN FLAME RELEASED
29 NOVEMBER 1974

Slade in Flame, *the soundtrack to the film of the same name, is Slade's fifth studio album and reaches No.6 in the UK charts.*

I WAS THERE: DAEV BARKER

I was born in the same year 'Merry Xmas Everybody' was released and so my first exposure to Slade was the best Christmas song ever, year after year. It is no mean feat to create a cool Christmas song. Other than the other big hits, I had no further exposure to Slade until I was in my twenties, when a work colleague and fellow Seventies Punk fan suggested I should give them a listen. I thought Slade were no more than a fun band with two or three well-known songs. I did borrow a copy of *Slayed?* and I didn't really hold much hope for enjoying it. But from the opening track, 'How D'you Ride', I was hooked. I loved the raucousness of the music, the crunching guitars, the stomping rhythms and Noddy's inimitable vocals. There are more subtle moments too. 'Look At Last Nite' is a great example, with fantastic harmonies and an intelligent song structure.

And *Slade in Flame* is an album that marks a maturity in songwriting and showcases the musicianship of the band. It is not an understatement to say Slade are an underrated band. Their body of work contains a large number of hits, but also a great collection of album tracks that span a larger range of genres than they are given credit for. The songwriting duo of Jim Lea and Noddy Holder is right up there with the best of them. As an inspiration for myself as a musician and songwriter, I couldn't ask for much more of a masterclass.

SLADE IN FLAME FILM RELEASED JANUARY 1975

The film Slade in Flame, *directed by Richard Loncraine, stars all four members of the band as members of the fictional band Flame. It is not well received critically on release, although it has been reappraised in later years.*

Flame *is a good film, but it's timed in the Seventies. I reckon we should have had a Slade* Hard Day's Night *caper, with Midlands humour. People like to see fun and humour.* **Dave Hill**

'HOW DOES IT FEEL?' RELEASED 7 FEBRUARY 1975

'How Does It Feel?' reaches No.15 in the UK charts.

I WAS THERE: KEVIN MOTTRAM

Slade's finest moment is the six minutes of majesty that is 'How Does It Feel?'. I started to click with it in the autumn of '96, a time of personal upheaval when I was undertaking an Access to Higher Education course at my local FE college and my folks were about to sell the home I grew up in. By the time moving day came around, the song fitted the mood perfectly, a mixture of optimism for a new start and sadness at leaving the old place behind, with a pinch of 1970s nostalgia thrown in for good measure. Moments after we'd locked up for the last time, my sister realised she'd left her favourite lampshade behind, so I volunteered to go back and fetch it, in the process having one last solo tour of the old homestead. In my head, this was a cinematic moment, the last bit of the film, 'How Does It Feel?' the soundtrack, like in the opening sequence to *Flame*. An empty house, with empty rooms, but rooms full of memories; each individual room lit up one last time, one last look inside each one, then it was lights out, and the doors shut, forever. Onwards and upwards to the next chapter.

I passed the Access course that summer, getting my first-choice place at the University of Manchester. Around then, the pilot episode of Seventies Midlands nostalgia sitcom *The Grimleys* aired, and as the lead character was a gawky schoolboy determined to get into university, the spirit of it happened to chime with my own joyous personal circumstances. It also featured a certain N. Holder playing a music teacher called Neville Holder (inevitably nicknamed Noddy by his pupils), bashing out 'Mama Weer All Crazee Now' on a gold top Les Paul plugged into a Marshall stack in an empty classroom; a fantasy perhaps, but a glorious one. A nice moment, a perfect moment even. And when it comes to such moments, the happy moments of our lives, Slade have always been there for us. Long may that be the case.

I WAS THERE: MERRIC DAVIDSON

I didn't think Slade (or Ambrose Slade) were going to be for me when they first appeared in the late Sixties. That skinhead look; the No.1 haircuts, the braces and boots, just didn't appeal to this fey folkie fan of Leonard and Joni and the Incredible String Band. But looks aren't everything, and never judge a book by the cover.

After this gimmickry failed and was replaced by the (hardly) Glam look we would soon grow to love, coupled with that glorious run of twelve top-five hit singles and loads of eagerly awaited appearances on Top of the Pops, Slade became irresistible. Ironically, given the No.1s, 2s and 3s of the previous three years, my favourite Slade single today, 'How Does It Feel?' – from the very fine and seldom-seen Slade in Flame movie – only made No.15 in 1975. 'How Does It Feel?' is not only Slade's finest song, but one of the finest of all pop songs. I doubted myself when I learned that Noel Gallagher also thinks so but, no, he's right, I'm right, it is!

STREATHAM ODEON

16 FEBRUARY 1975, LONDON, UK

I WAS THERE: JIM BOB, CARTER THE UNSTOPPABLE SEX MACHINE

Jim Bob wanted to be Jim Lea in the early Seventies, and still wants to be in Slade now

It feels like Slade have always been there. One of my life's constants. On all those *Top of the Pops* I watched as a kid and soundtracking my Christmases since forever. When I went to Streatham Odeon in 1975 to see *Slade in Flame*, it was the time in my life I'd decided I was definitely going to be in a band. I was going to be the bass player. Like David Essex's character in *Stardust* and like Ray Stiles from Mud, who lived on the same road as my old primary school. And Jim Lea in Slade. The bass players seemed like the coolest band members. Years later, in 2020, Jim Lea had seen the video for my song 'Kidstrike!', was getting a video made and wanted to know who made it. He'd apparently said he liked the song too. I don't know if that's true, but I still boast about it whenever the subject of Slade comes up.

In 1999, if it wasn't for Slade, my band Jim's Super Stereoworld's second single 'Could U B The 1 I Waited 4' would have been called

'Could You Be The One I Waited For'. Boring. And now, bang up to date, there's a song on my new album called 'Bernadette (Hasn't Found Anyone Yet)'. When we were recording it, the song reminded me a bit of 'Coz I Luv You', so we added a military type snare drum and a violin to make it more like it. We even talked about putting a microphone in the dance studio upstairs to record the kids' dance class stamping along with the bass drum. Yes, 40 years after seeing *Slade in Flame* at the pictures, and I still want to be in Slade.

ABC CINEMA

FEBRUARY 1975, ENFIELD, UK

I WAS THERE: KEVIN ACOTT

This is your music. You're 13. The furthest, furthest away you've been is Lowestoft. You've (sort of) loved one girl in your life. And the only red light you've ever seen is the one upstairs in that boozer in Edmonton, the one with bullet holes in the front, the one they'll knock down soon, right after Punk.

Kevin Acott a couple of years earlier, presumably on his way to a Bay City Rollers audition, 'displaying my usual sartorial flair'

Music has been there, though, kissing and embracing you, every day of those 13 years. Your mum and your dad love music. They both sing, sometimes. Not often enough, but when they do, it's a sign they're happy. They love their music. Though not your music; they say they don't really like your music. They don't like His hair, of course. Or His cockiness. Or His hat. Or The Other One's teeth. Or Their trousers. They don't like the way these so-called musicians talk. Northern. Rough. You realise right then, as Mum tuts, that you want to be Jim. Or Don. And that it's never going to happen.

They did quite like that Christmas song though, Mum once said. But you don't care what they think; this... this is *your* music. Yours. You don't know how. Or why. But you go to watch *Slade in Flame* at the ABC on Southbury Road, Enfield, full of thrill and fear, and you sneak in – it's a double A – and soon you don't know what you've just seen but all the adult world's sex and darkness and violence and harsh scrambling-for-joy starts to enter you, engulf you. And so does its sadness and its regret, it's sweetness and laughter and melody and harmony, its sillinesses and seriousnesses, its out-of-timeness. Changed.

Ha! How does it feel? HOW DOES IT FEEL?! I don't know, Noddy mate, I don't know. I didn't know then and I don't really know now. But: when I listen to you these days, I miss my parents and I smile and I understand at least a little more than I did. And I realise the Flame you helped light in so many of us still burns. And that makes me feel good.

This was our music. And it's still our music. OK. Yesterday was yesterday. But this was our music. And it's still our music.

STUDIO 1 CINEMA

FEBRUARY 1975, SUNDERLAND, UK

I WAS THERE: PETER SMITH

I began to lose faith in Slade during 1973 and 1974. They had become too much of a teen pop band. I didn't feel it was 'cool' to go and see them live at the time. I'd lost that fine, loud raucous rock band to the teenage girls who would scream at Noddy and Dave, going to their concerts sporting top hats with silver circles stuck to them, Slade scarves and tartan baggies. So, while all the girls at school were going to see them at the City Hall, telling me how great they were, I resisted the urge. I didn't fancy standing in a hall full of screaming girls. Anyway, I told myself, I'd seen them before they 'sold out' to celebrity status, when they were a proper rock band. I secretly wanted to go and see them again, but consoled myself by going to see Deep Purple, Led Zeppelin, The Groundhogs, Uriah Heep and lots of other 'proper' rock and 'underground' bands.

The next time I (sort of) saw Slade was when they made a personal appearance at a local cinema to promote their film, *Slade In Flame*, telling the story of a fictitious late 1960s beat group, Flame, who make it to the top only to break up at their peak of success. The film begins with the future members of Flame playing in two rival bands, one fronted by a singer named Jack Daniels (played by Alan Lake), the other, The Undertakers, fronted by a singer known as Stoker (played by Noddy Holder). Flame formed from remnants of the two bands and had the same line-up as Slade. It's entertaining and pretty funny in places, with some great songs. One moment which sticks in my mind is when Stoker is brought on stage in a coffin, the lid of which gets stuck and Stoker can't get out. The idea was borrowed straight from Screaming 'Lord' Sutch, who, of course, borrowed it from Screamin' Jay Hawkins, although I never saw Screaming 'Lord' Sutch get stuck!

I went with a group of mates to see Slade introduce the film. We were cutting it fine, time-wise, and as we arrived at the cinema, a big silver Rolls-Royce pulled up outside. Noddy, Dave, Jim and Don jumped out, ran straight past us, and made their way into the cinema. We quickly paid our money to the cashier (probably £1 or so) and followed them in, just in time to hear them say a few words to introduce the film, then run out as quickly as they came in. I think they told us they were off to another cinema in the region to do the same thing. Strangely, given the band were making a personal appearance, the cinema was nowhere near full. Or maybe their popularity was already starting to wane.

I finally relented from my Slade abstinence and went to see them in concert a few months after seeing the film.

ALBANY HOTEL

10 MARCH 1975, GLASGOW, UK

I WAS THERE: JOHN MILNE

Me and my friends were all Slade fans from when 'Get Down And Get With It' came out. When *Play It Loud* came out, they were dressed as skinheads and we all dressed the same; that's the way we were. My mum and dad used to get me my Slade singles, and when I was 21, they bought me the American version of *Play It Loud* because I didn't have a copy. Me and my pals would go to concerts together, and in 1974 I met Jessie, who I married later that year, and we started going to concerts together.

I missed seeing Slade perform 'How Does It Feel?' on *Top of the Pops* on 6th February 1975 because I had to go to hospital to see my wife and our new baby, Neville John Holder Milne. Next month, Slade came to Glasgow to promote the film *Flame*. The DJ Richard Parks was on top of a horse-drawn hearse with Noddy, who was dressed as an undertaker. The rest of them followed in a big black Rolls-Royce.

They started going down Bath Street from where they were staying at the Albany Hotel towards the Apollo, where the film was going to be shown. All the fans were running down the road with the hearse, including me. I was running quite close to the hearse. I had on white skinners and a *Slade in Flame* t-shirt and I had a wee tartan gonk I was going to try and give to Noddy.

As the hearse slowed down at the traffic lights I managed to jump up and I gave him the gonk. My white denims got covered in oil because I was jumping up the wheels.

There's a photo of me that was in the local paper running after the hearse. Me and Jessie kept running and running and running until we got to the Apollo.

We decided to go home and get changed and then go to their hotel. We got there and the place was swarming with fans. We walked up to the main door and we could see them walking about inside so we just walked in. We went to the lift and the lift opened and Don Powell got out. We got a picture of him. He looked at us as if he got a fright. We said, 'Where's the rest of the band, Don?' He said, 'They're in there getting something to eat.' So we went to their table and who should be sitting there but Noddy, Jimmy and Dave Hill. And I've got a picture of me sitting with Noddy with Dave standing behind us. And the fans were hitting the windows because they were so jealous.

I showed Noddy my son's birth certificate, and he said, 'Has your son got fair hair and blue eyes and long sideburns like me?'

CAPITOL THEATRE
21 APRIL 1975, CARDIFF, UK

I WAS THERE: ALUN PERKINS, AGE 13

I became a proper Slade fan in 1972 at the age of ten when 'Mama Weer All Crazee Now' was released, the first Slade single I ever bought. I had been aware of them since 'Coz I Luv You', liking that single and the subsequent two records. However, it wasn't until 'Mama…' that I really got into them. I've never been the same since!

Alun Perkins was 13 when he first saw Slade

I first saw them live at the long since demolished Capitol Theatre in 1975. They had played in Cardiff before but I'd been too young to go. *Slade in Flame* had recently been released and they were touring to promote it. My friend Mark and I were obsessed with them and had been to see the film at the Capitol a couple of months before. These were the days when you had to go to the box office and queue for tickets. We eagerly trekked into town when they went on sale one Sunday morning and got tickets in the fourth row.

Memories of the gig are a bit hazy, but I know for certain we had a great night. It was amazing to see our idols live on stage. Bear in mind, in those days there was no internet or streaming and very few pop music shows on TV, so seeing your favourites anywhere could be quite rare – mostly just *Top of the Pops* and other TV shows. So, to see them live on stage was absolutely incredible – I remember thinking, 'Wow, that's actually them up there on the stage.'

I don't recall a lot about the set list, although they were promoting the *Slade in Flame* album amongst previous hits. They previewed a new single, set for May, 'Thanks For The Memory' and also played B-side 'Raining In My Champagne'. I remember Noddy announcing it would be the first time they had played that live – what an honour, we thought, getting to hear a song that other fans had yet to hear.

I also vividly remember 'Get Down And Get With It' at the end, an absolutely storming and exciting track. I had arranged for my sister and her boyfriend to pick us up after the concert and take us home by car. They had been having a drink in the pub next to the theatre and I remember my sister remarking how they could hear Slade from next door and Noddy had been screaming 'allllriiiiight!' at the end.

I WAS THERE: CHRIS HARRIS

I was fortunate enough to attend the Welsh premiere of the film at the Capitol Theatre in Queen Street, Cardiff, a short distance from where I first saw the band live in June '73. This was thanks to my dad, a photographer at the time for the *Western Mail and South Wales Echo*. How lucky was I? All four members of Slade were there in person. I managed to meet them briefly and have the album signed by each one of them. What a day that was, meeting the band, watching their film and tucking into a buffet! To my shame, I no longer have the signed album.

I went back to the Capitol in April 1975 to see Slade in concert. I remember fans en masse trying to pick up small pieces of Dave Hill's discarded colourful face glitter that littered the stage and floor, all no doubt eager to take home a small souvenir of a fantastic evening. Sadly, the Capitol was closed down in January 1978 and demolished in 1983. What an absolute waste of an historic building. Shockingly, it was eventually turned into a faceless, half-empty indoor shopping centre.

I got to see Slade again in October 1979 at Cardiff Uni's Students' Union, and then in December 1981 at Sophia Gardens, an indoor venue situated near Bute Park, a stone's throw from Cardiff Castle.

NEW VICTORIA THEATRE

26 APRIL 1975, LONDON, UK

I WAS THERE: SIMON HARVEY, AGE 14

When Slade first hit the charts in June 1971 with 'Get Down And Get With It', I didn't realise as an eleven-year-old lad what an impact the band would have on my life. The band were just starting out on their chart career, their self-belief sending them on a journey to international fame. Hit single after hit single followed in rapid succession, with no less than six UK No.1s following. Thursday evenings were spent watching *Top of the Pops* in hope of Slade being on with their new record, and Tuesday lunchtimes listening to BBC Radio 1 on the 247 MW frequency as Johnnie Walker announced the new chart countdown to hear what position Slade's new record had entered.

Simon Harvey's ticket for Slade at London's New Victoria Theatre

Then there were Friday evenings listening to Rosko's *Roundtable*, the self-styled Emperor playing new releases, judged by an 'expert' panel as to the possibility of chart success. He loved Slade, having a cameo appearance in their 1975 cinematic film outing, *Slade in Flame*. There were also evenings spent listening to Radio Luxembourg 208 MW on a transistor radio with an earpiece under the bed covers after lights out at 9pm (I had to be up early to do my paper round before school).

In the words of 1976 Slade hit 'Let's Call It Quits', I was 'trapped hook, line and sinker' and desperate to see Slade live. Having saved my wages from my paper round, I was able to afford to make my dream come true at London's New Victoria Theatre, travelling in from Slough with school friend Kim Bryant on public transport. We arrived at the venue mid-afternoon to be greeted by the sight of hundreds of chanting Slade fans outside the theatre, the assembled throng demanding 'we want Slade!' to the amusement of the attending police, security staff and passers-by.

Fans were dressed in Noddy Holder mirrored top hats, glitter-encrusted outfits, Slade t-shirts and silver-studded stack-heeled boots. It was like walking on to the set of an apocalyptic film, with life's most weird and wonderful people all gathered in one place.

Eventually access was allowed into the theatre, where I was in awe of the beautiful Victorian splendour. The largest entertainment establishment I had been inside prior to the New Vic being our local village hall. After watching support act Bunny and what then seemed like an eternity, Slade hit the stage to a barrage of amplified sound and lights, tearing into 'Them Kinda Monkeys Can't Swing' with a ferocity that was incredible to behold – Holder in full, unstoppable flow.

I was mesmerised at actually being in the same room, seeing Slade in the flesh as opposed to on TV – a mind-blowing experience that changed the course of my life. The set that night consisted of some of Slade's big-hitting tunes, including 'Far Far Away', 'Gudbuy T' Jane', 'Everyday', 'Thanks For The Memory', 'Mama Weer All Crazee Now' and a stripped-back, haunting keyboard and guitar-led rendition of 'How Does It Feel?' which was spine-tinglingly beautiful.

The gig and tour were recorded by BBC Radio 1 and remain available to listen to online via the *Six Days on the Road* documentary, with commentary by Stuart Grundy. That day started my Slade live journey in style, the first of 98 such sightings between 1975 and 1983 up to their final gig together at the Royal Court Theatre, Liverpool, promoting No.2 chart hit 'My Oh My'.

I saw Slade play full to concert halls, thousands at festivals, and near-empty clubs, but that gig at the New Victoria Theatre will always hold a special place in my heart as the day I got SLAYED.

CIVIC HALL

27 APRIL 1975, WOLVERHAMPTON, UK

I WAS THERE: IAN PETKO-BUNNEY, AGE 15

I discovered them around 1973, the time of 'Cum On Feel The Noize' and 'Skweeze Me, Pleeze Me', going on to buy 'Merry Xmas Everybody', 'The Bangin' Man', and *Old New Borrowed And Blue*. Then

I bought *Sladest* and *Slade Alive!* – as good a live album capturing a show as anything. They weren't touring in the UK then. They made *Slade in Flame*, and they'd been touring a lot in the US. But to promote *Flame* they did a tour. I lived in mid-Wales and persuaded my dad to drive me and a buddy from school to Wolverhampton. That was something I'd never experienced.

I didn't see them again until I was at Cardiff University in '78, on a much smaller stage. It was all standing and we were all moshing. That was knockout. They hadn't really had hits for the longest time. Then came Reading, and the revival. I'm pretty sure I saw them twice in one week in '79. I went with a couple of buddies, notably including Russell Pierce, who I still talk to and who runs part of a radio station in Lyme Bay, Dorset. We hung around for the soundcheck but got kicked out pretty quickly.

After that, I saw them at *Monsters of Rock* at Donington and, on before Blue Öyster Cult, Slade killed it. I remember Noddy talking about AC/DC's *Back In Black* and how they had the big bell on stage, complaining as the rain dripped down from the bell. It was just a sea of people and that was a great, great show.

KING'S HALL

29 APRIL 1975, BELLE VUE, MANCHESTER, UK

I WAS THERE: IAN EDMUNDSON, AGE 16

Slade's *Flame* tour show at Belle Vue in Manchester was a very special gig for me. They were my idols. I bought their records on release from either Derek Guest or Javelin Records in Bolton. They rolled into town amidst some fanfare. There was quite a lot of radio station promotion in advance. Maybe that was a sign that they were beginning their downward slide and they needed to shift some tickets, but we'd all have laughed out loud at that idea back then. As far as we knew, they were still by far the country's top band, though you have to remember that 'How Does It Feel?' hadn't reached the Top Ten, and that was a bit of a blip for them. The press leapt on that and sharpened their knives.

I travelled in from Bolton, and on reaching the King's Hall, I dived into the merch stall and came away with a *Flame* poster (I saw the film a couple of times on release), the tour programme, and a 'Cum On Feel The Noize' badge which some swine mugged me for on a train near Bristol a year or so later. I went and took up a place on a stairway off to the right side of the room, out of the crush and with a really good view, and where I could put my swag down without losing it. All the hall stewards were too busy in the carnage down at the front to be bothered with where we were standing.

The support act were Bunny, who I enjoyed. They were close to being booed off by the crowd. After what seemed like an age, Slade took to the stage. In fact, they didn't just take to that stage, they seemed to explode onto it. I reckon it was the crowd that was exploding. The welcome was deafening. Then it was Slade's turn to be deafening. In about 50 shows that I saw, they never showed much restraint as far as decibels went.

The sound at Belle Vue was always an utter mire. The hall was huge and cavernous, and the sound just echoed around and around. I'd also suffered through Roxy Music struggling with the acoustics there. But I shrugged off the terrible sound of the room and got on with enjoying the show. They started off with 'Them Kinda Monkeys Can't Swing' from *Flame* – a great opener, high energy, just right.

Nod was wearing a white suit with dark spots, and the biggest tie you've ever seen. Dave was wearing a dark glittery suit with studs all over it. When I married fellow Slade fan Julie years later, she showed me one of the studs that she had managed to pull off it. I still have it somewhere. That suit must have just been in tatters by the end of the tour. Jim and Don dressed more conservatively, in white and white striped outfits.

While the stewards fought in vain to control the masses, Slade played 'The Bangin' Man' and 'Gudbuy T' Jane', familiar tunes that were greeted like heroes, then another from the film, 'Far Far Away'. Nod told us that he and Jim hadn't really fallen out like they had in the film. A lot of dim people seem to have thought the film was a documentary. Jim took to the Fender Rhodes piano, and they played the new single, 'Thanks For The Memory'. That song was just too long and wrong for a single for me, but we all still loved it. Jim stayed on the piano for 'How Does It Feel?' and the mirror ball over the stage did its work as the crew put a spotlight on it.

Everyone reverted to their own instruments for 'Just A Little Bit'. Slade showed everything that they knew about dynamics on this song. It went from quiet to deafening and back again several times. A singalong with 'Everyday' gave everyone a welcome breather, before two newer songs, 'OK Yesterday Was Yesterday' and 'Raining In My Champagne', baffled a lot of people who didn't know them. The show closed with 'Let the Good Times Roll'/'Feel So Fine' with *that* bass intro. Years later, I heard the Amen Corner version and was shocked to see where Slade had lifted it from. Not that it matters.

There isn't a better show-closer than 'Mama Weer All Crazee Now', so that was a no-brainer. Slade hammered their last tune home and when the lights came up, the crowd began to slowly drift out of the hall. As the room cleared, we saw the seats where we should have been were wrecked, so we had done the right thing in keeping out of the way.

My ears rang for a few days afterwards and the Slade gig was all that we talked about for the next couple of days at school. We could just about hear each other.

The gig left quite a big impression on me. I was drifting towards taking up bass guitar, and Jim Lea was an obvious role model. When I later fronted bands, chatting to crowds like Noddy Holder did came in very useful. One of those nights that you just don't forget.

I WAS THERE: DIANE RUTTER

Me and my best friend Angela spent weeks making Slade jackets for this Tuesday night gig. I still have mine, a bit worn for wear these days, and it definitely doesn't fit me anymore. Tickets were £1.60, including a booking fee, and coloured blue.

Angela was lucky as her parents let her go to two previous gigs, in November 1972 at Manchester's Free Trade Hall and February 1973 at The Hardrock in Stretford, the day that 'Cum On Feel The Noize' went straight to No.1. But this was my first gig.

After the obligatory boiled eggs and soldiers for tea, we started getting ready. At the time I had a Dave Hill-style haircut (a *Slade in Flame* look) and both of us were absolutely covered in silver glitter – faces and hair – and wearing our homemade Slade jackets and platform boots, which we'd sprayed silver, and carrying our Slade scarves. At last, we were ready to go, with Angela's dad taking us in their car. We arrived at Belle Vue and there was a huge queue of Slade fans. We joined the queue until the gates were opened and everybody ran like mad to get in.

The King's Hall was also used for the circus, so the auditorium was circular in shape. We had tickets very near the front, Row D. Support band, Bunny, came on stage, but all you could hear was, 'We want Slade! We want Slade!', chanted non-stop.

At last, Bunny departed and the roadies came on, sorting out bits of equipment and twiddling knobs on the amps. Then the moment arrived, the lights dimmed, shadowy figures could be seen, making their way onto the stage. And suddenly, in a flash of bright light, there they were… SLADE!

With the aid of gig info online, I can tell you the setlist was, 'Them Kinda Monkeys Can't Swing', 'The Bangin' Man', 'Gudbuy T' Jane', 'Far Far Away', 'Thanks For The Memory', 'How Does It Feel?', 'Just Want A Little Bit', 'Everyday', 'OK Yesterday Was Yesterday', 'It's Raining In My Champagne', 'Let The Good Times Roll' and 'Mama Weer All Crazee Now'.

Diane Rutter's homemade jacket for her first Slade show, and top, among the audience that night

It didn't matter in those days what seat number your ticket said, because everybody swarmed to the front. I was stood very near to the stage – about two or three rows back – and started the gig on Dave's sidem but by 'Thanks For The Memory', I'd managed to get over to Jim's side. Gazing up at our heroes was fantastic for 15-year-old (me) and 16-year-old (Angie) schoolgirls. We sang along with every song. I'm also fairly certain Nod did a rendition of 'The Banana Boat Song' ('Day-O'), years before Freddie Mercury, who nicked a lot of his stage ideas from Nod. At one point, all the stage lights were switched off. Then, in complete darkness, a strobe light flashed. It was like watching a silent movie, except it most certainly wasn't silent!

All too soon, the show came to an end and everybody made their way to the exits. We were absolutely buzzing. What a brilliant night. A famous photo of the band appeared in the *Manchester Evening News* the next day, showing all the broken seats in the concert hall. I remember when the lights came up, I looked round the hall and about the first half-dozen to maybe ten rows of seats had been completely trashed. They looked more like piles of firewood than seats. It wasn't done out of violence or wanton destruction though, just screaming excited fans (mainly teenage girls) dancing and having a good night.

There was also a photo in the next day's *Oldham Evening Chronicle*, showing a lot of the audience, including me and Angie. BBC Radio 1 recorded a show, compiled from most of the gigs on this tour, called *6 Days on the Road*, which was broadcast a few weeks later. It was two years until I saw them again, but the memories I have of that very first time will stay with me forever.

CITY HALL

30 APRIL 1975, NEWCASTLE-UPON-TYNE, UK

I WAS THERE: JOHN CRAVEN, AGE 14

I only saw them once, with my mate Paul. It being my first ever gig, I thought all concerts were going to be like that. But they weren't, not even Bowie or Iggy or the Ramones. My first and my best, and I've seen everyone I want. Shame it all came to a messy end with Dave and Don. A bit like *Flame* really. I even met Noddy at a book shop, and he shook my hand. Nice bloke.

I WAS THERE: PETER SMITH

In April 1975 I finally relented, saw sense, put 'cool' aside, and went along to see Slade again. This was my one and only experience of Slade and their audience during their Glam rock, mega-pop, teen sensation period. When sold out, as it was for Slade that night, the City Hall holds 2,400 people; I swear there were 2,200 screaming girls, and me and 199 other guys. The guys were either with their girlfriends, feeling very out of place (like me) and looking around sheepishly (also like me), skinheads who had followed the band from the start, or full-on Slade fans (who stood out as they were the guys dressed as Nod or Dave). I swear every single girl was wearing a Slade scarf, tartan trousers or top (or both) or Slade badges. Or, even better, a Slade rosette, often home-made, with pictures of Noddy cut out of *Jackie* or *Fab208*. Of the 2,200 girls, I reckon 1,500 of them were wearing top hats or bowlers with mirrors stuck on them.

I was seated upstairs on a side balcony, looking down on the stage. Not the best position in the house, and it only added to me not feeling fully part of the event. I felt so out of place and self-conscious, but what the hell; I was at a Slade concert again, and I knew how hard these guys could rock on a good night.

'WE WANT SLADE!' When they stepped on stage the place went completely crazy. The truth is Slade's popularity was starting to decline and their last single, 'How Does It Feel?', had only made No.15 in the UK charts. But as a live act, and in Newcastle that night, Slade remained massive.

Noddy was on top form. No one could work a crowd like him. And some of his banter with the crowd was pretty filthy in those days. 'Hands up all those girls with red knickers on… Hands up all those girls with blue knickers on… Hands up all those girls with NO knickers on!' Today, this feels dated (probably bordering on illegal), but back then the crowd screamed and screamed and screamed with excitement. They waved their scarves in the air, and everyone sang 'Everyday'. I stood watching, taking it all in. Sometimes I felt I was part of it, but mostly it was as if I was outside looking in. I couldn't quite relate to the madness and craziness of it all.

The set had changed completely from the early days. Slade no longer started with 'Hear Me Calling' or finished with 'Born To Be Wild'.

However, elements of the old Slade came through now and then; those old rockers hidden behind the Glam pop teen swagger. After all, deep down I knew Nod was still the cheeky raucous rock singer, Dave was still the big kid who wanted to show off, Jim had always been a real musician, and Don remained unphased by it all, the solid rock rhythm holding it all together at the back. But I left with a strange feeling; it was as if I'd been to a kid's party where I didn't know anyone, no-one spoke to me, and the party went on in full swing, completely ignoring me.

This was Slade the pop band at their height. Happy days.

EMPIRE THEATRE
5 MAY 1975, LIVERPOOL, UK

I WAS THERE: DENISE SOUTHWORTH, DJ

I've always loved the radio, and my passion was always music and buying records. Growing up I shared a bedroom with my sister, who was a year older than me. It was the Glam rock era and we'd listen to T.Rex – *Electric Warrior*, *Tanx* and all that – and Gary Glitter, Slade, Sweet, Mud and Alvin Stardust. My sister liked Sweet but I liked Slade because the music was loud and rocky. I love a good beat, and I love the drumbeat in 'Take Me Bak 'Ome' and 'Gudbuy T' Jane'. I started following them in about 1973 and my first gig was at Belle Vue in Manchester. It was back in the days when you had to go and queue for tickets, and if T.Rex or Sweet were playing, all the kids from school would go and queue up to try and get tickets When The Osmonds came, the school was half empty!

I remember being on the balcony at the St George's Hall in Blackburn. I just happened to wave to Dave Hill and he waved back. That made my day. Afterwards, all the fans were waiting outside, hoping to catch a glimpse of the band, and it was mayhem. My mum and stepdad had driven me and my sister up to Blackburn and were waiting outside for us. My sister wanted to wait behind as my stepdad's car pulled out and he was saying 'get in the car quickly'. He was worried about the car getting crushed under all the weight of these hysterical girls. I wagged off school on the day after their Manchester gig. They were stopping at the Post

House Hotel in Manchester (now the Britannia Airport Hotel). That was the first time I met them and I got their autographs.

At the Liverpool Empire, right outside the train station, I was hanging about outside before the show. One of the roadies, possibly Swinn, gave me a pound to go across the road to the WH Smiths in the train station and buy him some Sellotape or something. I brought him back the Sellotape and the change. It was only afterwards that I thought, 'I could have run off with that pound.'

''THANKS FOR THE MEMORY (WHAM BAM THANK YOU MAM)' RELEASED 9 MAY 1975

'Thanks For The Memory' reaches No.7 in the charts and spends seven weeks in the charts.

GRANADA STUDIOS

2 JUNE 1975, MANCHESTER, UK

I WAS THERE: CHRISTOPHER ANTHONY JAMES, AGE 13

I'd regularly pop in to visit my dad, who worked in management services at Granada TV. Basically, he was responsible for the running of the building – anything from security to window-cleaning and ensuring Anne Kirkbride and co's dressing rooms were tip-top. He had to go off and do a couple of things in the building, so he sat me at a table in the canteen to eat some beans on toast, where a lovely man already sat down chatted to me – Noddy Holder. Alas, I didn't get my Kodak Instamatic camera until I was 16!

That day, I'd sat through the Bay City Rollers rehearsing for their show, *Shang-a-Lang*. I didn't really appreciate at that age the privilege of watching a TV show being rehearsed, being the only audience. When my dad collected me later, he said we would have to leave by the rear of the building. Noddy did, and on our way out my dad took me past the front reception to show me why. Right across the front of the large glass front entrance were hundreds of screaming girls adorned in tartan, waiting to be let in for the recording. The windows didn't look strong enough. We made a safe exit via the rear!

Disillusioned by their lack of success Stateside, Slade fly to New York in late June, their tour opening on 5th July at South Bend, Indiana, sharing billing with Aerosmith, Black Sabbath, Blue Öyster Cult, Fleetwood Mac, REO Speedwagon, Ten Years After, and ZZ Top and looking to build the same reputation for live performances they enjoy in Europe, only returning home to plug new records.

WHITE PLAINS MUSIC HALL
20 JULY 1975, WHITE PLAINS, NEW YORK

I WAS THERE: STEPHANIE MORSE

My cousins came to the States from Germany. With that arrival, they brought back a copy of *Slayed?* and I was wowed. I couldn't believe how much I liked that album.

Steph Morse (second left) and her friend TJ met Dave and Jim at the White Plains show

My friend called me to come to the RKO, a small movie theatre in White Plains, New York, where they were rehearsing for a concert. Before I knew it, I was face-to-face with the group. I thought that was crazy. My sisters were with me and Dave actually asked us to watch them rehearse… which we gladly did. I was mesmerised by the music. Dave was the chattiest of the boys and my sister TJ and I clicked with him. We chatted away after the rehearsal, him telling us about *The Return of the Pink Panther* movie, which we ended up seeing at his recommendation.

We went to two shows at the RKO that summer. At each show the audience was electrified. We loved Slade… and so it began. Looking at newspaper ads I saved, tickets were $6.50, $5.50 and $4.50, compared to the outrageous pricing today. I never realised how many records I'd collected by them, and the items I have. Crazy girl. But great memories.

Slade were also special guest stars for Steve Marriott at Asbury Park Convention Hall in July and August '75. Then in April '77 we saw them when ZZ Top headlined. Slade were booed by ZZ Top fans and had empty beer bottles thrown at them. My sister and I thought Slade were good, but the crowd didn't like their clothes, loudness or songs. It was a terrible match-up and painful to watch. Slade playing their hearts out and the raucous crowd were so rude.

At Calderone Concert Hall, Hempstead, New York, on 31st October 1975, ZZ Top again headlined, the crowd a little more tolerant. My sister and I loved them, of course. They were loud and unforgiving.

CONVENTION HALL

9 AUGUST 1975, ASBURY PARK, NEW JERSEY

I WAS THERE: DAVID JURMAN

This is one of my saddest concert memories ever. In the 1970s, United States booking agents had a tendency to tour artists that never should have been part of certain bills, and pairing ZZ Top and Slade was a prime example. Slade were touring their *Slade In Flame* LP but the audience was overwhelmingly there to see ZZ Top. These were the type of fans who intensely disliked artists like David Bowie, Slade, Mott The Hoople, etc. After each Slade song concluded, loud booing could be heard throughout the venue. It was particularly painful as one of my all-time favourite tracks, 'How Does It Feel?' was met with incessant booing throughout, which could be loudly heard as it is a ballad. I was disappointed, and we left a few songs into ZZ Top's headline set.

David Jurman remembers Slade getting booed by ZZ Top fans

RICHMOND COLISEUM
27 AUGUST 1975, RICHMOND, VIRGINIA

I WAS THERE: TOM SAUNDERS

A friend had four older brothers and sisters who always brought new music to my attention. I was 15 when, through them, I discovered Black Sabbath, Pink Floyd, Montrose and others that were not on our radios. They had one of those huge console stereos which I always thought sounded huge for what they were. I was at their house one day and someone put *Slayed?* on. When the needle dropped on the first track, 'How D'You Ride'... Holy Crap! That guitar intro hooked me, then the rest of the band kicked in. I'd never heard a voice like Noddy's. It sounded huge, beefy and full. I was an instant fan. Their cover of 'Move Over' is epic and Jim Lea's bass on that... wow! It's sttill my favourite album of theirs.

About a year later, a concert was announced in Richmond, Virginia – Aerosmith, REO Speedwagon and Slade! This was Aerosmith's *Toys In The Attic* tour. We lived about 20 miles from there, I had just got my driver's license and got permission to drive me and my buddies to the show in my family's 1972 Gran Torino. I was able to get my dad's Minolta SR-T 101 35mm camera into Richmond Coliseum. We were able to get right up front to catch Slade and snap a few photos. It was awesome. After Slade, I must have run out of film!

COLISEUM
12 SEPTEMBER 1975, GREENSBORO, NORTH CAROLINA

I WAS THERE: DAVID JURMAN

I was starting my initial year as a student at the University of North Carolina at Chapel Hill, with Slade the middle act of a triple bill that included Kiss as headliners and Gary Wright as the opener. Slade played the same set as when I saw them before, supporting ZZ Top, but this time they were warmly received, and I was pleased as the American South was the area of the country where Slade were least well known.

Photos: Tom Saunders

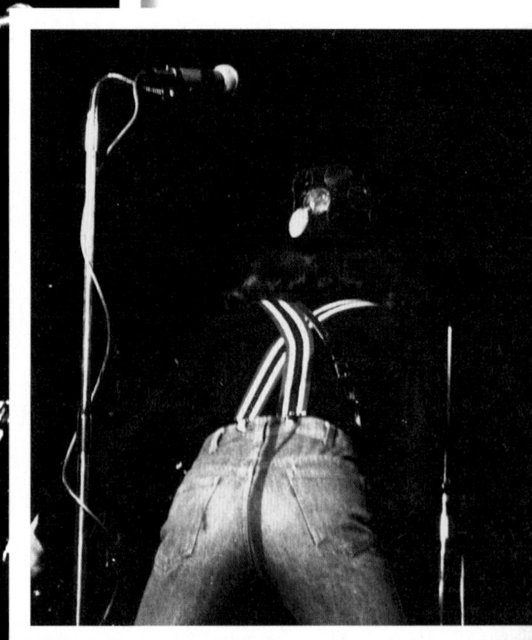

Slade in action in August 1975 in Richmond, Virginia

PALACE THEATER
29 SEPTEMBER 1975, WATERBURY, CONNECTICUT

I WAS THERE: MICHAEL YUKON LALIBERTE

I only saw them that one time. I can't remember who it was they opened for, but they were all glitter, and a good band but, wow, they were loud!

'IN FOR A PENNY' RELEASED
14 NOVEMBER 1975

Just missing out on the Top Ten, 'In For A Penny' reaches No.11 in the UK charts.

NOBODY'S FOOLS RELEASED
5 MARCH 1976

Five weeks after its second single, 'Let's Call It Quits' also stalls at No.11 in the UK chart, Slade's sixth album climbs no higher than No.14, its title track then becoming their first single not to chart since 1971.

I WAS THERE: IAN ASHLEIGH

Nobody's Fools was recorded in New York in 1976, and the album has its merits. 'Do The Dirty' shows the American influence the band was trying to capture at that time, imploring us to 'boogie' before Dave Hill's guitar kicks off the rock-funk. 'In For A Penny', released as a single, just failed to make the Top Ten in the UK, but its' lyric was very English music hall risqué. Meanwhile, 'Get On Up' is the very English Slade trying too hard to sound American.

Having failed to 'crack' America, Slade returned to England in 1977 to find a different landscape to the one they left two years earlier. The punks had moved into the space formerly occupied by Slade and the other Glam Rock bands. A piece of graffiti seen in London gave the ironic name of next album, *Whatever Happened to Slade?*. The album was not quite the return to form the band had hoped for, but it did have some good tracks on it. The band had hoped their fan base had moved with them, but they had spread their listening wings and were exploring other music.

Opening track, 'Be', is derivative of Led Zeppelin's 'Trampled Underfoot', over which a quick-fire lyric has been written. 'Dead Men Tell No Tales' is 'Slade do Americana…' and that's not meant to be detrimental; it's a fun piece of music as against some of the more earthy lyrics found on the album. Noddy was never shy about describing the pleasures of the flesh.

I WAS THERE: GERED MANKOWITZ

I didn't like the *(Nobody's Fools)* sleeve. Between them, Polydor and Chas messed that up. I wanted the black and white version with coloured red noses, which I thought was a vastly superior photograph. I think it would have worked really well. But record companies wanted colour for some reason, and they did a horrible thing to the picture. But I liked the session very much, and thought the band were looking extremely polished at that point in their identities, their images visually really refined. I've always loved the black and white pictures from that session. That stands up, and *Play It Loud*, because that was quite a breakthrough picture at the time. It wasn't a sort of natural cover image. I was very proud of that.

CAPITAL THEATRE

8 MAY 1976, PASSAIC, NEW JERSEY

I WAS THERE: STEPHANIE MORSE

This was a 'John Scher presents' show, at which Blue Öyster Cult headlined. Dave was the friendliest and kind, Don would smile and nod hello, Jim was around but seemed shy – and Noddy? We didn't bother with him much. But Dave invited us backstage, where we were able to watch the Cult from high above the stage. It was surreal being there with Slade. We couldn't wrap our heads around it. The group were polite to my sister and I always, never asking for anything (if you know what I mean). Thank goodness everything was on the up and up. And no hanky-panky, otherwise it would've left a bad taste. So our friendship continued.

Blue Öyster Cult were a much better fit for Slade than ZZ Top had been. Everyone seemed to really enjoy Slade. After the show, Dave asked if we could give him a lift into the city. He ended up hopping in and I drove him to the hotel in New York City. He invited us up and again we chatted and signed autographs. We chatted about so many things. Crazee.

Seats at the Capital Theater in Passaic, with Blue Oyster Cult, were $4, $5 and $6. Imagine! At Felt Forum, part of Madison Square Garden, New York City, on Saturday 22nd November '75, a 'ZZ Top Fandango', Slade were special guests at a good show. Top fans must've got used to Slade playing with them by now, and the crowd was tolerant. Of course, there were Slade fans there besides my sister and I.

Slade in action at Ontario's London Arena

THE WAREHOUSE
2 JUNE 1976, ASBURY PARK, NEW JERSEY

I WAS THERE: DAVID JURMAN

The Warehouse show would mark the final time that Slade would tour in North America. Sadly, after playing mid-size venues in North America in earlier years, the band's popularity had dropped significantly and they were relegated to playing such clubs. Prior to the concert, a fellow UNC – Chapel Hill student and I were able to do an interview with all four members of the band, which we turned into a Slade broadcast special that aired in the fall of 1976 on our campus radio station.

I was ecstatic to meet and get to interview the members of one of my all-time favourite bands. However, I was disappointed that, touring the *Nobody's Fools* LP, they played an abbreviated set which didn't include the title track, a favourite of mine. My lasting memory of that show is a melancholy one; it was sad seeing them play in a drab half-empty club on the Jersey Shore when I felt that, all along, the band deserved to be playing arenas in North America.

It is important to note that although Slade were considered a pop group in the UK, their airplay was mostly on FM rock stations in North America; the typical American Slade fan was someone who listened to David Bowie, Alice Cooper, Queen, Lou Reed, and Mott the Hoople, all considered cool artists then. As much as I liked Slade, many teenagers my age shunned the band, instead favouring artists like The Grateful Dead, Bob Dylan, Neil Young and those that were part of the Woodstock era. I believe their move to Warner Brothers Records from Polydor Records in the United States was a disaster and contributed to them not breaking through here. *Stomp Your Hands, Clap Your Feet*, *Slade In Flame* and *Nobody's Fools* were virtually ignored by the Los Angeles-based Warner Brothers Records; a shame because 'When The Lights Are Out', 'How Does It Feel?' and 'Nobody's Fool' were singles that had huge airplay potential in the United States.

Part of the blame for Slade not breaking through in the United States in the 1970s however is with the direction of the band commencing in 1974; *Sladest* is the pinnacle of their artistic creativity and I feel the North American fans after *Sladest* were expecting more boot-stomping tracks like 'Mama Weer All Crazee Now', 'Cum On Feel The Noize', and 'Skweeze Me, Pleeze Me'; later similar tracks such as 'Just Want A Little Bit' and 'Them Kinda Monkeys Can't Swing' were weaker imitations of those aforementioned tracks.

An anthem played for many years at arenas in North America was Quiet Riot's version of 'Cum On Feel The Noize'. Whenever I heard it while attending ice hockey games, it put a smile on my face, suggesting Slade had finally made it in the North American arenas.

THE PLACE

30 & 31 JULY 1976, DOVER, NEW JERSEY

I WAS THERE: STEPHANIE MORSE

This was a small bar-type venue and a good place to rock 'n' roll, but sad in a way. The Runaways appeared as back-up band – Cherie Currie, Lita Ford, Joan Jett; rough type girls but a good sound! My sisters and I were invited to the dressing room. The guys seemed pleased to see familiar faces in this foreign US music market. There we met Chas Chandler. I kept telling myself to be calm, don't faint. Swinn was there also; in fact, he was the one who asked us in. He seemed to always look out for my sister and I. We sat on the couch and Jimmy started playing my favourite tune, 'How Does It Feel?' on electric piano. I had to pinch myself.

Don, Dave and Nod were in conversation, I couldn't concentrate on that. I was watching, listening to Jimmy play. He played another tune I can't remember. Of course, we had a blast when Slade came on. We were such innocents, I had no idea about this groupie stuff. But Dave assured us we were not groupies. It remained all on the up and up, nothing else went on. We went to a lot of Slade concerts, as we never knew when we would see them play again.

Slade were fun guys, almost brotherly types. They helped me through a very rough patch, for which I am grateful. During the Slade mania, I received a letter from the UK from a girl who said she knew the group. We corresponded for years until my rough patch. I moved and we lost contact. I tried getting in touch for several years, to no avail, but looking at pictures posted on the internet, there to my happy eyes was a picture of my writing friend, with Dave Kemp, so I found a way to contact him, waiting patiently, biting my nails. And, one day I received an email from Dave. I was thrilled. A connection. He asked me questions, I answered everything he asked. I explained what I was trying to do. He reached out to my long-lost pen pal and we reconnected.

Dave Kemp then checked in with me to see how things were going with me and my buddy. I happily told him and how happy I was he could help out. He was very pleased to hear it. I thanked him profusely and thought what a really genuine man he was. I had read so many good things about him. It was to my complete and utter dismay that I learned Dave had passed away. I was truly upset. I worked in kidney dialysis for two doctors and when I read you could buy a t-shirt to go towards the Kidney Foundation, I quickly did. Plus, Jimmy was on the shirt (always my Slade favourite).

Through the magic of the internet, I got to see Jimmy play the Robin 2 some time ago. It was so good to see him play my favourite tunes, and I was glad to hear he was feeling better after his battle with cancer. I also got to see Jim and enjoy his fiddle playing with Kornastone, a wonderful group.

My sister and I tried what little we could for the boys. We went to local radio stations and gave them Slade records to play, which some did. Our local K-Mart would play 'Merry Xmas Everybody' frequently but that store's now gone. I did hear 'How Does It Feel?' on the radio in 2021 though.

Slade were the best. I'm glad I got to experience the little I did and collect what I did. Slade remain close to my heart. I'm sorry they're not together anymore.

BBC TELEVISION CENTRE
17 JANUARY 1977, LONDON, UK

Slade appear on the BBC children's programme Blue Peter *to promote the single 'Gypsy Roadhog'. Complaints over references inappropriate for children lead to the record being banned by the BBC. It stalls at No.48 in the UK charts.*

WHATEVER HAPPENED TO SLADE RELEASED 21 MARCH 1977

Released on Chas Chandler's Barn Records, Slade's 'comeback' album failed to chart. Its title is taken from graffiti seen in London. The LP receives mixed reviews. But Slade's eleven-date May UK tour and mainland Europe dates – including a fortnight stint in Germany – prove a hit with their loyal fanbase.

COLSTON HALL

1 MAY 1977, BRISTOL, UK

I WAS THERE: PAUL GOVERD, AGE 12

I saw the original band eleven times, three times at both the Colston Hall (in '77, '78 and '81) and Webbington Hotel and Country Club (in '78 and twice in 1980) and at Bath Pavilion, Donington, Bournemouth, Exeter University and, finally, Chippenham Golddiggers in 1982. I was twelve at my first Slade gig and 18 at my last, so they were coming-of-age gigs and all incredible nights out.

But the stand outs were meeting the band at the Webbington, talking to Don for over half an hour, and getting his drum sticks at Bath, Noddy shouting at me during a gig to shut up (!) and Donington and the plastic bottles bombardment.

They will always be my derivative band and the foundation on which I judge artists. I've seen everyone except The Beatles, Elvis, Zeppelin, Hendrix, Bolan and the Doors. It's easier to name who I haven't seen than who I have. I love music and proud to say I genuinely love Slade. Always have and always will.

Keep on rockin'.

CITY HALL

3 MAY 1977, SHEFFIELD, UK

I WAS THERE: NOMIS BAURLEY

The first record I bought was the *Slayed* album in 1971, from Woolworth's. They were my first love and have stuck with me all my life. But I didn't see Slade until 1977, on the *Whatever Happened to Slade* tour, their first after trying to crack the States. I was 15, going on 16. They had played locally before, in Bradford and places, but living in Leeds in 1975 it was a long way to walk, and my dad didn't have a car. So, May 1977 in Sheffield was the first time I saw them, a date firmly entrenched in my memory. My dad and I went on the train, and he waited outside the gig.

I was front row centre on the balcony. I'd never been to a gig before and didn't know what to expect. I can't remember who the support was. The lights went down at 9pm and a band came on stage. It took me a couple of minutes to realise it was Slade. Dave Hill had a shaved head and Nod was in a Napoleon-type outfit. I think he had a parrot on his shoulder. And it was so loud, I simply couldn't make out what the song was. My dad walked around town for a while then came to the hall to find me. It was still mid-gig, so the guy on the door said he could come in and stand at the back of the stalls. We still talk about it to this day – how he opened the door into the auditorium and the sound nearly blew him over; he couldn't bear more than a few minutes. He said the volume was excruciating, and so loud he could feel it rippling his skin. We missed the last train home and ended up sleeping on the station together, in a photo booth, getting the first train home to Leeds in the morning. It was quite a father-and-son bonding thing.

That was the start of my journey. I was 17 and earning a small wage. From then on, I saw them absolutely shedloads of times, even though I was in between jobs, in and out of work, and didn't have any money.

FREE TRADE HALL

7 MAY 1977, MANCHESTER, UK

I WAS THERE: RICHARD GOMERSALL

When I was very young, and for as long as I can remember, my family would gather round to watch *Top of the Pops*. That's where my lifelong love of the mighty Slade began. I was roughly six when I first saw them, around 1972. I couldn't tell you the exact song playing, but it was love at first sight – and sound – for this young lad. It was their colour, their passion, their power, their vibe. They just looked like four pals having the absolute best times of their lives. The biggest thing for me was that man Noddy. His Dickensian eyes, his permanent smile, his command on vocals, and that voice! How could any human have a singing voice like that? It was glorious. It seemed like he'd swallowed razor blades and some nuts and bolts then washed it down with oil. And the power… I was hooked.

Richard Gomersall was at the Free Trade Hall

My two older brothers had the Stones and The Beatles, but Slade were my band. Along with my Man United posters, I had Slade all over my bedroom wall. My family would buy me Slade albums, or I would save my pennies to put towards buying them myself. At the time Slade were huge. Six number one singles, three of them entering the charts at No.1, and 17 consecutive top 20 hits. I loved them, buying and listening to anything Slade-related. I went to watch *Slade in Flame* at the pictures with my gran, and I was only nine! They gave me wonderful memories.

Good times don't last forever and sadly the hits dried up. They'd conquered more-or-less everywhere apart from the big one – America. So, in order to try and crack it there, they said farewell to the UK for a couple of years and lived in the States. For various reasons, they never really made it over there and when they came back to these shores the landscape had totally and completely changed. Punk and disco were now the order of the day and the boys from the Black Country were out of favour, big time. They couldn't get any radio play to save their lives.

I remained a big fan, but with absolutely no internet or social media in those days and just three TV channels, news of my heroes was almost non-existent. It even got to the point where I assumed they'd split up.

Flipping through the LPs in Bradleys record shop in Rochdale, I was overjoyed to come across a new album, appropriately titled *Whatever*

Happened to Slade. Not quite eleven years old, I remember saying to my dad, 'Dad, Dad, look! They've not split up!' He bought the album for me, I took it home and to this day I reckon it's their finest album. Gone were their Diddy Men costumes and so-called Glam anthems (I never saw them as Glam, they were way too talented for that label), this was a more musically serious, mature Slade, and even at my young age I could see their progress.

That was March '77 and, one Saturday morning two months later, my having just turned eleven years of age, my mum shouted me down from my bedroom. 'Richard, can you come down a minute, we've got something to show you!' I had no idea what this was to be. I went down and there she stood with a Slade ticket in her hand and a big smile. I was almost speechless. 'What, why?' 'It's a Slade ticket,' she explained, 'you and Dad are going to see them!' 'What, really? When?' I replied, totally shocked and massively happy at the same time. 'Tonight, at the Free Trade Hall.'

To say I was happy was an understatement. I was going to see my heroes. But this total joy for an eleven-year-old became the total opposite at some point that day. I must have done something really, really bad and naughty, as I recall my mum saying, 'Right! You're not going now!' and ripping the ticket in half. Noooo! I was devastated. But I somehow wormed my way back into my parents' good books and me and my dad set off to Manchester. Later, Mum told me how terrible she felt at doing what she did, saying she made sure she strategically ripped it so as not to limit my chance of entry, ripping the part that would be given back anyway. Please note, my mum was the kindest, most caring mum you could wish for. So whatever I did to bring that on must have been really out of order. Sorry, Mum!

My dad never drove, so we went on the train from Rochdale to the Free Trade Hall. This was at a time when Slade were at a very low point in their career. But I can honestly say it's probably the best gig I've ever been to. I was in awe and it is without doubt still the loudest gig I've been to. Our ears were ringing all the way back to Victoria Station and the next day too.

Far from being downtrodden with their recent lack of success or media coverage, Slade were absolutely on fire, smashing through an ear-blitzing set, mixing mighty hits 'Mama Weer All Crazee Now', 'Gudbuy T' Jane', 'Take Me Bak 'Ome' and 'The Bangin' Man' with songs off their new album, the crowd loving it. Even my dad was blown away, and he was Frank Sinatra's biggest fan!

Seeing my childhood heroes at last was unreal, and the sight of Dave Hill stood topless on top of the amps with his new freshly shaved bald head giving it some on guitar and my hero Nod and his totally unique chainsaw voice commanding the crowd was magical! Then there was Jim 'the maestro' Lea on bass, violin and vocals, and the power machine that was Don Powell, chewing his gum… fantastic!

It was a wonderful night and an extremely happy memory to this day. If you wanted to try and find the meaning of life, you wouldn't go to see Slade. But if you wanted pure raucous, loud fun and thrilling entertainment, Slade's your band!

CITY HALL

8 MAY 1977, NEWCASTLE CITY HALL

I WAS THERE: PETER SMITH

Slade had been away too long, over in America working the US market and taking their eye off the ball in terms of their home fans. As a result, their popularity was waning. They realised this, and in early 1977 came back home to England and recorded their sixth album, *Whatever Happened To Slade*. The new album was a return to their rock 'n' roll roots, and received positive critical reviews, but failed to make the UK album charts. Musical tastes were changing in the UK, the Glam craze had passed and 'dinosaur' or 'old fart' bands were being passed over for new bands, the fashion of the day being Punk rock. Some of us could see the similarities between the rawness of Punk, early Slade, and the original skinhead image; however, to the majority of the music public Slade were a forgotten band, a thing of the past.

Undeterred, Slade decided to go out on a national tour, returning to the theatres and concert halls they were selling out just two or three years earlier. The tour called at Newcastle City Hall and I went along with a few mates. Support for the tour came from Liar, a rock band formed by a former member of Edison Lighthouse and featuring Clive Brooks, previously in Egg and the Groundhogs. The City Hall was far from full, which was a shame, as Slade were on fire, working so hard to regain their fans, demonstrating just how great a rock band they were. The stage was set with one of the biggest backlines of stacks I'd seen. I knew this was going to be loud. The lights went down, and Slade walked on stage.

The first thing I noticed was the appearance of guitarist Dave Hill. His hair was gone; he was completely bald with a shaved head and the biggest dangly earring I'd ever seen. He was wearing a leather jacket and jeans, and he looked amazing! Noddy was wearing a Napoleon hat and jacket! What was all that about? Then I heard the opening chords of 'Hear Me Calling' and everyone was up on their feet. And away we went. For an hour or so Slade showed us exactly how and why they made it big the first time, by playing loud, good, honest, raucous rock, like only Slade could. They even finished with 'Born To Be Wild'. It was just like old times, as if the last five years had never happened. The loud, heavy rock band that was early Slade was back.

Yes, Slade were playing excellently, but it was a few years before they would rebuild their fan base and return to the charts. During the period between 1977 and 1980, Slade entered their 'wilderness years', playing up and down the country in clubs, dives and cabaret. But they never gave up. The work ethic of this band remained strong, as did their belief in themselves. A small fan base stayed with them. It was still, it has to be said, an uphill struggle. But one which they would win.

APOLLO THEATRE

9 MAY 1977, GLASGOW, UK

I WAS THERE: JOHN MILNE

Jessie and I went to the concert and got backstage with them and presented them with a silver tray which had 'Welcome back to Glasgow' inscribed on it, with their names engraved round the edges. And we had Neville with us – he was two years old by then – and the band remembered us and treated us really well.

RAINBOW THEATRE
12 MAY 1977, LONDON, UK

I WAS THERE: TREVOR BRUM

Once upon a time, a nine or ten-year-old boy was in his bedroom, listening to music on his crummy transistor radio (hard to tune in). Then suddenly, like an almighty storm... 'Aaaaaaalright everybody...' What the fuck was that? 'Let your haaaaaair down!' Wow. My world changed in that moment. I'd been brought up playing brass in a Sally Army band (I'm grateful for that, as I now teach a bit of ukulele, and I have had years of writing and performing in bands). I'd been buying seven-inch singles with my pocket money and wages (I had to work for) for some years. And one day, I bought my very first album, *Slade Alive!* Oh, my God! Me and my mates would play it in my bedroom over and over. It was, frankly, life changing considering the dross on radio before…

It took me a few years before I escaped and sneaked out for my first Slade gig. The Rainbow Theatre, London, 1977. I was 15 or 16 and already addicted to Slade from radio and *Top of the Pops*. Everything they did had a magic to it. But even in those early years, I realised, Slade on *TOTP* or radio were a completely different animal to Slade live. In those early years I saw them live nine or ten times, including Hammersmith Odeon (twice), The Marquee (twice, that was mad, as it was a very small venue that Slade more than filled), Sheffield City Hall, Southampton and Reading University. I'd think nothing of travelling the length of the country to see them, when missing trains sometimes meant I didn't get home till midday the next day. Sorry, Mum!

There were times when my hands were literally red raw from clapping, my throat hoarse and aching from yelling, singing, chanting, shouting, and my top absolutely drenched in sweat. And that was before the band walked on stage. Such was the atmosphere Slade would conjure up at gigs.

By the early 1990s, I was performing in bands with a big following. Some of our fans and mates who were in their teens and twenties also liked Slade. But one day, at an after-gig party, I put on *Slade Alive!* on vinyl, and they couldn't believe the difference, from the singles they knew to this monster of a live band. 'Is that Slade?' 'It sounds like Slade!' Yep, that's them, live. I told stories from those early years' gigs. Even the mighty Quo would say 'fucking 'ell, they're fucking louder than us!' Yep!

Slade would involve the audience like an extra member of the band every time I saw them. Through the years, I've been lucky enough to see all the greats – the Rolling Stones, Lynyrd Skynyrd, Deep Purple, Black Sabbath, Led Zeppelin, and many more. But the greatest live band ever will always be Slade, my first true loves. Thanks for the memories.

I WAS THERE: COLIN GRANT

I saw Slade just once (I don't count Dave Hill's current band). It was at London's Rainbow, after the *Slade In Flame* film. Despite what appeared to be a full house, Slade were not as massive as they had been. Dave Hill had shaved his head and one of the audience threw a wig onto the stage, which he proceeded to wear. He was quite keen on his guitar solos, which were adequate but hardly stunning. Overall though, it was a good show.

Colin Grant remembers Dave Hill's shaved head

I WAS THERE: SIMON HARVEY

I had front-row tickets for this show, for me personally one of Slade's finest hours, the band on electric form, storming through their set on the *Whatever Happened to Slade* tour with a renewed energy after their recent travels across America, their new album – a hard-edged rockin' masterpiece – deserving to be so much more successful, far superior in my humble opinion to some of Slade's forays into the world of pop music.

The set was a mixture of old, new, borrowed and blue material (see what I did there?), and this gig is in the top five of the 98 times I saw Slade live between 1975 and 1983.

GAUMONT THEATRE
28 MAY 1977, IPSWICH, UK

I WAS THERE: PHILLIPE D'HOERARNE

I've been a Slade fan since the release of 'Cum On Feel The Noize' in 1973. I was only 13 and I was immediately hooked but regrettably I was too young to attend their most famous Belgian gigs. Also, my parents were rather protective and I couldn't see any rock 'n' roll gig until I was 16.

That's when the band had their American period and it had become impossible to see them in Europe, because they lived in the US. In May 1977 they were back with their *Whatever Happened to Slade* UK tour but nothing was scheduled for Belgium so I wasn't very lucky. But enough was enough and it became a matter of life or death (well, for me), so I listened to *Slade Alive!* once more, took a deep breath and ran away from home.

I decided to make my way to Ipswich (!) because I knew there was going to be a Slade gig at the Ipswich Gaumont. This was of course without my parents' permission, and it was illegal because I was only 17. But it worked. I first spent a few days in London, calling my parents on the phone to tell them everything was okay, and then I went to Ipswich. This was a real challenge for the very young man that I was, as I only had a few pounds in my pocket. But on the day of the gig, I arrived at the Gaumont in late afternoon only to discover that what was going to be my first ever Slade gig had been cancelled, Noddy Holder having lost his voice!

I think that only happened twice in his career with the band in 25 years. Shall I say that was a little bit disappointing? But I did eventually get to see my favourite rock band at the Rainbow in London, only a few days later. And what a gig that was.

It was well worth it. I took the opportunity to fall in love with London, made friends there, and even worked in places like the Marquee Club. I don't regret a moment.

I also built the band's first official website many years ago, and Dave Hill and Don Powell have become personal friends. Don even quotes me in his autobiography.

I WAS THERE: DAVID GRAHAM

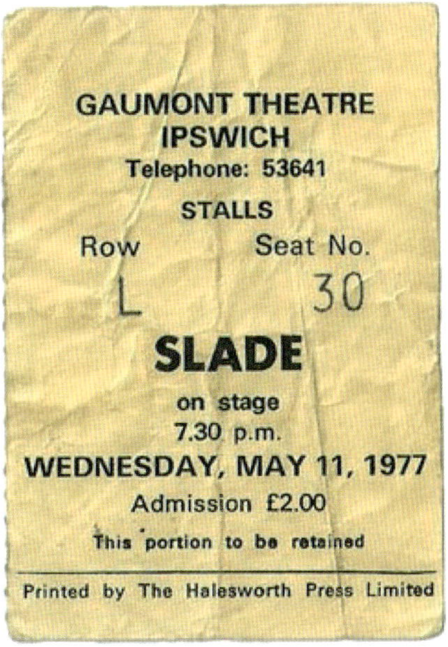

David Graham's Ipswich Gaumont ticket

I'm no different to most Slade fans. I don't mean those people out there who maybe bought a few of the records and had a little liking for the band. I mean *the fans*, those of us who stuck with them through thick and thin, good times and bad. We stayed true and loyal while all around us found it more than odd! If we could convert someone along the way, that was great, but most of the time the band's image – in fairness, mostly Dave Hill's image – meant people wouldn't give them a proper listen. It was never easy being a Slade fan, and it was much worse when the band were suffering their worst popularity crisis since hitting the big time. We all had to put up with the mostly good-natured jibes and banter from friends who just didn't get Slade.

It was certain sections of the serious music press that reserved the most sneering and snobbish remarks and reports. This was 1977, and a new wave of music was sweeping across the land. The snobs – failed art students that plied their trade as hacks writing drivel for the music press – loved Punk and hated Slade. For them, Slade represented all that was wrong with music, and they felt Slade should be swept away, discarded and forgotten about.

Slade hadn't helped themselves. They abandoned these shores and headed to America. I had last seen Slade live in 1975 at their two New Victoria Theatre 'farewell' shows in London. Two shows then they were gone, across the Atlantic to find the streets were not paved with gold discs after all. By 1977, they had been gone for two years trying – and failing – to conquer the American market.

The long hot summer of 1976 came and went. Bands like The Eagles, 10cc and Peter Frampton ruled the airwaves. Mainstream radio, previously home to Slade, barely played any of their releases and held no interest for me. It was down to pirate radio station Radio Caroline, transmitting from the good ship Mi Amigo, anchored off the coast at Harwich, to throw up an occasional album track. They mostly played wall-to-wall Zep and Stones records, but at least it was rock 'n' roll and not snotty-nosed, pimply, spikey-haired talentless dirgemeisters. Slade were out of sight and out of mind.

Each week, I would visit WH Smith and scour the music press, searching out any snippet of information or news, but there was nothing save two-line mentions from America. It was a bleak and desolate landscape in which to be a Slade fan. It really did feel like we had been abandoned. Too old to like the chartsters that usurped Slade from their throne, too young to be interested in the pomp of the Zeps and their ilk, it was left to bands like Thin Lizzy and AC/DC to tickle my fancy.

I had broadened my tastes and experimented, listening to the likes of Streetwalkers and Boston, played to death on Caroline, when news broke that Slade were returning to the UK with a new album and tour. That was great news, and in the days before mobile phones and the internet, these things trickled down to the fans very slowly. You might get a few lines in one of the papers about it then not read a thing about it for months. I remember having to pre-order *Whatever Happened To Slade* and going into town to pick it up on the day of release. I sat on the bus and read every word of the lyric sheet, looking at the groove on the LP, trying to work out if the track was fast or slow, a rocker or a ballad! It was a rather brilliant album, I thought, save for a couple of clunker tracks that seemed rushed, not living up to the rest.

That said, it was a good album and I couldn't wait to see them again. They were even coming to Ipswich Gaumont, my nearest venue. The day arrived, but Slade didn't, Noddy Holder (or 'Nobby Hooker' as the aged doorman at the Gaumont described him) had lost his voice, and the gig was put back a couple of weeks. What a let-down... but we stole most of the LP covers stapled to a billboard inside the theatre foyer once he disappeared, along with rather nice ones for support act Liar, a stockinged thigh being branded with the group's name.

With the gig re-arranged for the end of the month, in the ensuing fortnight I eagerly lapped up reports in the music press, although all seemed to say Slade were basically crap and too old to rock 'n' roll anymore. The press generally always gave Slade good copy, but now some of them couldn't wait to lay into them. Regardless, I managed to convince a Kiss-loving friend to come along to the Gaumont to give him a chance to be converted. As for me, the iffy press just regalvanised and enhanced my affection and loyalty. I couldn't wait to see them again after a two-year absence.

Dave Wyllie, a complete sceptic, accompanied me to the Gaumont that afternoon, where we managed to waltz in through the side doors and sit quietly in the shadows as we watched the roadies set up. No one bothered us and, after 20 minutes, one of the roadies came over and gave us three £1 notes and asked us to nip out and buy as many sausage, pie and chips as the money would pay for. Sausage, chips and a couple of pies safely delivered gave us the opportunity to walk about inside the Gaumont and mingle until H and Jim appeared on stage, Don following, all three running through parts of 'One Eyed Jacks With Moustaches'. We scuttled off to one side in case we were chucked out now some of the band were there. It was incredible to be inside an empty theatre, smack-bang in front of Slade's huge stack of equipment, Lea's bass notes leaving his huge speakers and physically hitting you in the chest.

After a while, Noddy ambled slowly down the centre aisles from the back of the hall, wearing jeans and a red t-shirt with a leather jacket slung over his shoulder. He was greeted and beckoned on stage by Jim, who said into the mic, 'Finally! Hello... Come and have a wank, Nod!' All four were soon on stage, running through various bits and pieces. It was a fantastic privilege to be able to sit and watch.

With the soundcheck over and the band free, we managed to chat with them all and got various pieces of paper and cigarette packets signed, although Jimmy tried as hard as he could not to have to chat with us, and the sum total of Holder's contact was a quick, 'Hello lads, have you come far?' as he signed whatever we thrust in front of his nose. Dave and Don stayed longer and chatted properly, telling us they had been touring in Germany on a bus with The Rubettes, of all people, since the last show was cancelled, but it was going to be a great show tonight as they were fresh after a week or so off since returning, batteries fully charged.

Once they departed, we turned our attention to the mixing desk, an island of technology amongst the seats in the middle of the auditorium.

I wasn't that interested but Dave was, so we chatted at length with 'Charlie' Newnham, the band's long-time sound engineer, a really nice bloke who had a lot of time for us. He told us the show was to be recorded through the mixing desk for possible inclusion on a double live album the band were thinking of releasing the following year (that ended up being *Slade Alive Vol II*) and told us to make sure we made a lot of noise as they wanted a great crowd sound. When it was time for us to go, we were asked to do one more job and we readily agreed. We were handed wads of flyers advertising *The Slade Papers*, to be offered for sale for a knockdown tour-only price of 75p. It wasn't easy to get these pieces of paper onto tip-up seats, but we did our best and then it was back out into late afternoon Suffolk sunshine to find a Wimpy bar.

The Gaumont was a 1,500-seater, and at the time about the only East Anglian venue name bands played. No matter who played, it was nearly always a sell-out. I noticed that the audience queuing to get in looked different from the last time I saw Slade, at the New Vic in 1975, where the audience included lots of teeny-bopper girls who seemed unsure whether to still follow Noddy and the boys or new kids on the block, the Bay City Rollers. This time around, the majority of those patiently waiting for the doors to open were male and older, the 'screamers' not there. And when the doors finally opened, it was clear the bouncers employed that night were not going to have it their own way. We were not only an older crowd, we were also bigger and not so easily pushed around anymore!

Once inside, the fans gradually filled the seats in the circle and stalls and our flyers soon folded into paper aeroplanes, squadrons of which filled the air until either the crowd got bored or the aircraft became so trampled and crumpled that they became un-airworthy.

Liar had been replaced by the dodgy Cock Sparrer as support, a bunch of pseudo-punks from London who did themselves no favours by swearing at the audience and telling us Slade were shit... needless to say, their set didn't go down well and they were roundly booed off when they finally (mercifully) left the fray. They also bored us rigid with an excruciatingly bad, overly-long take on the Stones' 'Starfucker'.

There was already an air of excitement as the assembled throng readied itself. 'Rocky Mountain Way' boomed out of the house PA, the odd paper aeroplane relaunched into space and some floated onto the stage, one or two making their way right to the back and landing to be precariously balanced on the cloth covering Powell's kit. As the house lights dimmed, the noise from the audience rose in a crescendo to a full-on Anfield Kop roar, the dark shadowy figures of a gaggle of roadies were seen through the gloom on stage removing the black cloth covers from the wall of amplifiers and Don's gleaming silver custom-built Ludwig kit.

I don't know what it was about that night, but the sight of the stage being readied sent the crowd mental and into some sort of collective shared hysteria, generating enough primal electricity to power East Anglia. The band hadn't even walked on! It was truly incredible to be a part of it, the air crackling as the silver chrome of Don's kit picked out every scrap of available light, red LED lights on the front of the equipment glowing brightly in the blackness and the bouncers already fighting a lost cause trying to get people back to their seats. It never got heavy. People just wanted to be ready.

First through the murk came Don, all in white, taking up his position; a couple of taps on the bass drum followed by a paradiddle on snare confirming he was there. It was now pandemonium in the crowd at the front, row after row of seats vacated as fans spilled into the aisles and ran forward, taking out half a dozen or so bouncers that tried manfully to hold us back. They were absorbed, Borg-like, into the crowd and barely seen again for the rest of the evening.

Without further ado, the rest of the band entered, plugged in and we were off. The opening bars of 'Hear Me Calling' boomed from Holder's SG, filling the theatre with a malevolence, easily drowning out the whoops, hollers, whistles and cheers. A pinky-purple spotlight picked out just his head and shoulders, the sound so crisp, perfectly mixed, as first Hill then Powell joined in... This was really it, the two-year wait over, the opening bars giving way to an explosion of noise and pyrotechnics as lights, strobes and dry ice meant it was well and truly game on.

It was hard to know where to look, and harder to stay in one place as the crowd surged, jostled and surged again at the front. Jimmy Lea, in red and blue paisley-patterned satin jacket, light blue jeans and bluey-grey Cuban-heel boots, topped off with a red and white handkerchief in the waistband of the jeans, was stage left, bouncing around, that Gibson EB3 slung from his shoulder, involving every one of the multitude in front of him. The opposite side belonged to Dave Hill, completely bald, leather-clad and studded, sporting a gigantic hooped earring, already leering and gooning around, playing to an adoring crowd. The man at the back was wearing a white vest and was just smashing the shit out of his kit as he always did... But most of all it was Noddy Holder that held the attention.

Centre-stage, Holder was the man, the showman supreme. Gone were the jeans and t-shirt, replaced by a three-quarter length blue satin frock coat, sporting a bicorne hat, standing square in the middle, looking more an effeminate Napoleon than a rock icon. He was armed with that phenomenally loud, dangerous sounding cherry red Gibson SG junior, which disgorged chordage so powerfully it almost melted the bone marrow of those at the front. Abso-fucking-lutely fabulous!

The spectacle was awesome. Slade had always been a shit-hot live band, learning their trade slogging the show around for years before it paid off. They knew how to rock, they knew how to produce and they did. America may not have warmed to Slade, but from the first minutes it was clear to see their stint there had turned them into an incredibly finely-honed rock machine. Tight as a cod's arsehole, they tore through 'Hear Me Calling', the track they made their own, the best opening track the band ever employed bar none, a proper clarion call to arms to those there to pay homage.

Then they were straight into 'Be', the first new song and the opening track from *Whatever Happened To Slade*, incredibly powerful. To see Nod and Jim share the mic to belt out the tongue-twisting lyric was something else. And when Holder got to the 'Stand Up, stand up, stand up and be yourself' bit, those still seated at the back of the hall all seemed to get up and run down to the front on command, quite a lot from upstairs, to get as close as they possibly could. It was a really wild scene, and 'Get On Up' was next, giving Jimmy a first opportunity to wow us all with his fretboard dexterity.

Holder took a few moments to survey what was going on underneath him before a 'Good to be back in Ipswich again', immediately correcting himself, saying, 'I don't think we've ever played here before... let's do a little bit of 'Take Me Bak 'Ome'.' Cue more complete mayhem as the familiar strains of this '72 No.1 began bludgeoning everyone present. Hill, grinning, pogoing and goofing around, was no longer the perambulating Christmas tree of old, but a shiny-domed whirling dervish lapping up the adulation and devotion of those who came to pay homage, the song played at 1,000 mph.

That gave way without a break to 'My Baby Left Me', Holder uttering the immortal words, 'Take it, grasshopper' as Dave Hill played his guitar break. Then it was 'One Eyed Jacks With Moustaches' from the new LP before Holder decided it was time for his customary 'It's hot in here, innit' – bottles of beer swigged from then tossed into the crowd. The band took a breather and while Nod had his banter with adoring fans, it was time for Hill and Lea to strip to the waist and for Holder to discard his coat and show us his frilly shirt. A storming rendition of 'Gypsy Roadhog' was followed, as on the LP, by 'Lightning Never Strikes Twice' with its false endings, multiple echoed vocals and a few wolf howls for good measure.

Hill in particular excelled himself, climbing on to the speaker stacks and throwing himself around without missing a note. It was pure theatre, pure spectacle, and we loved every second. There was a point that it seemed the band and crowd became synergetic, all as one, working together, each enjoying and needing the other.

Fuck me, what a band this lot had become, a tour de force unstoppable juggernaut feeding off the audience's pure unadulterated joy at being in the same space. There was definitely something in the air, the band, the crowd, all of us in it together, a joyous night of balls-to-the-wall rock 'n' roll dished up by the best rock band ever to play live. No band could walk on to a stage to the same manic reception as Slade had done without playing a note.

Slowing it down, letting us gather our collective breath, Holder announced it was time for a 'sing-song', with 'Far Far Away' giving us a chance to wave arms aloft in unison and belt out the chorus as one. But this was Slade, one ballad and one sing-song always enough, Holder promising they'd be 'rockin' all the way' from there, starting with 'oldie but goodie', 'Gudbuy T' Jane', like 'Take Me Bak 'Ome' earlier blasted out at speed before a heavy version of 'Burning In The Heat Of Love'.

It was relentless, 'The Soul, The Roll And The Motion' giving Lea a customary fiddle solo, playing that lime green Barcus-Berry violin behind his back, through his legs, upside down, on his back on the floor, while running back and forth across the stage. He was on his back when Holder and Hill returned, an hour gone by all too quickly, and now it was time for traditional show closer, 'Get Down And Get With It'. As before, it was bedlam, and that was the first time I saw a seat hurled into the air, picked up half a dozen times and tossed around between fans as Holder extolled the virtues of clapping your hands and stamping your feet at the same time.

You've been really wonderful, you've been really great, you've been rockin' and rollin'... and pissing it up in Ipswich tonight... We've gotta go now... Alright!

The band stood before us, all four saluting the crowd, who were saluting them, Don threw his towel into the heaving mass, and it was swallowed up immediately... the night fucking magical, the first chants of 'WE WANT SLADE!' starting as they exited, growing louder and more intense. We all knew they were coming back but wanted them to know we demanded it! it was echoing around the theatre, reverberating off the walls, and I'm sure everyone was baying for their return.

They didn't let us down, returning for three separate encores, each more appreciated than the one before. We had 'Mama' first, then the mandatory 'Give yourselves a big cheer' and a rendition of 'You'll Never Walk Alone' before 'Cum On Feel The Noize'. Finally, a seemingly unending rock 'n' roll medley featuring a run-through of Holder's favourite Little Richard tracks, culminating in 'Born To Be Wild'. It truly was a night to remember, and 45-plus years later remains fresh in my memory.

When it was over and they had finally gone, Gene Kelly's 'Singing In The Rain' filling the hall and the house lights up, the scene of devastation down the front was plain to see, at least the first three rows of seats mangled, many broken. It really had been Bedlam at the sharp end.

We made a dash for the side stage doors and were allowed backstage by Swin and the other roadies, who remembered us from the afternoon, the band in a rush to get away but staying long enough to sign autographs for those that managed to get that far. Jim asked what we thought of the show while Nod and Don looked around for cigarettes, then all four left by the window and were driven off into the night.

We missed the last train home to Colchester, so waited for the milk train and read every word at least three times in my newly acquired but creased 75p *Slade Papers*.

My ears were ringing, which lasted three full days as Slade's mind-numbingly loud volume completely discombobulated my ears. It was, in the words of my newly converted mate, 'Fucking brilliant!'

In my time I saw Slade before, during and after their heyday, but there was never a night to rival that. Those first five tracks belted out one after another that night provided the best opening to any gig I've ever witnessed. That night, we loved them, and they loved us. It was a different Slade for sure, but my lifelong affection, fidelity and affiliation for the band was well and truly cemented. While they had been away, I'd seen Priest, Lizzy, Nugent, AC/DC and Kiss, in fact just about every new 'thing'. Only AC/DC and Lizzy gave shows worth mentioning though, and no one ever came close to Slade live. Slade were the Guvnors.

I WAS THERE: DAVE HOLDGATE, AGE 14

So where did it start? I guess 1972 and *Top of the Pops*. It was 'Mama Weer All Crazee Now', those growling vocals from under a glittery top hat, driving drums and bass, and a grinning guitarist in a tin-foil suit. Wow. Music at home was always part of our lives. The radio was always on at mealtimes, so I listened to The Beatles, the Stones, The Animals, Cream… But this? This was different. This wasn't for my parents. This was for me.

Christmas '72 came, and my parents bought this ten-year-old lad his first LP. I'd got singles with my pocket money before, but there, in my hands on Christmas morning, was an album in wrapping paper. I unwrapped it and my excitement soared. I was holding *Slayed?* It went on the turntable straight away. It was amazing. My love for Slade was born.

A few years later me and a mate, Bob, also a Slade fan, pestered our parents so much they got tickets to see them at the Gaumont. We were too young to travel up from Halstead in Essex so our mums took us. Were we embarrassed? A bit, but when we walked to our seats in the stalls all that went away. The excitement was building, the lights dimmed and – bang! – Slade hit the stage. What a first gig for a 14-year-old to attend. The place rocked from start to finish, and I was exhausted. My ears rang for days but I didn't care. I had finally seen my favourite band.

I WAS THERE: MARK BLEAY, AGE 16

I got into Slade with 'Coz I Luv You'. My first ever album was *Old New Borrowed And Blue*, on cassette. I still have it. My first ever gig was Slade at Ipswich Gaumont, the spring that 'Gypsy Roadhog' was released, in 1977. My mum gave me a lift, but the show got postponed as (I was reliably informed at the door) Noddy had 'laryngitis'. I went back a week or two later. To this day it's the loudest gig I have ever heard.

I saw them 17 times. None of my friends liked Slade, so I was the odd one out. I was there at the Reading Festival, having taken four mates with me, and I got my voice on the EP, as Dave was tuning up. I shouted out, 'It's close enough!' and Noddy repeated it to Dave. That got a laugh. I followed them all around the tiny venues too. I followed them all around London in the wilderness years, mostly for university gigs, as well as West Runton Pavilion for the tour when 'Ginny Ginny' was released.

I still have all the ticket stubs. I used to scour *Melody Maker* for the release of each single and album. I have most of the singles on vinyl, but foolishly sold the vinyl albums to make more shelf space on the request of my (now ex-) wife. Grrrr! I was really sad when they announced that Noddy and Jim had left the band. The end of an era.

'MY BABY LEFT ME/THAT'S ALL RIGHT'
RELEASED 14 OCTOBER 1977

Released as a tribute to the recently deceased Elvis Presley, 'My Baby Left Me' reaches No. 32 and spends four weeks in the charts.

TOWN HALL

21 MARCH 1978, BIRMINGHAM, UK

I WAS THERE: MICHAEL VAN OVERSTRAETEN

My first Slade gig. I'd not long moved to the UK from my homeland, Belgium. I was 20 and a long-time fan when I saw Slade for the very first time, having not got a chance to see them first time round. My mum got me the ticket. I went to Birmingham with a friend, on the bus. I remember a black Rolls-Royce parked at the back of the Town Hall and had to pinch myself that I was about to see my all-time heroes. Queuing to go in, I was so excited. I can't remember the support band, but I do remember the fans chanting, 'WE WANT SLADE!' They'd just come back from a two-year stint in the States and were promoting new album *Whatever Happened To Slade*. When they came on, I was gobsmacked to see them in the flesh – and Dave Hill with no hair!

Michael Van Overstraeten's pride and joy is his Super Yob guitar

Their sound was heavy and very loud. A totally new look and sound for this fantastic live band. They went down a storm, playing new songs like 'Be', 'One Eyed Jacks With Moustaches' and Burning In The Heat Of Love' and all the classics. What a gig. I was not disappointed at all. My ears and chest were still ringing and thumping three days later. I will never forget that gig.

I saw Slade again in 1979, 1981, 1982 (twice) and 1983, and then at their 25th anniversary celebration in 1991 when they played 'Johnny B Goode' live for the very last time together. I have wonderful memories about this great live band, meeting Slade personally for the first time in 1982 and afterwards many times as the original band and Slade II. I just wish I'd had a camera at that first gig.

TIFFANY'S NIGHTCLUB

22 MARCH 1978, PURLEY, UK

I WAS THERE: IAN MCIVER

They were the first band I ever saw, at the Rainbow in London in 1977. Soon after I saw them at an unusual venue for a gig – a nightclub in Purley which Queen also played on their *Crazy* tour of London in

1979. Dave Hill shocked everyone with his bald head. It's about the only gig I've ever been to where the band emerged afterwards and just nattered with everyone. Great guys.

LEAS CLIFF HALL

5 APRIL 1978, FOLKESTONE, UK

I WAS THERE: DAN WELLER

By rights, as I sit here writing this, my left forearm should bear a tattoo of Noddy Holder's signature. I managed to meet the boys once at a soundcheck (Kent University) and after the great man administered his biro scrawl, it was erased in a boisterous and very sweaty mosh pit. I was crestfallen... because I was a Slade nut.

I'm pretty sure I'm remembered by old primary school classmates as 'that kid who liked Slade'.

Proudly sporting a pair of homemade red-and-black chequered loons that my mum thought resembled Nod's, hair that sat on my shoulders à la Dave Hill and a badge the size of a small dinner plate, I went about my business with a blissful ignorance that shielded me from the effect of any harmful quips from unenlightened teachers.

I played my *Slade Alive!* cassette on a portable tape recorder everywhere I went (along with an Arcade compilation that included 'Take Me Bak 'Ome'). Pocket money was spent on *Popswop*, *Disco 45* and *It's Here and Now*, and pictures of the lads soon hid the astronaut-themed wallpaper my dad had proudly hung in my bedroom.

Then, one May morning in 1972, a bright red poster appeared on the wall of the local chip shop advertising their concert at Margate's Dreamland. At nine years old, I was deemed too young to attend, but my dear dad drove me up and down the seafront in his Vauxhall Victor on the evening of the show in the vain hope of catching a glimpse of the band.

I had to wait another six years before I finally got to see Slade in the flesh. Like many fans in the mid-Seventies, I felt like a jilted lover when the group decided to leave our shores to set up home in America. But when they returned to the UK (unfashionable, but armed with a fantastic LP, *Whatever Happened To Slade*), they continued to tour extensively, and on 5th April 1978 they played Leas Cliff Hall in Folkestone. That evening, my schoolfriend Andy and I had become concerned by an absence of tour buses at the loading bay as we clutched our £2 tickets. Then, as light (and hope) began to fade, we were alerted to the group's safe arrival when the riff to 'Be' rang out unannounced, piercing the chilly clifftop twilight. That feeling of excitement and anticipation has never left me.

Dan Weller (pictured right, with Don Powell) was 'that kid who liked Slade' at school

Inside the hall, we made our way to the front of the stage, 400 loyal fans having come to watch their old friends. The tension grew to a climax as the house lights dimmed and four shadows stepped out of the wings to that familiar cascade of notes that would fall as the opening bars of 'Hear Me Calling'. The crowd stamped and clapped along until the moment the stage lit up in an explosion of colour... and there before our eyes was Nod the God, gurning in a tartan jacket, eyes as big as Marty Feldman's. To the right, a hairless Dave Hill (black studded leather, pirate earrings and toothy smile), Jim on the left (white trousers, red neckerchief and sandals) and Don, the least visible (though his gum shield was unmistakable).

My chief memories of the show are 'Them Kinda Monkeys Can't Swing', Nod conducting the crowd as we sung a belated happy birthday to Dave, a silk scarf from their heyday being thrown by the guy next to me and duly tied around Jim's mic... and a ringing in my ears at school for days afterwards.

We saw them again at Chatham later that year, when Nod was still sporting a black eye from a bouncer at Porthcawl. I watched them at Camden Music Machine on my 17th birthday after they appeared on stage at midnight (resulting in a freezing cold night wandering the streets). There were gigs at Canterbury Odeon and Ashford Stour Centre too.

Years later, I may not have that tattoo on my arm as a souvenir of those days, but I am happy instead to own the jacket Don wore on *Top of the Pops* when 'Cum On Feel The Noize' was No.1 in the charts.

EMPIRE

12 APRIL 1978, SUNDERLAND, UK

I WAS THERE: PETER SMITH

'Rock fans wreak havoc in Empire,' The *Sunderland Echo* wrote. 'Seats and brass rails were smashed and twisted at the Sunderland Empire last night, as rock group Slade worked a young audience to fever pitch.' It went on, 'The youngsters tend to stand on the arms and backs of the seats which smashes the framework, and the sheer weight of numbers pressing against the brass rails bent then easily.' Although there was an audience of only 800 – less than half the theatre's capacity – they had been very involved in the performance and at times some became carried away with the highly-charged atmosphere.'

Support came from local rockers Geordie. Slade took to the stage and the audience went wild. Their highly charged, extremely loud set seemed to whip the crowd into a frenzy. I was quite close to the front, with a group of mates, and we watched the first few rows of seats collapse under the weight of fans pushing, shoving and generally going Crazee. By the end of the concert all that was left of the first five or so rows were a pile of smashed-up wood. The local news reported that it cost the Empire hundreds of pounds to replace the front row seating, a lot of money in those days.

Back then, Sunderland Empire issued tickets with simply a date on, and no name of the act appearing. Very strange, I always thought. The date of the concert was changed as well. Slade were excellent that night, and the crowd knew it; hence the crazy reaction and the damage. They were back to starting with 'Hear Me Calling' and included all their hits along with new songs. It was great to see them again. And the carnage added to the craziness and the excitement.

CIVIC HALL
24 APRIL 1978, WOLVERHAMPTON, UK

I WAS THERE: GRAHAM CROYDON

I've been a Slade fan since 1972. I saw the original band live on 14 separate occasions, mainly in and around Wolverhampton and Birmingham. In 1978 I attended Wolverhampton Civic Hall with a bunch of schoolmates. We were all in our last year, so aged 15-ish. I was really excited about seeing Slade again and wasn't disappointed by their performance.

When towards the end, Slade did 'Cum On Feel The Noize', the place erupted and people started climbing on the stage. I was one of these people and I remember being topless (I was in much better shape then!) and trying to shake Noddy's hand. The thing I had overlooked in all the excitement was that Noddy was playing guitar. He just gestured down to his guitar with his head and smiled. Next thing I remember is being thrown back into the crowd and being briefly body-surfed. It all seemed like a dream afterwards, and one of my friends still laughs about it to this day.

Keep on rockin'!

I WAS THERE: NOMIS BAURLEY

The second time I saw Slade was at Wolves Civic in April 1978, my first solo venture away from home. I remember practising a Midlands accent, based on how I'd heard Slade talk in interviews, so I was confident I could ask for directions from the train station to the venue. This time I queued and got right to the front, tapping Nod's foot throughout the gig, which didn't please him. This was a ground-breaking moment. The band I'd only seen on TV and from far away on the balcony in Sheffield were now there for me to touch.

I slept on the station again, probably with a handful of other fans. I also saw them at Sheffield Uni and Bradford Uni that year, where I managed to sneak in and watch them soundcheck for the first time before getting booted out by JJ, one of the road crew. In all, I saw them seven or eight times in 1978. At the end of that year, they did a tour of the universities. I saw them at Sheffield Poly, where I got to talk to them for the first time, then Bradford Uni a week later. And they recognised me!

THEATRE ROYAL
25 APRIL 1978, LINCOLN, UK

I WAS THERE: MARTIN BROOKS

The first single I ever bought was 'Skweeze Me, Pleeze Me' from WH Smith in my hometown of Boston in Lincolnshire, aged nine. It cost 45p and came with a bright red Polydor label and sleeve. It was fast and loud! When I turned it over, I heard music like I had never heard before. What was this crazy sound? 'Kill 'Em At The Hot Club Tonite'. So began a lifelong passion for the music of this amazing band.

'My Friend Stan', 'Merry Xmas Everybody', 'Everyday'… the hits kept coming, but even as a kid I could sense a subtle change in direction. I bought Slade sheet music if I could find it, learning to play some of the songs on piano. But then the chart positions dwindled and there was less and less about Slade in the news, in the papers and in the music press when they moved to America.

Three events in a period of about six months changed my life. First, in autumn 1977, I switched on *Top of the Pops* and the first act was Slade, playing 'My Baby Left Me', the whole performance so powerful. They were back! Maybe not in the eyes of the masses, as that single struggled up to No.32 in the charts, but my heroes had returned.

Then, in Easter 1978, on a family holiday in that little-known outpost of rock music, Menorca, my dad asked if I wanted a record. My parents normally bought me and my sister a little present when we went away, but at 14 I was growing out of souvenirs. We went in a little record shop down a back street, where there was a copy of *Whatever Happened To Slade*. The shop had a record player with headphones, which had gone out of fashion in the UK by then. The shop assistant passed me the headphones, and seconds later the introduction to 'Be' blew me away. The guitar riff, the power chords and… what were those vocals in stereo? I'd never heard anything like it! To this day it's my favourite album of all time.

Within days of returning home, I saw an advert in the paper for Slade playing the Theatre Royal in Lincoln. My auntie took me and from the opening notes of 'Hear Me Calling' I was on a different planet. Incredibly, my auntie knew one of the bouncers and got me backstage to meet the band after the show. Starstruck, I politely asked each band member for an autograph, not daring to ask why they weren't having hits anymore.

For the next two and a half years I suffered abuse for my loyalty. Each week, I scoured the music press for news, where I'd discover news of tours of clubs, colleges and universities, maybe the occasional three-line paragraph announcing a new single which would die without trace, sometimes a short gig review. Into this desert of information, I came across an oasis in the shape of Dave Kemp's Slade News, Issue 1 of which (dated January/February 1979) was advertised in *Record Mirror*. The arrival of each issue was eagerly anticipated, and I became good friends with Dave, always telling him how important that magazine was to me and so many others.

My love of the group and their music has continued, and I've had the pleasure of meeting all the members on various occasions over the years. I organised two school trips to see Slade – Dunstable in 1979 and West Runton in 1980 – and was lucky enough to see them live at Leicester De Montfort Hall and Hammersmith Odeon, as well as three times on their final UK tour in 1983. I have made numerous friends through their music, too many to mention, but it would be remiss of me not to mention Nomis, Mark Richards, Danny Bloomfield, and Pouk Hill Prophetz co-founders, Nigel Hart and Trevor West, our little beat combo paying tribute to the music of Slade and others. Noddy, Jim, Dave and Don – you guys rock! Thank you for the huge part you have played in my life.

POLYTECHNIC

29 APRIL 1978, PLYMOUTH, UK

I WAS THERE: PAUL RIDLEY

I saw Slade live at the Plymouth Polytechnic. To be honest, I can't recall a great deal about it. I was 19 or 20 and Slade had been pretty big a few years before. I do recall Noddy wearing his top hat, him and the rest of the band in normal stage clothes. My memory is dodgy – lots of cider and beer from the wood on the night.

NORCALYMPIA
27 MAY 1978, NORBRECK CASTLE HOTEL, BLACKPOOL, UK

I WAS THERE: STUART RUTTER

Stu Rutter saw Slade 36 times

I saw 36 Slade concerts spread over ten years. They were so loud, so powerful, so tight as a unit. It was incredible. Blackburn's King George's Hall in June 1973 was my first one and they came back in May 1974 and in the summer of 1981 as well. And between those, they played eight times at Blackburn's Cavendish Club (aka Bailey's, the chain that owned the club then). There should have been an extra night, but Dave Hill set fire to his arm in his garden on the Thursday, so they had to cancel that night!

I'll always have very fond memories of seeing them when they played Norbreck Castle in Blackpool, a place called the Norcalympia, which was like a big aircraft hangar around the back of the hotel. The hits had just started to dry up and they were starting to think, 'What are we going to do now?' But no matter how much trouble they had trying to get into the charts at the time, they always produced an absolute piledriver of a concert.

Over time, they started to recognise us, the fans who went regularly, and you'd start chatting after the gigs, and it was Slade that brought my wife Diane and I together. She'd also been a Slade fan all her life. There's a pub in Bilston, Don Powell's hometown, called The Trumpet, which would be packed if it had 40 people in it, but that's where they used to go to celebrate their big hits, big releases, and any special events. They didn't go for champagne receptions in London, they went for a tiny little jazz bar on the outskirts of Wolverhampton.

I remember hearing the first three Slade hits on the radio. then my

Stuart Rutter's flyer from the Norcalympia show in 1978

older sister was watching *Top of the Pops* as she was a T.Rex fan and I saw Slade doing 'Mama Weer All Crazee Now'. The power of Nod's voice and of the guitars on that intro got me hooked. And the volume and the pace of the songs. There was probably some peer pressure too. I would have been ten and all the boys were Slade fans at school.

The quality of the hits was just so consistent that I soon latched on, like a lot of my friends did. And we were never really disappointed… even though there was one infamous release, a bit embarrassing, their version of 'The Okey Cokey' – they were that desperate for a hit at the time!

As well as 15 shows in Lancashire, there were three shows at Bradford University, one at Leeds University, and I've been down to London and up to Lancaster. I moved to Scotland in the early Eighties, and the last time I saw them was in Glasgow. I wouldn't call it an obsession, but it's certainly been a lifetime interest.

I saw them live once a year during their fame days, so '73, '74, '75, '77. Then it really ramped up when they were reduced to playing all the dives and fleapits. They'd just returned from the USA, and then Punk wrecked their success. It was great to meet them often, as they were far more accessible.

GRAND PAVILION

25 AUGUST 1978, WITHERNSEA, UK

I WAS THERE: DAVE HEMINGWAY, THE HOUSEMARTINS & THE BEAUTIFUL SOUTH

Slade. Wow. To this day probably the best live band I've ever seen. Maybe you could say I'm looking through rose-tinted glasses because I was just a young teenager seeing one of the first bands of many,

Dave Hemingway, pictured at the launch of the first Sunbirds LP, was in awe of Slade as a live band

but I don't think I've ever seen any band better, tighter, louder, or more enjoyable. I saw them twice. The first time was at Withernsea, where they opened up with a tight spotlight to just pick out the faces of Noddy and Jim. For 30 seconds or so it stayed like that while they sang a slow intro, before the stage exploded into white lights and ear-shattering guitars. Brilliant.

The second time was when I was a student at Goldsmith's College in New Cross, London when they played the students' Christmas party on 8th December 1979, when they were assumed to be past it, has-beens. Not a chance.

The students' hall they played had a really low roof, and was long and narrow, with Slade at one end, and I was lucky enough to be around ten yards from the front. I say lucky, but my ears were ringing for two days afterwards. They got a girl up on the stage and Noddy, Jim and Dave just rocked out at her while she danced.

The film they made, *Slade in Flame*, was much underrated and much unseen. The acting was good, the songs were great, and the opening sequence to maybe one of their best songs, 'How Does It Feel?' was right on the money. I suppose you can tell they had quite an effect on me. They made you want to be in a band. Thank you for the memories.

STONELEIGH CLUB

28 AUGUST 1978, PORTHCAWL, UK

I WAS THERE: JULIAN GITTINS

When I first saw them in the Stoneleigh night club in Porthcawl, it was a fantastic loud gig, the best gig I've been to, to this day… and I've done hundreds. Noddy invited us to dance on stage with them. The bouncers tried to kick us off the stage, Desmond Brothers, the bouncer breaking Noddy's nose in the corridor off stage. They all spent the night in the

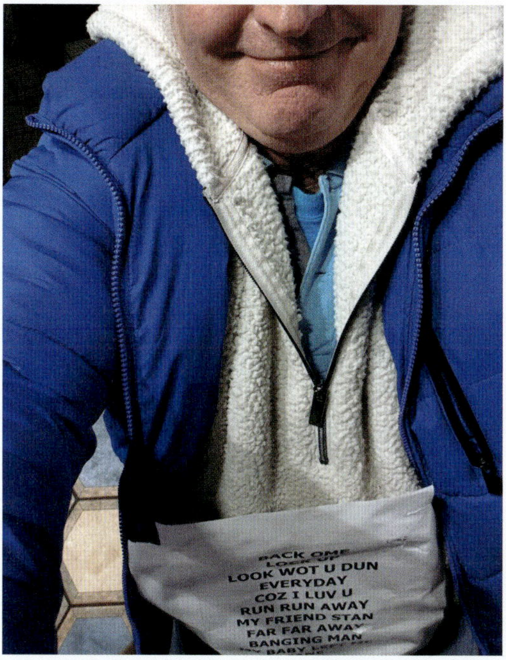

Julian Gittins saw Slade in 1978 and Dave in action as Slade more recently

Porthcawl nick. The bouncer got a three-month sentence.

My ears were ringing two days after that 1978 concert. They had us all dancing on the tables after the first song and were brilliant live. I saw Dave Hill's Slade play a Christmas show recently, still very good but missing Noddy. We're all getting on a bit.

BAILEY'S

24 - 30 SEPTEMBER 1978, WATFORD, UK

I WAS THERE: GLENN STARK, AGE 16

I went to many Slade gigs in the Seventies, but the week they played Bailey's in Watford in late September 1978, I went every night, heading up from Kingston. My mum said one night, 'Where you going tonight?'

I said, 'To see Slade.' She said, 'But you went last night.' I replied, 'Yes, and I'm going again tomorrow night!' That night I got a drumstick from Don. I was so excited. I showed my mum and dad, and Mum said, 'But it's broken!' To me it was priceless.

At the end of the following month (30th October 1978) I saw them at the Music Machine in Camden. I was sat in a nearby Wimpy when Noddy went walking by. I ran out and called him. He stopped and I asked if he could sign a photo for me, a pic taken at Bailey's earlier that year. He said yes, asking if I was going that night. I said yes and he said, 'Hope you enjoy it.'

I went to many gigs in and around London from there, and when Don and Dave started Slade II, I started seeing them. One memorable gig was the Tower Ballroom, Blackpool in December 1998. Myself, my partner Gwen and our friends John and Jane Sales were there quite early, and the lorry turned up with the gear but there was no road crew to load in. They were stuck in a motorway traffic jam, so we offered to get it all inside. That was my first time as a roadie, and I went on to help Don and the band for a few years after that.

In June 2005, Don asked us to go over to Denmark to help out with a gig, and he and Hanne put us up for a week. We had a fab time.

BAILEYS

2 - 7 OCTOBER 1978, LEICESTER, UK

I WAS THERE: DAVID FEARN

There were various gigs later in the mid-Seventies, from Birmingham to Leicester to Coventry. Slade were still magnificent, but now they couldn't sell a record for love nor money. That didn't stop us disciples getting the word out though. I lived in Leicester in the latter part of that decade, when cabaret club Baileys announced that the best band in the world had decided to do a week's residency. I went every night.

Sometimes they were playing to just 30 to 40 people tucking into chicken-in-a-basket meals. But by the end of the set everyone – and I mean everyone, including your 70-year-old granny – would be up on the tables, singing and dancing along with everybody else. Slade proved so popular they were booked again for another week later on – and, yes, I went again every night. Every time I heard people say, 'Best band I've ever seen.'

I followed Slade to places I didn't even know existed, and to the *Monsters of Rock* concert at Donington, where they were big news again and, as I suspected they would, they stole the show. I then met my future wife who, having never seen Slade, was in for a treat. They were playing Leicester again, this time at the De Montfort Hall rather than some little cabaret club. We had front row balcony seats, in the middle, but the band cancelled. It was the end.

I still loved them. I've been to all the conventions, even winning a prize in a Slade *Mastermind* competition. I saw them together for the last time at Walsall Town Hall. But it's not any of the gigs that I think of when I think of Slade. It's walking over that hill towards the village fair and hearing Slade for the very first time.

CAVENDISH CLUB (BAILEY'S)
9 OCTOBER 1978, BLACKBURN, UK

I WAS THERE: STUART RUTTER

In more recent years, down the pub with Jim Lea (as you do), I told him I was at the gig with Slade's smallest ever crowd – 19 in a 1,000-seat nightclub in 1978. And he was very interested. I told him I'd seen dozens turned away at the door for the wrong dress code and that's why the crowd was so small. He laughed and said, 'I thought it was cos we were crap!'

Those wilderness years are the favourite gigs of most fans I still know. They were usually in small places, not used to handling a rock band of Slade's history. They'd generally start in a similar but better way to early gigs. When they opened with 'Hear Me Calling' in the early days, they'd walk on stage, plug in, shout hello and wave, etc. But in the later years there'd be more drama.

As it got nearer to stage time, the lights were slowly dimmed to pitch blackness. The amps and Don's drums were covered by black voile curtains, which you could see being pulled off by the crew, and the 'We Want Slade!' chanting would start. The tour manager, Haden (Donovan) or Swinn (Graham Swinnerton), would stand in the dark behind the drums and flash a small torch at Charlie and Boogie on the desks. This was it!

A roar would go up and you saw dark shadows appear on stage, maybe a couple of hits on Don's kick drum. Then out of the darkness the opening chords of 'Hear Me Calling' boomed out, just like on the

Photos: Stu Rutter

Slade in action at the Cavendish Club October 1978

Slade Alive! album, but earsplittingly loud. The very second the first verse started (by Nod and Jim in unison), two spotlights in green and blue lit just their faces.

Then at the end of the line, 'And if you don't come soon, I know my love is through,' the whole stage exploded in lights and sometimes a couple of thunder flashes, one on each PA column, went off. The whole crowd would be jumping, shouting, cheering and at the front, jostling for position to get nearer the stage. I still remember the smell of leather soaked in beer and sweat from those days.

Stu Rutter saw Slade at the Cavendish Club

Guitarist injured in garden fire

Pop group Slade were unable to appear at Blackburn's Cavendish last night after lead guitarist Dave Hill was burned in a petrol fire.

Dave was in the garden of his Wolverhampton home lighting a bonfire with some petrol when flames burned his arm. The group will be back on stage tonight.

Photo: Stu Rutter

Slade in flames

When Slade's star dimmed in the late Seventies after they came back from America, Punk had happened, and they couldn't really sell any records. They were shocked when the first record they released on their return failed to get into the chart at all, and the album didn't even bother the Top Ten. They then went on a big tour in '77, where I believe most of the venues were only half sold out. After that, they lost their record deal with Polydor, so Chas Chandler started up Barn Records, distributed by Polydor initially, but then that was dropped. And somewhere in the middle of all that, the Slade fan club collapsed.

But a few months, possibly a year after that, one fan, Dave Kemp, based in London, advertised in *Record Mirror* that he'd started a newsletter for 25p. I wrote in, as did almost 300 others, and one of the guys that wrote and started appearing quite regularly was Nomis – Simon backwards – who worked for a printer in Leeds. He started getting Slade badges made. I wrote to him for some badges, and we've kept in touch ever since. He's actually my best mate. I've known him since I was about 16 or 17. He used to take so much time off work to go on Slade tours that he ended up being adopted by the Slade crew, going to 110 Slade concerts in total.

And the fan club began to snowball. Myself, Nomis, Dave and quite a few others kept in regular touch. I was also in touch with Haden, the tour manager and a personal friend of Noddy Holder, and a few years later he mentioned in one of the newsletters he did that Nod said something along the lines of, 'It was good to see some of the old guard in last night,' to which Haden said, 'What do you mean, 'old guard'?' Nod replied, 'Well, the fans that stood by us. It's always good to see them in the crowd.'

That name stuck, the fans Dave Kemp rallied around and provided newsletters for the Old Guard – the ones that didn't desert them, the ones that slept on train station platforms, park benches, and phone boxes… I've slept in many a phone box, and when they played Blackpool three times, myself and my friends Shaun, Tom and George slept in the tram shelter near the North Pier. Obviously, alcohol would have been involved.

Sadly, we lost Dave Kemp a couple of years ago, but he was very highly regarded by just about everybody I know, including the band. I was in touch with him right up until a few days before he went into hospital and died. We were very close. If it wasn't for Dave, Slade would not have survived long enough to have made that miraculous renaissance at Reading Festival in 1980.

The concert at Bailey's where there were 19 of us in the crowd? When Slade came on, Nod put his hand to his eyes and gazed out into this just about empty 1,000-seat club and his first words were, 'Jeez! Did you all come on the same bus? I'll tell you what we'll do, since there's so few of you, we'll do the golden oldies, alright?'

They played the concert though, just as blistering. Dave Hill was wearing a bandana that night – the stubble was coming, and by October the following year, it had grown quite a bit more. It was a bouncer that later told me there were 19 in that Monday night. And that was the night Dave Hill started thinking he was leaving Slade. He said so much later in a fan club newsletter, looking at other means of income, ending up with hiring himself out as a wedding chauffeur with his Rolls-Royce. And yet, on the Saturday, six nights later, they turned away 500. In the same club. An incredible transformation.

If Dave Hill was thinking of leaving in October '78, there's no way they would have survived until August 1980, unless the fans that were left pulled together and started touring the country to support them… which we did.

I WAS THERE: CHRIS SELBY, SLADE HISTORIAN

I first encountered Dave Kemp via his Slade newsletters. In the late 1970s, most Slade fans felt like loners. The group had disappeared from the charts and radio, and TV appearances were rare. Fans would meet up at gigs, if you managed to find out about them, but that was pretty much it. One day in 1979 while reading *NME*, *Melody Maker* or whatever music paper was at hand, I came across an advert for a 'Slade Fan Club'. A voice in the wilderness. My

Dave Kemp with his younger self in matching Slade t-shirt. The first shot dates from March '73 and his first Slade gig, the second from 2020

interested piqued, I sent off the required postal order and fairly soon received my first fan mag. I missed out on the original A4 sheets. That was the start of a 'relationship' with DK. I sent a few things to him and occasionally he'd print them. He built up the club.

Dave Kemp in his management role, behind the bar serving Slady in 2020

I started talking to him on a regular basis in the late 1980s. He would phone me, asking if I knew something, was in contact with someone, or just have a good moan. We would put the world of Slade to rights, despairing at some things and giggling like the eternal schoolboys we were at others. I still have his messages on my phone from the last few says of his life. He's missed by all that knew him, and I honestly feel sorry for those that missed out on the double pleasure of seeing the original Slade line up live and knowing Kempy. 'Those that know are blessed.'

GREAT BRITISH MUSIC FESTIVAL WEMBLEY ARENA

29 NOVEMBER 1978, LONDON, UK

I WAS THERE: RICK BUCKLER, THE JAM

We came across them more and more, because they were signed to Polydor, the same record company as us. The first time I saw them, they were supporting us (Slade billed as 'special guests'). And, for the first time, I actually appreciated how good they were. The songs were great, they performed really, really well. They had the audience in the palm of their hands and they were really fantastic. So, just disregarding them as a pop band was obviously a mistake on my part! They were good. You can see that they came from the class of bands where they actually learned to play and could perform on stage… really, really well.

Rick Buckler, pictured signing copies of *The Jam*: 1982, saw Slade in a different light at the Great British Music Festival in late '78

I WAS THERE: CATHY CASSIDY

Slade were the kind of band that gave hope to working-class kids in the early 1970s. Maybe you didn't have to be rich or beautiful to make something of yourself. Maybe you could just go for it anyway. When I was growing up, Slade seemed to be pretty much a weekly fixture on *Top of the Pops* and the pages of *Jackie* magazine. Loud, cheeky and lovable in their clumpy boots and cartoon costumes, they made my parents roll their eyes – but every girl wanted Dave Hill's impossibly perfect page-boy haircut and satin jacket, and every boy wanted Noddy Holder's jokey confidence.

Cathy Cassidy, pictured way back then with her mum, little brother Andy, and Kash the 'mad rescue my dad found', is transported back to Christmas '78 when she hears 'Merry Xmas Everybody'

And even when Punk began to elbow its way onto the scene, Slade remained a staple – at Christmas especially. When I was 16, I saved and saved and bought myself my first high-heeled shoes. They weren't platforms – they'd fallen from grace by then – and I tottered dangerously as I made my way to the big Christmas party. I felt like a giraffe in those shoes. I towered over every boy there, and no way could I dance... but when Slade's 'Merry Xmas Everybody' came on, I'd had enough. EVERYBODY had to dance to that. It was the law. I kicked off the shoes and danced, and a boy danced with me. He walked me home through the snow, me in my stocking feet and him with the hated shoes in his pocket. My feet were blue and bleeding slightly, and I had a cold that Christmas, but my first boyfriend was a lot better than my first (and last) pair of high-heeled shoes. Thank you, Slade. I never did try the page-boy haircut, and that's probably a good thing!

BAILEYS

3 MARCH 1979, WATFORD, UK

I WAS THERE: GAVIN FLETCHER

I was born in May 1963 and first started watching *Top of the Pops* in summer 1972, so my earliest memories of that show would be seeing performances of 'Metal Guru' by T.Rex, 'School's Out' by Alice Cooper, and 'Starman' by David Bowie, when he famously put his arm round Mick Ronson. My first memory of Slade was seeing *Top of the Pops* performances of 'Mama Weer All Crazee Now'. Noddy was probably the most memorable, with his top hat with mirrors, long sideboards, and the way his powerful voice screamed, 'Mama, mama, mama, mama, mama, mama, yeah!' towards the end. The next most memorable was Dave, with glitter on his forehead and his outfits always entertaining. As I became more familiar with Slade, Dave's

Gavin Fletcher always looked forward to seeing what Dave would be wearing on *Top of the Pops*

latest costume, whenever they were on TV promoting their new single, was always eagerly awaited.

By the end of 1972, I liked all the Glam rock bands, with Slade my favourites. I bought my first album with some Christmas money. It was an Arcade compilation, *20 Fantastic Hits By The Original Artists*, and I bought it because it had 'Gudbuy T' Jane', 'Blockbuster!', 'All The Young Dudes' and 'The Jean Genie' on it.

I remember hearing about Don's accident in the summer of '73. We were on holiday in the Isle of Man, where my grandparents had retired. We went there every year but were there unusually early that summer as it was the only time my dad could get off from work, so we avoided the Summerland fire in early August, when we usually stayed there. Unfortunately, I was too young and didn't have the money for a ticket for Slade's live performance on the Isle of Man a few days later, when Jim's brother Frank stood in for Don. I remember seeing a photo of Don's car, all smashed up, on the front page of my grandparents' newspaper.

For some reason, probably financial, I didn't buy a single until autumn '73 – 'The Ballroom Blitz' by Sweet. The first Slade single I bought was at Christmas that year – 'Merry Xmas Everybody', of course. It stayed at No.1 for several weeks, into January, and was eventually replaced at the top by The New Seekers' 'You Won't Find Another Fool Like Me', which I absolutely hated then – and now!

We had a regular babysitter for my younger brother and me, a Mrs Armstrong. She must have been in her fifties, but still liked her pop music. She was babysitting one Thursday in January '74 when we were watching *Top of the Pops*. The New Seekers were performing 'You Won't Find…' in their first week at No.1, when Mrs Armstrong asked what I thought of that song. 'Rubbish!' I replied, 'nowhere near as good as Slade's 'Merry Xmas Everybody'!' She said, 'Yes, but this can be played anytime, whereas 'Merry Xmas Everybody' can only be played at Christmas, and now Christmas is over you'll never hear it again.' I wonder how many times I've heard it since!

Through his work, my dad knew an Australian music writer called Richie Yorke, who visited our house in early '74 and asked who my favourite groups were. 'Slade and The Sweet,' I told him. A little while later, he brought me a copy of *Old New Borrowed And Blue* along with some 'Skweeze Me, Pleeze Me' and 'My Friend Stan' stickers and a 'Slade Talk to Melanie Readers' flexi-disc. It was the first Slade album I acquired, and I played it over and over. I remember them performing 'Everyday' and 'We're Really Gonna Raise The Roof' on *Crackerjack* in spring that year.

Early in 1975, my mum took my brother and me to see *Slade In Flame* at the cinema. I don't think she enjoyed it much, but I certainly did. It was quite bleak, which suited the time, and the ending has always stayed with me, when Noddy says, 'I think we've all had enough.'

Sadly, Slade's fortunes declined in the second half of the Seventies, but I still bought their records – singles like 'Gypsy Roadhog', 'Rock 'n' Roll Bolero' and 'Ginny Ginny', and albums like *Whatever Happened to Slade* and *Return To Base*.

By 1979 I was 16 and had started going to gigs with school friends. Around this time, I went to see Slade at Baileys nightclub in Watford. It was a chicken-in-a-basket-type venue, but that was what they were reduced to by then. The place was half empty and I remember Noddy asking the audience if they had Bostik on their arses, with everyone being glued to their seats and not getting up! Things didn't improve for the group until late summer 1980's much-publicised Reading Festival set.

STUDENTS' UNION

8 MARCH 1979, HULL UNIVERSITY, HULL, UK

I WAS THERE: KEV PICKERING

I discovered Slade at my local youth club when I was 13. People used to take their records for the DJ to play. Someone took *Slade Alive!* and the DJ played the whole LP. That was it for me. The best thing for me was the Hull college concert, with about 300 people there. It was only a small venue, very loud, but maybe that was because I snuck past the security and sat in front of one of the many speakers for most of the night.

OSCAR'S

29 MAY 1979, LIVERPOOL, UK

I WAS THERE: PAUL COOKSON, POET LAUREATE FOR SLADE, DON POWELL'S OCCASIONAL FLAMES

I arrived relatively late to the Slade party. 'Cum On Feel The Noize' was the awakening, although I'd been aware of 'Gudbuy T'Jane' and 'Mama Weer All Crazee Now'. To be honest, football was the over-riding obsession – playing it, watching it, talking about it. But Slade changed all that. Forever!

A flyer for Paul Cookson's first Slade gig in May '79

I didn't have a record player until later but had a trusty cassette player that, like everyone else, I'd tape *Top of the Pops* on, getting my family to be quiet, a lesson I'd learned in 1970. At the height of my football obsession and the World Cup, England had recorded 'Back Home' and were No.1. I'd never watched *Top of the Pops* before and didn't know the No.1 was always played last. Plus, the music didn't interest me. Dad had set up a NASA-sized reel-to-reel tape recorder with hand-held microphone so I could record my footballing heroes. At last – after countless Dad interjections of 'Rubbish!' and 'Is that a boy or a girl?' – the mighty England came on and Dad pressed record. Because I was holding a hand-held mic towards the telly, it didn't occur to me that other sounds would be recorded too. So I was surprised to hear my own voice when we played it back with the commentary. 'That's Bobby… Nobby… Mooro… Bally… Banks…'.

Later, I'd tape all the singles on my cassette player and watch every episode of *Top of the Pops*, *Supersonic*, *Lift Off With Ayshea* … even *Shang-a-Lang*, the Bay City Rollers' show, in case Slade were on. They even played 'How Does It Feel?' on *Crackerjack*. And I'd buy the fold-out posters – I've still got them, framed in my study! Or I'd ask my sisters or their friends for *Popswop* pages.

But we never went to concerts, it just never occurred to us. I was in Walmer Bridge and Preston, eight miles away, seemed a world away when you're 13. Plus, we were a family of church-goers and the only concerts our parents considered involved church choirs. And none of my footy mates or their brothers went to gigs; that's the way it was. So I never saw Slade in their Glam rock heyday.

However, as fashions were changing and some lads probably needed cigarette money, I managed to get *Slade Alive!*, *Slayed*, and *Slade in Flame* for 50p.

Slade fell from favour, but not mine. I very nearly got to see them in Blackburn in 1977 but the folks, who were driving, pulled out as it was massively stormy. So it was 1979 in Liverpool when it happened. I was at Edge Hill College. I remember the excitement of seeing they were coming to Liverpool – not a big rock venue but Oscar's nightclub. I went with my then girlfriend, who, truth be told, wasn't that bothered.

This was before they had their comeback at Reading, before 'We'll Bring the House Down', although they had released a six-track twelve-inch single, the *Six of the Best* EP, its lead tracks 'Night Starvation', 'When I'm Dancin', I Ain't Fightin'' and 'Wheels Ain't Coming Down'. I bought this from a tiny record shop by the bus station in Ormskirk and was gutted to find out Noddy had made a personal appearance the day before – I'd missed the tiny sign advertising it!

Also, they had still had a massive skinhead following and these featured in two prominent incidents that night. The first involving my girlfriend's handbag. We'd gone to the bar or the loo and she realised the bag was at the table we'd been at, now populated by a dozen tough-looking skinheads. I'd like to say I was the hero and recued said bag… but she just walked up and asked them, and they smiled and posed with it before giving it back.

The second… as they began 'Wheels Ain't Coming Down', there was loads of dry ice and suddenly Nod shouted, 'Stop! Stop now!' We thought there was something amiss technically, but two skinheads were knocking seven bells out of each other just to the front of the stage. 'Will you effin' stop your effin' fighting! For eff's sake, we're here to have some effin' fun!' shouted Mr Holder. And they did. 'Right, we'll effin' carry on… One-two-three-four!'

It was loud, very loud, and it was gloriously exciting to see these guys up and close. It wasn't Glam but it was rock. Over the next few years, I'd see them several times in Liverpool – from Eric's, where it was downstairs and sweaty, to the Royal Concert Hall on the *Till Deaf Do Us Part* tour. And then again when 'My Oh My' rode high in the charts for their Christmas tour.

Nod was always in charge and a great frontman, one of the best. The opening of 'Rock 'n' Roll Preacher' was a tour de force. Jim really came alive with his bass and violin solos. Dave was, well, Dave, and Don was the powerhouse heartbeat. 'Get Down and Get With It' was never my favourite track, but live – it was just incredible – as they would later prove at Reading Festival the following year.

ALLIED BREWERIES CLUB
31 MAY 1979, BURTON-ON-TRENT, UK

I WAS THERE: NOMIS BAURLEY

In 1979 they toured extensively from March until June, and there was a second tour in October. I saw them 15 or 16 times that year, along with other bands like Motörhead, Saxon and Quo, mainly on the college circuit but also at a couple of nightclubs and chicken-in-a-basket places, where shirt and tie were required to gain entry (which were taken off to reveal homemade Slade t-shirts when the band came on!).

At Burton-on-Trent's Allied Breweries Social Club I was the *only* genuine fan there. Everyone else sat at tables. I stood alone in front of the stage, and only a handful of folk stood up from their seats for the encores. I again went to Bradford Uni, met them and chatted. By now, I was helping out a few local bands in Leeds, so as the tour went on, I was thumbing lifts to gigs, getting there any way I could.

I did 110 gigs before they stopped touring in the UK. I know people have done 80 and 90 gigs but, far as I know, nobody else did as many as me. Some people say I cheated, because I probably only bought tickets for about ten Slade gigs in my life. I'd turn up in the afternoon in my scruffy jeans to see what was going on and got to know the road crew. They were quite frosty at first, and longstanding tour manager, Johnny Jones (known as JJ) was particularly ferocious. He was only about five foot two but he was the one you knew not to cross and not give any shit to so I used to really avoid him. Then one time he came up to me, gave me a kick up the arse and said, 'You're always hanging about, you. What's the story? Take your hands out of your pockets and give us a hand shifting some of the stuff out of the van.'

He saw that I wasn't gonna be an arsehole and overstep the line so he invited me to help load in and out in return for entry to the gigs. I was in seventh heaven. It was a typical student gig. The load-in crew had either not turned up or weren't interested in doing what they were meant to do. From there, it was absolutely great. The crew were great to me. 'Where are you going to next?' I'd say, 'Well, I've only got a tenner in my pocket and I'm trying to get to…' wherever the next gig might be. I'd thumb lifts up and down the country and I got a Young Person's Railcard to get me to some of the gigs. I would just turn up at gig after gig. I'd turn up in the afternoon, say 'hello', help with the load-in, then get in for nowt. That's how I did the other hundred-plus gigs.

I got the occasional lift with the band in whatever hire transport they had. And I'd talk to the support band, get straight in there and try to help them load in and out. Support bands like Vardis and Spider also took me under their wing and let me travel on their buses to get from gig to gig. Saxon supported Slade a couple of times too. At Cardiff Uni, Saxon bought me a breakfast. I had nothing in my pocket, and they had only slightly more.

In time, I got to know the band really well, especially when they were playing the little clubs, in front of 200 or 300 people. And when it exploded again, after Reading Festival and 'We'll Bring The House Down', they were playing the Odeons again, and I still had the same kind of access.

By now the band knew me. I called myself Nomis – Simon spelt backwards, which was a nickname from school. By 1980 I was working full time. I managed to get the number for Slade's office so I'd ring every few weeks and get advance notice of all the upcoming gigs in order to ask my boss for odd days off here and there to get to as many gigs as possible. I'd often do a gig and get the first train home in the morning and go straight into work, then take the train to another gig that night.

Towards the end of the year, they were playing bigger venues based on the success of that year's Reading Festival. In May, they played to fewer than 300 at the Cedar Club in Birmingham, but by December they had sold out Birmingham Odeon. We felt so proud to be part of this remarkable resurgence, which continued into 1981 on the back of 'We'll Bring The House Down'.

There was still a great camaraderie in the band. They were very close-knit right until the end. Whether they were touring in the Seventies, with a huge articulated truck crammed full of gear, or the Eighties, when they were driving around in a couple of battered old Ford Cortinas, they would always share a car, two of them in one car and two in the other. I never ever saw any kind of despondency. They knew where they were. Nod and Jim were pretty much putting their hands in their pockets to fund it when they weren't selling loads of tickets, but they were always forever hopeful that they would turn the corner.

There was a little group called the Magic 300, which was apparently how many people were in the fan club at that point in time, when Dave Kemp was running it. Then *Slade News* came out, which increased the numbers a little.

In 1978, I saw Cheap Trick and in 1979, I saw bands like Motörhead, Status Quo, Ozzy, Saxon; the new wave of British heavy metal. But when something's in your blood, it's in your blood, and you did everything you could to fight your corner for Slade through all the bad times, doing things like sticking stickers on bus shelters for the new singles when they came out. That's how it was in them days, and I consider those years, from '78 through to '83, the best of my life.

MUSIC MACHINE
20 OCTOBER 1979, CAMDEN, LONDON, UK

I WAS THERE: BRETT 'BUDDY' ASCOTT, THE CHORDS & THE FALLEN LEAVES

Brett 'Buddy' Ascott couldn't get over the size of fellow drummer Don Powell's sticks

As my childhood reluctantly gave way to adolescence, I naturally started to become more interested in pop music. But at 13 years old I wasn't a willing subscriber to Glam Rock – Bowie freaked me out, The Sweet were just creepy, and Bolan looked like a girlie. To this newly minted teenager the only group who didn't scare me to death – and seemed vaguely comparable to my beloved Beatles – were Slade. They also seemed to be having the most fun on *Top of the Pops*, my sole glimpse into music other than Radio 1. The misspelling of their song titles further endeared them to me, and I was soon a regular singles-buyer of theirs. Their hits just kept coming, each more rowdy and joyful than the last. Their film was pretty damn good too!

Fast forward to October 1979 and I'm stood at the bar at the very top – and the back – of Camden's Music Machine. I cannot be further from the stage unless I'm serving over-priced drinks, but still my ears are pounding – Slade are the loudest group I will ever see in my life (and I was at The Who at Charlton in '76!). I look down at the distant stage and Don Powell appears to be using two freshly-hewn tree trunks as drum sticks – they are enormous. How he manages to even lift them is beyond my comprehension. He must've had bionic wrists fitted after the tragic car crash that so nearly took his life a few years earlier. He's an inspiration to us all. The show is a triumph, of course, but my ears are still ringing over 40 years later!

Larger-than-life; big, bold and brassy as hell. Slade – I salute you!

CIVIC HALL
21 OCTOBER 1979, DUNSTABLE, UK

I WAS THERE: MARTIN BROOKS

Martin Brooks and Don Powell sporting matching Pouk Hill Prophetz beanies at a Don and the Dreamers launch gig in London, March 2023

I was seeing the mighty Slade for the second time, as part of a school trip I organised with legendary Boston Grammar School teacher Richard Anderson. Slade had just released 'Sign Of The Times' as a single and were promoting a new album, *Return To Base*. They couldn't get arrested at the time – no radio play and blanked by the 'trendy' music papers, with more chance of West Ham winning the League than Slade getting back in the charts or on *Top of the Pops*. But when your favourite band walk onstage in front of 800 crazee hardcore fans, plug in and open with 'Hear Me Calling', you know you have made the right choice and you are part of an elite group of believers.

If you were there, you know... If you weren't, imagine your favourite team scoring two goals in injury time to beat your biggest rivals and win the FA Cup, and you might have a slight idea of what it was like back in the Barn days. This gig was the inspiration for my first group, Conflict, at Boston Grammar School, with Philip Bullen, Nick Pogson and Graham Corlett, and 40 years later I am proud to be playing guitar in Pouk Hill Prophetz with Nigel Hart and Trevor West, and still playing songs by this incredible group. Return To Base indeed!

MUSIC MACHINE
29 FEBRUARY & 1 MARCH 1980, CAMDEN, LONDON, UK

I WAS THERE: GÉRARD GOYER

Gerard Goyer was at the Music Machine

I'm French and have been a Slade fan since 1972, but I missed the chance to see their last concert in France, two days after my 19th birthday, on 16th December 1974 at Paris Olympia, because I was doing compulsory military service. Instead, I saw Slade for the first time at London's Music Machine in 1980, getting backstage to see him. The following day, I also saw the film *Flame* at the Essential Cinema on Wardour Street.

I knew Slade from the jukebox in the bar, which included 'Take Me Bak 'Ome' and 'Mama Weer All Crazee Now', which sold well in France. It was the voice of Noddy and the catchy music that made me love the band. I bought my first album, *Slayed?* in December 1972, and the next day *Slade Alive!*. In 1973 I bought my first single, 'Cum On Feel The Noize', then went to Lille to buy the singles from 'Get Down And Get With It' through to 'Gudbuy T' Jane'., when I realised each European country sold those singles with a different photo. And, having started work at 16, I had a little money to start buying their records from around the world. That's where my collection started.

I WAS THERE: NOMIS BAURLEY

I notched up another 29 or 30 gigs in 1980, mostly at universities. They played two nights at Camden's Music Machine and me and a mate got volunteered to sleep on the stage between the two gigs to guard the equipment, as Nod had a guitar stolen a few days before. We felt pretty special, but to be honest we didn't get much sleep. It was scary as hell in the pitch black, listening to the old building creaking and cracking as it cooled down. I don't know what on Earth we could have done anyway if anyone had tried to steal anything, but we were grateful of somewhere more comfortable to sleep than train station benches, etc.

U2 supported them at London's Lyceum. There was a very small backstage bar, and I bought a pint for about 30p, leaving myself enough to get a burger later. I knew nothing about U2. These Irish guys appeared. I went for a piss, and when I came back my pint had been drunk. I guess they were as skint as me.

I could now just turn up at any gig and get a pass and help out when I could. Jobs they gave me were things like polishing Don's lovely silver Ludwig kit every night and painting all the scuffs on the huge PA every few nights.

I saw them a further 27 times in 1981, mainly playing clubs and the uni circuit. I hitched from Edinburgh to Aylesbury and got there with half an hour to spare. Sometimes, I'd help the merch guy to get an extra £10 to help me get to the next gig. I slept in the back of the merch van a couple of times amongst all the t-shirts and stuff. In June they played Birmingham Cedar Club to a couple of hundred people. But then they had that resurgence after Reading Festival and they sold out the Birmingham Odeon in December. By 1981 they were back in the bigger venues – City Halls and Odeons again.

It felt great to be a Slade fan again after the wilderness period when we were known as 'the 500', those that stuck with them through the lean times. They toured from January to March in '81, followed by a few gigs in May then December, ending with nights at Hammersmith and Birmingham Odeons. I think I saw them 27 times, including Castle Donington.

NEW WEBBINGTON HOTEL & COUNTRY CLUB

15 JUNE 1980, AXBRIDGE, UK

I WAS THERE: STEVE COBBETT

Steve Cobbett was right at the very front

My mate Paul Goverd and I were at the Webbington gig. We were right at the very front, sat on the edge of the low stage, right under Nod. Paul would shout out requests at every opportunity, prompting Nod to inform the crowd they had a 'right noisy bastard down the front'. After the gig finished, we hung around and managed to catch Dave Swinnerton's eye as he cleared the stage and convinced him to let us go backstage to meet the band. On entering the dressing room, Nod groaned and said, 'Fuck's sake, Swinn, why'd you let the Noizy Bastard in?' To me, Paul will always be the Noizy Bastard.

We got various items signed by the band. Dave asked why I had bought a copy of *Play It Loud* to be signed rather than newer stuff. I said it was because it'd probably be worth more than newer stuff. Dave laughed and said to Noddy, 'Did you hear what this cheeky cunt just said?' Fortunately, that's not been a name that stuck with me!

NORBRECK CASTLE

18 JUNE 1980, BLACKPOOL, UK

I WAS THERE: TOMMY MCMEEKIN

They played at the Norbreck Castle when I was on holiday in Blackpool. A group of us went along. I remember it being really hot and they were the loudest band I'd heard up to that point. They were supported by Girlschool. It was a good week, music-wise. I also saw the Tom Robinson Band, The Hollies, Gerry and the Pacemakers, and The Nolans! The only song that sticks out from the Slade gig is 'Get Down And Get With It'. It was mighty!

Tommy McMeekin (right) saw Slade at Blackpool's Norbeck Castle with William Shiels

ROCK GARDEN
24 JUNE 1980, MIDDLESBROUGH, UK

I WAS THERE: PETER SMITH

In the late 1970s, the Rock Garden in Newport Road in Middlesbrough opened its doors and became the main venue for Punk rock in the North-East. Everyone (The Sex Pistols, The Clash, The Damned, Adam and the Ants, 999) played there. It was an old Bierkeller, basically a room with a stage, a bar, a few tables and benches, and a small kitchen serving burgers. I spent many memorable nights there, but it was a scary place. If the skinheads didn't get you, the Rock Garden burgers would almost certainly finish you off. A visit to the Rock Garden was an experience not to be forgotten; a fight or two was guaranteed as part of the evening's entertainment, alongside performances by some of the finest Punk or heavy rock bands around at the time.

Slade were on their never-ending tour of clubs, pubs, cabaret and ballrooms. From 1977 to 1980 were their 'wilderness years'; Slade were down on their luck and receiving next to no money. Their records were no longer making the charts and they were forced to play small halls and clubs around the UK, their only income coming from royalties from the old hits, most of which will have gone to Noddy and Jim, as the band's two songwriters. Their single releases from this period were not their best and included 'Give Us A Goal' and 'Okey Cokey'. However, live in concert they were as great as ever, perhaps more so as they fought and played hard to win new fans and win back their place in the charts.

The Rock Garden was packed with skinheads. My mate Norm has vague memories of the support act being pelted off stage, having to hide behind the bar while the skinheads continued to throw handfuls of ice at them. But the skinheads loved Slade, and Noddy managed to keep them in order. When a scuffle broke out, he would tell the hard guys to behave, and they would listen to him and take notice. They saw him as one of their own.

The Rock Garden stage was tiny, and Slade came with masses of amps, which they still had from the days when they would pack out big halls. So, Nod, Dave, Jim and Don were limited to playing in a tiny area in front of a massive back line, surrounded by big PA speakers. And they were deafeningly LOUD. I swear my ears were ringing for days afterwards.

The set was a mix of their hits, recent tracks and a few covers. The place went crazy. Slade were called back for several encores and finished with 'Born To Be Wild', just like old times.

A couple of months later I was at Reading Festival, when a lucky break gave Slade the chance to show everyone just how great a live band they still were, and put them back in the music public's eye, this time as heroes of the heavy metal brigade.

We didn't know we were doing this fucking gig 'til about three days ago. **Noddy Holder**

READING FESTIVAL

24 AUGUST 1980, READING, UK

I WAS THERE: BILL ADAMSON

I officially became a pop fan and began studying the music charts in 1969, ten-year-old me purchasing my first single, 'Sugar Sugar' by The Archies. Slade's first album, *Beginnings*, out under the name Ambrose Slade, was released that year, but I confess it completely passed me by. My first exposure came with their second UK Top 20 hit and first UK No.1, 1971's magnificent 'Coz I Luv You'. This not only kicked off my love for these boys from the Black Country, it also launched their cheeky habit of spelling things wrong in the song titles. I always thought that misspelling was a fun thing to do, but it seemed to really upset the prim and proper brigade, led by Mary Whitehouse and Lord Longford, who I recall claimed it would have a negative impact on children's education in the UK. Wel it didnt afeckt myne! In fact, the band referred to it in 'Skweeze Me, Pleeze Me' with the lines:

Bill Adamson, seen here carrying fellow attendee Bryan Jones, was at Reading in 1980

Can't you learn to spell?
Take me bak home, you got it all wrong, coz we sing that as well!

Top of the Pops is where I first saw Slade, although I'd heard 'Coz I Luv You' on the radio a lot by then. On the show they weren't fully glammed up like at their peak, although Dave Hill was looking rather camp, a few months before he acquired his famous Super Yob guitar. It was also before Noddy Holder bought his original and incredibly stylistic mirrored top hat. In an interview with *The Guardian* newspaper, he said the hat 'was sold to him by a young man he knew called Freddie, who ran a market stall in Kensington. That man went on to become Freddie Mercury.' Apparently, Freddie said to Noddy during the transaction, 'One day I'm gonna be a big pop star like you,' to which Nod replied, 'Fuck off, Freddie!'

As a teenage school kid, I could only afford seven-inch singles rather than albums, with Slade and Hot Chocolate the two bands for whom I bought every single. After 'Coz I Luv You', I bought every release up until 'In For A Penny' in 1975. Slade really took to the whole Glam rock thing when it took off, but for me they were always so much more than just a pop or Glam band. The press sometimes dubbed them the new Beatles, as they did with so many new bands. But with Slade I believe that was a fair description, the quality of Noddy and Jim Lea's songwriting grade A to start with and immeasurably better with every new release.

Noddy's vocals sounded like they were forged in the bowels of Mordor. There was no one around with a voice anything like his. Could anyone have sung 'Cum On Feel the Noize' any better? I really doubt it.

Whilst I love the pounding anthemic sound of their biggest hits, my favourites are those where they veered away from what many saw as their signature style, and in particular 'Far Far Away'. It has everything. Great lyrics, great sound, magnificent production, and some melancholy and reflective words. The band took a real departure when they embarked on the film *Slade in Flame*, billed as something to rival The Beatles' films, albeit with a more real and gritty story. It was not particularly well received when it came out but has become something of a cult classic. And the soundtrack was first class, including the aforementioned 'Far Far Away' and fully orchestral 'How Does It Feel?'. Both tunes showed a huge development from the biggest hits, Noel Gallagher calling the latter 'one of the best songs written, in the history of pop, ever.' Listening to it again while writing this, I can see where he's coming from.

Around that time, Slade had become disappointed with their lack of a breakthrough in the US and relocated to America for what turned out to be a couple of years. However, despite recording and touring stateside they never broke big there. Their only Top 20 US hit didn't arrive until 'Run Runaway' made it to No.20 in 1984, a few months after US metal band Quiet Riot took a cover of 'Cum On Feel The Noize' into the US Top Ten. Personally, I think America missed out hugely, not 'getting' Slade, who deserved to be huge on the scale of The Beatles and the Stones.

I was lucky enough to see the band live twice, first in April 1975 at the New Victoria Theatre in London. My Aunt June, who worked in London, got tickets for me and my school mate Jonesy (the late, great Bryan Jones). As we were still just 16, she rather embarrassingly came to meet us at Victoria Station afterwards to ensure we got home to Hillingdon safely. We were so rock 'n' roll, right?

And the second – and last – time I saw Slade was considered by many to be one of their finest ever live sets, at Reading Festival, stepping in when Ozzy Osbourne pulled out. By all accounts, the band were ready to call it a day, but Chas Chandler persuaded them to play. I'm so glad he did.

It was an incredible set and an unbelievable performance that won the crowd over almost from the start. A lot of the big hits – 'Cum On Feel The Noize', 'Mama Weer All Crazee Now', 'Take Me Bak 'Ome' and 'Everyday' – were there. But the icing on the cake was a standout version of first chart hit 'Get Down And Get With It', which might have given birth to the first ever mosh circle. I was there, and I reckon that is true! Then there was a singalong of a rather rocky version of 'You'll Never Walk Alone'. But perhaps the most uplifting and surreal moment of that day was when Slade launched into 'Merry Xmas Everybody'. Yes, we sang along to that Christmas classic at the end of August! But seriously how could the band not play that song? Even now Christmas doesn't start in our house until Noddy has uttered his immortal, raucous and guttural, '*It's Chriiiiistmaaaas!*'

I did eventually buy a secondhand copy of 1972's *Slade Alive*, and my girlfriend at the time gave me a cassette copy of *Slayed?* at Christmas 1974. So I suppose I kind of caught up. I never met the band, but I did write an article about Betty the Tea Lady at Wessex Studios. Betty is no longer with us, but I spoke with her daughter, who told me Betty thought Slade were nice, polite lads. She also once told the band while delivering tea and biscuits to a recording session, 'You boys make big noise,' a comment that inspired the title of their final studio LP in 1987.

My overriding memories of Slade are of them being a truly great band missing out on the worldwide acclaim that their energy, skill, and musical ability should have brought them. They might well have been a Seventies Beatles in a parallel universe. But I'm sure we will always remember them as a band that made the best and most raucous party anthems in the history of the world! I look back on my love of Slade and say, 'So it was alright, yeah, it was alright!' Yeah, take me bak 'ome to 1972, and I would be happy.

I WAS THERE: SIMON HARVEY

On Thursday 21st August 1980 I purchased all the weekly UK music publications – *NME*, *Melody Maker*, *Disc*, *Sounds*, etc. – as was normal for me at the time and in the hope of finding out anything new happening with Slade in the near future. A few lines in the press nearly slipped under the radar but, thankfully, I noticed that Slade would be playing at Reading Festival that very weekend, late replacements for Ozzy Osbourne's Blizzard of Ozz. I bought a ticket from my local record shop in Slough, who were acting as agents for the event, and duly arrived at the festival site that Sunday, catching some of the acts before Slade were due on stage about 5pm.

Mid-afternoon between bands, wandering around the festival site taking in the wonders of Reading Rock, Noddy Holder and Jim Lea came and stood by me. We struck up a conversation, me having been a regular at Slade's gigs in the Seventies, getting to know the band, roadies, and fellow fans. And whilst Nod and Jim were slightly apprehensive about playing to an estimated 65,000 crowd that day (one of the biggest of their UK career), they brimmed with confidence, having been playing clubs, universities and half-empty concert halls for far too long, and eager to get the opportunity to show a big crowd that Slade could still 'kick ass'.

Reading changes

SLADE, White Spirit and **Ange Witch** have been added to this weekend's Reading Festival line-up to replace Ozzy Osbourne who's pulled out (see separate story) and Angel City who've been withdrawn for "mysterious reasons that have something to do with their record company CBS." **G-Force** have also had to cancel because Gary Moore's three band compatriots are all American and have had trouble getting work permits.

Slade and Angel Witch appear on the Sunday 24th, while White Spirit play on Saturday the 23rd.

The music press story that tipped Simon Harvey off about Slade's Reading Festival appearance

And from the moment the band opened their set with 'Dizzy Mama', they sent the crowds dizzy with a dazzling display of pure showmanship, knocking out hit after hit, including 'Take Me Bak 'Ome', 'Mama Weer All Crazee Now' and 'Everyday', new tunes including 'When I'm Dancin', I Ain't Fightin'' and 'Wheels Ain't Coming Down', responded to with much enthusiasm from the crazee crowds, as were classics like 'Get Down And Get With It' and 'Cum On Feel The Noize', which the assembled did that day, the unforgettable moment being 65,000 people singing along to 'Merry Xmas Everybody' in late August.

Slade were the underdogs of the day who came out on top, the music press and new-found fans giving the band a new belief in themselves. Slade were soon back in the charts, back on *Top of the Pops* and back selling out big concert halls, playing to a similar-sized crowd at Castle Donington's *Monsters of Rock* festival the following year, a soggy day but one that much like Reading Festival 1980 was a day I shall never forget.

I WAS THERE: DAVE HOLDGATE

The years went by and albums were bought, but I missed opportunities to see Slade again for various reasons. Then, in 1980, my mate Graham and I went to Reading Festival. It was at the beginning of the New Wave Of British Heavy Metal, with bands like Iron Maiden and UFO on the bill. The Blizzard of Ozz were due to be last-but-one on the bill, before Whitesnake closed the weekend, but word got out that they weren't appearing. Rumours started to go around the campsite about who was being lined up to replace them. No, surely not. Can't be. And then, an announcement on the Saturday that Slade would indeed be on Sunday's line-up. Boos around the field. What? No. They can't boo Slade.

Sunday came and Slade appeared on stage to a mainly empty field. Noddy strode to the mic and roared, 'Are you ready to rock?' and off they went at 100mph into 'Dizzy Mama'. Suddenly the magic happened. The beer cans stopped flying, the cheers got louder, the crowd got bigger, and everyone was singing along to hit after hit. We even sang 'Merry Xmas Everybody'. It was surreal.

They had done it. They had turned a crowd and quite simply stormed it with an electric set. It's possibly the most talked about set in the history of Reading Festival, and I was there. I was buzzing. They were back.

I only saw them once more – back at the Gaumont in Ipswich in March 1982, just under five years after the first time. I still have the t-shirt, although it appears to have shrunk over the years. Thank you, Slade. You made growing up fun. When it comes to my funeral, I guess there will be at least one Slade song played. Until then, I will play the vinyl as it was meant to be played – LOUD – and will educate my two young granddaughters about times past when music was great – really great.

I WAS THERE: DAVID GRAHAM, SLADE IN ENGLAND

Reading Rock '80 was without a doubt one of Slade's finest hours, literally and metaphorically. As far as their history as a band was concerned, perhaps only their ground-breaking appearance at the Great Western Festival at Bardney, Lincolnshire (aka Lincoln Festival) had as much impact on their standing with the public and the music writing press.

Festivals back then were not the well-organised sanitised events of today. Little regard was given to various Health & Safety Acts, let alone basics such as food, water and ablutions, and the the wall-to-wall facilities that festivalgoers enjoy now are light years away from the spartan conditions offered in a few fields in the heart of Berkshire's countryside in 1980.

'Reading weekend' was for us an annual event, with a half-dozen of us heading off from Essex, or as many as could be squeezed into a battered ex-Post Office Telephones Bedford van. The 1980 event started as all previous Reading festivals began, running the gauntlet of Thames Valley Police between Reading town centre and the location. The previous year had seen a fair amount of trouble, with pitched battles between punks and heavy metal followers breaking out sporadically throughout the weekend. This year, the police were not going to take any chances, stopping all suspect-looking vehicles en route... and that meant just about all of them! The occupants were searched and checked at the roadside before being allowed to continue or in some cases arrested for outstanding warrants or minor drugs offences.

Unlike previous years, the 1980 festival was to be a complete heavy metal event, sprinkled with the cream of the so-called New Wave Of British Heavy Metal and featuring 'wunderkinds' Def Leppard as well as stalwarts and old hands such as Rory Gallagher, Gary Moore and Ozzy Osborne and his Blizzard Of Ozz, with main headliners Whitesnake bringing up the rear, so to speak.

Arriving at the festival grounds, the usual scramble for a good parking spot and a place to pitch tents was in full flow. It was sunny, hot and the feeling around seemed to be that this was going to be a great weekend of music and a spectacle. It didn't take long for the festival rumours to start. And after a million Chinese whispers, they bore no relation or similarity to the truth. The first rumour was that Ted Nugent had been seen buying a burger and was set to play with Gary Moore. It had to be true, how could it not be? A bloke who knew a bloke who used to go out with another bloke's sister overheard someone else saying so...That rumour soon fizzled out but like sharks' teeth, as one fell away another took its place. Tony Iommi had been spotted milling around backstage and would be joining Ozzy onstage on Sunday... As day turned into night, the main rumours became that Gary Moore and Ozzy Osbourne had pulled out. By 8pm on Friday, it was pretty much confirmed that Ozzy's Blizzard had indeed pulled out and a 'name' band would take their place. And by midnight, from somewhere, whispers started... the name band brought in to replace Ozzy's Blizzard… Slade.

I had gone to Reading with a best mate I converted from Kiss to Slade three years before, when Slade returned from their American sojourn and barnstormed their way across the country with their 1977 vintage rock on the *Whatever Happened To Slade* tour. He had become as much of a fan as I was after witnessing the band live for the first time, battering Ipswich into submission. Neither of us could believe Slade, our band, were going to play at Reading Rock Festival. It seemed so leftfield that it couldn't be true. This was Reading with 80,000 metal heads, bikers and down 'n' dirty HM monsters... Were Slade really coming to town?

Slade were at this time in the third year of their doldrums, having become as relevant to the music scene in 1980 as Adam Faith had become by time the Sixties flicked over into the Seventies. The 500 'Old Guard' fans that fervently and loyally followed the band up and down the country to the sweaty nightclubs, university halls, Young Farmers dos in marquees, miners' welfare social clubs and chicken-in-a-basket nightspots were all that had kept Slade alive, and we began to think Slade appearing at Reading could be the final nail in their coffin... pop jesters thrown to the ravenous hordes... sacrificial lambs. It seemed all so surreal.

Despite waking up with a dreadful hangover and the sort of aches and pains you only get from cheap sleeping bags on hard but damp ground, we regained some positivity. If it were true, Slade would blitz and blow everyone else off stage, if given the chance by an audience that took annual delight in 'canning' those they didn't take to with cans of piss. It was medieval at times, but it could be funny... One year, a full West Indian steel band from the inner city had been one of the first acts on as the afternoon kicked off, and it didn't take long for the cans of piss to be seen arcing through the air to clatter into their steel oil drums – a real cacophony of noise.

As news that Slade were replacing Ozzy gathered pace, not one person I spoke to about it (with the exception of Gary Marsh, a fan from Edmonton) had a good word to say about Slade, especially not hairy, bearded men wearing denim jackets that were bedecked with a myriad of patches and badges proclaiming their affection for some rock legend or other. The worst were those proudly displaying their assorted Sabbath denims or Ozzy t-shirts. None seemed to be exactly overly enamoured that it would be Noddy and not Ozzy. Everywhere you turned, every queue for the bogs, the beer, the burgers, it was, 'Fucking Slade? Slade? I mean, fer fuck's sake! Those fucking Merry Xmas clowns? Blah, blah, blah...' it seemed that everyone was muttering the same or similar blasphemy!

No one seemed to be able to find out for definite if Slade were going to be sacrificed to the HM Reading crowd, but then again no one had heard of any other band being announced. And sometime during Saturday evening, I was told that Whispering Bob Harris had confirmed over the PA that Slade were deffo appearing. I was still unsure, but my fears for them seemed to subside, a few gallons of Watney's Party Seven giving me the ability and confidence to collar hold of anyone I heard dissing Slade and tell them they would surprise them. 'You like loud, you like heavy... You've never seen Slade? You're in for a treat!'

Sunday came around a lot quicker and earlier than I managed to do, the previous evening's fare of loud music, dodgy bacon sandwiches, Watney's gnat's piss ale and cheap low-grade grass keeping me in my pit past midday. But around 2pm I was woken by my mate, Dave, who claimed to have seen Graham Swinnerton, or Swinley as we knew him, Slade's road manager, by the backstage area. He knew Swinley by sight as well as any of the 500, and if Dave had seen him, it was fact... Slade had arrived! That was enough for me.

We found out they'd be appearing on the second stage. Reading always had two, so as one band walked off the next band would walk onto the other while various road crews and stage managers readied the vacant stage for the next act. Stage Two was the right-hand stage, and in between them was a large JumboTron-type screen that worked some of the time, relaying the images that the festival cameramen were filming from the stage (although sometimes there was too much sunlight shining directly onto the screen for it to be seen, while at other times the screen was black despite the cameramen seemingly filming whoever was currently playing).

As their allotted time drew closer, the general consensus of opinion was that Slade would be the first band that day to be mercilessly canned off, in order to get rid of them as soon as possible and get the real bands on. Apart from perhaps 200 people, the massed ranks of hairies, bikers, pseudo-Hell's Angels and the unwashed in general had no appetite for Slade and nothing was going to change that.

On Stage One was a painfully bad band called Girl, a standard spandex and hair band and the type of typical support band that could have pitched up at any NWOBHM gig. They laboured their way through a half-hour set to little acclaim or interest. I stood and watched them regardless, making sure I could be as close as possible to Stage Two when Slade, who were next up, hit the decks. As Girl droned their way to a standstill, attention shifted. At festivals, and certainly at Reading, the crowd is spread out and thousands of festival-goers are in the camping areas – the tent cities – way off in the distance, especially during the day when lesser bands are on.

Even though a huge name band like Slade were due on next, the thinly spread crowd all seemed to turn as one, like a herd of wildebeest on the African plain, and start heading away from the stage area and towards Tent City. It was early evening, and it seems that those in attendance decided now would be a good time to go for a dump/meal/beer/shag... anything, in fact, that didn't involve watching Slade.

Front of Stage Two was sparsely populated and, being a resourceful sort, I managed to blag my way into the press pit using a magic card I always carried in those days. Behind the barriers outside the press pit, a few hundred more seemed to have stayed, but the mass exodus carried on as thousands turned their backs, the proverbial mass 'putting on the kettle at half time' syndrome.

Although the stage lights had been used all day, it was only now, as day turned slowly to night, that they could be seen properly... and then it was on. Slade, resplendent attired in stripes and yellow, breezed onto the stage. the few hundred immediately in front of Stage Two giving a few cheers and shouts of approval as the band plugged in and took their positions. Holder, sporting a black jacket and hat, glanced out over the festival site as DJ Bob Harris introduced the band.

Without any more delay or due process, the opening notes of 'Dizzy Mamma' cut through the still evening air...

We're gonna rock ya, we're gonna fuck ya up
We're gonna rock ya, we're gonna fuck ya up...
A one, a two, a one, two, three... WHAM!

The loudest noise of the weekend blasted its way out of the Reading sound system. It was so loud, the soundwaves seemed to rip through the weak and feeble bodies of those in front of the stage before travelling away off into the distance, where it literally stopped people in their tracks. As one, the herd of heavy metal wildebeest who had dismissed Slade as the day's token jesters started running back down the hill towards the party… and I mean running, to get as close as possible to the stage now occupied by Slade, masters of their craft.

It was a sight to behold, and by the time 'Dizzy Mamma' crashed to a rousing finale of immensely powerful crunching power chords, the crowd in front of Stage Two had swelled from hundreds to thousands, with thousands more making their way there.

As the dust from the first grenade settled, Holder, showman supreme, stood centre-stage, silently scanning the audience for reaction. He'd seen what had happened during 'Dizzy Mamma', and without further ado or ceremony the band quickly treated the still-growing crowd to 'My Baby Left Me', then launched straight into 'Take Me Bak 'Ome'. The scene was set.

The crowd continued to swell through 'When I'm Dancin' I Ain't Fightin'', now probably around the 20,000-mark, all crammed into the immediate area around the stages and beyond, all jostling and already forgetting that a quarter of an hour before that they thought Slade were a Micky Mouse Christmas novelty band.

By the end of 'Wheels Ain't Coming Down' or maybe halfway through the 'Somethin' Else' medley, Slade's audience was the whole festival. All 65,000... 75,000... 85,000… depending on which reports you believe. For me, everyone there was watching Slade. No, not just watching, that would be painting the wrong picture. They were all joining in – big hairy, dirty bastards, multiple tattoos, all seemingly wearing denim jackets weighed down with a zillion enamel badges featuring HM bands, all jumping up and down, stomping, waving their hands at Holder's behest. He had them all in his pocket, Holder and his chums turning an apathetic crowd into a frenzied mass of dancing whirling dervishes. And the one thing that struck me while crowd-watching? Fuck Ozzy Osbourne – he couldn't do this to a crowd.

Holder, was, as always, in complete control, from the top of his hat, through the tailcoat, down the slippery black trews to his favourite blue suede boots, he cajoled and coaxed those in attendance to pay homage to him and his band of men. And what a band they were. Jimmy Lea, as ever, was all over the place, using the huge Reading stage to good effect, criss-crossing with H in a never-ending spectacle of goofy pogoing and pirouetting while belting out thunderous basslines and dirty little guitar riffs, all held together by Powell's drumming and up front by Holder's murderously crunching SG.

And the crowd forgot it was Slade, forgot that Slade were that shit Merry Xmas band, forgot that it wasn't cool to have a ball at a gig. By the time we got to 'Get Down And Get With It', everyone as far as the eye could see was stompin' and a clappin'. No one stood with hands in pockets looking at the stage trying to be cool, everyone lost it. It was one huge party, a celebration of unabashed enjoyment by all in attendance.

With the party in full swing, off they went to an appreciation unheard of. We knew they were coming back to do the one encore the name bands were allowed. And after a brief run through of 'You'll Never Walk Alone', orchestrated by Holder but sung by the Reading crowd, it was straight into a 100mph version of 'Mama Weer All Crazee Now', then once again they left the stage to a fabulous ovation… game over.

But not quite. For the first time that weekend, a band returned for a second encore. The crowd demanded it, and so back they came. The crowd wanted 'Merry Xmas' and so they were dutifully asked to sing it themselves, which they did, all of them, every last man and woman there that night sang 'Merry Xmas Everybody', at the end of August in a field in Berkshire! With the juices flowing, the band then launched into a double encore of 'Cum On Feel The Noize' and that old festival favourite, 'Born To Be Wild'. Crash, bang, wallop... it was finally over and the band left the stage, arms aloft, acknowledging the Reading crowd they had won over completely with their masterful set.

As the band waved their goodbyes, Gene Kelly's 'Singing In The Rain' gently wafted from the PA. As an afterthought, Holder took two steps back towards the microphone and ordered the crowd to sing along. 'Sing it!' he commanded, and as one, thousands and thousands of voices joined together to sing along, a sea of smiling faces, arms gleefully waving in the air. It brought a tear to my eye!

As the band finally vacated the stage, it did actually start to rain, just a few spots of drizzle before it evaporated away, leaving the huge swirling entity that the audience had become to ponder what they had just witnessed and been part of – knackered, exhausted and thoroughly entertained

Def Leppard tried manfully to follow on, but the adrenaline coursing through the bodies of those watching could not be dampened down by Leppard's relatively limp-wristed heavy metal, and for a large part of their set the chants of 'WE WANT SLADE!' could be heard from small enclaves within the mass.

I never thought Slade capitalised on their festival-stealing performance that year, bad management and poor decisions squandering what serendipity had brought their way. But, that day, for nearly an hour, they were without doubt on top of their game, a tour de force… nay… a force majeure, simply unstoppable, and as tight as a duck's arse. They stole the show, blew all the other bands and acts that weekend into oblivion, and it was a privilege and pleasure to have witnessed it first-hand. Until the day I die, I will never forget the sight of all those people turning as one and rushing back to the stages to join in, that crackle in the air as the excitement generated by the band fed the crowd, and the crowd fed the band... a perfect symbiotic relationship.

Slade, long may they be remembered and revered.

I WAS THERE: PHIL BRENNAN

As much as I loved seeing Slade in 1972, I never saw them in concert again until they were announced as a late replacement for Ozzy Osbourne at Reading Festival in 1980… although my mate Barney, also there, said that technically they replaced Gary Moore on the bill. Both

Barney and I were quite happy that Slade were going to play but John, one of Barney's mates who came with us, wasn't at all happy. As we sat drinking at the end of the first evening, he said, 'They were shit years ago and they're probably still shit now, and don't get me started on that fucking Christmas song. I suppose the good thing is they will get booed off at worst and get cans thrown at them at best.' I did tell him that Slade were easily one of the loudest bands I'd ever seen, and he was sure to be pleasantly surprised.

The following morning, Barney made us all some breakfast, a great cure for a hangover and the aching I had from sleeping rough for two nights on the trot. John got out of the tent to the two of us chatting away about how Slade would be received by the masses at the festival. 'They'll hopefully get drenched in piss from all the fucking cans definitely going their way, that's if they actually have the bottle to walk out on to the stage,' he growled.

'Fucking hell, John, are you always so happy?' I asked. 'I just don't like fucking Glam rock or any type of soft shite like them, mate,' he replied. 'I wouldn't mind betting that you've got a Kiss t-shirt,' I ventured. 'Just fuck off and let me eat my fucking breakfast, will you. You'll see I'm right later, when everyone else agrees with me and they get hundreds of cans thrown at them,' he sneered, ignoring my dig at the American Glam rockers.

As John ate his breakfast, Barney and I decided to leave the site for a walk: one reason was that neither of us were that bothered about the first few bands due to play, the other was that we had both become a bit tired of John's constant moaning.

Barney put all the sleeping bags and anything of value back in the van, locked it and shouted across to John, 'We'll see you down the front later, mate.' We didn't wait for a response and just walked away, enjoying a relaxing couple of hours mixing with throngs of people enjoying a similar break from the festival.

One of the highlights of our walk had been watching drunken bikers and rockers jumping off one of the road bridges into the flowing River Thames below. How nobody received any serious injury was beyond me. Having resisted the urge to join in, we arrived back at the festival site and stopped to buy a burger, where we could hear more people like John with the same misgivings about Slade being added to the bill. A group of long-haired rockers muttered about the fact that Reading Festival had no place for Slade. It was the same on our walk down towards the double stages. There were more people walking away from the front than walking towards it, almost all of them complaining bitterly about the appearance of Slade at a rock festival.

By the time Barney and I reached the front of Stage Two, there were only a few hundred people waiting for Slade to come out, and I was certain that some of them were only there to throw cans at the band when they came on. Then, suddenly, they were there, a matter of feet away from us, and launched into their opening number. And wow, it was loud!

By the time 'Dizzy Mamma' had finished, the crowd around us had grown considerably and, as far as I could tell, not one can had been thrown. The next two songs, 'My Baby Left Me' and 'Take Me Bak 'Ome', ensured that anyone that had misgivings about the band playing at the festival had been wrong. The whole place was bouncing, and with every beat there were more people flocking towards the stage. Noddy Holder was clearly enjoying himself and even joked that if the music wasn't loud enough, he would get it turned up, receiving loud cheers of approval from the newly converted. The band raced through their set with real power and not a single person stood still. The whole crowd were stamping their feet, clapping their hands and singing along, and before we knew it the band were walking off to a huge ovation that hadn't seemed likely earlier in the day.

They were soon back and Noddy began the band's encore by getting the crowd to sing 'You'll Never Walk Alone' before bursting into the loudest version of 'Mama Weer All Crazee Now' I had ever heard.

Again, they walked off stage to a tremendous ovation from a crowd that obviously wanted more. Bands rarely came back for a second encore at Reading, but this was a crowd that demanded another encore, and they got one! Bizarrely, the song that had been the butt of most people's jokes earlier in the day started being sung by the people around me. It was August Bank Holiday, yet gangs of hairy rockers all around were singing 'Merry Xmas Everybody'. The opening bars of 'Cum On Feel The Noize' dragged us all back into reality and the place was again bouncing. There was only one song Slade could finish with, one of the first that had drawn me to the band, and once again they delivered 'Born To Be Wild' in brilliant style.

This time they left and weren't coming back. They didn't need to. They'd stormed their way back into the hearts of people that had written them off. It was probably the greatest comeback in music history. As they walked away, Gene Kelly's 'Singing In The Rain' started playing, and I looked at Barney, who had tears in his eyes. We hugged and as we did so I looked over his shoulder and there were hundreds of grown men hugging each other.

I had never seen so many happy faces at the end of a gig before, and I couldn't stop myself from bursting into tears as I whispered in his ear, 'Thank you so much for talking me into coming, mate, I will remember this for the rest of my life.'

I didn't bother staying at the front for the next bands, Def Leppard and Whitesnake. I took the van keys off Barney and walked back to the tent. I grabbed the last of my cans of beer from the van and sat drinking them in a contented manner. It had been a trip that I hadn't really fancied, but one I was extremely happy to have made.

I WAS THERE: CHRIS COLES

I have been a Slade fan since 1971, and the first single I bought was 'Coz I Luv You'. I first saw them at Nottingham University. It was hot, sweaty, smoky, very loud, with plenty of foot-stomping. 'Get Down And Get With It' was the big highlight for me. I saw them again at Reading Festival when they stole the show in August 1980, and I've seen Dave Hill's Slade numerous times, most recently in Salisbury then Southampton with my 16-year-old son, who also loves Slade. I'm definitely a Seventies Slade fan, although I saw 10cc recently and they're always superb too.

I WAS THERE: KENNETH MARKWELL

Blizzard of Ozz cancelled and Slade stood in. Me and my friends were sat about halfway down the field. Slade came on and the whole festival field came alive, with everyone up and dancing to every song played. It was my highlight of the festival. Just brilliant. They had the crowd by the balls and rocked the place. I'll never forget it, even though we were all pretty sozzled by the time they came on. I'm so glad I got to see them though, my one and only time.

They were one of my favourite bands in the past. I went to four Reading Festivals, from 1980 to 1983, and this was the first time I saw everybody dancing. It was like a big party and they were the best band there. Everyone knew the lyrics so everyone was singing along. Who cared that Ozzy wasn't there? Slade nailed it. Those festivals were at a great time in my life. I think we paid about £12.50 for three days – unbelievable now!

I WAS THERE: STEVE CLAYTONSMITH, AGE 17

Born in 1963, my memories of Slade began with *Top of the Pops* in primary school days. Then, in 1980 whilst on leave from the Royal Navy, I went to Reading Rock Festival with a couple of mates. It was rock and heavy metal back in those days, drinking beer out of cans. Slade were a last-minute fill-in. They came onto the right-hand stage in the afternoon and were great. They really got the crowd going, with 50,000 peeps on their feet, most topless, in the brilliant sunshine, singing 'Merry Xmas Everybody'. It was an awesome set. The next band, on the left-hand stage, was the up-and-coming band from Sheffield, Def Leppard. They got booed and canned. They couldn't follow the Slade set. I even managed to launch a plastic bottle, full of urine, spinning onto their stage as the curtain closed. I was 17 and drunk.

Steve Claytonsmith didn't take the piss when Def Leppard came on - he gave it!

I WAS THERE: PETER SMITH

Their singles weren't selling and their concerts were no longer drawing in the crowds. At the time they received the last-minute call asking them to appear at the 1980 Reading Festival, Slade were on the verge of splitting. It's safe to say nobody could have predicted what an impact their Reading set would have upon the music scene.

Reading Festival had become a heavy metal extravaganza. Headliners were Whitesnake, UFO and Rory Gallagher, a full supporting heavy rock cast including up-and-coming new wave of British heavy metal (NWOBHM) bands Def Leppard and Iron Maiden. Metal legend Ozzy Osbourne was billed to play on the Sunday with his new band Blizzard of Ozz, but rumours started to go around the festival site that Ozzy wasn't going to show. Soon those rumours started to hint at who might replace Ozzy, and the name in the frame was … wait for it … Slade.

At first this seemed implausible. Slade were out in the wilderness, playing in small clubs, and had apparently lost their mojo. How would a staunch heavy metal crowd react to them? The festival organisers wouldn't take the risk, would they? But the more I thought about it, the more I began to hope it would happen and the more I began to think it might really work out well for Slade. After all, I'd seen a similar thing happen eight years before at Lincoln, when Slade turned around a potential disaster and secured themselves a special place in the heart of rock fans. I had no doubt that they had the ability, the songs, the passion and the supreme rock 'n' roll sensibilities and credentials to do the same again.

I'd seen them play Middlesbrough Rock Garden a couple of months earlier, so I knew Slade were performing well, powered on all four cylinders, and ready to rock. And if anyone had the bottle to face the Reading crowd, and a potential shower of Party Seven cans, it was Noddy.

I think it was on the Saturday night that DJ Bob Harris (or it may have been John Peel; they were both there) confirmed Slade would be replacing Ozzy, to massive boos from the crowd. Slade, those guys who sing the Christmas song? How could they replace a metal legend like Ozzy? The crowd was having none of it. I'm sure many were already plotting how they were going to show Slade exactly what they thought of them. This would no doubt involve lobbing cans at the stage, and probably filling them with piss first.

Sunday afternoon came. Slade were to appear after glam heavy metal band Girl, and just before new heroes Def Leppard. My mate Dave and I were willing it to work out. The field wasn't that full as Bob Harris announced that Slade were taking the stage. Their entrance was greeted with a hail of cans. Noddy wasn't fazed at all by that, and asked everyone if they were 'ready to rock'. Then they launched straight into 'Dizzy

Mama'. And then it started to happen. Slowly at first, the crowd began to cheer. People wandering around the outskirts of the site started to be drawn towards the stage. It was evident that Slade knew they had to win the crowd over and were working so hard, rocking so hard, and playing the hits. The area around the stage was soon completely rammed and the whole field was going crazy.

It was amazing. Slade absolutely nailed it, and in the space of one hour made sure they were well and truly back. Dave and I couldn't quite believe what was happening. It was clear that we were witnessing an important moment in rock history. I stood there, overwhelmed, tears in my eyes. They nailed it, and they were back!

The music press that year only had one word to say regarding Reading. Slade! Reports were unanimous in their love for the band's performance, and it was clear that their set had pulled them from the cusp of obscurity and placed them back at the forefront of the music scene. The event was recorded, a few tracks released as an EP, leading to chart success, and next time Slade toured it was no longer in half-empty clubs, but in packed-out concert halls.

The set-list was a mixture of hits and new songs and included 'Merry Xmas Everybody'. Well, they had to play it, didn't they, and the crowd sang the chorus; a surreal moment, a field full of denim singing that Christmas song along with Noddy; it was wonderful. They finished with, as in the early days, 'Born To Be Wild'; a perfect closer and a perfect end to an amazing set. Slade had returned. All their hard work had paid off and my heroes were back on top, where they belonged.

I WAS THERE: PETER HAWKINS

I lived in Reading at the time, and 1980 was a very important year in my life. I married my lovely wife, Debbie, who thankfully fancied Jim Lea, so we saw Slade six times that year. She took the attitude, 'If you can't beat them, join them.' My mother phoned me on the Thursday before the festival started to tell me she had heard Slade were a last-minute replacement for Ozzy Osbourne. My first reaction was of great excitement, then panic – how to get tickets? I went into a local record store (remember those?) on the off chance they still had festival tickets. The guy first said no, but must have noticed my disappointment and went away, returning to say they only had Sunday tickets. Yay, the day Slade were performing! He then advised me to not tell anyone where we purchased our tickets. And when Debbie and I arrived at the festival site, on entry we were surprised that our tickets were backstage passes!

We found ourselves in the backstage grounds with all the groups (including an unknown band called Iron Maiden). The difference out back was amazing, with white picket fences, comfy chairs and posh food and drink. Debbie and I were sat on the grass when we spotted Don Powell. We finally went over to talk to him, and how I wish we had a camera. We met the whole band. Dave Hill wouldn't stop talking (nerves) while Noddy Holder hardly said a word (nerves).

When Slade were about to go on, we went out to the front of the stage. To say Slade took control was an understatement. This gig even surpassing Earl's Court. When the crowd shouted for 'Merry Xmas Everybody', Noddy refused but asked the crowd to sing it, which we did. I admit when I turned around to see the crowd singing, I cried.

In hindsight, I wish Slade had called it a day then, to go out with a bang.

I WAS THERE: DYLAN WHITE

In '74 I saw them again at Hammersmith Odeon. I went with another mate, but don't remember much about it. But as Marc Bolan discovered, the kids had grown. We were getting into Deep Purple, Led Zeppelin and Floyd. We weren't teenage Glam-head teenyboppers anymore. We'd moved on in our growing up. My hair grew long, my clothes changed, and then I started working in the music industry. I did security at Reading Festival. It was run by The Marquee – I wrote to them and got a job. You got to put your tent in the workers' area backstage, so you weren't quite amongst the melee. I did that in '77, '78 and '79 and that was great because all the Punk bands played there. So I was front of stage, security or whatever, for The Jam, Dr Feelgood, Tom Robinson. It was great.

And, lo and behold, we got to 1980 and the story is well known that Slade weren't on the original bill. But Ozzy Osbourne was ill or something and couldn't do it, and they went and got Slade. Chas Chandler had to persuade them to do it. Dave Hill in particular was reluctant, I believe. Slade turned up at Reading and I saw them backstage – my teenage idols. I didn't speak to them. Then they came out and delivered, and this rock crowd went nuts. I was so proud and pleased for them. They were going down a storm playing 'Cum On Feel The Noize' and all the rest of it. All the hits, like 'Take Me Bak 'Ome', and at the end of it, this wave of toilet rolls was thrown out into the audience. Typical Slade style.

They absolutely conquered it. And there's the EP, and that set them on the way back, with a whole new rock kind of crowd really. And a new rock sound. And another wave of success.

ALIVE AT READING RELEASED 3 OCTOBER 1980

This three track EP, culled from the band's Reading Festival appearance earlier that year, reaches No. 44 in the UK singles chart.

LYCEUM BALLROOM

19 OCTOBER 1980, LONDON, UK

I WAS THERE: GAVIN FLETCHER

I saw them two months later with a school friend. The support acts were an awful punk band called Discharge and an unknown band from Ireland. We thought they were quite good, but we weren't sure whether that was because they were genuinely good or because anyone would have seemed good after Discharge. This band was U2. Slade themselves were as good as ever. The only disappointing part of the evening was that we had to leave just before the end to catch the last train home. We lived in Aylesbury, and this was a Sunday night so there were no late trains.

I WAS THERE: PAUL A SMYTH

I saw the original line-up live at the Lyceum Ballroom when their supporting act was a new young group called U2. And I saw them at the Hammersmith Odeon in the early '80s. I also have every British vinyl release from 1964 onwards with Steve Brett and the Mavericks. And the one and only Slade monopoly set!

PLACE D'HOURAINE

25 OCTOBER 1980, LESSINES, BELGIUM

I WAS THERE: PHILIPPE DE KEMMETER, AGE 16

When Slade did a mini–Benelux tour, me and some friends went to see them on both days. The first show took place in Lessines and we took the train there from Brussels, having some beer and whisky and coke to get in the mood. A marquee had been erected in the middle of the square. We got in the first row. I had my camera with me. The place was packed, with 600 people, and the atmosphere was great. Noddy was just in front of me. I could touch his shoes. It was a rocking gig and at the end the crowd started a chant which (according to road manager Haden Donovan) gave Slade the idea for 'We'll Bring The House Down'.

My father had told me to be home before midnight but there were no more trains to Brussels so we decided to hitchhike, splitting into pairs. Me and my friend Marc left first, walking along the road. Some cars passed us but none stopped. Then a

Philippe de Kemmeter took shots of Dave Hill and Noddy Holder when they visited Belgium in 1980, and still has his ticket for the Lessines show

van sped past, flashing its lights. It was the Slade van, but they didn't stop. We kept walking for hours, and there were few cars passing by and no lights, just trees along the road. Everything was closed when we reached a village where we found an open pub with three people inside. A drunken guy at the bar said he could drive us back for 1,000 Belgian francs (25 Euros). It was more than we could afford so we kept walking to the nearest train station, taking the first train home in the morning. We walked about 20 miles that night.

ANCIENNE BELGIQUE
26 OCTOBER 1980, BRUSSELS, BELGIUM

I WAS THERE: PHILIPPE DE KEMMETER

I got home at 7am and my father was angry, telling me I couldn't go to the concert in Brussels that night. I felt really down and was in a bad mood all day. I told my mother I needed to visit a friend and ran from home, taking the bus and then the Metro to the centre of Brussels, where Slade were to play the Ancienne Belgique. The concert had begun when I arrived. It was a great atmosphere, with toilet paper flying throughout. When Slade left the stage, the lights came on but the audience kept shouting and stomping. They eventually came back to play 'Hear Me Calling'. It was absolutely great. There was a time when I would do almost anything to see Slade live. I would even lie to my mum and dad. I don't regret it.

SLADE SMASHES! RELEASED 1 NOVEMBER 1980

Released by Polydor to cash in on the renewed interest in the band following their Reading Festival appearance, Slade Smashes! *reaches No. 21 on the UK album charts.*

CIVIC HALL
7 DECEMBER 1980, WOLVERHAMPTON, UK

I WAS THERE: TREVOR WEST

I was fortunate to see the original line up of Slade 38 times. My first Slade gig was my first gig, full stop, at Sheffield City Hall at the tender age of 15. The date of Tuesday, 3rd May 1977 is burned in my memory. My last gig, in December 1983, was at the Palais in my home town of Nottingham. I met the band many times pre- and post-gig both during those years and at various TV shows and other events afterwards and, with a couple of fellow Slade fans, I formed a band, Pouk Hill Prophetz, in deference to Slade when we were all in our fifties.

I've seen pretty much every band or artist on my wish list, but Slade as a live act were peerless. No special effects, no dancers, no big screens or pyros (okay, they used a single one on the Christmas 1983 tour). They just let the music, their energy and their showmanship do the talking for them. Dave Hill preening, Jimmy Lea running around like a banshee whether it was with a bass or a violin, stripped to the waist, the musicians' musician. Don Powell beating seven bells out his kit. And then, there was Nod. Noddy Holder, the greatest front man I've ever seen. The best crowd controller. A voice that could blister paint from 20 yards away. The only singer I've seen who could stand at the back of the stage, ten yards from his mic, and still be heard above the band anywhere in the venue. He didn't just shout though, as even a cursory listen to the *Slade Alive!* album will testify. He could sing. It's just that he could sing far louder than anybody else! He needed to. The band as a whole were loud. Incredibly loud.

Three shows stand out. They played two shows over consecutive nights at Cleethorpes Bunny's Club in August 1978 and me and a mate went to both. Nod made it onto the front page of *The Sun* newspaper whilst we were there, having had his nose broken by a bouncer a couple of nights before during a gig in Porthcawl. With his nose suitably patched up, Nod said 'the show must go on'. And it did. Bunny's was a typical chicken-in-a-basket venue with an audience mainly suited and booted. Slade played there several times over the years. On one occasion they had a small riser built at the front of the stage. It lasted less than five minutes before it was stormed by fans and collapsed.

After the City Centre Club gig in Coventry in May 1979, I had to sleep overnight in a freezing cold bus station, as happened on many occasions post-gig. Me and Nomis (another one of the 'Magic 500') got on stage with the band to sing the choruses of 'Cum On Feel The Noize' at Dave Hill's mic. I couldn't hear our voices, which was probably just as well! It wasn't unusual for fans to get on stage with them, and the band often tolerated it. It's not something I could imagine any bands doing nowadays.

Their hometown gig at Wolverhampton Civic in December 1980, following their Reading Festival appearance, sold out instantly. I've never witnessed an atmosphere like it, before or since. Within a couple minutes of the support band finishing their set, and a good 30 to 40 minutes before Slade were due to take the stage, the entire crowd (and I do mean everybody in the crowd, not just those at the front) burst into 'You'll Never Walk Alone'. It made the hairs stand up on the back of the neck. The band were on fire, as they always were. They played five or six encores that night as the crowd simply wouldn't let them leave the stage. It was my favourite Slade gig of the lot.

SHOULDER OF MUTTON

8 DECEMBER 1980, HARDSTOFT, UK

I WAS THERE: JOHN RANDALL

I saw Slade in concert at the Shoulder of Mutton. It was a small venue and at the time they were riding high after appearing at Reading Festival. I remember the venue being absolutely packed with fans, and everyone had such a great time. Slade were always brilliant live, and this was no exception. I also remember the venue floor being covered with glass beer bottles, and not one was broken. Great memories.

I WAS THERE: RICHARD LEIVERS

My brother's ten years older than me and was bringing Beatles records home so I was a big Beatles fan. But next to The Beatles, Slade are my favourite group of all time. What attracted me to Slade was the fact that they wrote their own music and they had these cosmic number ones. In the Seventies, I grew my sideburns and grew my hair the same as Noddy Holder. I played guitar. And my friend from work was the double of Dave Hill. We used to stand in his bedroom and I'd play guitar and he'd play drums to Slade records.

They were going on tour and did a couple of warm up gigs in the Shoulder of Mutton at a little place outside Chesterfield called Hardstoft. The tickets went on sale in Chesterfield for five pounds each. I think the first show was the beginning of November. They were just getting everything ready, tightening things up for the tour. They sang 'Merry Xmas Everybody' in November. Noddy Holder was shouting, 'You're all mad! You're all crazy – it's November!' – with a few well-chosen swear words in the middle, but he was conducting everybody and everybody was singing it. They did some new stuff but a lot of the old stuff, 'Gudbuy T' Jane' and all this.

And they came back on 8th December to do another show, because they had a few more things they wanted to tidy up. I remember waking up the next morning and hearing that John Lennon had been shot. It was one of those 'you remember where you were' moments. They'd met Lennon in America. They were in this studio recording when he came in. Noddy Holder said John Lennon liking them was the best tribute they ever received.

ROTTERS CLUB

15 DECEMBER 1980, MANCHESTER, UK

I WAS THERE: DENISE SOUTHWORTH

They were very much down on their luck and playing a nightclub on Oxford Street in Manchester. The audience was mostly students who would go to any gig rather than particularly Slade fans. Right at the end, for the encore, Noddy came out dressed as Father Christmas, and he said, 'You didn't think we were gonna forget this one, did ya?' and launched into 'Merry Xmas Everybody.'

I've seen them several times since, as the two man Slade, but I don't want to see just with Dave. I want to keep my memories. I've seen Slady and they were great. They came to Manchester and I interviewed them for my radio show. They're nice girls.

I've met all the members of Slade. I've interviewed Don a couple of times via Zoom in Denmark. Nod doesn't do interviews now but I've interviewed Suzan. And I went all the way to Birmingham to meet Jim a few years ago where he was doing something on the BBC and I spent 15 minutes just chatting to him.

Denise has met Jim, Dave and Don

UNIVERSITY OF SURREY

16 JANUARY 1981, GUILDFORD, UK

I WAS THERE: DONNA JONES

At 14 and three-quarter years old, I considered myself a seasoned gig-goer, having seen Blondie and OMD the year before. Oh yes, I was down with the adults now! I was wearing my new Indian-style padded jacket and thought I was the bee's knees. My friend Jackie's older brother Alan took us to this and several gigs in our teens, which was incredibly kind of him considering he was a lot older than us. We must've really destroyed his street cred in hindsight. This was the second gig he took us to, and I knew who Slade were but mainly from a very special Christmas song that I believe is still quite popular.

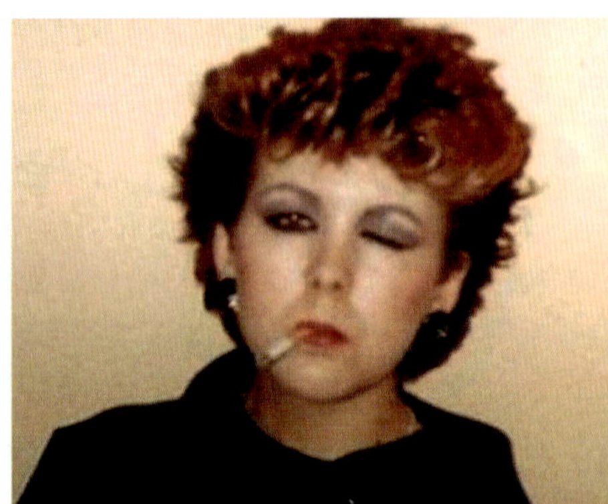

Donna Jones had a thing for Don and Jim which deterred her from going to the stage door

Well, I wasn't prepared for the pure rock 'n' roll I hadn't experienced at the former events. Proper guitars and banging drums, nothing synthesised at all, starting with 'Dizzy Mama', I believe. I was fascinated by Dave Hill. Whenever I'd seen Slade on TV, all I could see was his fringe, earring and platform boots. He didn't disappoint and I think he might have had a cheeky cowboy hat on that night. And Noddy. What a showman. A voice like no other, entertaining was an understatement. I quite fancied Don Powell and Jim Lea, and when I was asked if I wanted to go to the stage door for an autograph, I declined because of my girly new-found admiration. I knew I'd go to pieces.

Some highlights for me were 'Gudbuy T' Jane' and 'Mama Weer All Crazee Now', along with a great cover of 'Somethin' Else'. I can still remember looking around in awe at all the rock fans, those cool men with long hair and denim. It was then that I started growing my hair and became a right royal headbanger by the end of the year. Great times. All thanks to the magic of Slade.

I WAS THERE: STEVE CARVER

Glam rock, eh? I guess it all started with Bowie. My first grown-up concert was Ziggy Stardust at Guildford Civic Hall, May 1973. I started buying the music of David Bowie and Alice Cooper. But Alice was from Phoenix in the USA, and Ziggy was from Mars. I didn't actually think that rock stars could be normal, regular, human beings. Then there was Slade…

Steve Carver, photographed with close friend Paul Weller, was at the University of Surrey to see Slade in January '81

Trying to bask in the light of Bowie's trailblazing glory, every two-bob band in the land started to dye their hair, ditch the denim, order some cheap and nasty nylon threads, slap on some eye shadow and lipstick, and empty a bucket of glitter over their barnets. God, there was some crap out there. Some got it so wrong, like the ridiculous Rubettes, shocking Showaddywaddy, and Mud. What was with the Teddy Boy Glam Revival? Then there was Sweet, obviously a frustrated heavy rock band, Smokie, Wizzard, Mott the Hoople ('Did you see the suits and the platform boots?'), and Roxy Music for the boys (and Suzi Quatro?), and The Bay City Rollers, Marc Bolan & T.Rex, and The Osmonds for the girls. (Are we even gonna mention G*ry G****er?). And then there was Slade…

I guess they entered most music fans' radar in 1971 with 'Get Down And Get With It', when they were flirting with a short-lived skinhead image (which didn't do Dave any favours), and followed up the same year with 'Coz I Luv You', which still has one of my favourite opening lines, 'I won't laugh at you when you boo-hoo-hoo…'.

And that was it, five years of non-stop hits, five years of being the resident house band on the BBC's *Top of the Pops*, five years of rockin' good 45s, equally at home with the foot-stomping, fist-pumping hand-clappers – 'Look Wot You Dun', 'Take Me Bak 'Ome', 'Mama Weer All Crazee Now', 'Gudbuy T' Jane', 'Cum On Feel The Noize', 'Skeeze Me Pleeze Me' – as they were with the beautiful ballads, like 'Everyday' and 'How Does it Feel?'.

Maybe, just maybe, 'Merry Xmas Everybody' done them a disservice, future generations thinking they were a one-hit wonder, novelty Christmas band (although the annual royalty cheque must help).

I only saw Slade in concert twice, including one at Guildford's University of Surrey on the *We'll Bring The House Down* tour. It was summer, and the place was like a furnace. The band came back for an encore, and Noddy asked for requests. Somewhat predictably, the sweat-drenched audience demanded 'Merry Xmas Everybody'. Noddy laughed and said, 'Shall we?' As the steaming crowd bellowed every word, I couldn't help thinking, that surely happens every gig.

About ten years ago, I caught a Slade/Sweet winter tour. I sat next to Andy Scott in the pub. By now, Slade were just Don Powell on drums and Dave Hill. It was a trip down memory lane for me, a chance to hear those magnificent songs one more time. Once again, they encored with 'Merry Xmas Everybody'. I had to smile. Dave wore a hat through the entire show, exited stage right and reappeared with a Santa hat. I wondered to myself if his flowing locks were actually attached to both pieces of headwear.

And then there was Slade, one of the finest British bands to ever tread the boards. Maybe they don't always get the credit they deserve. PLAY VERY LOUD.

GAUMONT THEATRE
17 JANUARY 1981, IPSWICH, UK

I WAS THERE: MURRAY FORSYTH

I saw them at the Ipswich Regent in the early Eighties. It was a long time ago and my memory is a bit hazy, but out of all the live bands I've seen, they are close to the best ever! Each member was at the peak of their abilities and Jimmy Lea was outstanding! His violin and bass guitar playing was out of this world, the first time I saw a bass player play bass like it was a lead guitar. However, the rest of the band were also awesome, better and much louder than I ever expected, as a lot of their contemporaries are not as good live as they are on recordings. Quite the opposite with Slade, who were much better live than in the studio!

'WE'LL BRING THE HOUSE DOWN' RELEASED
23 JANUARY 1981

Slade's first UK Top 40 single since 1977, peaking at No.10.

FRIARS
24 JANUARY 1981, AYLESBURY, UK

I WAS THERE: GAVIN FLETCHER

I didn't have to wait too long to see them again. My friend Neill Brown and I went to see them at our local haunt, Aylesbury Friars. During the gig,

Dave broke a string on his guitar and while he was sorting it out Jim began an impromptu version of T.Rex's 'Hot Love'. 'Marc lives!' shouted Noddy, when Jim finished. We'd heard just prior to this gig that if you hung around for long enough there was a chance you might be allowed into the dressing room to meet the group. In case this was true, I took the cover of my *Sladest* album in the hope of getting it signed. While we were waiting to be allowed in, we saw a heavily built guy in a brown leather jacket go past and down a nearby staircase. My friend shouted, 'That's Chas Chandler!' so we caught him up and got him to sign our album covers.

Shortly after, we were allowed into the dressing room. Jim and Don were talking quietly with what looked like friends or family. Noddy briefly acknowledged us and was drinking Jack Daniels, swigging straight from the bottle. Dave was really friendly and spoke to us for quite some time. 'We'll Bring The House Down' had just been released and Dave was eager to know if we'd bought the single yet (which we had) and was interested in which shop (WH Smith).

We also saw Slade in Oxford, probably in May 1981. We had seats in the front row of the balcony. The only thing I remember is that we could literally feel the balcony bouncing up and down in time with the music. Fantastic! We usually found we had ringing in our ears for about two days after each gig due to the loudness.

The next time we saw them was December 1981 at Hammersmith Odeon. We'd been to see Adam and the Ants at the Theatre Royal, Drury Lane a few days earlier, where the stage set was similar to what you might find at a pantomime – a shipwrecked galleon in the first half, then a recreation of the set from the 'Prince Charming' video for the second half. The Slade set at the time was more down to earth – a picture of an ear with a nail through it, hanging up behind the band!

VICTORIA HALL

19 FEBRUARY 1981, STOKE-ON-TRENT, UK

I WAS THERE: NICK LATHAM

I first got into Slade in the early Seventies, when they were always having hits. My friend and next-door neighbour, Chris, was already a fan and asked me to listen to some of the records he'd bought of theirs. At the time, 'Mama Weer All Crazee Now' was at No.1. And that was it, I was sold. I started collecting all the records (on the red Polydor label), then started to play them to all my friends, and they jumped on board too. Slade's music was great, all the tunes catchy. We'd go to our local youth club and dance to their stuff when it came on (which was a lot), all wearing Doc Martens boots, jeans and t-shirts, which Slade kind of embodied until they started getting outrageous with the glam rock outfits.

Nick Latham was at the Victoria Hall

When the film *Slade In Flame* came out, I remember being dead excited about its release. I was 14 or 15 and went to the cinema on my own on release and fully enjoyed it, feeling it gave a great flavour of what it was like to see them live. I bought it on DVD a few years ago, the first time I'd watched it since the Seventies, and I still really enjoyed it. It still stands up, whereas a lot of those types of films with bands in them can fall flat when you watch them now.

As it was, things died down a bit towards the mid to late-Seventies when disco seemed to take off, largely down to John Travolta and *Saturday Night Fever*, and around the time Slade were trying to conquer America. When they returned, the music scene had changed, the Punk scene was taking off and we had the beginnings of the New Wave Of British Heavy Metal. And for a number of years they were, I guess, unfashionable.

I moved on myself, with nightclubs and pubs and chasing girls deemed more important. Having been born in 1962, by the end of the Seventies I was in my late teens and I'd started working as a figure painter for Wedgwood. Like most people of my age, I was influenced by what was on TV or played in bars and so on, so for a short time funk and disco took hold. And back then, if it wasn't on the radio or TV, you heard little about what was going on in the music scene.

Then came 1980 and Reading Festival, by which time a lot of my friends were listening to heavy rock and I moved away from funk and disco, starting to listen to the likes of AC/DC, Rainbow, Deep Purple, and Whitesnake. Then, partially due to Slade's success at Reading and the LP that followed, *We'll Bring The House Down*, they magically adopted the heavy rock scene, and it was as if they'd never been away, climbing the charts again.

By this point I hadn't been to any live concerts. I was 19 when Slade announced a tour for the aforementioned album and a show at the Victoria Hall in Hanley. It was relatively local to me, living in a small village called Madeley, near Keele University, and I wasn't going to miss this one. I can't remember the opening song but the atmosphere in the hall that night was palpable. They rocked the socks off us all night, and their performance and a good-looking girl in the balcony giving me the eye all night made for a magic moment I reflect back on even today. Noddy Holder was one hell of a frontman, and I've seen a lot since then – including Freddie Mercury – but none have I seen pull a crowd in and get them up and moving like Noddy could.

I didn't get the girl that night. I lost sight of her in the crush to get outside. But that night sparked off my love for seeing live music.

WEARMOUTH HALL, SUNDERLAND POLYTECHNIC

21 FEBRUARY 1981, SUNDERLAND, UK

I WAS THERE: PETER SMITH

Slade were starting to fill concert halls again, and toured relentlessly throughout 1981. Wearmouth Hall was ram-packed with students and heavy rock fans who gave Slade the returning heroes' welcome they deserved. It was great to see them back filling halls again, and you could tell how much Noddy, Dave, Jim and Don were enjoying their new-found stardom.

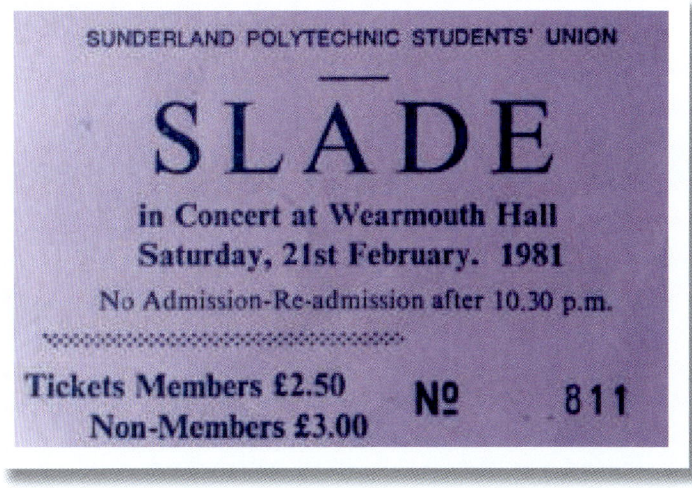

Peter Smith saw Slade at Sunderland Poly's Wearmouth Hall in 1981

Even the programme for the tour emphasised the heavy nature of the new, reborn Slade. The cover featured a fist pushing its way through a shield, the knuckles tattooed with letters spelling 'SLADE'. The sound was much heavier, as were the new hits. The band had clearly latched on to their success at Reading and were determined to capitalise on this by taking on a new heavy rock, almost heavy metal image and sound. This worked well. The new hits were great. The performance was loud and rocky as before, and Noddy was on top form, clearly enjoying his renewed fame. These guys knew the business, knew how to rock, and were having a ball!

CARDIFF UNIVERSITY

28 FEBRUARY 1981, CARDIFF, UK

I WAS THERE: ALUN PERKINS

The second time I saw Slade I went on my own. They had suffered a bit of a decline in recent years but in early 1981 they were back in favour, and this was an absolutely storming gig.

The last time I saw them live was again in Cardiff, on 14th December 1981 at Sophia Gardens Pavilion. This was another great night and, again, I went on my own. By chance I bumped into about half a dozen school pals in the hall when the band was on and I remember us dancing and singing together when Slade played 'Merry Xmas Everybody'. It was really good to see Slade enjoying success again after some lean years.

I also had a ticket to see them at Cardiff Top Rank/Mayfair on 30th November 1983, but the gig was cancelled after Slade were invited to appear on *Top of the Pops* to promote 'My Oh My'. I didn't find out until I arrived at the venue. What a disappointment, and it was never rescheduled.

APOLLO THEATRE
5 MARCH 1981, MANCHESTER, UK

I WAS THERE: PAUL GUY BEDFORD

I must have been 12 or 13 when I first heard them on the radio, and I loved the Glam Rock sound. Coming from a large family and being the youngest, I have a wide range of musical taste, but really only had one love – rock. I think it was 'Coz I Luv You' or 'Gudbuy T' Jane' that I heard first. I was only a youngster, but it was a new sound, catchy and (Glam) rocky! I saw them on the *We'll Bring The House Down* tour and they were absolutely awesome! It was a packed house.

WE'LL BRING THE HOUSE DOWN RELEASED
13 MARCH 1981

Released on the appropriately-named Cheapskate Records, Slade's ninth album has a running time of just over 30 minutes and recycles some tracks from 1979's Return To Base. *It reaches No.25 in the UK album charts.*

I WAS THERE: IAN ASHLEIGH

We'll Bring the House Down capitalised on the 1980 Reading Festival interest and attracted new fans. Some of the tracks were from 1979's disappointing *Return to Base*, but the band sounded rejuvenated and back on form.
The title track gave Slade a Top Ten UK hit single, while 'Wheels Ain't Coming Down' told of a real experience Holder and Lea had flying from Los Angeles to San Francisco, and 'When I'm Dancing, I Ain't Fighting' is the Slade us original 'Sladeheads' knew and loved, every one of their heyday singles rolled into one, and just a huge smile of a song.

WH SMITH
MARCH 1981, GUILDFORD, UK

I WAS BAK 'OME: ALEX CHESTERTON

I grew up with music around me. My father was tone deaf and insisted on singing along to folk songs by The Spinners, who managed to sound even more tuneless in their rendition of 'I'm A Rambler'. My mother listened to the soundtracks of musicals like *Cats* and *Evita*, and I soon knew the words to 'Don't Cry For Me Argentina'. My brother was fairly conservative in his tastes, with ELO and Pink Floyd occasionally heard from his bedroom, but his first love was (and is) football, hence my ability to recall the lyrics of 'Blue Is The Colour'.

But my big sister had some proper tunes, including a lot of David Bowie, so 'Life On Mars' and 'Space Oddity' are amongst my favourite tracks. She lent me her AC/DC albums and *Man in the Bowler Hat* by Stackridge when I was about twelve. (I must give them back one day.) In these influential days, my mother randomly bought me two singles; ABBA's 'Knowing Me Knowing You' (aha), followed by a thankfully much cooler 'Rat Race' by The Specials.

But it was 1981 when I finally walked a mile into Guildford town centre, up to WH Smith, to purchase my first two (99p) singles with my own money! One was the appallingly un-PC dreadful novelty record by Joe Dolce, 'Shaddap You Face'. Luckily, I redeemed myself by purchasing 'We'll Bring the House Down' by Slade. And, of course, it is the latter that I list as the first record I ever bought.

STADTHALLE
30 APRIL 1981, OFFENBACH, GERMANY

I WAS THERE: JÜRGEN PETTKE

I saw Slade as the opening act for Whitesnake in Offenbach, Germany. They were fantastic and on fire. The encore was totally enthusiastic!

Jurgen Pettke saw Slade at Offenbach

LOCHEM FESTIVAL, DE ZANDKUIL OPENLUCHTHEATER

28 MAY 1981, LOCHEM, NETHERLANDS

I WAS THERE: KEES DE WIT

The primary bands at this festival were The Kinks and Mother's Finest, but Slade stole the show, playing 'Gudbuy T' Jane', 'Hear Me Calling', and 'Mama Weer All Crazee Now'. Afterwards I was so sick because the weather was bad and I had too much alcohol in my body. That, and standing very close to the speakers! I have also seen Slade II in Enschede. They played the old songs and their new songs. It was nice but they were so much better with Jim Lea and Noddy Holder.

MONSTERS OF ROCK FESTIVAL

22 AUGUST 1981, DONINGTON PARK, UK

I WAS THERE: CAZZY

I grew up with Slade – their posters were on my wall, *Slade Alive!* was the first album I ever bought, closely followed by *Play It Loud*, which wasn't easy to get hold of – I had to order it from our local record shop. They were the first band I ever got into. You could say that they set my life path. I first saw them

Cazzy was at Donington

on *Lift Off With Ayshea*, an after-school children's TV show, playing 'Coz I Luv You', and it was like being hit by lightning. *Slade Alive!* was so much heavier than seeing them on TV, so getting into heavy rock was a natural progression.

I actually won tickets to go to *Monsters of Rock* at the Sounds Atomic Rock Show featuring More, at a backstreet club called The Stone Garden, near the Apollo at Ardwick Green, Manchester. The contest involved pretending to be Angus Young… and I won. It helped that the others didn't take it seriously.

It had been absolutely bucketing it down, as is traditional for the great British summertime. It was also cold, or maybe it was just that we were so wet. We had taken bright dayglo-orange survival sacks to keep dry, so we held sack races to warm ourselves up. Then Slade came on and suddenly the cold didn't matter.

I had never seen them live before, and they were pretty much bottom of the bill, but I just remember the sheer energy when they hit the stage! We weren't close to the front, but we had a pretty good vantage point to see the crowd start bouncing.

After a while, with the cold and the damp, they were actually steaming. It was like watching a pot simmer. I can't remember the whole set list but seem to remember 'We'll Bring The House Down' and 'Run Runaway'. The crowd were going absolutely mental at the end – no piss bottles for Slade! I couldn't stop smiling. Everyone around me was smiling, it seemed. I said it had been raining. That would be understating the case – the place was an absolute mud bath. There were two hairy biker types – they might've been Hell's Angels, but with the mud it was difficult to tell – stripped to the waist, wrestling in the middle of a colossal mud puddle at the top of hill on the other side of the racetrack, close to the old Dunlop Bridge.

Donington 1981 was the muddiest festival I ever attended. We looked like swamp donkeys when we got home. But it was a great day. Slade went up on that stage before rock aristocracy like Whitesnake and AC/DC and played an absolute blinder.

I WAS THERE: LEE RUFUS

I was quite close to the front at Donington. They stole the show. It was chucking it down. I'll never forget Noddy Holder between songs saying, 'Well, seeing as it's nearly that time of year...' and then proceeding with 'Merry Xmas Everybody', during which the roadies were throwing toilet rolls into the crowd and we were throwing them back. It was an endless stream of tissue – just brilliant. They were on top form, playing all the hits. They were better than Blackfoot, Blue Öyster Cult, Whitesnake and even AC/DC. And I was a massive AC/DC fan.

I WAS THERE: HUW HOWELLS

It was the highlight of the weekend, to see my favourite band from my teenage years at Reading. I had seen them a couple of times before, at Swansea and Llanelli. They rocked the stage that day, the noise was incredible, and fuck, they were back! I felt sorry for the next two bands. They tried, but everyone wanted the Slade back. I saw them at *Monsters of Roc*k too after, and they rocked that stage as well. A great band and great times. And the early Seventies were special – T.Rex, Sweet, Ian Hunter… know what I mean?

I WAS THERE: NICK LATHAM

The next time I saw Slade was the first of many times I attended the *Monsters of Rock* festival, the fore-runner to what is now *Download*. Back then it was a one-day event and I'd mainly gone because Slade were on the bill. They were low on the billing, with Blue Öyster Cult, Whitesnake and AC/DC above them, the latter introducing Brian Johnson as frontman in Bon Scott's place on their *Back in Black* tour. It pretty much poured down all day, but when Slade came on, they got everyone in the mood, Noddy throwing toilet rolls into the crowd, which were then thrown around the crowd of some 30,000. They were without doubt the best act, Noddy at one point pointing out that the bell used by AC/DC on 'Hell's Bells' was 'fucking leaking water' on them due to the rainfall.

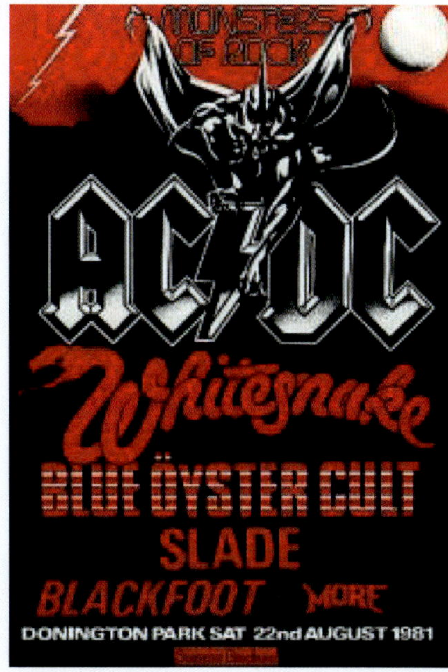

Peter Smith saw Slade again at Monsters of Rock

I WAS THERE: PETER SMITH

By now Slade were well and truly accepted as bona fide members of the heavy metal fraternity, and denim jackets stared to sport Slade patches alongside those of Motörhead, AC/DC, Judas Priest and Iron Maiden. Slade were back and loving it.

Although they were only fourth on the bill, my mates and I made sure we watched their performance. One of my mates (name withheld to protect the innocent) worked for a delivery company and organised a delivery in Birmingham early that morning. We tagged along in the back of his Transit van and, after he dropped off the gear in Birmingham, we went along to Donington. I remember he was quite worried in case anything happened to the works van when it was parked in the field, as he would have been in trouble for taking a van-load of lads along to a pop festival!

Slade used the opportunity to solidify their position as a new heavy rock band. They had a bunch of new songs, including 'When I'm Dancin' I Ain't Fightin'', 'Lock Up Your Daughters', and 'We'll Bring The House Down'. All of these were poppy but also heavy and rocking. The band had started wearing denim and leather stage costumes. Noddy, and Dave in particular, just loved dressing up! Some of the hits remained in the set, including 'Mama Weer All Crazee Now' and 'Get Down And Get With It', and they would still finish with 'Born To Be Wild'. The crowd lapped it up; I am sure they made some new friends that day.

'LOCK UP YOUR DAUGHTERS' RELEASED 4 SEPTEMBER 1981

'Lock Up Your Daughters' reaches No.29.

TILL DEAF DO US PART RELEASED 13 NOVEMBER 1981

Slade's tenth studio album reaches No.68 on the UK charts.

I WAS THERE: IAN ASHLEIGH

Till Deaf Us Do Part gave a minor hit single and a future live set favourite, 'Lock Up Your Daughters', but for fans who had embraced heavy rock this was Slade not sure whether to go the whole way and reinvent themselves as a heavy rock band or continue to try to appeal to the fans they attracted ten years before, with 'A Night to Remember' a case in point, a piece of quality heavy rock that could have been at the core of the album.

LATE 1981

Chas Chandler sells his Cheapskate shares and negotiates Slade's deal with RCA, the band effectively managing themselves.

We've a lot of lovely memories with Chas, and he was so integral in what happened to us. He really believed in us, even though it took a few years before it happened. He kept on slogging away, and he'd been there, done it, got a t-shirt. **Don Powell**

WINTER GARDENS

13 DECEMBER 1981, BOURNEMOUTH, UK

I WAS THERE: STEVE SLATER

Growing up in the early Seventies, I got to hear a lot of chart music thanks to my much older brothers – Wizzard, Sweet and even Paul Gadd, aka Gary Glitter were just a few that were played. But one group stood out – Slade. From 'Coz I Love You' to 'Far Far Away', I loved them from the age of five!

Time moves on and musical tastes change, and although Slade hung on through Punk, Disco and New Wave, it seemed that by 1979-80 they were all done and ready to split up. But filling in for Ozzy Osbourne at the 1980 Reading Festival at the last minute, Slade took to the stage and blew the audience away. There were no magic stage shows or lighting, just a plain rock 'n' roll group that really needed to be seen live to appreciate their power. Some months after Reading, they released a live EP and did a small tour. I'd never seen a really famous band before (Val Doonican doesn't count) and I was twelve and just getting into the 2-Tone/skinhead youth cult when my brother Dave surprised me with a ticket to see Slade. I was both excited and a little nervous at the thought of seeing this band that had been a constant in my life since I was five years old. In the run up to the concert, I remember studying the tickets my brother had purchased:

Steve Slater was a 12-year-old skinhead when he saw Slade at Bournemouth's Winter Gardens

Slade at Bournemouth Winter Gardens, December 13, 1981, price £3 standing.

The night came and, after queuing for half an hour, we got in and made our way downstairs at the Winter Gardens. (In my opinion, one of the best small to medium-sized venues in the UK; the sound was phenomenal but it has sadly been demolished and all we have now is the awful Bournemouth International Centre.) With a crowd around 1,200 to 1500 in attendance, I was somewhat out of place being so young and with my grade one crewcut, Harrington, Ben Sherman, Sta-Prest and DMs. I remember David gently pushing me to the front of the stage. (There was no health and safety nonsense then.) I was right at the front and feet away from Noddy and co. The band were everything I thought they would be, basically doing the live Reading set plus a few other of their classics.

Halfway through the set, after Dave Hill climbed down off his Marshall stack, I noticed he was staring at me. He then proceeded to walk over to the front of the stage and started rubbing my almost bald head. He proceeded to keep on doing this at the end of every song!

Thanks to my brother David, I have a wonderful memory to look back on and a personal interaction with Mr Hill. Years later, Dave released his book and I attended a book talk and signing session where I reminded Dave what he had done. He didn't remember it but he said, 'Oh, that sounds like something I'd do!' So there it is, a small but very cherished memory of my first gig, and all of the thanks goes to my brother David, for surprising me with the ticket.

SOPHIA GARDENS

14 DECEMBER 1981, CARDIFF, UK

I WAS THERE: IAN PETKO-BUNNEY

The last time I saw Slade was at Sophia Gardens in Cardiff, at the time of 'We'll Bring The House Down'. The day after, the weight of the snow on the roof of Sophia Gardens meant the roof fell in – so they did indeed bring the house down. It was so intense seeing them live. They'd stopped wearing a lot of the Glam outfits. Noddy was funny, with a lot of the patter between songs. And the songs were always happy, get-up-and-go kind of songs. Basic rock 'n' roll. I loved it then and love it now.

They were pretty well recorded, not too serious, and always a lot of fun. Whoever wrote the script for *Slade in Flame* really got a good sense of who they were. I think it surprised them. Jim became even more cerebral. Who knows where Noddy's head was at when he decided to call it a day? Everybody now thinks he wanted to do other things, such as the acting. I wonder what he thinks now? But he made his money and perhaps he just didn't want to do it anymore. It must be tiring, and it must get boring. The three times I saw them, they started with 'Hear Me Calling', a great song, but it was a very formulaic show. You kind of knew where it was going. But I liked that. I still like that.

CITY HALL
18 DECEMBER 1981, NEWCASTLE-UPON-TYNE, UK

I WAS THERE: PETER SMITH

The last time I saw the original line-up live in concert, Slade were where they should be, performing to sold-out concert halls up and down the country. It was great to see them back at the City Hall after years of playing much smaller venues. They were very clearly enjoying themselves, and it being close to Christmas festivities, of course they played *that* song. We were a few rows from the front, and my ears were ringing for days afterwards. The set was very similar to that I saw them perform at Sunderland Polytechnic some months earlier. But, although I didn't realise it, the end of the band was soon to come.

DE MONTFORT HALL
25 MARCH 1982, LEICESTER, UK

I WAS THERE: STEVE MASON

I saw Slade live twice, first at Baileys in Leicester in 1979 and then again following their Reading success at De Montfort Hall, on the *We'll Bring The House Down* tour. There were about 50 at the first event, and a full house that next time. I managed to get on stage at De Montfort Hall during the encore, and I didn't get chucked off!

APOLLO THEATRE
26 MARCH 1982, GLASGOW, UK

I WAS THERE: NOMIS BAURLEY

I saw them another 23 times in 1982, a March tour of the bigger venues followed by another tour in December, at a mixture of colleges but also now city halls, finishing with two nights at Hammersmith Odeon and two at Birmingham Odeon.

By now, my duties included blowing up balloons (with no pump) and runs to Hasty Tasty to get Dave Hill his regular milkshakes. Slade's riders in the late Seventies were almost non-existent. I often got sent out shopping with £20 to buy a bottle of vodka, a bottle of whisky and as many beers as I could with what money was left. I was sent out bog roll shopping many a time, and also to go and buy Scholl foot pads that Don stuck on his bass drum skin to stop it splitting. I helped with a spotlight a few times when that was the task of whoever was available (usually the truck drivers) to earn a few quid.

Nomis (Simon Baurley) has seen Slade more than anyone else

That March tour included my first time at the wonderful Glasgow Apollo. They were still riding the wave. I did seven gigs in March, bearing in mind I still had a full-time job and was seeing lots of other bands. I managed 15 gigs that December in a mixed bag of venues – from universities to those Odeon finales. They hired a whole suite in what was the posh Midland hotel for their two nights in Brum, although they all lived local. Don got so drunk that they only found him an hour before stage time for the second gig, the last of the tour. It was my 21st birthday and Don gave me a half-drunk litre bottle of Smirnoff. Wish I'd kept the bottle.

They let me sleep in the back of the merch van between gigs, although I got a bollocking for leaving the light on and flattening the battery.

I WAS THERE: JOHN MILNE

The band were fantastic that night. I asked Haden Donovan if my son could meet Slade so we went into their dressing room and Noddy said 'your son has grown up'. We chatted away and they offered us food and drink. A couple of years later, on 6th March 1985, Don Powell Milne was born. We had 'Mysterious Mr Jones' played on the radio for him. Two days after that, Nod and Don were in Glasgow to promote the single.

The Milne family meet Mr Holder

VICTORIA HALL

1 APRIL 1982, HANLEY, STOKE-ON-TRENT

I WAS THERE: MARK MILLICENT

I was now a 21-year-old art student, at the same Victoria Hall venue in Hanley. Styles had changed but Slade were back on top, and I was back down the front. That was all that mattered. The crowd surged, as before but maybe more. 'We're in Noddy's army!' was chanted over and over as well as the intro to 'We'll Bring The House Down' as the lights went down...

The little red power indicators of the Hiwatt stacked equipment glowing beneath black covers were the only illumination. Anticipation – a brief quiet then the roar as you knew they were taking the stage in the darkness – wham! – noise – lights – action! The 'Rock And Roll

Preacher' was laying down a sermon that would be ringing in your ears for days. The first few chords of that stormer rang out from Nod's Gibson SG. Down at the front, 'Nod's army' swayed and jumped as one. Slade did what they did best and rocked the post-Reading Festival renaissance that was the early Eighties, playing the first track from new LP, *Till Deaf Do Us Part*.

Years of touring and honing their skills made Slade live a surgical attack on the senses, Nod in this incarnation dressed in black as the Southern preacher, frock coat, flat black-brimmed hat, bootlace tie, blue Kickers boots, knees bent and a maniacal smile as the energy shot through the crowd like a thunderbolt of sound.

The enthusiastic crowd again surged in waves of adulation as before, but this time there were no seats. You had no chance of remaining in the same spot as you were crushed and dragged by the sheer power of the energy that a solid mass of jumping post-teenage rocking headbangers can generate. It was hot, it was sweaty, it was Slade!

Dave preened and strutted as before while Jim pounded out the bass and some virtuoso violin to Don's driving drums. The wall of sound that fills your ears and the 4,000-seat auditorium still rings in my head clear and loud, and if I'm honest my heart today. The set was electric, finishing with an encore of 'Cum On Feel The Noize', and we the attendant crowd did. I still do. Two encores and an hour and ten minutes later it was done.

Gene Kelly's 'Singing In The Rain' drifted over the PA, as it did after every Slade gathering. Ears ringing, I was soaked in my own sweat and probably that of a few other people, and just like that an era was over. Thanks for the memories, Nod, Jim, Don, and Dave.

UNIVERSITY OF EAST ANGLIA

3 DECEMBER 1982, NORWICH, UK

I WAS THERE: PETE KEELEY

I was eight-and-a-half (the half was very important back then) when Slade first encroached on my world. *Top of the Pops* was watched religiously on a Thursday evening in our house, and in the middle of

1971, we sat down to watch and suddenly this foghorn voice blared out.

Well alright everybody, let your hair down…
Want to see everybody get up off their seat,
Clap your hands, stamp your feet, get down get with it!

And the way they looked! I was full of wonder and hooked from that moment. Although I don't think my parents were that impressed with the stomping around the room, me and my brothers would do every time it came on the telly or the radio over the next few weeks. For the next three or four years, the week was always improved when Slade were on *Top of the Pops* (it seemed that they were on most weeks), and there was a constant stream of misspelt hits (I loved the misspelling) to fall in love with. Then they stopped having hits and the *Top of the Pops* appearances dried up. But Punk was just around the corner, and I'd find a new obsession.

I was too young to see Slade live at the height of their fame, but in December 1982, in my last days as a teenager, they were doing the college circuit, and played the UEA in Norwich for a Christmas gig. By then I was working in a record shop and lapping up the latest Post-Punk and Indie singles by the bucketload. But I couldn't resist the chance to see Slade live, helped by the fact that I could get in free. They didn't disappoint and I was pleasantly surprised to see a large contingent of the Norwich punks at the gig, along with a lot of the John Peel-listening customers from the record shop. They didn't disappoint, and Noddy's voice sounded terrific. They did 'Get Down And Get With It', and the thrill was still there for me, same it was as an eight-and-a-half-year-old. And they finished with the obligatory 'Merry Xmas Everybody', and I felt like a kid again.

These days, the Slade single I most return to (and still play it regularly, despite the fact it's disappointingly spelled correctly) is 'How Does It Feel?'. This was the first Slade single not to go top ten after they broke through with 'Get Down And Get With It'. Its wistfulness still gets me every time, and although I still love all those raucous hits, it's their ballad that most speaks to me and remains one of my favourite-ever singles.

STUDENTS' UNION KEELE UNIVERSITY

7 DECEMBER 1982, STAFFORD, UK

I WAS THERE: NICK LATHAM

The third time I saw Slade was on their tour to promote *Till Deaf Do Us Part*, again at the Victoria Theatre, Hanley. It kicked off with Noddy's back to the audience, the sound of thunder, and lightning streaking across the stage. He'd dressed all in black, with a black preacher's hat on, wearing a vicar's dog collar, opening with 'Rock and Roll Preacher (Hallelujah I'm On Fire)', belted out 'for those about to rock and those about to roll in Hanley tonight'. Then there was a loud bang and the rest of the band came out, the audience soon moving as one and the two-hour party off and running, never straying from that high tempo. It was a great night, and I couldn't wait to see them again. Unfortunately, there was no lovely lady to wink and wave to in the gallery this time.

Later that year, I heard they were playing the Students' Union at Keele University, just up the road from where I lived. I wasn't going to miss that, and went with the usual suspects, the event made more special by it not being long before Christmas. I wasn't to know it, but this was to be the last time I saw Slade with Noddy fronting the band, and it turned out to be the best time, and possibly the best concert I've ever seen. Not because they had amazing lighting or any gimmicks, but because of the intimacy of the venue which, being pretty small, only held perhaps 500 or 600.

We got in early and were very close to the stage. Noddy repeated his 'Rock and Roll Preacher' opening and, like last time, it was a party from beginning to end. We danced, sang and jumped around for the whole two hours. Noddy swapped his famous mirrored hat for a Santa hat for 'Merry Xmas Everybody', which was all the more poignant at that time of year.

I got separated from my friends, so walked back to the car alone, waiting for them to turn up. It was a cold December night, with a light snow falling. The denim jacket I'd worn was soaked through with sweat from being in a crammed crowd and moving around all night, and it was now steaming.

In the early 2000s, I got to see Dave Hill and Don Powell's Slade. Jim's place by then was taken by a guy who used to play for Mud and Noddy's by a singer who looked like Brian Johnson. The show was once again in the Victoria Hall, where I'd seen them twice before all those years earlier. I bumped into a friend I'd gone to those gigs with, having not seen him for years, and it was good to catch up. Gig-wise though, it was quite a let-down, much as I loved Dave and Don. Sometimes you're best remembering them as they were in their heyday.

I got to see Noddy again too, when he did a talk in Buxton, around 2013. That was brilliant, with him telling stories of his life with Slade along with ones about Ozzy Osbourne and a stuffed bear, and another about Noddy and the rest of Slade arriving in America and getting in a van at the airport meant for the crew rather than the Cadillac laid on for the band.

On entering this venue, there was a chance to write down a question and put it in a box. As it happened, mine got read out, asking if he'd really been offered the lead singer role with AC/DC in 1980 after Bon Scott's tragic death (I was a massive AC/DC fan). It was an excellent evening, and when I left people were queuing outside, as there were rumours Noddy was going to sign autographs. I joined the queue and sure enough he came out, so I got him to sign his autobiography and a *Slade Alive!* CD. I shook his hand and thanked him for making amazing music and so many memories.

Would I like them to reform for one last concert? Yes, of course. Do I think that will ever happen? Very unlikely, even more so after Dave sacked Don.

I WAS THERE: MICHAEL WEST

They were past their glory days, but we were all young teenagers when they were at the top, so it was the perfect gig for a bunch of 20-year-olds. The Students' Union was full to the brim. They played all the standards and you could tell they were having a ball, pumping out the tunes. We were pushed right up against the stage, singing all the words with Noddy. And we sweated buckets!

SLADE ON STAGE RELEASED 11 DECEMBER 1982

Slade on Stage *is released, recorded live at Newcastle City Hall on 18th December 1981. It reaches No.58 in the UK album charts.*

CORNWALL COLISEUM
14 DECEMBER 1982, ST AUSTELL, UK

I WAS THERE: ALAN KENT

The Coliseum was a legendary Cornish music venue that could hold about 3,000 people, situated at Carlyon Beach, the hall basically right next to the beach and the ocean. I remember this gig particularly well. I would have been 15 and my friends and I were all into metal and rock. It was *de rigueur* to be into any kind of music of that type in the china clay mining villages around St Austell, as the music seemed to reflect that kind of heavy industry. My parents liked Slade a lot and had a few of their albums, but my interest was reignited in them because they'd become reinvented as new champions of the New Wave Of British Heavy Metal. They played Reading Festival too, which was important for me.

A visit to the Coliseum had some habitual events. It would begin by getting down there and nipping in the restaurant for a Wimpy. You'd always have a stroll on the beach as well – part of the atmosphere. In December it'd be freezing, but it was traditional. Then you'd always have a wander backstage where the barriers and security were, and where the dressing rooms were. My dad's mate, Murray, was a beast of a guy and on security down there. He knew me and would usually be able to get various things signed, but I was too disorganised at that point to bring an album down for the band to sign. At that stage I had *We'll Bring The House Down* and *Till Deaf Do Us Part*.

After trying to see the band backstage, you queued around the front. This was the only way to get down the front of the stage, which we loved. The crowd outside was already going nuts and having fun. It was close to Christmas, with everyone dressed up. It was a very innocent party atmosphere, no drink or drugs or anything like that.

Murray would be on the door for the big opening, and everyone would run in. You'd hand over your ticket, get your stamp on your hand and run down to the front. You wouldn't look at the merchandise stand – that could wait until later. The odd thing about the Coliseum was that, although it was a relatively modern venue, there was this massive pillar in front of the stage about ten metres back from the edge of the stage. If you needed to meet someone at a gig, you'd always say 'meet by the pillar'.

We, however, headed to the front barrier. You needed to get there and hang on, because if you were between there and the pillar, you were in the moshing and pushing danger zone, and at gigs like this it was mental at times, with full-on, violent and aggressive moshing.

Slade began with a shadowy Noddy coming on then speaking the intro to 'Rock and Roll Preacher (Hallelujah I'm On Fire)', a track I loved. Jeez. It was loud – mentally loud. I don't think Slade had much of a production. Basically, it was just a wall of Marshall amps at the back – most false. But whoever was on the sound had it turned up to *Spinal Tap* levels of eleven. I've been to many metal gigs since, but still think Slade destroyed my hearing at an early phase. We were right in front of Noddy and Dave. From what I can remember, Dave was on the right and Jim was on the left. Don's kit was big with lots of old-fashioned wooden drums and lots of cymbal stands etc. There were no projections or images behind the band. Dave was dressed up in his gear; he had a hat on and lots of shiny stuff.

For 'When I'm Dancin' I Ain't Fightin'', the place went nuts. Slade had a very mixed audience. There were metalheads, proggers, people who'd known them in the 1970s, and lots of dangerous skins and punks too. Perhaps not the best mix. I reckon there were a few fights, with the place going apeshit. It was the same with 'Take Me Bak 'Ome'. It only slowed down when, and we got a breather for, them playing 'C'est La Vie', their current single.

Sometime during this half, Jim got out his electric violin, which me and my mates thought was ultra-cool. He did a kind of solo thing. The violin was florescent green. I remember Jim wearing an open-chested shirt with a length of black scarf around his neck. It was somewhere at this point that they did 'Far Far Away', the whole audience swaying, their arms in the air. You could look around and see everyone doing this on the two balconies (seemingly where the older people sat). I think the next song was 'A Night to Remember'.

Noddy would certainly have said hello to the St Austell crowd. This always amused me because St Austell was a small Cornish market town and it always looked funny on the tour shirts next to all these big cities like Birmingham and Manchester. But the Cornish were proud of it because it put them on the map. You have to remember that the Coliseum was also the main gig for anyone from Plymouth and Exeter too.

The maddest and most metal section of the show followed, when they did 'Lock Up Your Daughters', 'Gudbuy T' Jane' and 'We'll Bring The House Down'. I remember the rolling force of Don's drum on the intro to the latter songs. The Coliseum went nuts and I had to grip the barrier rail just to stay in position.

They played 'Get Down And Get With It' next, then encored with 'Mama Weer All Crazee now' and 'Merry Xmas Everybody'. The place went nuts again. Noddy came out wearing a Santa outfit and I remember some kind of confetti coming down from the ceiling. The set didn't seem very long. Slade's songs were generally short, so maybe they could have squeezed a few more in. There were more songs I'd have liked them to have played and I remember being a bit disappointed that some of their other 1970s hits did not get played.

We always hung around after the gig to see if the band came out. Jim and Noddy came out to sign a few things and I remember filing past and shaking their hands. I wish I'd got their autographs, but I learnt my lesson that night. I went home with ears ringing and couldn't hear much the next day in school. It was only later that I realised how amazing it had been to have been at a Slade gig. I'd grown up with them on *Top of the Pops*. To my parents they were recognisable pop stars, not like the rest of the metal I was listening to.

At the end of the gig, I bought a shirt which I wore to death. It fell to pieces and my mother later threw it away.

HAMMERSMITH ODEON

17 & 18 DECEMBER 1982, LONDON, UK

I WAS THERE: GÉRARD GOYER

My third Slade concert was in October 1980 in Lessines, Belgium. Again, I got backstage. My last two Slade shows were at Hammersmith Odeon, where Noddy gave me permission to take a picture of him at the same time as the official photographer. Travelling from Paris to London by train and boat took me three and half hours. A few weeks before my Christmas '82 visit, an article appeared in Wolverhampton's *Express & Star* newspaper about this

Gerard Goyer got backstage at Hammersmith

French fan's passion for Slade.

I WAS THERE: ROY CAPEWELL, AGE 20

I only got to see the original line-up of Slade in concert once. I discovered them via school friends the week 'Cum On Feel The Noize' went straight in at No.1. My liking for them fuelled the basis of an early rebellious phase that should have occurred in my teenage years. After this show, I saw Slade II a couple of times with their first line-up.

I WAS THERE: GAVIN FLETCHER

The last time we saw them live was a year later, December 1982, Hammersmith Odeon again. Elton John was playing a Christmas season there and had had the building wrapped up, so it looked like a huge Christmas present. He had a couple of nights off and on those two nights Slade played. When the group returned for the encore, Noddy was dressed as Santa Claus. He shouted to the audience, 'Has anyone got any requests? You'd better say 'Merry Xmas Everybody'!' After the show was like being in the crowd at a football match. The subway to Hammersmith tube station was absolutely packed with Slade fans, everyone singing the chorus of 'Merry Xmas Everybody'. Brilliant!

I WAS THERE: BRUCE PEGG

This was on my first trip back to Britain after leaving for the US the previous year. Accompanying me was my American fiancée, who was from a small village in central New York State. She had never before stepped foot in the UK. Our first stop was London for a few nights, with my old friend Glenn Williams. On arriving, he told us he'd blagged backstage passes for Slade, and were we interested in going? 'Err… yes, please!' Saturday night was epically sorted.

Saturday evening arrived, and we were among the first to get to the backstage bar. I explained to my fiancée that we were probably going to meet some pretty big stars. 'Just be cool,' I said. 'They're just humans like us.' At that moment, in walked Ozzy Osbourne, with wife Sharon in tow, and I started blithering, 'Fuckin' hell! It's fuckin' Ozzy!' in a voice loud enough for the whole room to hear.

Photo: Richard Houghton

Bruce was backstage at the Odeon

Eventually, we made our way toward the back of the stalls and the band was in full swing. My fiancée didn't know any of the songs, not even set closer, 'Mama Weer All Crazee Now'. As it was the weekend before Christmas, all 3,500 of us in the audience (apart from my fiancée), knew what was going to happen next… a spontaneous sing-song, 'So here it is, Merry Xmas, everybody's havin' fun!', broke out in the crowd as two beautiful young women walked on stage in scanty Santa Claus outfits.

At this point, the whole place went bananas. The band then walked on and launched into 'Merry Xmas Everybody', and everyone (but my fiancée) screamed all the words back to Noddy and the band. 40 years on, I don't think she's fully recovered from the culture shock of that moment.

Afterwards, we went back up to the bar, where Bruce Dickinson of Iron Maiden regaled us with stories of jumping out of elevators and hitting fans with plastic samurai swords during the band's recent Japanese tour. Then we all headed out into the cold London night, where Bruce, Denise Dufort (Girlschool's drummer), Glenn, my fiancée and myself all piled into a nearby phone booth to stay warm while ordering taxis home.

If my fiancée hadn't been traumatised enough by what she had just seen, the 70mph taxi ride on the left of the road through empty London streets early that Sunday morning put her completely over the top. The relationship may have ended a few years later, but the memory of that night lives on forever.

I WAS THERE: TONY ROACH

The last time I saw them was at what was then the Hammersmith Odeon, in December 1982. This was a year or so before their massive return to favour with giant hits 'My Oh My' and 'Run Runaway'. They were flaunting their heavy rock sound from *Till Deaf Do Us Part*, but it was regularly punctuated with Glam stompers like 'Gudbuy T' Jane', 'Mama Weer All Crazee Now' and 'Far Far Away'.

Two immediate memories from that occasion: first, they were loud! You really did Feel The Noize. It vibrated through your ribcage like an earthquake. Second, the cross-section of the audience impressed me. There were kids and pensioners, hippy chick girls, black dudes, Japanese fans, middle-aged couples rubbing shoulders with Mohican-haired punks, Hell's Angel types in studded biker leathers, dancing and joking with bovver-booted skinheads in denim and braces. Really, the most cosmopolitan crowd you could imagine, every one of them having a ball! There wasn't an ounce of trouble, just a groundswell of bonhomie which seemed contagious. The atmosphere in the audience itself was brilliant, let alone what was booming out from the stage...

I've never seen anybody work an audience better than Noddy Holder. He teased us, he jested with us, he thrilled us. My God, that voice – like a pitch-perfect, melodic concrete mixer. If he stood next to the runway at Heathrow, he'd drown out the jet planes! Don Powell behind on the drums: immense, relentless. He had those trademark stick-of-rock stripey drumsticks and he was like a runaway juggernaut. Finally, twin imps springing in, out, up and down either side of Circus Ringmaster Noddy. Jim Lea gave a good impression of Spring-heeled Jack, playing his violin like a man possessed. And he was matched in energy by whirling dervish Dave Hill – resplendent in giant brimmed hat, bandolier and stack-heeled snakeskin boots. I remember him bouncing all over the stage that night, like Tigger on speed, his guitar breaks breath-taking.

All in all, it was the most exhilarating concert I ever attended. We were visited by a musical cyclone that evening, and I didn't see a single person leaving who wasn't smiling and dripping with sweat. A fantastic night.

THE ROUNDHOUSE
1983, CHALK FARM, LONDON, UK

I WAS THERE: GRAHAM JONES, HAIRCUT 100

Graham Jones, back with Haircut One Hundred in 2023, 40 years after that Chalk Farm meeting with Slade in 1983

I was always a Sweet, Slade and T.Rex fan. I was in the Slade fan club as a kid in the early Seventies, and I remember the initial thrill of sending off your stamped, addressed envelope and seeing what would happen, and getting a cartoon image of the four of them and a letter.

I bought 'Skweeze Me, Pleeze Me' with my pocket money, off the racks in the local newsagent in Sydenham, having turned twelve in early July '73 when that – the second of three Slade singles released that year that went straight in at No.1 – was at the top of the UK charts for a second week. I never got to see them live. I was too young, still at school in Forest Hill, South East London. We just had to make do with the wacky outfits. That's what everyone wore in those days – high waisters, tank tops – and there were also some really whacky high-heel creepers that people used to wear.

It's not as if I went out every weekend and bought a record. I think my sister bought a record one month, then I did. It wasn't the kind of thing you did all the time. In those days, they'd sell records on a little carousel in some newsagent's, or you'd buy something from Woolworth's or from specialised record shops. You'd buy it, take it round your friend's house, put it on, you'd play it again and again and again, then listen to the B-side and go 'oh, that's rubbish,' but you might get to like it a bit later on. There's all sorts of things you did with just one record!

The whole class was into Slade then. I was more into rock music, and I was fascinated by Don Powell spinning his stripey drumsticks. I was a massive Sweet fan as well, and Mick Tucker was my favourite drummer. My best mates, Mark and Kevin Trype, lived over the road. They'd come over mine and we'd play a record. I'd have a set of drumsticks – because I was learning drums at school – we'd put a record on, then have a go at drumming along on a pillow, then put it on again and the next person would have a go, and so on, drumming along with the record – the daft things you did!

I only had that one Slade single. You couldn't afford to buy them all. But the charts then… they were exciting times for kids. There wasn't much else to do, really, other than go over to the park or play with your Matchbox cars in the gutter!

In 1983, Haircut 100 were back in the studio at The Roundhouse in Chalk Farm. We were now under the Polydor label, after departing from Arista and recording an album, sadly without Nick (Heyward). Polydor had secured some cheaper studio time, so we'd go there in the evening and go home in the morning. We soon realised we were sharing the complex with Girlschool, who were in the studio down the hallway and were being produced by Jim Lea and Noddy Holder.

We would sometimes hear the heavy guitars blasting out when they opened the studio doors. To let off a bit of steam in between recording, we would record little out-takes and jokes, one of which was a well-known heavy metal track from which our engineer had removed the main vocal using EQ. Les (Nemes) was singing over it for a laugh. Jim Lea suddenly poked his head around the door and said something like, 'Hey, this sounds alright,' until he realised we were just mucking about.

I was in the loo one time when Noddy came in to take a leak, 'Alright, mate, how's it going?' he said. I can't remember my reply.

Nick (Heyward) recently said to me, 'You won't believe who I've been speaking to, Jonesy – Dave Hill!' I said, 'What? Slade Dave Hill?' He said, 'Yeah, we've been having these little chats!' They've become good mates.

'MY OH MY' RELEASED 11 NOVEMBER 1983

Slade's penultimate Top 10 single reaches No.2 in the UK charts.

I WAS THERE: KEVIN MOTTRAM

I was minus seven in 1966, and my folks hadn't even met when the band were known as The 'N Betweens, fellow sons of the historic county of Staffordshire, although in cultural terms, our heroes' Black Country stomping ground (faggots, chips and payz, Banks' Bitter, Highgate Mild) and my own North Staffordshire manor (oatcakes, Draught Bass, Marston's Pedigree) were worlds apart, albeit all housed in one convenient county, which certainly made life fun (especially when Stoke City and Wolves played one another). Nevertheless, that chasm didn't stop our heroes making semi-regular trips up the A34 in the late 1960s to play such long-gone venues as the Golden Torch in Tunstall, the Place in Hanley, the Waggon and Horses in Meir, and my own favourite, the Greenway Inn, a huge 1950s boozer on a miners' estate in Baddeley Green, seven miles down the road from where I type these words (don't look for it; it's not there anymore).

They would have been a tough old crowd, who after a hard week's work down t'pit would have been demanding serious entertainment (and rightly so, it was a bloody dangerous job). This might have crushed the wills of most acts, but only served to sharpen the stagecraft of our fledgling heroes, in particular the MCing skills of future mirror top-hatted ringmaster, young Neville Holder of Walsall. But once you've grabbed the attention of a pub full of miners and got them eating out of the palm of your hand, the small matter of dealing with 18,000 screaming rowdies at Earl's Court was hardly going to be a problem. Just a bigger hall and a bigger crowd, that's all.

But if I wasn't there at Slade's beginnings (or should that be beginningz?), they were there at mine. Alright, Noddy, Jim, Dave and Don weren't in the delivery room at North Staffordshire Maternity Hospital as I literally burst into life on the evening of 21st March 1973. But they were, at that very moment, *numero uno*, toppermost of the poppermost, kings of the heap, the biggest thing since pre-cut bread hit the streets. 'Cum On Feel The Noize' was still at No.1 as I was making my entrance. My mum assures me I was born about ten days early; if I had appeared on schedule, the No.1 would have been 'The Twelfth Of Never' by Donny Osmond, which really wouldn't have been as good.

By the time I became aware of Slade, the glory days of Earl's Court, the Empire Pool and literally shaking the London Palladium to its rafters were long in the rear-view mirror. I recognised some hits from listening to *The Golden Hour* on Radio 1 in school holidays, but probably couldn't have told you who did them. It was in the wake of their second wind, courtesy of Reading Festival 1980, that I started to know who they were, especially after 'We'll Bring The House Down' stuck them back into the Top Ten for the first time since the winding down of the '71-'75 golden era. I didn't really get round to investigating them properly until late 1982.

Slightly disillusioned with the charts, nine-year-old me was going down the retro route and I investigated the 1970s via one of the double LPs my folks had lying around.

K-Tel's 1975 40 *Super Greats.* (I've still got it!) Slade weren't on it, but my interest in the era was piqued, and shopping trips to Hanley in the holidays would involve buying a regular supply of retro singles from the record department in the basement of WH Smith's, one such choice being a Slade maxi-single with 'Cum On Feel The Noize' on it.

I'd also started delving into the Guinness chart books, so I knew Slade were No.1 on the day I was born, and they were (six No.1s, twelve straight top-four hits!). But as I was on the verge of getting stuck in, December 1983 jolted me back to the present day.

Ten years after the Christmas record topped the pile during the Great Glam Rock Christmas that was 1973-74, Slade came so close to repeating that particular card trick. Myself and a couple of mates dutifully bought 'My Oh My' in an attempt to nudge them towards the top, but The Flying Pickets' acapella take on Yazoo's 'Only You' won the all-important granny vote. (Does your granny *really* always tell you that the old songs are the best? Perhaps not in this case!). Our heroes got stuck in the Christmas runners-up slot at the crucial moment.

For good measure, I bought a copy of the 1973 Christmas No.1 to make doubly sure; okay, 'Merry Xmas Everybody' didn't quite repeat its 1973 performance, but it still nudged into the Top 20, a respectable performance for a record that almost every person in this country must have bought at some point in their lives in the preceding decade and the four decades since. For me 1983, not 1973, was well and truly Slade's Christmas.

THE AMAZING KAMIKAZE SYNDROME RELEASED 3 DECEMBER 1983

The Amazing Kamikaze Syndrome *reaches No.49 in the UK album charts.*

I WAS THERE: IAN ASHLEIGH

In 1983 we saw the release of the curiously titled *The Amazing Kamikaze Syndrome* (released in America as *Keep Your Hands Off My Power Supply*), giving Slade a No.2 hit single with the anthemic 'My Oh My', while follow-up 'Run Runaway' would prove to be their final original Top Ten hit, and 'All Join Hands', the lead single from the next LP, *Rogues Gallery*, their final Top 20 hit. From there, 'Radio Wall of Sound' in 1988 just missed the Top 20, their last studio album of new material being 1987's *You Boyz Make Big Noize*.

Slade never did recapture the success of the early 1970s, and the albums slowed down, although they were always an exciting band live. But for four years in the early Seventies, Glam Rock ruled, and I will argue the kings at the high table were Slade. No other band could touch them.

SHOULDER OF MUTTON

11 DECEMBER 1983, HARDSTOFT, DERBYSHIRE, UK

I WAS THERE: NOMIS BAURLEY

In 1983 they announced only one tour, and it turned out to be their final tour, involving a strange mix of venues, mainly universities… although the Hardstoft Shoulder of Mutton was memorable. 'My Oh My' was at No.2 in the charts and this was basically a large pub venue in Derbyshire. I was helping out doing a spotlight on this tour, earning a tenner pocket money each night. That night I had one foot in the sink in the pub's kitchen, with the spotlight pointing through a serving hatch!

PALAIS

12 DECEMBER 1983, NOTTINGHAM, UK

I WAS THERE: MAGGIE BOURNE

I was also lucky enough to see them at the Palais de Dance in my hometown, Nottingham, at the second attempt. I was working there at the time and couldn't believe my luck. The gig was scheduled for 16th October 1980. After I was calmed down by the then manager, I offered to work for free as long as I could go to the gig. The Palais had two areas then, upstairs for gigs dancing, and downstairs the Bali Hai with a revolving dancefloor. At that time, we had heavy rock nights, and the whole crowd knew I was a really big Slade fan.

On the big day I was in early, listening to the soundcheck, only to be told they had to cancel because Noddy was ill. It was last minute, so all their fans were at the main door, and I had to tell everyone the gig was cancelled. It went very well though, no one gave me any grief, thank God. I was more peed off than anyone else!

Then the day came when they were going to do the gig again. I came in early but had to work in the heavy rock bit until the gig started. I listened to the soundcheck again, but have to say I noticed a bit of tension in the air. The management knew I would be going upstairs the minute Slade were going on stage, and the crowd in the heavy rock venue knew this. They were watching me like a hawk. They knew the minute I went upstairs was when to follow me, and that's exactly what happened. I don't think the promoter was very happy.

After getting up to the stage, their roadies wouldn't let me go to the front, but the bouncers that worked there did (a big thank you to Colin). I had a great time, and Slade being the professionals they were, they didn't show any of the tension I witnessed earlier. All the heavy rockers had a great time too.

QUEEN MARGARET UNION

16 DECEMBER 1983, GLASGOW, UK

I WAS THERE: STUART RUTTER

My last Slade gig was at Glasgow's Queen Margaret Union at Christmas 1983, the third-to-last full UK show. By then they were playing to a formula, and even Nod's stage banter was the same at each gig. It was hard to pinpoint but it just seemed like his heart wasn't in it, though I've been told since that he had a bad cold that night. It was still a fantastic show. They never lost that incredible sound, and they played so tight together as a unit. Very recently, Jim Lea said in a Radio Boom interview that Nod had started getting severe headaches from the strain of singing that loud for so long, so it must have started being more of an ordeal for him.

I WAS THERE: JOHN MILNE

I was there for the load-in and I said to the roadies, 'Do you want a hand?', and they said 'sure', so I was a roadie with them for that day. As a thank you, I was given tickets for the show that evening, so I went home and said, 'Do you know where we're going tonight?' and she said 'no' and I said, 'We're going to see Slade.' Jessie and I went with a friend and his wife. I met Don Powell that night and asked if we could see the rest of the band but he said they were quite busy. But he got the band to sign photos for me, and the cover of 'My Oh My'.

SATURDAY SUPERSTORE

17 DECEMBER 1983, SALTAIRE, UK

I WAS THERE: JOHN BARKER, SLADE ARE FOR LIFE – NOT JUST FOR CHRISTMAS

I didn't discover Slade until 1983. Keith Chegwin was doing an outside broadcast for the BBC's *Saturday Superstore* from Saltaire, in West Yorkshire. It was only about a mile from where I lived, so I thought I'd pop along and meet some school friends there. I found out that the band appearing with Cheggers that day was Slade.

As a 13-year-old into Adam Ant and other popular Eighties acts, I knew 'We'll Bring The House Down' but I didn't really know 'Merry Xmas Everybody' and so on. Seeing them do a playback performance of 'My Oh My' that day changed my life forever. There was a sense of fun about them, and Noddy's personality shone through. He was wonderful with the crowd, even when the cameras weren't rolling. That afternoon I bought the 'My Oh My' single from my local record shop and found

John Barker with Don Powell and Jim Lea in 2023 at a video shoot for a new single by the Don Powell Band

a secondhand copy of *Slade Smashes!* on the market. From that moment, I was a Slade fan.

My collection grew quickly, and I discovered just how great they were as recording artists. Sadly, I never saw the original Slade play live, as their final UK show was the day after that *Superstore* appearance, at Liverpool's Royal Court Theatre.

I joined Facebook in 2010 where I found a few Slade-related groups and pages, but nothing that I thought celebrated the band properly. The Official Slade page was for the then current touring line-up with Dave and Don, while other fan groups didn't seem to support the current band. So I created *Slade Are For Life – Not Just For Christmas* to be a Facebook group that supported all aspects of Slade, and all band members. The name was my usual response to people when all they mentioned or knew about Slade was 'Merry Xmas Everybody'.

The group quickly grew and when it reached 5,000 group members and hit the limit set by Facebook, I had to create a Facebook page instead. That also proved popular with fans worldwide. It seemed that others also wanted a page supportive of all things Slade.

I continued the page with regular updates, but it wasn't until 2015 that I realised it was being appreciated by Slade's record company, some band members, and management. I helped promote the *When Slade Rocked The World* box set. This was appreciated by BMG, and I've continued to work with them, promoting subsequent releases. I also provided them with a couple of my foreign singles for the creation of *Feel The Noize – The Singlez Box*. I have a similar relationship with Jim's record company, Wienerworld, and last year it was a pleasure to put them in touch with

Don's Denmark-based band, Don & The Dreamers, Wienerworld distributing their debut album, *It's Never Too Late To Be A Rock Star*. It's great to think that two members of Slade are now with the same record company, and to have had a small part in that.

Today, the page has over 127,000 followers. There are also linked Instagram and Twitter accounts, but it is Facebook that is the priority. I now work closely with Don to promote his bands and share his personal news. He really is the nicest man in rock, and it's a pleasure to call him a friend and work with him and his band members. He appreciates the page, and the time and effort that goes into it. We even do the Euromillions lottery together. It was a pleasure to have been one of Don's guests at his Q&A event with Jim Lea in August 2022, and at the Don & The Dreamers album launch event in March 2023.

Noddy's wife, Suzan, is also in regular contact to share his news and let me know what's happening. He's never had a personal social media account, so it's great to share his information and personal photos on the page. Dave's manager is also a regular contact, and very helpful when wanting a response or information from Dave. I've been fortunate enough to have been invited backstage to meet him and his Slade line-ups several times over the years, promoting Slade's UK Christmas tours. I've seen the band many times, with all the different line-ups, and I've always had a really good night.

I also have contact with Jim's brother and manager, Frank, and it's so satisfying to see Jim and Don working together again on projects. It's been a privilege to have been in the company of them both, twice in the past year.

The page is also a supporter of all-female Slade tribute band, Slady. They're a breath of fresh air, helping keep the music of Slade alive and to find new audiences. Lead singer/band creator Danie Cox, aka Gobby Holder, has become a good friend. We even wrote a tribute song together, 'Slade Are For Life (Not Just For Xmas)'.

The page continues to grow with the philosophy of simply wanting to share news of Slade in a professional way to as many people as possible worldwide. I've made official contacts with the band and their representatives, improving the content and getting heartwarming feedback. My love of Slade is stronger than ever.

DUNELM HOUSE
17 DECEMBER 1983, DURHAM, UK

I WAS THERE: PETER SMITH

Slade played a couple more times in the North East, at Newcastle University in December 1982 and at Durham University Students' Union twelve months later. I was at the Durham concert and Slade were, as usual, excellent. A packed Dunelm House gave Slade a rapturous welcome. I didn't know it at the time, but it would be the last time I would see the original Slade line-up.

The night after, they played Liverpool's Royal Court Theatre in what proved to be the original band's last ever full UK show. A UK tour was scheduled for 1985 but cancelled. An era had come to an end and one of the greatest rock bands the world has ever seen were no more. Slade were truly one of the best bands I ever saw, and I carry many fond memories, particularly of wild shows in the 1970s. A class act. Their like is never to be seen again.

The front cover of the tour programme at Durham shows Slade on stage at Reading in 1980. The concert was recorded and released as the live album, *Slade on Stage*. They were clearly very proud of that performance and wanted to be remembered for it and their status as heavy rock heroes. I am somewhere in that crowd close to the front, but I can't see myself!

I WAS THERE: KEVIN THORNTON

I got into Slade after an argument over who was the best, Status Quo or Slade, in 1973 at school. I was hooked on Slade from there, collecting all their albums after that. It was the 1980s when I saw them. I'd been living in Gibraltar with my parents. I remember them walking on stage with two crates of beer and throwing them into the crowd. The place went wild, and for the next two hours they sang all their hits. Brilliant.

ROYAL COURT THEATRE
18 DECEMBER 1983, LIVERPOOL, UK

I WAS THERE: NOMIS BAURLEY

I saw them eleven more times that year, and only saw them less because they did far fewer gigs. The last was at Liverpool's Royal Court Theatre. It should have been Durham Uni, but gigs got switched to allow for *Top of the Pops* appearances in a bid to push 'My Oh My' to No.1. It didn't happen, but we came so close. I'm glad the last gig was in a big theatre. Durham Uni was a small sweat box. I travelled down from there with two of Slade's old crew, Haden Donovan and Mickey Legg, in a Smith's Self Hire van. We thought it would be a good idea to steal a Christmas tree from a service station to hoist above the stage in Liverpool at the gig.

Once again, it was another triumphant tour, with lots of back slapping and 'see ya next years'…' but it wasn't to be. Nobody knew at the time it would be their final UK gig. They got the call to support Ozzy in the States on the back of the success of 'Run Runaway' there, but a couple of gigs in, Jim got ill and they had to cancel. A tour was announced for 1985 and then got cancelled. The Liverpool gig was the last time the original line-up would play the UK.

Dave and Don carried on, but the band today is a pale shadow of what I believe was the best live band of all time. I have kept in touch with them all to this day, but I am still such a big fan of lots of bands, seeing around 120 gigs a year.

I took retirement at 50 after having a successful business from 1987. If Slade had kept on touring, I would probably have kept following them round, working shitty jobs, so at least some good came of it.

There was never an official 'Slade have split' statement. They just fizzled out. They were still putting albums out through the Eighties; *Keep Your Hands Off My Power Supply*, *Rogues Gallery*, all these. Most of it was being done by Jim. He was doing all the recording and all the producing. Dave Hill played very little guitar on a couple of the latter albums. They were a band in name, but nothing else really.

I WAS THERE: PETER FARRINGTON

I first experienced Slade like most people, through *Top of the Pops*. I was nine years old, so too young to see them at the peak of their stardom, but I followed them with interest. I collected their records and read articles and books until I considered myself an expert. It wasn't until the internet surfaced that I discovered I'm not. In the late Seventies, the wilderness years, the opportunity to see Slade never presented itself to me. I was pretty sure I was the only fan left, as I staunchly fought their corner at school. The Jam, Squeeze, The Clash and such like were the order of the day. All very good, but just not Slade.

In 1980, Slade famously triumphed at the Reading Festival. As that was going on, I was busily being a police cadet and was unable to attend. I saw Slade for the first time in 1981. I went with a long-suffering mate. His passion was Genesis and a dose of heavy metal here and there. Slade had found a level of respectability in the eyes of heavy metal fans though, so he was persuaded to come along, either to the Empire Theatre (23 February) or the Royal Court Theatre (10 December) in Liverpool. I'm not sure which now.

They came on stage to 'Dizzy Mamma' and were seriously loud. Holder had the crowd in the palm of his hand. He was wearing a wide-brimmed hat, black coat, yellow shirt and bootlace tie. He was dressed like a confederate gentleman but with blue Kicker boots on.

It was all new to me. The ad libs seemed hilarious. I had no idea they were rehearsed and repeated every night. I got home with ears ringing. I couldn't hear properly for days. But the next year I was back for more. Number one crew cut, t-shirt, braces, jeans and Doc Martens. The 1969 Slade look. I distinctly remember a bloke tapping me on the shoulder just before the band came on stage. I turned to face him and he handed me my police cadet ID card that had dropped out of my pocket. That was embarrassing.

This time, Nod was in the guise of the 'Rock And Roll Preacher', captivating the audience from the start. My two main pastimes were football and rock music. The passion of a Slade crowd was very like that of the Liverpool Kop, where I was a regular. Slade fans don't just watch the band – they support them.

This time I was with my girlfriend, later to be my wife. She didn't get it at all. She's learned to live with Slade and Liverpool FC though, politely humouring me. She's an Everton supporter and David Gray fan. The gulf is clear.

The third time I saw them was at the Royal Court Theatre in December 1983, the last hurrah. I later acquired a video recording of the event, which is a story in itself. On the night I had no idea it would be the last show. That June, I was involved in a serious motorbike accident. I spent three weeks in hospital and my leg was in plaster for several weeks. I was then on crutches and only returned to work late in November. I'd persuaded a doctor to let me back as I was worried I'd have my probationary period extended. I should not have been walking a beat as I couldn't run or even cross the road easily – stepping on and off kerbs was very hard. I couldn't bend at the knee. Nevertheless, such was the desire to see Slade, I took my chances.

Again, I was blown away by the sheer power and their exuberance. Holder is the greatest frontman of all time, better than Mercury, Jagger, Lydon or anybody else that might contest that accolade. If you've never seen Slade, you just can't grasp how different they were on stage to the *TOTP* sound and image most people know.

The name of Slade continued to be used by Dave Hill and Don Powell, enlisting an array of other personnel over the years. I've seen this act more than once. Never again though. The original Slade, however? I'd be in like a shot (from my gun).

I WAS THERE: ANDREW RIGBY

Did anyone ever see Slade play a bad gig? I doubt it. Although I missed them in their pomp, even in the doldrum years of the late Seventies and early Eighties they never failed to deliver, regardless of whether there were 100 people there or if it was at their Reading renaissance. For excitement and audience participation, I don't think I've witnessed anyone to touch them, and that's after nearly 45 years of concert-going. I would match them only with The Clash, Springsteen at his best and Thin Lizzy in their prime. And that's some company!

There are of course other artists with more credibility and respect, but no matter. Nod, Dave, Jim and Don had that something that made them untouchable as a live act, a bit like The Who. The sum of their parts together was never matched by them as individuals. Years of paying their dues up and down the M1, Nod's almost vaudeville-like approach to audiences, Jim's intensity and need for respect, and Dave and Don's pop background all made for an untouchable live sound.

I think I saw them twelve times in all. Highlights were the infamous Christmas gigs, where the roofs were literally blown away when they launched into *that* song, and the Reading and Donington festivals, where they were considered underdogs on both occasions, only to blow away all the opposition even without lights or stage gimmicks to rely on.

Slade's 'last stand' was a memorable gig for Andrew Rigby

My personal favourite is what was (regrettably) their last stand, at the Royal Court Theatre in Liverpool. It was another Christmas tour, complete with Nod in Father Christmas garb. You could literally eat the atmosphere when they hit the stage, and they gave a performance never bettered by a rock 'n' roll band. You could feel the balcony literally shake, but this was nothing new at a Slade gig. Anything less was not acceptable!

ROISSY AIRPORT

9 JANUARY 1984, PARIS, FRANCE

I WAS THERE: GÉRARD GOYER

I did see the classic Slade line-up live again, in January 1984 at Paris' Roissy airport, and the next day at their hotel and photo sessions at the Eiffel Tower, when the band came over for a television show to promote 'My Oh My'. Slade loved my passion for the band, and I have often been mentioned in fan club publications. In 1986, French magazine *Juke Box* asked me to write six pages to celebrate 20 years of Slade, while on 17th November that year, the *Evening Mail* in Solihull wrote an article

Gerard Goyer photobombed the official photo session in Paris

about my record collection, a few weeks after a mention of me in a Craig Brown column in *The Times*. And in 1995, three years after the original band split, the UK fan club released a book which featured my list of all the Slade records I had collected, from multiple countries.

I sold my singles, albums and cassettes, only keeping my CDs, VHSs and DVDs. I still buy CDs and DVDs. I have never calculated how much I have spent on my collection.

I have three children. You can guess why my youngest son is named Jimmy.

'RUN RUNAWAY' RELEASED 13 JANUARY 1984

'Run Runaway' is released and becomes Slade's last ever Top 10 single, reaching No.7 in the UK charts and No.1 on the US Album Rock Tracks chart.

Quiet Riot's success with a Slade cover leads to a US re-release of 'Run Runaway' as CBS sign Slade in mid-1984, peaking at No.20 on the Billboard Hot 100, *charting for 17 weeks and topping the US mainstream rock chart, their first and only top-20 hit there helped by heavy MTV airplay.*

In March 1984, Slade release a repackaged version of December '83 album The Amazing Kamikaze Syndrome *for the North American market, renamed* Keep Your Hands Off My Power Supply.

I WAS BAK 'OME: STEVE RUSSEY

I was a big fan, although they never seemed to catch on over here in the USA. I know they were very popular in Europe though. It's ironic that Quiet Riot had big hits with two Slade songs, encouraged to record them because Kevin Dubrow had a Noddy Holder 'sound' about his voice. I love the story Tom Jones told about Holder, praising his singing, glowingly, and saying something to the effect that while British vocalists were doing their best to hold their own, Noddy was kicking everyone's ass!

I never saw Slade, yet when they had brief success here with 'My Oh My' and 'Run Runaway' a friend saw them open for Ozzy and said they were really disrespected by the juvenile crowd. I guess Jim Lea was trying to do a violin solo and someone pelted him with a roll of toilet paper. Heathens! Still, I'm glad that 1984's *Keep Your Hands Off My Power Supply* converted me. I still love them! Great songwriters, performers, and all-round musicians.

13 OCTOBER 1984, BARMOUTH, UK

I WAS THERE: ALUN TAYLOR

The first album I bought was *Slayed* and it just blew me away. I was a fan from then on. They were never to be missed when they were on TV. Having first seen Slade in May 1977 at Wolverhampton Civic Hall, and then on every tour after, in 1984 I read an article in *The Slade Mag* regarding Slade fans getting married. I was due to get married to my woman while my mate was to marry her sister. I contacted Keith Altham, Slade's press agent, and he set it all up, our stories

Alun Taylor had a very special chauffeur at his wedding

filmed by a Welsh news team (Dave Graham has the footage somewhere). Dave Hill turned up on the day with his YOB 1 Rolls-Royce and came into my house for a refreshment, then went to pick the brides up, taking them to the church and then to Shell Island, eight miles away, for the reception. My marriage has long since been dissolved, but it was a good day and Dave was in fine form. I've met him a few times since and talked about that day.

'ALL JOIN HANDS' RELEASED 9 NOVEMBER 1984

Slade reach No.15 in the UK singles chart.

THE SHIP

DECEMBER 1984, WARDOUR STREET, LONDON, UK

I WAS THERE: ANDY STRICKLAND

I've been working as a freelancer at *Record Mirror* for a year. Slade hit the Top Ten earlier in '84 with 'Run Runaway', so there's enough interest from the editor to let me chase an interview for their 'All Join Hands' release – if, and only if, we can somehow roll it into our Christmas festivities and get some quotes about 'Merry Xmas Everybody'.

It's suggested that I go on a pub crawl with Noddy Holder. Oh, go on then. Slade's press officer is Keith Altham – possibly the most famous music journalist and now PR guru of the Sixties and Seventies. Keith tips me the wink that Noddy probably won't want to spend an afternoon trawling Soho's pubs with me, but he will meet me for a half in The Ship, outside the famous Marquee Club on Wardour Street.

Noddy is a joy. Everybody recognises him and it's not easy to keep his focus, but he's happy to talk about Slade's 'rebirth' since that 1980 Reading Festival appearance, and the new single, and to have a photo with me outside the pub raising a glass. Just a half for him.

Back at Keith's office, I get 30 minutes with an engaged Jim Lea. Jim

Photo: Joe Shutter

Record Mirror reporter Andy Strickland shares a festive ale with Noddy Holder in Soho

makes it very clear that he is the musical brain behind Slade and is delighted to tell me the story of writing and recording 'Merry Xmas Everybody'. I'd always imagined a snowy Olympic Studios in West London or similar, but Jim explains how the band were halfway through an American tour in 1973 and he woke early one summer's day with the song complete in his head. He rang Noddy and said, 'I've got our Christmas No.1.'

The band recorded it as soon as possible in a sweltering New York, using the hallway of the Record Plant studios to get the big sound that Jim could hear in his head. Slade were not big in the US in 1973 and studio staff thought they were crazy, singing about Christmas in August. Half a million advance orders later that year suggested otherwise.

YOU BOYZ MAKE BIG NOIZE RELEASED 27 APRIL 1987

After singles 'Still The Same' and 'That's What Friends Are For' fail to chart, the Roy Thomas Baker, Jim Lea and John Punter-produced album You Boyz Make Big Noize *spends just one week in the UK album chart, peaking at No.98. It fares better in Norway, reaching No.12.*

RADIO CLYDE

JULY 1987, GLASGOW, UK

I WAS THERE: JOHN MILNE

When 'You Boyz Make Big Noize' came out, I rang up Radio Clyde and asked them to play it and they said, 'Sorry son, we've no got it.' So we took it down to Radio Clyde and they then played my copy on air. I knew it was my record because I could hear the wee clicks and everything.

I WAS THERE: DAVID NEWTON, THE MIGHTY LEMON DROPS

I was first aware of them around the time of 'Look Wot You Dun'. Radio 1 was on in our house from around six in the morning until I went to school around 8.30am, so I'd hear all the Slade singles then. My dad left for work at seven or eight, but my mum would leave after I'd gone to school. She worked in a school kitchen. The first Slade single I bought was either 'Cum On Feel The Noize' or 'Skweeze Me, Pleeze Me'. With my 50p pocket money, I couldn't afford to buy chart singles at 60p or 65p, so I'd go through the ex-chart box, where singles were 25p or 30p and buy one record a week. I probably spent the rest on sweets! If it was a birthday or Christmas, with a little extra money, I'd buy an actual chart single. I definitely paid full price for 'Merry Xmas Everybody' when it came out, and I bought a few later, like 'How Does It Feel?'.

Growing up in Wolverhampton, it seemed that everybody knew somebody that knew somebody that knew somebody from 'The Slade', as they were known locally. It really was like 'our band'. And when I was a little older, in the early Eighties, there was this great pub by us in Bilston called the Royal Exchange, but nicknamed the Trumpet because a lot of live jazz was played there, and Noddy was a regular. You'd go in on a Tuesday night and he was always leaning up against the bar, having a pint, even when they got big again in '82 or '83. You'd be on nodding terms, so to speak!

One of my first jobs was working in Music Stop, a music shop in Wolverhampton. The owner's wife had run Slade's fan club when they were the 'N Betweens, pre-Ambrose Slade, and she gave me some items like little 'N Betweens ten-by-eights, and a promo copy of 'You Better Run'. But when I moved to America, I misplaced a lot of stuff, and can't find them for the life of me.

In 1976, Wolverhampton finally had its own radio station, Beacon Radio, and one of the first big things they had to launch it involved Slade doing a live on-air phone-in Q&A. I phoned in and got through, and remember the whole band were in the studio. You had to ask a question, and I had this on tape for years but again I cannot find it.

But the question I asked – I was twelve – was if any of them had ever thought of taking up a solo career. And I couldn't tell who was replying, maybe Dave or Jim, but they said, 'I'm thinking of getting into pirouette dancing, along with Freddie Mercury.' Not very politically correct.

I never got to see them live. I was too young. Even in the days of The Mighty Lemon Drops, we'd do all these European festivals with all sorts of bands on, from all eras and genres, but I had no recollection of Slade playing. I would have gone out of my way to see them in the early Eighties when they had their comeback. There was one I really should have gone to, in 1979 or 1980, when they did Monmore Green Stadium, a speedway track in Wolverhampton. Local rock bands Diamond Head and the Jameson Raid also played, and a lot of my friends went. But I thought it would be full of rockers and I was more about catching The Undertones or someone. There was an absolute crossover though, with Slade the band it was okay to admit liking!

In 2004, my wife and I went to a friend's 40th birthday, Mighty Lemon Drops and Blue Aeroplanes manager, Cerne Canning, who's the same age as me and now manages Franz Ferdinand and The Vaccines. I went as Noddy Holder and my wife as Dave Hill!

I last saw Dave Hill when I first met my wife, who's originally from America. She moved in with me in Wolverhampton and worked at the Victoria Park Hotel, and Dave and two of his mates came in and had lunch there one day.

When the Lemon Drops started spending a lot of time in London, in 1986 and '87, we stayed at the Columbia Hotel, popular with bands because it was cheap and they put up with you coming in late at night, and they'd open the bar late. Noddy was staying there on and off for like a year, when they were recording *You Boyz Make Big Noize*, and he would be jibbing with Joan, the legendarily stern waitress, because they stopped serving breakfast at 9.45 sharp, and all the bands who'd been up till two, three or four in the morning would only get out of bed at 9.40am.

Dave's Super Yob guitar was in the window of Musical Exchanges on the main street leading into Birmingham from the mid-Seventies right through to the early Eighties. Marco Pirrone from Adam and the Ants saw it in the window, and although it wasn't for sale, he said, 'I want that', making an offer they couldn't refuse. I think he still owns it.

DAVE WAKELING, THE BEAT

I was a Wolves fan… and so were they. I don't know what it was, I'd either fallen out with my dad, which happened quite regularly and stopped me being a Villa fan, or it was because I had a couple of mates who were Wolves fans who I went to games with. And I liked the colours – the yellow and black. You'd hear a lot of Slade and sing along with them. But I never saw them live. By then, you didn't see their name coming around as much as some of the others. There were a lot more Sabbath concerts, stuff like that. Then eventually they became a kind of TV-inspired thing, and Dave Hill's cartoonish-ness became bigger and bigger. But my Vox Teardrop, the first copy I had, was made by John Diggins, who did the Super Yob guitar, and anytime anyone said they liked my guitar, I'd say, 'This is the guy who made the Yob guitar!' and everybody knew what I meant. They were a band of the people. And in the Black Country, that's taken as a big strength, your affinity to your community.

ROGUES GALLERY RELEASED 29 MARCH 1989 (UK)

Showcasing Jim's studio craft and despite attracting critical acclaim, Rogues Gallery *falters at No.60 in the UK charts and stays outside the US Top 100.*

In late 1989, Noddy announces plans for a new album, but neither that nor a mooted tie-in tour materialise, Slade seeing out the decade with a No.99 showing for 'that song', in a year that Dave Hill features alongside ex-Wizzard keyboard player Bill Hunt in side-project Blessings in Disguise, with Nod on lead vocals.

In 1990, Jim Lea releases a new take on 'We'll Bring The House Down' under the name The Clout, and with Noddy co-produces (and appears in a promo video for) a 'Merry Xmas Everybody' cover by The Metal Gurus (mainly drawn from The Mission), artist royalties donated to Childline.

TOWN HALL
6 APRIL 1991, WALSALL, UK

A month after the release of RCA/BMG compilation The Slade Collection 81-87, *Slade's fan club organises a 25th anniversary party, the band back on stage one last time, covering Chuck Berry's 'Johnny B. Goode'.*

I WAS THERE: NN MARTIN

I saw them many times, but a Birmingham University graduation party they played was perhaps the most extraordinary. They came on stage at 4am, the audience being students celebrating the end of year, with ball gowns and suits. But once the show started, they were all raving, the scene afterwards as if they'd been through a hedge backwards. I only managed to get a ticket by fluke. It was students only. I wasn't a student.

The crowd was packed but small. Maybe 150 to 250 people, yet they had on their full stage gear, and were so loud! As usual, the show was very well run and controlled by Nod, who knew his audience well.

I was born in 1960 and first heard 'Coz I Luv You' on the radio. The clapping sound hooked me. I saw them aged 13 at Birmingham Town Hall, Alex Harvey supporting. I tried to see them every tour thereafter. I just adored the power and tight sound. And Noddy's range was fabulous. I think I saw them at least ten times. After their 'failed to conquer America' era they returned and I saw them do Barbarella's, Birmingham, a nightclub with no ventilation. I stood, or should I say was held up, the crowd packed in like sardines that night. Again, they were in full stage gear and extremely loud. I also caught their last show, the Wolverhampton fan gathering in 1991.

I WAS THERE: PAUL COOKSON

I can't remember how I first got involved with Slade's fan club conventions and compering them. I know I went down to London for a few. I'd started performing poetry on the alternative cabaret scene. A couple of poems referenced Noddy and Slade and somewhere along the line I'd performed them at a fan club event. I then got asked to compere at fan club events and so I was the compere at Walsall Town Hall with

Phil Dascombe, another Slade fan.

Paul Cookson, Slade's poet laureate, was a compere at Walsall Town Hall before Slade's final stage performance

About six months previous to this, I'd asked Noddy for an introduction to a poetry collection called *Over 21 And Still into Noddy*. He'd replied with a great introduction, but the book wasn't out by the time of the fan club event.

Slade weren't scheduled to play at the Town Hall but they appeared on stage to say hello, have photos, receive gifts and so on. Backstage, I'd said thanks to the man himself and his reply was, 'Some shit hot stuff there, Paul.' I was amazed he'd remembered and equally elated that he liked it. As I left the dressing room, a lady was coming in. She said I looked pleased, so I told her why. She then said, 'Oh, he's mentioned them at home.' It was Mrs Holder I'd been talking to!

Eventually, the band were persuaded to do a number – on borrowed instruments. They did 'Johnny B Goode'. Phil and I introduced them, not knowing it would be the last time all four would appear on stage together.

'RADIO WALL OF SOUND' RELEASED 7 OCTOBER 1991

Reaching No.21 on the UK charts, this is Slade's final hit single (excluding that song *reappearing in the charts).*

I WAS THERE: KEVIN MOTTRAM

'Radio Wall Of Sound' was Slade's final chart biggie and in its wake there was one last appearance on *Top of the Pops*, plus a very funny interview with Noddy and Dave in the *NME*. Were we on the verge of another renaissance? In his sleeve notes for the *Wall of Hits* compilation, Chris Charlesworth suggested the two new songs 'could herald a new era for the group'. But 'Universe', the other new song, stiffed as a single, and by the spring of 1992 there was a new era around the corner, but probably not the one fans anticipated; Sir Nodward of Holdershire decided it was time to do new things, and Jim followed Nod through the exit door. End of an era? You betcha.

Although the original four were no more a working entity, they've continued to endure. Not so long after, enter *The Smell of Reeves & Mortimer*. I'd wager that thanks to 'Slade in Residence', even if they didn't quite pick up a new generation of fans, sales of the back catalogue kept ticking over very nicely. To this day, it only takes finding a packet of Cup-A-Soup unexpectedly at the back of the cupboard to set me off, uttering lines out of nowhere in a Black Country accent such as, 'Teacher's pet, Jimmy,', 'shut yer face, mutton-chops!' and my favourite, guaranteed to ring in my head every time I buy washing up liquid, 'Everyone knows you need lemon to shift dirt.' It was obviously done with affection; one suspects Vic and Bob, plus Paul Whitehouse and Mark Williams, were most certainly living out 1970s childhood fantasies of being in a band through those sketches.

And if it's true that Noddy made certain suggestions when he received advance copies of the early scripts, so much the better.

Slade continue to endure in other ways. Every so often you'd get a member or two of the band pop up on Central News or Midlands Today, usually when some exhibition on local music was about to open or a civic commemoration of some sort was happening over Wolverhampton or Birmingham way. And you often hear a Slade song or two backing everything from Nexus tablets ('Everyday') to the most apt of the lot (especially considering how much time Slade spent in vans back in the day), the Ford Transit 'Backbone of Britain' ads ('Coz I Luv You'). Also, such a distinctive presence as Sir Nodward was always going to be a shoo-in for fronting adverts, ranging from (inevitably) Banks' Bitter to Iceland's Christmas campaign ('Not yet, Noddy!') and perhaps my favourite, the wonderful Nibble Nobby's Nuts advert ('Can't any of yow people rayyddd?').

WALL OF HITS RELEASED 11 NOVEMBER 1991

This Polydor compilation, alongside a video compilation, includes two new songs issued as singles – October's 'Radio Wall of Sound', written by Jim and originally for a solo project, which reaches No.21, and December's 'Universe', which fails to dent the Top 100. And while the album reaches No.34, Polydor withdraw an option on a new album and future singles.

GRANADA STUDIOS

DECEMBER 1991, ALBERT DOCK, LIVERPOOL, UK

I WAS THERE: GWEN DALE

The last time I saw them all together on stage was in 1991 on *This Morning* with Richard Madeley and Judy Finnegan. Me and my friend Di entered a competition with the fan club to get picked to go on the TV with them. We never got picked but went anyway, arriving at around 7am. We waited about two hours before someone asked if we were the Slade fans for the show. We explained that we were Slade fans but weren't lucky enough to get picked, but the woman said 'the more the merrier'. She invited us in, and we watched them turn this

Gwen Dale and Diane Rutter on the set of This Morning to catch Slade in December 1991

cold warehouse into an amazing Christmas scene. We were the only ones who got to see the soundcheck, as the others hadn't turned up by then.

Codsall High School

You are invited to the
Official opening
of
THE MUSIC CENTRE
by
Mr James Lea
on
Wednesday 12th May 1993 at 7.00 pm
R.S.V.P by Wednesday 5th May

Gwen Dale's ticket from Codsall High School from May '93, surprising Jim Lea somewhat

That was the end of Slade, and the beginning of Slade II. My friend Diane Rutter and I started going to gigs in England, Scotland, Belgium, Germany and Holland, getting to know the band really well. I've also been to Denmark to stay with Don and his wife, Hanne. Me and Di loved going along to support anything the boys were doing, usually charity things.

We once popped into Codsall School, where Jim went, as he was opening the new Music Centre there. We asked the headmaster if we could have tickets. He said, 'Why should I give you tickets?' We told him we were mental Slade fans, and with that he said okay, giving us two tickets. When we got there, Jim asked, 'How did you two get in?' We told him and he replied, 'You two can get places that cod liver oil couldn't reach.'

After 26 years in Walsall, I met someone who lived in Kingston-upon-Thames, packed up work and moved in with him in Surrey, along with my youngest daughter. I've been there 22 years now and still get to as many Slade happenings as I can. I haven't seen Dave for a while, but I'm not getting about as much, due to health issues. I did however see Don and the Dreamers' album launch at the Water Rats in King's Cross, London, a few weeks ago. My mum used to say, 'She'll grow out of it one day.' But, hey, I'm going to see Noddy at a sell-out show with Tom Seals in Walsall in July, 51 years after my first Slade gig.

Noddy announces that he's leaving Slade, with Jim following suit rather than continue without him. Don is working in a hotel that his then-wife manages

---

I was on the road for 25 years with the same four guys and I was touring with other bands before, so I was actually on the road for 30-odd years. I was getting bored, quite frankly. It was album, tour, album, tour, year in, year out, and I didn't foresee myself carrying on with it for the rest of my life. I was going through a divorce from my first marriage and my dad was dying so there was a lot of things building up on me, and I didn't want to be away from home, going round the world for the 30th time, so I had to make the conscious decision. **Noddy Holder**

UNKNOWN VENUE

11 DECEMBER 1992, UMEA, SWEDEN

Don rejoins Dave and they make their live debut as Slade II. Initially a five-piece, the name is later shortened to Slade and the band work solidly down the years, mainly in the UK and mainland Europe, but around the world, releasing one studio album, 1994's Keep On Rockin'. Several changes of personnel follow, Don remaining involved until early 2020, when he claims Dave sends a 'cold email' informing him his services are no longer needed, a version of events Dave disputes.

WESTFALENHALLE

27 DECEMBER 1992, DORTMUND, GERMANY

I WAS THERE: NOMIS BAURLEY

I went to the first proper Slade II gig, at the Westfalenhalle in Dortmund, Germany, although I think they played three small warm-up gigs in Sweden before. I was drafted in by a guy who ran the Dutch fan club at the time to do an interview with them. We went over and stayed with my friend in Holland for a couple of days, then drove down to the gig. I was completely in denial about what I was going to go see, and it was only when I got to the gig that it hit me, like a hammer. I literally collapsed when it dawned on me that Slade were no more. This was a new thing, with Dave, Don, a new singer and a new bass player. I sat in the balcony and cried. It wasn't Slade anymore, as I knew it.

For a couple of years, it was like I was mourning a parent. I was quite sulky and didn't want to talk to any of the Slade crowd. I didn't want to know what Dave Hill's band was doing. But the years softened me and, although the music wasn't as good, I realised I was missing all the camaraderie and all the people. I'd retained a great friendship with Don and missed his company. He would always make the time to sit down and talk and have a cup of tea or whatever, so I rekindled that relationship.

I'm proud to say I know all the guys on a personal level. Don is a fantastic guy. He is everything that people say about him, Mr Nice Guy, and he'll make the time for everybody.

Jim's been fairly quiet because of health issues within his family, but he's quite pro-active now. He's talking about doing a couple of small gigs, all the proceeds going to charity. He doesn't need the money. He and Noddy are both rich men. But there are quite a few fans, like myself, who are retired and whose kids have flown the nest, and who don't mind chucking a few quid in the pot and having a good night out seeing their hero.

I got to know Dave quite well when they were playing the clubs. He did things like borrow my leather jacket for a couple of photo-shoots, because it was better than the one he was wearing. Or I'd be sat on the front row at Birmingham Odeon with my girlfriend, blowing balloons up a couple of hours before the gig, and he'd chuck some money at me and say, 'Oh, can you go and get a milkshake at the Hasty Tasty?' We loved it with all the 'Dave's my mate' kind of thing. I personally think the current version of Slade is a step too far, the singer side-stage on a keyboard. I would rather they called it a day, but I can't knock the fact that Dave, at 77, is still prancing around the stage. A lot of people still go to the gigs and enjoy it. It's just not for me.

Then there's Nod, or 'Rent-a-Nod' as some people call him. Whenever there's a story to be told, he's there telling it, or a more elaborate version of it. The last time I saw Nod was at a thing he was doing in Harrogate, and that must be eight or nine years ago now. Everyone in Slade circles calls me Nomis, and he said, 'How are you doing, Nomis? How are you doing?' We had a bit of a chat. I keep an eye on what he's doing. He's looking quite well, quite dapper.

'COZ I LUV YOU' COVERED BY THE X SPECIALS 1994

I WAS THERE: RODDY BYERS (AKA RODDY RADIATION) THE SPECIALS & THE X-SPECIALS

I was in a pre-Punk days group called The Wild Boys, which were sorta Glam rock 'n' roll. I was a big T.Rex fan and then moved on to Bowie and Roxy Music. Slade were the working man's Glam rockers, I suppose, and seemed a lot tougher than the rest.

They came from not that far away from Coventry, and I always preferred their songs to the other bands at the time, such as The Sweet or Mud or Gary Glitter. (I didn't mind Alvin Stardust though.) I only recently bought a *Best of Slade* CD. I suppose money was tight back in the Seventies, so I could only afford to get a few 45s and albums. Sadly, I never got to see Slade live for the same reason.

Frank Lea, Jim's brother, got some of The Specials to do an album backing Desmond Dekker and then record a couple of CDs off Trojan's back catalogue. This was because Frank now owned Trojan Records, and that's how the Jim Lea production of 'Coz I Luv You' by The X-Specials came about in 1994. Jim really knew his way around the studio, even though he didn't seem to know much about reggae or ska. He would get Neville Staple, who did the lead vocal, to sing the same line at least five times, then pick certain words from each version that were the most in tune and put them together for the finished version. We were all very happy with the completed mix, but when it came down to business, we weren't happy with the deal, so it was never released. Somehow, a few were manufactured on CD though, and they still pop up on eBay for sale occasionally.

I WAS THERE: DAVID BATEMAN

I discovered Slade in 1997 as a child, watching *TOTP2* with my parents. I was seven years old, playing a Nintendo Gameboy in the living room. The song played that evening was 'Mama Weer All

Crazee Now'. When it faded in, my dad stopped in his tracks and let out a 'great song!' I remember it being like nothing I'd heard before. A fuzzy, noisy, terrace-shifting chorus, not to mention Noddy's growling vocal. It just got something inside of me, and I told my dad I enjoyed it. Next thing I knew, his feet were dangling out of the loft, and he was digging out a well written-on copy of *Slayed?* and *Old New Borrowed And Blue*.

By the time 1998 came, I was the youngest member of the official Slade Fan Club. By the time 1999 came, I had all the albums on CD and had started collecting the vinyl pressings. Fast forward 25-plus years, and I'm still as big a fan as I was then. Oh, and I should probably add that I had a Super Yob guitar custom-built a few years ago.

Dave Bateman was a Slade fan at the age of seven, and never looked back

My dad never saw them live, unfortunately. He was slightly too young, for the live shows at least. He's 61 now. I really wanted to see Dave and Don for a number of years, but being so young, even then, I was not permitted to be in the majority of venues, so it took until I was around 19 to finally see them. The gig was at Glasgow's Royal Concert Hall, a 2,000-seater venue, with only the front three rows sold. It was a good gig, but it must have been very disheartening for them. I've fallen out of love with how it's turned into the Dave Hill Show. Not for me.

Back to the early days though, and after digging the two LPs my dad brought down, he began to bring a Slade album back from Virgin each week until I had the entire studio album set. Having met all the band since, they've all tended to be very pleasant, especially Don. Jim seemed a bit startled to have any fans waiting for him when I found him outside a radio studio in Edinburgh, but he was happy to sign, shake hands and get on with his day. A lovely experience for me, but he and his wife Louise were caught off guard by a small group of us.

Noddy has also been very pleasant on both occasions I met him. He had known I was meeting him in 1999 at his book release in Glasgow, so when I finally walked up to him, he knew who I was. I took my Holder hat, made from a fancy dress top hat and some flattened milk bottle lids. The second time was brief, and 20 years later, so he didn't recognise me, and I didn't ask. Ha ha! This was when I obtained the final signature on my copy of *Play It Loud*. That's my most treasured musical possession, displayed proudly at home. Meanwhile, like a crazy fan, I chased Dave into a Premier Inn about five years ago. He was happy to come out for a quick picture and sign some items.

I first met Don ten years ago at his book release in Glasgow. When I sent the picture on to his official website, Don personally emailed back, saying thanks for being a fan for 20 years. I also met him around five years ago prior to a gig in Glasgow, where I showed him the picture from our first meeting. I was overjoyed when he said he remembered it. A lovely fella.

My Super Yob guitar is good to play, although I've never used it in a live setting. It needs a proper set-up, but it would be interesting to compare it against a John Birch model. According to Marco Pirrone, the original is awful, refusing to stay in tune, but he knows it's iconic.

I have no idea what appealed to me that first time I saw Dave and Don's Slade. I think it was a mixture of everything. The sound, the look, the gear. It just pricked up my ears and eyes instantly. Do I believe they're the greatest musical act ever? No, but they are my favourite, and they have a wonderful back catalogue filled with stomping romps, huge choruses, beautiful ballads, and hit after hit after hit. There's a reason they were the biggest selling singles band in the UK in the 1970s, but it's unfortunate that generally they are renowned for one sound (and a seasonal hit) when they were much more dynamic when you look at their output between 1969 and 1992 as a whole. They have lots more to offer than what we see on the surface.

MAINE ROAD FOOTBALL GROUND

27 & 28 APRIL 1996, MANCHESTER, UK

I WAS THERE: DYLAN WHITE

I didn't see them in any theatres or anything in the Eighties period, but I remember they had that single, 'Do You Believe In Miracles?' in 1985, written about Bob Geldof and Live Aid. It was a fantastic record, but it wasn't a hit.

Having attempted to become a rock star with my limited guitar playing and my limited singing, I hustled my way into being a record plugger with a guy called Gary Blackburn. I ended up working with The Beautiful South, Suede and The Farm, and then, because I'd impressed Alan McGee enough with Ride, I got to do Oasis. Every artist has a manager, a booking agent, a press agent and a plugger. And they now have a social media organiser. You represent the artist in the area that you're in, because it's crowded, so the press agent was pestering the music press to get reviews, gig reviews and everything else.

The record plugger was fundamentally pestering BBC Radio 1 to play the records, because that's all there was then, that and an element of Capital Radio, so all you were worried about was getting records on there. It was a massively crowded, complex place. These DJs were bigger than gods – the Simon Bates, the Steve Wrights, the Peter Powells. You name them, they were household names on the radio and on *Top of the Pops*. And when they walked in the building, there would be a series of record pluggers grovelling in front of them.

You'd have to take the producers to lunch. There was nothing corrupt, no payola going on, but there was a bit of, 'Oh yeah, you took me out to lunch the other day. What was that record you wanted playing?'

I was part of this new breed trying to get what was called Britpop on the radio. Luckily, I was very successful at it. I was voted Plugger of the Year in 1994 and won it eleven times with my team. We became very successful as a promotions company, promoting Britpop and dance stuff like Leftfield and Fatboy Slim.

In the Nineties, when the world was on CDs, I owned all of Slade's catalogue in that format and knew there were fallow years when the hits stopped and they kept releasing singles but nobody was buying them. I thought I could make an interesting box set, so I created this playlist on my computer via iTunes. I tracked down all their old records, and because I have access to the BBC, I could get certain records converted, having them played in the studio and put onto tape, things like 'Give Us A Goal'. There was a whole series of singles that weren't hits which were released on the Barn label. I compiled this for a possible four-CD box set of Slade's music, tracked down Colin Newman, their manager, and went to meet him. He thought it was a fantastic idea. Later, they released a five-CD box set. Slade still meant something to me, and I thought those lost singles sounded great.

Meanwhile, Oasis were becoming very successful, doing Knebworth and everything else. I was organising promotion for Noel Gallagher and we went into XFM, run by this tiger who wanted to play everybody first. As part of the promotion for their *(What's the Story) Morning Glory?* LP in 1995, Noel went into XFM for Mary Anne Hobbs' show. We had a multi-platinum disc for *Definitely Maybe* which said,

'To XFM, thank you for all your support.' We went marching in there and Noel presented this disc and did this interview with the host. He might've done a session as well, as he went there a few times, taking an acoustic guitar once or twice.

Mary Anne Hobbs turned around and went, 'Why don't you stay for the second hour? Go in the library, pick some CDs, and we'll play a few of your favourite records.' So me and Noel shuffled off into this little back room in the offices of XFM. He was looking through the CDs and I spotted Slade's *Greatest Hits*. I was quite surprised it was there, at this alternative grunge radio station that basically swore by Nirvana. So I went, 'Noel, Slade! You've got to play some Slade!' He took the CD off me and, lo and behold, played a Slade track and spoke about them in the second hour.

A few months later, Marcus Russell, the manager of Oasis, rang me and said, 'Dylan, come round the office, will you?' I went round and he said, 'I've got to play you something.' He played me Oasis doing 'Cum On Feel The Noize' and said, 'That's your bloody fault! Noel said, 'Dylan's been banging on to about me about Slade and actually it's quite good, you know, and it suits us.'' That became the B-side of 'Don't Look Back In Anger'. They famously did two songs on *Top of the Pops*. No band since The Jam had done that. And they did it on *Later with Jools Holland*. Liam had a dreadful sore throat and sounded like he was singing with razorblades, but it was great.

Oasis moved on to stadium gigs that summer and played Maine Road. Noddy Holder knew all about it by then. Marc Riley was DJing on Radio One with Mark Radcliffe in the evenings then, and he said, 'Look, I can get hold of Noddy.' I said, 'Okay, look let's bring him to Maine Road,' because Noddy lived up there. So we sorted it, passes and everything, and Noddy Holder came to Maine Road.

Oasis knew he was there, and for the encore they did 'Cum On Feel The Noize'. Noddy seeing 40,000 kids going nuts at his song? It was a great moment. And I had a great chat with him. He couldn't remember meeting me in 1973 though!

CHAS CHANDER'S FUNERAL
22 JULY 1996, CULLERCOATS, UK

I WAS THERE: ROGER CROSBY

Roger Crosby met Slade at Chas Chandler's funera

As a local band called The Crosby Brothers, Chas Chandler had been working with us for around eight years and we were impressed by his own musical success but also his management of Jimi and Slade. We'd never met Slade before but had heard loads of stories from Chas of their early days as skinheads. Chas talked about the moment Noddy transformed his stage persona with the addition of the mirrored top hat!

We were working with Chas when he died. His son Stef asked us to play at the funeral and keep the door at the church. Slade came to the funeral. Jimi Hendrix's father Al was there too. It was an odd but celebratory day for our friend, with a lot of musicians and celebrities from the Sixties, Seventies and beyond. Noddy made a wonderful speech about Chas and how he walked through walls for Slade (literally, in a Chinese hotel).

When we all went back to Chas's house, we said hello to the band but Noddy and Dave stayed in the background. Jim, on the other hand, was happy to grab a bass and jam through a few rock 'n' roll hits with us as we played in Chas's garden. We all ended up back in our favourite out-of-hours watering hole in Whitley Bay and had a ton of drink. It was an experience I will never forget and playing with heroes who had 'done the miles' with the same manager and friend as us really brought them to life!

Happy times, sadly too long ago.

BBC TELEVISION CENTRE
1998, WHITE CITY, LONDON, UK

I WAS THERE: MATHEW PRIEST, DODGY

I've met Noddy a couple of times over the years, generally through TV stuff. I shared a panel with him on *Never Mind the Buzzcocks*, got to meet him, and then he had a thing himself (*A Question of Pop*, BBC1, 2000/01), that I did. Because of my accent, all I have to do is speak to anyone from the Black Country for literally five seconds and (goes into the accent) 'I start speaking like that again, mate, y'right? Ah great!' He recognised that, we hit it off and he almost took me under his wing.

After one of the shows up in Manchester, he invited me out for lunch the next day, him and his wife, regaling me with wonderful stories of Ozzy Osbourne and Slade in the early days. One story which is probably in Slade myth but which he told me was true was when they first visited America. They got off the plane at JFK or whatever airport and there were stretch limos there for the band and a van for the crew and the gear. But Slade being Slade, they got into the van and the crew got into the stretch limos! (*adopts black Country accent again*) 'Ah mate, get into the fucking van, knoworrimean!'

Noddy's a lovely bloke, very screwed on, very down to earth… and very shrewd. I got the impression that he doesn't take fools lightly and no one really gets one over on him. The other time I met him was when I was managing Misty's Big Adventure, from Birmingham, this great, crazy band. They had this song, 'Fashion Parade', that needed a spoken bit in the middle. I asked Noddy and he did it for us. We went to the Langham Hotel, London, and we recorded him saying his bit. He appeared in the video as well, bless him. He didn't want any money for anything. Just a lovely bloke, and a survivor… and there's not many of them, really. He's lovely, and I'm proud to have met him.

WATERSTONES BOOKSHOP
3 DECEMBER 1999, GLASGOW, UK

I WAS THERE: JOHN MILNE

I was at Waterstones on Sauchiehall Street when Noddy came to promote his book. He signed it to 'John Milne and the Slade family – Merry Xmasssss!'

Noddy dedicated a piece of promo material to the Milne family

PALACE THEATRE
NOVEMBER 2001, MANCHESTER, UK

WE WERE THERE: DAVID & RACHEL HURST

Me and my daughter Rachel attended the press night of *Miss Saigon* in Manchester in November 2001. Sat behind us were Noddy and Liverpool councillor Derek Hatton. Rachel couldn't contain herself and wanted to speak with Noddy.

At the interval, she took the opportunity and chatted to him and obtained his autograph. After the show had finished, we were walking back to our car and suddenly there was a bellowing voice echoing down the street. At the top of his voice, in the manner of 'It's Christmas!', Noddy was hollering, 'Alright, Rachel?'

David Hurst and daughter Rachel on her wedding day in 2016, but there was no surprise visit from Noddy that day

THE ROBIN 2

SEPTEMBER 2002, BILSTON, WOLVERHAMPTON, UK

I WAS THERE: PAUL COOKSON

It's fair to say that poet Paul Cookson was Touched By the Band of Nod

I did a whole book of Slade poems – *Touched by the Band of Nod* – full colour and illustrated wonderfully by Si Smith, with endorsements and quotes from Mike Peters, Miles Hunt, Mark Radcliffe, Henry Priestman, the (much) re-used quote from Nod, and another from Don Powell. When the book came out, I sent copies to Slade's management for Nod and Jim. I was in a school in Bolton when I got a call. It was Frank Lea, Jim's brother, saying, 'James has asked me to let you know how much he enjoyed the poems, he was reading them out to his wife and mother over dinner.'

This eventually led to Frank asking me to write a poem to be performed before Jim did an event at The Robin in Bilston, to celebrate his DVD release. So, there I was, supporting Jim Lea!

I received a signed album and two-page letter from Jim sometime later, thanking me, saying he'd expected a nervous best man's type of speech but was blown away by my performance and presence!

GRUETUNET

9 AUGUST 2003, KIRKENÆR, NORWAY

I WAS THERE: GEIR ARNE AMUNDSEN

Geir remembers everybody singing along

Slade were playing a concert in Kirkenær, Norway, a small village north of Kongsvinger, 150 kilometres north of Oslo. Slade were a part of my life when growing up so I went. The first record I ever bought was *Sladest.* I still have it! They were playing all the old songs and it was a very good show, with everybody singing along.

KOKO

18 DECEMBER 2011, CAMDEN, LONDON, UK

I WAS THERE: PETER SMITH

The 2011 incarnation of the band featured guitarist Dave Hill, drummer Don Powell and a couple of new members. No Noddy Holder or Jim Lea. I wasn't too sure what to expect and thought twice about whether to take the plunge. Could they possibly recreate the raw energy their performances used to exude? Could they spark the excitement they achieved all those years ago? Most importantly, how could Slade still be Slade without Noddy? A few things made me decide to make the trip to London. Firstly, Slade shows in the UK were few and far between; they seemed to be playing mostly in Germany at the time, where they retained a strong following. Secondly, this concert saw them returning to the Music Machine, aka Camden Palace and now called Koko, a venue they had played several times in the Seventies and Eighties, so there was a sense of homecoming about the gig. Also, this was a charity gig in support of the Lord Taverners, all monies going to a good cause. Finally, this was the closest I was likely to get to seeing Slade again, with Dave Hill always a great showman, and Don Powell a great drummer, so why not?

Reading the Slade forum before the gig, it seemed that many members were, like me, going along after a long time away from the band. It was also being filmed for a DVD, which always makes things a little special. On balance, I was looking forward to the gig as a way of returning to my memories, and saying thank you to Dave and Don, although I did worry that, without Noddy, the gig would be disappointing. So why was I so apprehensive of seeing Slade without Noddy? I guess it says something about the power he had as a vocalist, and the presence he had on stage.

That night, I walked from my hotel and stopped off for a drink in the pub over the road from Koko, which was full of Slade fans. A Noddy lookalike was sporting a mirrored top hat and a tartan suit, and another had a Dave Hill haircut and an inflatable guitar. I made my way over to Koko, which was starting to fill up. At around 7pm, DJ Mike Read took to the stage to introduce the band. He also showed a video of charity work of the Lord Taverners. A few moments later Slade took to the stage, starting off with 'We'll Bring The House Down'.

The set was, as expected full of hits, all played well; it was great to hear them all again, although I thought it could have been louder. The singer did a good job, his vocals strong and pretty true to Noddy, although he left much of the talking to Dave, who had clearly become the front man. It was very obvious that this had become Dave and Don's band. Dave was on great form, clearly enjoying himself, running about the stage, getting the crowd to sing along and playing some great guitar. The place was pretty full, and the crowd was really up for the occasion, giving the band a great reception. During 'Mama Weer All Crazee Now', Dave strapped on his Super Yob guitar to a massive cheer from the audience (was this a new one? I am pretty sure Marco from Adam and the Ants had the original).

The set finished with 'Get Down And Get With It', and the encores were 'My Oh My', 'Cum On Feel The Noize' and the inevitable 'Merry Xmas Everybody'. Mike Read came back on to close the evening wearing Dave's old stage jacket, which had just been auctioned for £250 (a bargain; looking back I wish I had bought it!). It was great to see them again for old times' sake, but it did make me realise how good a full reunion could be.

I made my way back to the hotel and was up early in the morning to get the 6am train home. I'd enjoyed the event but realised things could never be the same. I bought the DVD and was quite touched to see myself on it, entering the venue at the start of the evening.

I have seen Slade since on a 1970s tour with The Sweet. Again, they were good, but my old memories always take me back to the original band. Slade were one of the greatest rock bands ever to come out of the UK. On a good night, in a sweaty ballroom, close down the front there was nothing like them.

I'm probably partially deaf now. Some of that is down to Slade. No regrets. Happy days. On reflection, Noddy is probably right not to reform the band. It could well be a disappointment, and that would be sad. We are best left with our memories. Having said that, good luck to Dave and Don, long may they continue to keep the Slade flag flying. Slade forever! Writing this has renewed my interest in Slade. Perhaps I will go and see the new version again one day. Just for old times' sake.

WATERSTONES
4 OCTOBER 2013, WOLVERHAMPTON, UK

I WAS THERE: SIMON HARVEY

I arrived at Wolverhampton train station in good time for a late morning book signing at Waterstones of Don Powell's *Look Wot I Dun*, followed by afternoon tea with the author at a Q&A session at the Quality Hotel. But outside the station, I bumped into Dave 'Super Yob' Hill, who was on his way to BBC Radio's Broadcasting House in London to meet Ken Bruce and record his selection of favourite tunes for the *Tracks Of My Years* feature on Ken's Radio 2 programme. We had a quick catch-up at the taxi rank, recalling some great times spent together, before he headed off to his train and I went off to meet Don. You just never know who you're going to meet wandering the streets of Wolverhampton!

Dave Hill in his Yob 1 Jenson Interceptor at Alfreton Leisure Centre, 4th October 2003 before a gig at the venue with his line-up of Slade.

The book signing was well attended, Don on fine form chatting to fans, signing books and memorabilia and generally being an all-round nice chap. Then at the Quality Hotel, he was interviewed by BBC Coventry & Warwickshire presenter Clive Elkin. All aspects of Don's professional and personal life were touched upon, and no stones were left unturned. As well as Slade's success, Don's personal tragedies were recalled and he twice had to regain his composure when discussing the 1973 car crash

Noddy Holder and Simon Harvey, at a Christmas lights switch-on event at Walsall's Manor Hospital on 5th December 2014 rather than Dr Who auditions

in which his 20-year-old fiancée Angela Morris died. It was an insight into the man himself that was so very endearing.

The Q&A session was a resounding success, with members of the audience asking some very obscure and bizarre questions which Don did his best to answer honestly – you had to be there to believe some of them.

I attended this event with lifelong Slade friends Dave Kemp and John Gibbings, the three of us having first met at Bailey's Nightclub, Watford in October 1978 as Slade commenced a seven-night residency at this chicken-in-the-basket cabaret club. I booked the front row centre-stage table for the full week, and night after night Dave, John, Juliet Harris and myself witnessed Slade in a tiny venue tearing up the club at full volume, to the dismay of some of the attendees.

It was an experience never to be forgotten. We met the band as they arrived every afternoon, attending soundchecks and after-show soirees in the dressing room, where much alcohol was consumed by all. The four of us soon realised the bond of Slade would cement firm friendships. We christened ourselves The Watford Four and began a lifetime of fun and frolics following our beloved Slade across the nation.

Dave Kemp was a true ambassador of all things Slade, becoming personal friends with all the band, especially Don and Jim. He ran the Slade International Fan Club from the late Seventies through to the late Eighties and was heavily involved in organising many successful fan club conventions across the years, touching so many fans' lives across the globe until his sad passing, aged just 60, in December 2020. I'm more than privileged and honoured to have been his friend for 42 years, and his memory lives on through his love and dedication to Slade.

TOWN HALL
24 JUNE 2014, WALSALL, UK

I WAS THERE: CHRIS HILL

I was lucky enough to be one of only 40 people allowed into the council chamber's public gallery to witness Noddy Holder receiving his Freedom of Walsall accolade from the Lord Mayor. Nod later appeared in the Town Hall in front of a big crowd to celebrate his award and address the public. He's never forgotten where he came from.

I have an un-played box set signed by all four Slade members, which took a while to complete. Don and Dave were easy to locate – they signed when I worked with them. But then there were Nod and Jim to track down. There were far too many people to attempt a Jim signing at the Robin 2 in 2017 and he was literally mobbed, so the hunt went on. I then saw Nod advertised as opening a shop in Darlaston, local to us, so out came the box set and my Slade t-shirt and off I went. Luckily, there was an *Express and Star* reporter there, who spotted my shirt and asked me to the front to pose with Nod for a few photos. I was in, and got the third signature and my picture in the paper, with Nod actually signing it.

And then there was Jim, the elusive one. I happened to mention to a friend of mine something about Slade and he mentioned how Jim would go in the cafe where his wife worked in Brewood Village, once or twice a week for his breakfast – usually the day the fishmongers' van was present. I went to the café, left the box set there, and a week later my mission was accomplished – all four signatures.

THE CALEY BAR
AUGUST 2015, EDINBURGH, UK

I WAS THERE: TERRY EDWARDS, THE NEAR JAZZ EXPERIENCE

A lot of people who got somewhere in Indie music and Punk rock like to think of there being a Year Zero and like to forget all that came before. But, you know what, when we were 13, we fucking loved The Sweet, Mud, and the really poppy ones… rather than the cool ones. You look through the charts, and a lot of these things you really liked were kind of novelty singles really. But we loved all that, and just liked the sound of the guitar. And we're not talking Jimi Hendrix or Eric Clapton here.

I was doing some shows in Edinburgh in August 2015, playing for a burlesque show (also starring former Dexy's/Serious Drinking keyboard player Pete Saunders), and then at eight o'clock there was a space available, so I did a show with Neil Fraser from Tindersticks, just straight music (as Edwards & Fraser). We kept our clothes kept on all the time! Then we did a late-night burlesque show, and Noddy Holder came up with his family.

Burlesque shows are family shows in a sense. There's no full-frontal nudity, it's all just end of the pier and *Carry On*-ish. It's very entertaining, very well done. It's not the centrefold of *Playboy.* It's an adult family show you can enjoy together, and you get mixed audiences, which is really brilliant. Anyway, we had a chat with Noddy.

I'd met him once before with George Peckham, as in Porky Prime Cuts, whose studio used to be not far from the BBC, on Portland Place. There was a little mews pub, and the back door of his studio almost went straight into the pub... and he did! That was just me, George and Noddy having a drink together.

I reminded Noddy of this when I chatted to him in Edinburgh, although of course he wouldn't remember me, and then he started talking about how Slade went to Hamburg in the early Sixties, after The Beatles had been there. He was telling us there were a lot of US Air Force and GIs there, many of them Black Americans, and they'd be asking for James Brown songs for the band to play, which they'd never heard before – we just couldn't get hold of that sort of music over here at the time.

He was saying, 'We learned a lot of these songs, and we learned our craft there.' And that made such sense to me, thinking Slade made such perfect pop songs. Because, like The Beatles, they did play loads of pop songs back in the day, and not a lot of people really know that. You then put two and two together and realise that's why they crafted such perfect pop songs, because they'd done that in their late teens or early twenties. That was their stock-in-trade.

It was just lovely to have a proper chat with him. He's aware that you know he's Noddy Holder, but he's very good with people, in the same way someone like Suggs is. You'll have that little chat, then the person who's had the chat for 30 seconds goes away happy, and nobody gets stuck with anyone! And he's quite happy with his fame and everything. And going back to the music, I thought the guitars on Slade's songs sounded great. They were just so in your face, weren't they!

ST SAVIOUR'S COMMUNITY CENTRE
25 OCTOBER 2017, EAST RETFORD, UK

I WAS THERE: STUART RUTTER

A few years ago, Don Powell was doing a *Pies, Peas and Performances* book night with Paul Cookson, a brilliant poet and another huge Slade fan. For reasons best known to myself, I went in a black frock coat, a Cadbury's purple metallic shirt, badges and a Slade belt. I met Don outside and he recognised me, came straight over, big hugs, and we had a quick catch-up. We got pictures taken together, but there was no comment whatsoever about what I was wearing.

We get into the venue and he's up on stage, with everybody sat there – maybe 200 or 300 people. He's got the microphone and it's all, 'Glad to see so many people

February 10, 1979 SOUNDS

Fan Clubs

SLADE NEWS — The new Slade mag!! Send 25p to: D. Kemp, 24 Ingham Road, London NW6.

here… thanks very much for coming and…' – pointing at me – 'it's especially nice to see Showaddywaddy sent a representative along.' And that's exactly his kind of humour – waiting until there's 300 people to laugh before passing comment!

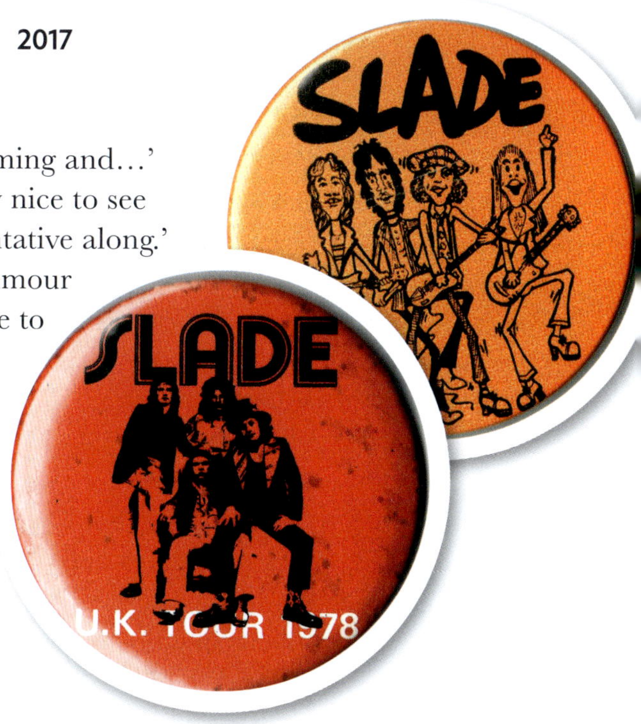

Part of Stu Rutter's collection of Slade memorabilia

ROBIN 2

14 NOVEMBER 2017, BILSTON, UK

I WAS THERE: COLIN FOSTER

I lived on the Bentley estate, just across the M6 motorway from Pouk Hill. Aged 14, I'd popped up to the shops. A friend was coming out of the sweet shop/tobacconist's, and we stopped to chat when we turned to see this posh car – a silver Jensen Interceptor – pull up, out of which stepped H, the one and only Dave Hill. He looked at the two of us, and my pal greeted him with, 'Worroh, Dave, how's ya doin'?' I remember Dave starting with, 'I'm doin' great,' and the majority of the rest of the conversation is lost in the mists of time… probably down to the beer I've drunk since. But I remember him standing there for around five to ten minutes, just chatting, telling us he'd stopped to pick up some cigarettes before heading to his girlfriend's, and if he wasn't careful he'd be late.

We were still standing there, starstruck, when he came out of the shop, thanked us for following the band and for being fans, and said he hoped we'd be able to get to the next gig. Then, with a brief wave, he'd gone. Up to that point, I'd been a 'bit of a fan', but that cemented them as the band for me. The fact that Dave had taken the time to have a chat with a couple of starstruck lads just blew me away. Slade were properly at the top of their game, and yet it came across that, off stage, they were 'just like us'.

I saw Slade several times at Wolverhampton Civic. I'm not sure whether my ears have ever recovered! One time, my mum and dad picked me up as it was a Friday night and we were then going to the caravan – they were good enough to delay a trip out to Wales until after the gig. I only spoke once on the trip out, as my ears were ringing so much, I was shouting and got told off!

When Dave was on his book tour, I saw him at the Robin 2 and, getting my copy signed of the book signed, I recounted the story of our first meeting. He chuckled and said that talking to fans when they were out and about at home was something they always tried to do, as they were always conscious that it was 'us fans' that got them famous.

My daughter mentioned that when she was at university, one of her fellow students regularly played Seventies and Eighties tracks as they drove to assignments (they were both trainee teachers) and she always wondered why she was word perfect whenever a Slade track came on… until she got back in our car for the end of term journey home from uni… Second track in, she realised why!

I've met the other members too – Noddy when he was signing his first book, Jim in a pub and Don at the Robin 2 watching a band the night before Slade II were on stage. I personally thanked each of them for being the soundtrack of my youth and these past 50ish years, and whilst we didn't have much time to chat, they were all still the same down-to-earth chaps. But that meeting with Dave, when they were at the height of success, always stays with me. I think it's more a case of, 'That's Dave, local boy made good!' than, 'Oh, my gosh' – screams of recognition – 'that's Dave Hill from Slade!' I guess that's just how us Black Country folk are.

BBC RADIO BIRMINGHAM

17 MAY 2018, BIRMINGHAM, UK

I WAS THERE: SIMON HARVEY

Jim Lea was booked into BBC Radio Birmingham's Mailbox for a mammoth all-day recording session to promote his six-track EP *Lost*

Top, Simon Harvey with Jim Lea, and above, Jim with Diane Rutter, right, and Julie Evans-Mulligan at BBC Radio Birmingham

in Space, recording interviews with regional BBC broadcasters to be aired at later dates. I arrived at the studios with my Slade friends Diane Rutter and Julie Evans-Mulligan, hoping to meet Jim during the day. We were all in for a massive treat when Jim took a break from recording and, passing through the reception area, kindly obliged our request for a few moments for photos and autographs. He ended up spending his lunch hour talking to us about many subjects, including Slade at Reading Festival 1980 and him replacing Alan Lancaster in Status Quo on *Top of the Pops* on 'Margarita Time' in 1983, the day Rick Parfitt fell into the drum kit during the broadcast.

It really was a unique experience for a Slade fan, and Julie, Diane and myself were fortunate enough to have that honour to ourselves. Diane and myself had met Jim many times over the years, but it was Julie's first time, fulfilling a lifetime wish.

Sadly, Julie lost her fight with the Big C in April 2019, but that day will always be a treasured memory for me, one shared with special friends and the unbelievably talented, down to earth multi-millionaire superstar James Whild Lea. A nicer person you couldn't wish to meet.

SWANYARD STUDIOS
SEPTEMBER 2019, RETFORD, UK

I WAS THERE: PAUL COOKSON

In September 2002, I met Don Powell face to face for the first time. *Pies, Peas and Performances* is a venue and event I've created and curated with friends in Retford, Nottinghamshire. It does what it says on the tin. The pies are wonderful, and we've had some great shows.

I invited Don over and we had a great chat and interview, and Les (Glover) played a couple of Slade songs as part of the event with violinist Graham Bottley (from *Gogglebox*). After the event, Don said how much he enjoyed it, and asked if he could come back and do another, as he hadn't told all his stories. Of course, he could!

Les and I had started writing songs by then, so we decided to write a couple of nostalgia-based songs – 'Rose Tinted Glasses' and 'Coz We Luv You'. We performed the latter at the next event with Don. We'd also got 'It Isn't Really Christmas Until Noddy Starts To Sing', which we wanted to do as a Christmas single. We asked Don if he would consider drumming on them if we recorded them and he agreed. On a borrowed drum kit in Swanyard Studios, Retford, he said to James Bennett, the engineer, 'Play it through, James, and I'll play along, see how it goes.' Two takes and he'd got both tracks – perfect. On 'Coz We Luv You?'' he said, 'Is it okay if I do the same sort of beat as on 'Coz I Luv You?' and on 'It Isn't Really Christmas…' he said, 'I think I'll do the same shuffle as 'Merry Xmas Everybody'. Is that okay, lads?' Of course, it was!

As he'd got both songs in quick time, he asked if we'd got any others, and we worked up a couple of demos with him there and then. Don said, 'We've done five songs today, lads – that's half an album… should we do an album?' Alright Don, if you twist our arms.

That was how it began, and here we are, two albums later, with another ready for later in the year. And when Jim and Don did an event at Wolverhampton Art Gallery on 6th August 2022, Les and I performed a piece called 'Time To Shine', about the two of them, perhaps the guys in the background before. I mean, with Nod and Dave, you've not much choice! It was part-poem, part-song, and went down really well. So much so, we've since recorded it.

ENGINE ROOMS

4 DECEMBER 2021, SOUTHAMPTON, UK

I WAS THERE: GARY STEWARD, AGE 17

In 1981 I was eight months into a career as an Air Engineering Mechanic in the Royal Navy. Based on the south coast at HMS Daedalus, during August we were given some down time, especially at weekends. On 1st August a few of us had travelled to the Heavy Metal Holocaust Festival at Port Vale FC's stadium, widely regarded as one of the all-time great festivals and the loudest. A few weeks later, the same few travelled up by train to Derby for the Donington Festival. Having no accommodation, Derby Railway Station waiting room was not a pleasant place for a kip (that on the back of sleeping at Stoke-on-Trent station a few weeks earlier).

Gary Steward saw Dave Hill's Slade 40 years after seeing the original line-up at Donington

The awesome line-up made Donington extra special. On getting to the site, we headed straight for the mosh. The festival had not yet got going and the massive crowd were not sure what they were going to get from Slade, who were on next. At Port Vale, we had witnessed anything and everything, including food stuffs and urine-filled plastic and glass bottles, being thrown around in the air, so a lovely prospect awaited. Slade blew everybody away that day, getting the crowd going in full-frenzied excitement and top throwing capability. Noddy and Dave were on fire. Noddy's fabulous voice was as gruff as ever, and his showmanship came to the fore as Dave and Jim bounced around the stage. All the classics were there, along with some truly gripping covers, such as Eddie Cochran's 'Somethin' Else'. By the time Noddy and the band banged out 'Merry Xmas Everybody' in the middle of August, that year's Donington was special and a hard act for Blue Öyster Cult, who were on next, to follow. I left that day knowing that Slade had truly got people talking. I also left with a smile on my face, as well as being covered in all sorts of stuff and fluid that we won't mention.

Winding the clock forward 40 years to December 2021, the only remaining original member was Dave Hill. His diminutive frame still housed that larger-than-life character and the classic Slade songs still sounded so good. Climbing onto the front of stage amps, he could still get the crowd going. It took me back to 1981 and a reminder that Slade truly were one of the great rock bands.

2022
BUTLINS
16 OCTOBER 2022, SKEGNESS, UK

I WAS THERE: DAVID MURRAY

I saw Slade many years ago and as recently as October 2022 at a Seventies weekend at Butlins, where I also saw Lindisfarne, The Glitter Band, The Three Degrees and Showaddywaddy. Most of the groups only had one or two original members, but all were brilliant. Slade only had Dave Hill as the original member, having now taken over as frontman and lead singer.

He was totally mental… in a good way – very energetic and involving the crowd to sing along, and best of all, my ears were ringing for an hour or so when they had finished. They were very loud and very good.

ST SAVIOUR'S COMMUNITY CENTRE
29 OCTOBER 2022, EAST RETFORD, UK

I WAS THERE: PAUL COOKSON

I'd contacted Suzan Holder about her book, *Shake It Up, Beverley* and she came along and did a great event. So much so that when her follow-up, *Rock 'n' Rose*, came out she asked to come back. How could we refuse? We were setting up when she came in and said, 'Hi Paul, I've brought a friend – hope you don't mind,' and in came Nod with a 'hello, my man, how ya doin'?'

Paul Cookson duets with Noddy Holder and an out-of-shot marrow in East Retford, late 2022

Nod was great and gave Suzan centre-stage… until the raffle that he'd agreed to do at half time. (We always have a raffle with prizes of varying quality.) It started at 8.30pm, and by 9.10pm Noddy was still telling stories, brilliantly and comedically interrupted and joined by Suzan.

We'd had a church fair earlier on that day so had two sizeable matching marrows available as raffle prizes. Much hilarity was had at their expense, and in a moment of fun and opportunism someone suggested a pic of Noddy and a marrow. I mentioned that it sounded like a George Formby song. I had my ukulele there and started strumming in a Formby style as me and Nod had our pic taken. He began singing along, 'Me and my marrow are friends!' A duet… of sorts. I write a daily poem, so shortly after I wrote an intellectual ditty, 'Hello, Mrs Holder – Have You Seen My Marrow?', which was performed by Henry Priestman, Les Glover and I at a later *Pies and Peas!*

Some of Dylan White's singles collection

EXTENDED PLAY

I WAS THERE: STUART DEABILL

A fucking great band who managed that rare thing, a hard-edged physicality of sound and a tenderness of touch throughout, with no quarter given. God bless Noddy, Jim, Dave and Don. They lit up my Seventies like a Ford Capri with go faster stripes!

I WAS THERE: NICK HORTON, THE SHAKESPEAROS

So here it is… Slade were the first 'contemporary' band I really got into, having been raised during the 1960s on a heady diet of *Two Way Family Favourites*, James Last and, thankfully, The Beatles and Jerry Lee Lewis. The matchless run of smash hit singles during that glorious epoch of 1971 to 1973 coincided with my elevation from junior to senior school after passing my eleven-plus in 1972, and they were the initial inspiration for my long-lasting love of popular music and my wanting to learn to play the drums. The thrilling spectacle and deafening racket of Slade on *Top of the Pops* had me sprinting downtown to Woolworth's the next morning, flinging my pocket money over the counter. Dave's gurning Super Yobbery, Jim's cool musicality, Don's fabulous and inimitable shuffling drums and Noddy's unmistakable roar and mirrored top hat were just what this snotty eleven-year-old oik, suddenly transported to a stuffy, pseudo-posh, all-boys grammar school, was looking for.

Photo: Paul Caldwell

Nick Horton, in action with The Shakespearos, a big Slade fan in his formative years

I distinctly remember the '0/10, See Me After Class' from my English teacher when I attempted my own Shakesperean-style sonnet homework, written in the misspelt style of a Slade single. Well, I fort it was grate…

I also recall being sent home from school for wearing the regulation black platform boots I'd persuaded my mum to buy from, I think, Freeman, Hardy & Willis in Weymouth after seeing Noddy wearing a pair on *TOTP* that week. To her eternal credit, she sent me back the next day with a note explaining they were NOT the prohibited platform boots but heavy duty shoes as, 'Nicholas tends to go through a pair very quickly these days.'

Slade were part of the Glam avalanche (Glam-slide?) which opened my ears and eyes to such brilliant artists as T.Rex, Sweet and, ultimately, Bowie and Roxy Music… The rest is hysteria.

At school, I volunteered to take part in a 'Show and Tell' during a General Studies period where I argued the merits of Slade, Sweet, Bowie, and Gary Glitter (okay, no one knew at the time, all right?) against those of the twiddling tedious prog pomp of Yes, ELP and King Crimson, as preferred by pals' older brothers. I can't remember if I was successful during the debate, but I think history has proved me right. The classic hits, 'Take Me Bak 'Ome', 'Cum On Feel The Noize', 'Mama Weer All Crazee Now' and 'Skweeze Me, Pleeze Me' still sound fantastic today and were, I'd argue, outriders for the Punk movement only just a couple of years away. And I'll stamp my platform boots in disgust if you don't agree that 'Everyday' and 'How Does It Feel?' are brilliant songs by anyone's yardstick.

And you know the festive season is just around the corner when you hear 'Merry Xmas Everybody' in the shops every flipping September…

I WAS THERE: PRENTICE JAMES

Slade hold a special place in my musical journey and are without doubt the band that captured perfectly the wonderful era that was Glam rock. When I started high school in the early Seventies, Glam rock was in full swing and bands like T.Rex, Sweet and Slade were a constant presence in the Top 40. Every Thursday evening, *Top of the Pops* was my must-watch programme, and if anyone was to ask which band epitomises that era, without hesitation I would always say Slade.

They were everything TOTP was about – they were fun, great on stage, and produced pop magic time and time again. One of my earliest seven-inch purchases was 'Skweeze Me, Pleeze Me', at the age of eleven. Music has that unique ability to leave permanent deep memories of particular times, places and feelings, and when I think of Slade, I am back there reliving the magic that was '70s Glam rock – happy daze. They were a truly special band who define an era of music magic. Simply put, they were pop perfection and TV gold, and hold the accolade in my personal musical journey of 'the band I never saw, yet the band that for me defined an era I loved.'

I WAS THERE: TONY MICHAELIDES, BROADCASTER & PODCASTER

I never saw Slade live, but I loved their look and their crazy energy. It was high-speed, full-on entertainment! Some might have lumped it in with Glam Rock, but I blended the two and prefer to call it Slam Rock! I thought their music had instant appeal. I have always loved bands who looked like they were having a good time. And Slade were most definitely that band. Noddy Holder stood out, not only because he was their lead singer, but he had an incredible aura about him, which wasn't just how he dressed or his crazy hair but his appetite to entertain and that unique ability that great frontmen have where you just can't take your damn eyes off them! He 'worked' the audience in a way that he appeared to be looking at all of them. And that naughty, cheeky little grin didn't do him any harm. He clearly needed no training, and I'm sure they were a huge influence on a multitude of bands back then.

Tony Michaelides in Piccadilly Radio days. He was very impressed with Noddy Holder when they worked together at the station

My favourite Slade song has to be 'Cum On Feel The Noize', the ultimate classic, singalong anthem. How could you just stand there and not jump up and down and bounce off the person next to you whilst bawling out that chorus? It was good to see the Gallagher brothers reintroduce the song to a new audience many decades later.

Noddy got to do his own show at Piccadilly Radio in Manchester at the same time I was on air, so I got to see him quite a few times in and around the station. He was always cordial and happy to talk to you, and none of it was at all contrived. And he never lost that cheeky grin. He made you feel that he was happy to see you. He would always try and make himself available to play in the radio station's charity cricket matches too, whenever possible, which I thought was really cool. He was the perfect pop star, so equipped to deal with fame. No airs and graces.

Having been around successful musicians for many years, it's easy to identify those who were destined to be Rock Stars. Noddy Holder was such an iconic star of the Seventies and Slade would be deserving inductees in the Rock and Roll Hall of Fame. They released 21 singles and 15 albums, all with the same line-up. That is a worthy achievement in itself.

I WASN'T THERE: ANN NAZARIO, PODCASTER

Being originally from the Philippines, I didn't know anything about Slade until I moved to Manchester in 1996, not even THAT famous Christmas song! They never got played on the radio. Our generation had heard of 'Cum On Feel The Noize', but we knew this as a Quiet Riot song. Imagine my surprise when, now living in Manchester and watching *Top of the Pops 2* one evening, I saw Slade doing that Quiet Riot song! I got to know more of their music via 'oldies' programmes on the telly. And, yes, since my first Christmas in Manchester, I've learnt to scream, 'It's Christmaaaaaaaaaass!'

Fast forward to 2022, into the second year of my *Ask The Drummer* podcast, and I was blessed to have Slade's Don Powell on the show (with massive thanks to Don's Occasional Flames' bandmate, Les Glover). By now, I already knew how much of a legend Don is. When I was writing my script for the show, I speed-read (overnight!) *Look Wot I Dun*, and was so shocked and equally amazed with everything he'd gone through.

It also made me so nervous, thinking 'I am not worthy' of doing this podcast with such a legend. But when we finally got connected, and I saw him on the screen, we had a little chat before we went live, and he was so lovely.

I loved the way he talked, his accent so sweet, and he soon made me feel at ease. Don Powell is such a beautiful soul. The hubby still can't believe we got an invite to go and see Don Powell and his family in Denmark! We should really do that soon. I'd love to meet Don in real life and give him a BIG hug! He's such an inspiration. Perhaps, someday, I'll get to learn more about his bandmates too. But, for now, Don Powell is my favourite in Slade! Oh, and I do believe 'Merry Xmas Everybody' is now being played in the Philippines a lot over Christmas.

I WAS THERE: MIKE PHILPOTT

Trouble is, when I was nine, I always preferred Gary Glitter. There's all sorts of public bar jokes to be inserted there, and with the benefit of hindsight it's an opinion I have had to submit back to myself for reconsideration for many a long year now. But Slade used to give me the right hump. They'd release a single at around the same time as my hero, and it would always outsell his. Only just outsell, but outsell, nonetheless. And don't even start me about the bloody Sweet. But Slade? They couldn't even spell their song titles properly, for Christ's sake.

Let's look at the facts. For context, pop music didn't exist until 1972. I grew up with classically trained, classical musical loving, classical parents, and only a chance encounter with *Top of the Pops* in late 1972 changed my perception of what actual tunes could sound like. It would be the middle of the Seventies before The Beatles even existed in my life.

So in 1973, when 'Do You Wanna Touch Me' appeared on *TOTP*, performed by the tin-foil-suited yet-to-be criminal, I was delighted to be able to say I'd found a favourite pop star. It reached No.2 in the charts, which apparently was important (I was still learning). And then, immediately, those oiks from Wolverhampton trumped it when 'Cum On Feel The Noize' went straight in at No.1 and stayed there for four weeks. They repeated the trick with 'Skweeze Me, Pleeze Me', despite our Gaz having said hello and been back again in the meantime. And although there was a brief respite when the leader of my own perfect imaginary gang back then beat the Midlands yobs' friend Stan to the No.1 spot, they well and truly went and placed the nail in my sparkly, spangly idol's commercial coffin that bloody Christmas.

You-Know-What spent five weeks at No.1 at the end of 1973, knocking my soon to be ex-leader's masterpiece off the top of the charts after it had only been there for an ignominious four weeks. Spurred on by this injustice, I pushed myself hard in an effort to exact retribution, and duly came second in a Gary Glitter impersonation contest at my primary school, miming to 'I Love You Love Me Love'. I'd have won it too if it wasn't for that pesky Italian girl that everyone really liked. But you get the picture. Always the runner-up. That bloody Christmas song has since spent over half a million weeks in the charts and scientists have had to commission several new unpronounceable valuable metals to make commemorative records in frames every time it sells another five billion copies or so.

But, but, but... thing is, though, y'know… whisper it quietly, but… Slade were quite good actually, weren't they? We grow older, the mind expands, we wander through our memories, and we realise how lucky we once were (and still are) sometimes, and we forgive, we mellow, and we revisit.

Truth is, I always liked Slade, even back then as a nine-year-old, for all of their sins. I liked pretty much everything I saw on that half-hour long weekly TV treat that was all I had to help me discover the world of rock 'n' roll back in 1973, but Slade were always a highlight. That singer and his silly hat and sideburns, that posing guitarist with his equally silly hat (the guy that I knew my teacher fancied, whatever that meant, because someone told me she did), that dude on the bass and that drummer who just chewed and chewed on gum at the same pace as he beat those skins. Those songs, that sound, the Glam. Ah yes, the Glam. Funny how we all kicked against that in 1977 when we were older and wiser and more street, man, and we wanted to consign those bands to the dustbin of history.

But it sounds alright now, doesn't it?

With hindsight, Slade were one of many, many bands from pre-history without the sum of whose parts Punk and everything that followed would never have happened. I pride myself on my eclectic and educated musical tastes these days, but when all's said and done, give me some electric guitars, at least one show-off playing one of them, a bassist and a drummer who can combine and bang out metronomic 4/4 rhythms with the occasional accomplished twiddle and flourish, some basic bluesy chords, a bloody good tune and a middle-eight that hooks you back into the song till it's over, and you know what? I'm happy as Noddy.

I WAS THERE: JOE SHOOMAN

Neal Kay, who was instrumental in the birth of the New Wave Of British Heavy Metal. He promoted many bands at the Metal, took the view that 'they were a fucking rock 'n' roll killing machine onstage'. And he would know. Never mind the cheesiness of the famous stuff, Slade were a mighty unit providing roaringly aggressive guitar rock whilst most NWOBHM acts were still in short trousers.

About 2006, I interviewed a band in Wolverhampton and they took me around the sights, sounds, venues and important musical places that made them who they were. The band I forget – they had a couple of indie singles and disappeared – but I will never forget the buzz of excitement that went around a particular coffee shop we were in. Literally like all conversation stopped and there was a hush – I turned around and there was Dave Hill, waving happily at everyone. Obviously, the band got pics with him. I wish I had.

Everyone goes on about Oasis loving The Beatles and being Fab Four wannabes. Actually, if you listen to *Definitely Maybe* and *(What's The Story) Morning Glory?*, the predominate influence there, sonically, is Slade. Walls of guitars, catchy choruses, streetwise posturing, and a disdain for bullshit? Come on. It's Slade all over, though Slade's spelling is on a par with the Ladybird-book rhyme schemes of Noel's lyrics. And Oasis were at their very best when they sounded like 1975 Slade.

I WAS THERE: DAVID STARK

My main memories of Slade in their heyday are of being as gobsmacked as everyone else by Dave Hill's outrageous costumes on *Top of the Pops* and Noddy's mirrored top hat and especially his voice, which reminded me of John Lennon's. I also loved his and Jim's songwriting, their clever lyrics, brilliant melodies, and the great fun attitude of the band in general.

Thanks to BBC Radio 2 (mainly Ken Bruce, but also Johnnie Walker)

David Stark with Noddy Holder and Mike McCartney

Photo: David Stark

Noddy and Suzan Holder

I became aware of what quickly became my favourite track of theirs. I'd completely missed out on 'How Does It Feel?' from *Slade in Flame* first time round, having never seen the film at the pictures, only on TV many years later. The record is an absolute masterpiece of composition and arrangement which always makes me stop whatever I'm doing whenever it comes on the radio, usually Radio 2 again.

It was also only many years later that I unexpectedly became pals with Noddy and Don Powell thanks to us all attending a bi-annual music veterans' lunch in Barnes. They were regulars there well before me. I also recall Dave Hill being there on one occasion, the nearest thing to a Slade reunion. Being a drummer and avid Beatles fan like Don also means we can talk shop whenever we meet up. He's rightly still very proud of playing with Ringo on one occasion when the All-Starr Band played in Copenhagen.

I also know Noddy and his lovely wife Suzan from attending Graduation Days at the Liverpool Institute for Performing Arts (LIPA), co-founded by

Paul McCartney, which I'm closely involved with. Nod and Suzan's son Django studied there and he's now making headway in the music business himself, a lovely lad. Suzan and Noddy are a great couple who I've shared more than a few laughs with over the past few years.

I WAS THERE: PETE ASTOR, THE LOFT & THE WEATHER PROPHETS

I guess Jim Lea was the person I visually looked up to when I was twelve or 13. He struck me as the cool one. Noddy was always a bit of a clown. That's not criticising, but he didn't have the vibe, whereas when you're growing up you need role models, and Jim was super-cool.

I WAS THERE: JC CARROLL, THE MEMBERS

I remember them from the very early days when they did a Yardbirds cover, 'The Shape of Things to Come', and thinking 'this band are really good'. Then they just exploded into this monster that was Slade! They were a rock band, then they suddenly went pop, very similar to Sweet, a fantastic rock band that decided to make pop records with Chinnichap (producers Nicky Chinn and Mike Chapman). And like there's two sides of Sweet, there's kind of two sides of Slade, but they fitted in so well into that groove. They had great songs, great deliveries, and some surprises in the catalogue.

JC Carroll of The Members was taken with Slade from an early age

Punk rock was very similar to Glam, in that anybody that was into the Punk rock scene was into Glam. There weren't too many guitar solos… just great beats. There were quite a few bands that didn't break through to the mainstream that made great records too, like Hello, and The Arrows, who did 'I Love Rock 'n' Roll'. But Slade were the biggest group, although unlike T.Rex, they probably slightly more appealed to the boys than the girls.

Jim Lea is an amazing musician and songwriter, and he was a really big part of what they were doing, writing some fantastic songs with Noddy Holder. He was kind of the Paul McCartney. I remember seeing him playing violin on *Top of the Pops*, on 'Coz I Luv You', which is a great song. I've covered that for my live streaming shows.

My Glam rock group at school used to do 'Gudbuy T' Jane', in that same period when The Jam would have had those big fat ties! In the first half of the Seventies, we were playing Woodham Church Hall, and Cobham, and Horsell, and all those places.

I used to do a panto every year in Notting Hill, and we'd always do the Christmas song ('Merry Xmas Everybody') at the end. But I would also choose 'Coz I Luv You' as my favourite song. It's a perfect pop song, and they taught me a lot about songwriting, I guess, listening to their music.

When I first saw Jim Lea, I was thinking, 'Why's he playing the violin?' But then it was like, 'Well, this is brilliant!' It's just an A minor and a D minor chord, but there's just something about the way he puts the chords together. Also, songwriting-wise, there's a little thing that happens in the chorus of ('Merry Xmas Everybody') that's like, 'Whoa! What are they doing there? What's going on here?' There are little bits in it that are like, 'This is the secret!' Little bits that make it really, really work. Bits of magic. And the songs are quite basically recorded but just really good. And their film, *Slade in Flame*, was great.

I WAS THERE: NIGEL CLARK, DODGY

They were an amazing live band. They did that live album, didn't they, *Slade Alive!*, with a couple of covers on it. I also do a version of The Lovin' Spoonful's 'Darling Be Home Soon'. And I loved the singles. I remember hearing one, thinking, 'Who is this? It sounds like me.' It was on an advert not long ago, a brilliant song. 'Dun, dun … 'Coz I Luv U'! And I've always thought of myself as the Noddy Holder of summer, having 'Good Enough' and 'Staying Out For The Summer' as consecutive hits in '95 and '96.

I WAS THERE: JOHN COGHLAN, STATUS QUO

I always got on with Don. We go right back to the early Seventies. I remember when we played in Australia and New Zealand, in early '73 –

Don Powell and John Coghlan, fully paid-up members of the Drummers' Union and great pals

Slade, Status Quo, Lindisfarne, and Caravan. I don't know how much that would have cost in those days, but I don't think they could do a bill like that now! We really enjoyed it, and the funniest thing was that the airline we flew on employed four or five undercover police on the plane, everywhere we went. There were four bands and four road crews, so quite a lot of us, all with long hair, t-shirts and all that, and I think they were waiting for us to get out of hand, get pissed and do something. But we were very friendly and very well behaved. I think that pissed them off! I remember getting off the plane when we were due to go back to England, and it was, 'See you, guys. Did you arrest anybody? No? Good! Bye!'

Me and (John's wife) Gillie had a programme on BBC Radio Oxford that went on for five years. We'd invite guests from what we call the Old Boys' Lunch in London twice a year. I'd say, 'Would you be prepared to come to the studio in Oxford to pre-record a show with me?' Look, there's no money in it, we'll just take you next door, have lunch in this Italian restaurant.' And it went down well, Don coming along to talk about Australia, Quo and Slade. It was so much fun that we ended up doing two hours. We had so much to talk about. The producer was pleased because he got two shows out of it.

Noddy Holder came down from Manchester for the show, and again we had so many things to talk about. I never had a script. When you're talking about something you love, what do you need a bloody script for? It was often a case of carrying on where the conversation left off last time you spoke… and probably things that wouldn't go live on air now!

Slade made loads of great records, and I just think they were an extremely good band. But the first one that comes to mind would be

'Cum On Feel The Noize'. It's just its rawness. I don't think there are any guitar overdubs on it. It's just as they did it. Anything to do with recording now is all bloody computers.

I WAS THERE: GARY CROWLEY, BROADCASTER & DJ

Gary Crowley, regularly on air on BBC Radio London and Soho Radio, and a huge Slade fan from his formative years onwards

Growing up in the early Seventies, even if you only possessed a passing interest in pop music, you could not escape Slade. They were a veritable hit-making machine… and everywhere. Blasting out of the radio, the TV, and staring out of magazines. Chalking up something like a dozen top-five hit singles between 1971 and 1974, three of which went straight to No.1. Now, not many could match that. Not that my younger sister Soo and older brother Steve wanted to escape them. In our North-West London council flat, we devoured the pop music of the day, and Slade were top of the pops for us. Shared favourites for all three of us, which was something rare in our home.

Soo was utterly nuts about Jim, Steve loved crazy Dave and coveted that Super Yob guitar and that Rolls-Royce of his, whilst Noddy in his mirrored top hat and with that rasping voice was the epitome of excitement for me. And then there was drummer Don, at the back and keeping the beat that kept us all (and countless pals) appreciatively stompin' along.

There was nothing complicated or arty-farty about Slade. Their brand of no messin' pop was unadulterated feel good. The essence of rock 'n' roll. Memorable, fun, a breath of fresh air. They were a respite from the power cuts and economic gloom of the Seventies. Completely in step with their audience and deft at releasing singles.

'Coz I Luv You' and 'How Does it Feel?' are just two of many of their classics that still make the hairs on my neck stand up. And time hasn't dimmed one iota their uniqueness.

Love you Slade.

I WAS THERE: CARL HUNTER, THE FARM

It's always a joy chatting to Noddy. He is as funny and as charming as you think.

Carl James Hunter, bass player for Liverpool band The Farm, and an award-winning film director, with fellow chart-topper Noddy Holder

I WAS THERE: RUSSELL HASTINGS, FROM THE JAM

Me, Rick (Buckler) and Bruce (Foxton) bumped into Dave Hill and co. at a service station on the M40 around 2007. When we got in the car afterwards, we said to each other, 'Did that just happen?' And Dave Hill looked like Dave Hill!

I WAS THERE: MILES HUNT, THE WONDER STUFF

I was too young really, so don't remember ever talking to Uncle Bill (Hunt of The Move and Wizzard) about him knowing Slade or anything, but it was pretty obvious to us that they did. And because we lived in an area of Birmingham, just south of the Black Country when we were growing up, we knew Slade just lived up the road. That was really exciting. And they were omnipresent back then, weren't they? They were on the radio and on *Top of the Pops* all the time.

Miles Hunt, the Wonder Stuff frontman's Uncle Bill's appearances on *Top of the Pops* set the tone for a life in music and love of Glam era contemporaries Slade

So yeah, there was a bit of pride in that, and they weren't up themselves. I suppose the path was being laid for me. They were normal guys. Okay, there's obviously something wrong with Dave Hill in the clothes he wears – ha! But they seemed like normal guys, we'd all seen the movie, *Flame*, and they could all act but came across so naturally, and it was like, well, they've done it, and there doesn't seem to be anything in our way, does there…

It was all we knew, having an uncle on *Top of the Pops* and the like, and me and my brother were really into the pop music of the early Seventies when we were growing up. And as well as Bill, one of the biggest bands in the country at the time was Slade, and there was a sense of pride that they were from where we were from.

They were working-class guys catapulted to national fame. The music they played had such an energy, and we were just the right age to catch it.

I WAS THERE: NIK KERSHAW

They were great musicians, but not only that – it coincided with me being a skinhead for a while, so you were into Slade and reggae. In fact, the first band I was in used to perform a couple of Slade songs. 'Look Wot You Dun' and 'Mama Weer All Crazee Now'. I think Jim Lea was kind of regretful that he never got the kind of credit that he was due for some of those songs. 'Coz I Luv You' was the first one I got into. The first band I was ever in that I called 'my' band, Thor, had one gig. It was at Rushmere Village Hall, and I remember two of the songs that we played – 'Coz I Luv You' and 'Jean Genie'.

Nik Kershaw had a thing for Slade, long before he found fame in the early Eighties

I WAS THERE: ROLO MCGINTY, THE WOODENTOPS

Noddy Holder's voice was nuts, like he was always yelling, always full caps, the titles, the spellings, the stomps, the Slade, usually fun to watch on a mime, but from the live LP you could tell they really could cut it on a stage. The secret weapon was Jim Lea, an all-rounder musician who could whip out the violin and give Slade a touch of folky class. That elevated them somehow, melodically, and you got a dose of the musical tension in the Nod's voice, 'Cos I Luv You' being one. But if you go back to before the sequins and round mirrors and top hats to, say, 1969 you get a different band all together. Its folky almost African hi-life sounding guitar riffs on songs like 'Martha My Dear' or inventive arrangements for 'Know Who You Are' or 'Wild Winds Are Blowing', a prototype yeller.

Slade were definitely a band who had plenty of ideas, good guitar and always the back beat from Don pushing it along. Dave Hill was doing his best to make Yob culture a peaceful thing, colourising that very greyscale implication, and a superb guitar player, let's not forget. I loved them as a coming into rock 'n' roll age teen. There was plenty of high-end talent around then, and Slade wafted around with the best of them. A working-class, class act.

I WAS THERE: ROB PURSEY, THE CATENARY WIRES & HEAVENLY & SWANSEA SOUND

I remember gazing at the poster on my older cousin's bedroom wall thinking, 'That must be what a rock band looks like.' They looked quite menacing to a seven-year-old. Later on, they seemed like people you'd want to have at a party. I put it down to Noddy's beautiful smile and that top hat with shiny circles on it. I met Noddy many years later, when I was making TV programmes – he was mates with Amanda Holden, who acted in one of my shows. He was a really nice bloke.

I WAS THERE: DYLAN WHITE

I got to know Noddy quite well. I went to a Phonogram record party that Slade were at, because they had this back catalogue coming out, and I had a long chat with Dave Hill all about it. I went to Don Powell's book launch in Wolverhampton with Miles Hunt from the Wonder Stuff. And Miles is a massive Slade fan. I had a great chat with Don Powell at that. I've not met Jim Lea again since 1973 but I'm working on that, because I'm doing some work for Weinerworld and they release Jim Lea's solo stuff and I said, 'You've got to get me in front of Jim Lea.' I'm absolutely still a fan. It's T.Rex and Slade all the way for me.

I WAS THERE: MARK RADCLIFFE, AUTHOR & BROADCASTER

He's the only celebrity person who's a proper friend. People like Guy Garvey and that are friends, but Nod's the only kind of iconic person who's a friend. But I am beyond that now really. You can't go anywhere without Nod being recognised, and people are always so pleased to see him. But I just like his company – he's just a nice fella.

I WAS THERE: JOHN ROBB, THE MEMBRANES & LOUDER THAN WAR

I know people tend to rewrite their history as only liking David Bowie, but my generation loved all the Glam bands. You'll get people, before they were in really cool bands, being into Slade when they were like twelve, 13 or 14. Every single thing that came out of *Top of the Pops* would end up dominating the playground talk, like when Sparks did 'This Town Ain't Big Enough For The Both Of Us'. The next day everyone was going, 'Wow! Who was that new band?' We had no idea that they had been going for six years. I remember really clearly watching *Top of the Pops* and everybody going on about every single thing. And I remember in the youth club, people smashing bottles along to Slade. They brought out a lot of teenage frustration, because they were so exciting.

Photo: John Middleham

John Robb recalls the hold Slade had on his fellow teens in Blackpool

On one level, Glam didn't take itself too seriously so there's always a danger of overlooking just how good that music actually was. And because they kind of played the comedy card and didn't take themselves too seriously, people overlook how absolutely musically brilliant Slade were. They were an amazing singles band and Noddy Holder is one of the greatest British vocalists of all time. His voice is pretty astounding. And there's that weird thing that he was actually a roadie for Robert

Plant's in his Band of Joy – two really powerful Midlands singers. Don Powell was a real powerhouse drummer, wasn't he?

That early '80s comeback was really amazing – that famous story about the Reading gig, where they thought they were going to get bottled off but they just blew every single band off the stage. They were just a brilliant live band. It's also interesting that the bass guitar changes position in music around then, where the bass is playing the melodies. Every instrument was equally important, whereas with old school rock bands the bass is playing a lot of interesting stuff. That changed with Punk, where the bass kind of sat in the mix.

I WAS THERE: BOB YOUNG, STATUS QUO

We met in the early Seventies, and they became more successful than Quo for a while, which is why we supported them when we did gigs with them. I'm not sure exactly what the first gig they did together was. It may have been in Bristol. I remember a double that night – that was the second gig, with the first on a farm over in Wales. I remember a bit of a party after. In May '72 we supported them at the Orchid Ballroom in Purley. I've a feeling that was one where there was a stage that went round. It was only a short while later, the end of January '73 on the *Piledriver tour*, that we went off on tour with Slade to Australia. It was breaking new ground, with a bunch of people you really got on well

Slade, Status Quo and Lindisfarne had a blast Down Under in early '73, and Bob Young was at the heart of it

with… and they all knew how to party. There's a photograph, on a bus in Australia, having spent the afternoon at a vineyard. They took us to enjoy ourselves and see how wine was made. Well, they showed how wine was made, and we showed them how wine was drunk!

We became good friends and stayed friends. In May '73, not long after the Australian shows when we did our first tour of America, one of the early shows we did over there was supporting Slade at the Civic Auditorium, Santa Monica. And it was great to be able to meet up over there. Whenever you got together it was like time hadn't passed.

There were so many great songs… but 'Far Far Away' – that's fantastic. I think of the lyrics and the music, amongst all the noise. What a belter that is. They've had so many. An enviable catalogue and a great, unique band.

I WAS THERE: KRIS JOZAJTIS

Slade were never a cool band, in the sense cultivated by, for example, the Mods of the 1960s. But just as Mod style influenced the Skinhead sub-culture that Slade had a dalliance with before their breakthrough, the band's attitude and confidence in their own worth could easily accommodate the Mod ethos of working-class kids 'living well under difficult circumstances' that has informed every great British youth sub-culture since. And their classic '70s music retains qualities not so easily dismissed as mere nostalgia. The early hit singles like 'Coz I Luv You' may have been basic and simple in comparison with the complex Prog flourishes and sonic exploration of the Yes and Pink Floyd albums carried around by sixth formers and designed to be heard on proper hi-fi systems. But Chas Chander's productions were made to sound good through the cheap record players and small transistor radios which were all that oiks like me had at the time, and translating the live excitement of a great band onto vinyl as well as he did is still a feat worthy of respect: many of those records still sound like a wild party compressed onto a seven-inch single.

To that end, Don Powell and Jim Lea provided a rock solid, if not brutal, rhythmic base, honed by endless gigging, that, like the great soul rhythm sections of Detroit, Memphis and Muscle Shoals, never let you down. The crunch and raunch of the twin guitars easily matched that of the 'heavier' bands of the time like Sabbath and Free, and that sound – loud at any volume – remains a personal touchstone whenever I plug in. But because they provided the perfect setting for the sheer exuberance and power of Noddy's singing, what set Slade aside were the songs.

For a while at least, Lea and Holder were the masters of writing songs that enabled the making of great pop records. 'Mama Weer All Crazee Now' may not have been subtle or deep, but it was effervescent, bubbling over with the kind of humour and defiance that would soon inform Punk.

That subsequent movement may have been a step too far for a much older band like Slade to negotiate when it came along. But how many punks turning 18 in 1976 like me were Slade fans three or four years earlier?

Actually, I think some of Slade's best material emerged once they'd achieved a kind of immortality with 'Merry Xmas Everybody' (a song I had to learn to play a few years ago for a Christmas concert with my school's staff band). Along with some great, inventive arrangements that moved away from the initial party band template, there's an emotionally convincing directness and honesty to songs like 'Far Far Away', 'How Does It Feel?' and 'In For A Penny'. And I'd often add a bit of good cheer to my Post Punk-era mixtapes by throwing in something as playful and witty as 'Thanks for the Memory (Wham Bam Thank You Mam)'.

Just as our development as people depends on the nature of the relationships we form as we grow up and older, so our various musical loves are integral to who we become. Indeed, everyone who falls in love with music will have particular songs or artists that marked shifts in their perception of things. And those musical events are so much more intense and charged with meaning as the hormones kick in and we start to work out for ourselves who we are, what we might want to be, and what this thing called life is all about. It's one reason why each generation requires new music to call their own. As with everything else, what that might be depends on fortune.

I'd say I got lucky. I may have changed beyond all recognition since I first heard 'Take Me Bak 'Ome' in 1972, but I'm still grateful that, for a short time at least, Slade were 'my band'; four larger than life exemplars of the joy, good humour, creativity and resilience needed to make life worth living. As the fan pages say, 'Slade are for life, not just for Christmas.'

I WAS THERE: STEVE SMITH, THE VAPORS

I first became aware of Slade when one of the music papers did a feature on their earlier incarnation, Ambrose Slade. They looked like a gang and certainly not one that you'd want to meet down a dark alleyway. But they'd made an impression.

Photo: Paul Caldwell

Steve Smith, here in action with The Shakespearos, was aware of Slade as early as their Ambrose Slade days, and stuck by them

Most of the music I listened to at that time was on Radio 1, and it was there I first heard Noddy blasting out the intro to 'Get Down And Get With It'. Then the band came crashing in and I was hooked. They sounded loud and brash and like they were having the best time. That record opened the door to a stream of brilliant singles that were the soundtrack of my teenage years.

I bought the *Slade Alive!* album and played it to death. They were still a gang, but it was a more inclusive and fun one. The *Top of the Pops* appearances were a case in point – four mates having a laugh and dressing up but also making some great music. They were so big at one time they were allowed to make a film. I'd grown up watching a lot of

Sixties bands in films and with a few honourable exceptions they were terrible, but *Slade in Flame* was a grittier more realistic depiction of life in the music biz. The soundtrack album featured some more thoughtful songs like 'Far Far Away' and 'How Does It Feel?' but it was still undeniably Slade.

I felt sadness when Noddy left – it was like a great British institution was gone. But they're all still alive and Noddy said last year that he'd love the original line-up to get back together for Glastonbury's legends slot, so who knows?

I WAS THERE: JOHN MILNE

I heard that Dave Hill was going to chuck the band before they broke up, because he was into the Jehovah's Witnesses thing. There were rumours that he'd had enough. When I heard they were breaking up it broke my heart. They were my life and I felt my life going apart. They were like family to me. I still love them all, even though they're all doing different things. I'm still supporting them 100 per cent.

I WAS THERE: STUART RUTTER

It was Slade that brought my wife Diane and I together. She'd also been a Slade fan all her life. We went to concerts together all the time, without actually knowing each other for quite a while. I was at her first Slade concert, but we didn't know each other for a very long time after that. It was at Belle Vue in Manchester, April '75. It's all disappeared now – all knocked down – but it was in a concert hall called the King's Hall, part of the Belle Vue complex. We were kids then. She went with her best friend and I went with mine.

Slade stopped touring in '83, and Diane was one of those that had fallen by the wayside during the dark days, whereas I carried on being a fan all the way through. Don and Dave didn't get much in royalties off the hits or any recordings, so they were obliged to carry on playing live, and very quickly formed Slade II. The rumour goes that it was Noddy Holder's tongue-in-cheek idea to call it that. He wasn't serious, but they did it anyway. They started going out on tour and recorded an album, re-released at least once or twice under different names.

Diane started going to see them, and I started going to their concerts when they were nearby, just an excuse to meet up with old friends from the original Slade days. That's when Diane and myself came across each other and very loosely kept in touch. And then the Slade fan conventions started happening, usually in The Trumpet or somewhere in Wolverhampton.

We got to know each other more and more, kept in touch and then, four years ago, she had a cardiac arrest and I was her nearest friend that could go into visit on a regular basis. I'd known her since the mid-Nineties and we'd been friends for a very long time, but it was Diane's illness that brought us together. Things went on from there, and here we are, a married couple! We married last November. We have a heck of a lot of mutual friends, probably numbering well over 100, through being Slade fans.

Jim Lea and his wife, Lou, have been especially kind, as has Don Powell, keeping in regular contact, and they all sent us cards for our wedding last November, when Jim and Lou had the words to 'Everyday' printed out in the form of a love heart, which they then had framed and sent to us as a wedding present.

SLADY

In conversation with Danie Cox and Wendy Solomon, aka Gobby Holder and Jem Lea of Slady.

So here it is… you're clearly far, far away too young to have caught Slade alive in all their pomp. What were your first memories of Slade? Was it 'that record', as Don would say? And was it on the radio, the telly or played at home? Were your folks Slade fans?

Danie: My first memories of Slade were when I was a kid and trying to count how many choruses of 'that song' till the 'IT'S CHRISTMAAAASSSSSS!' part, just so I could perfect it. It wasn't until I was about 14 and watching *TOTP2* on BBC 2 back in the mid-2000s that I saw them doing 'Cum On Feel The Noize', just when I was getting into Bowie and Alice Cooper and Buzzcocks. And I just loved that sexy rugged rock 'n' roll, almost punky approach to Glam, where it wasn't about make-up but about dressing like farmer clowns and metallic nuns and screaming about having a good time.

Wendy: Same for me really! I think the Christmas song is kind of so ingrained into popular culture that it is almost impossible to grow up in this country and not be aware of Noddy and Slade. It wasn't until much later that I even realised they were a serious band! I think that is the real double-edged sword of a hit like that – young people still very much have those misconceptions about Slade. Being a child of the late Eighties, I kind of missed the gritty rock 'n' roll years and only caught the tail end with the big hair and studded belts! My folks were definitely not into hard rock 'n' roll, they were more Sixties kids into The Beatles and Peter, Paul and Mary! I was very much into Post-Punk stuff like Buzzcocks and The Undertones. It's been a pleasure getting to know them though, for sure! I just wish it had been sooner.

I love what I've heard of Slady, not least your spin on (occasionally) rather 'of their time' lyrics from a different era (e.g. your subtle rewording in 'Skweeze Me, Pleeze Me'). Was that foremost in your mind when you came up with the concept? And why did you think this idea might work (because it clearly does)?

Danie: It's a great song and Slade hardly ever played it live, so we make sure we play it every set in its full glory, without glorifying a right to rape really. The lyrics were meant to be funny, I guess, but they're not the greatest from Nod and Jim. I can't sing, 'And I thought you might like to know, when a girl's meaning, 'Yes', she says, 'No'.' That's just gross.

Wendy: I agree. It's all too easy to just say, 'Well, it's of its time' and let it go, but it's definitely not something we could shrug off. In terms of being a tribute, we like to think we are more than just a copycat band. We are 100 per cent authentic but we also have our own personalities and banter, which comes through in our stage shows. I like to think we keep the passion of the music but rather than just going through the motions and trying to replicate something, we have our own identities stamped firmly on it, with big 'ol bovver boots. We are a band in our own right who play Slade songs, rather than just a tribute – if you know what I mean!

It was Danie that came up with the idea and approached me. Being less clued up about Slade, I agreed, not really knowing what I was letting myself in for in terms of learning the Jim Lea basslines! It was a bit of fun initially, but we quickly realised that people loved the concept and really got behind us, which encouraged us to go further with it. We were lucky enough to get a good response from the majority of long-term Slade fans, with only very minor hostility from the ones who felt threatened or lacked imagination (!), so it felt like a stamp of approval.

Did your love and understanding of the original band grow as a result of your Slady experience? Did you truly appreciate the Holder/Lea partnership before? They were clearly great performers, but there's plenty of songwriting genius in there too.

Danie: I think, since learning the songs, I can really appreciate that despite how simple the chords are, they are structured together so differently and have their own style. It's really cool and also so much fun to learn.

Wendy: I had no idea of the total genius of Jim Lea. The diversity within the material is astounding too, from pure sweaty headbangers to melodic and tender love songs with a bit of cabaret sprinkled on top. It's been a challenge, but I have loved every minute.

You've been at this for five years now. I've heard positive words from Don and endorsements from Nod's Suzan. Have you had a chance to speak to all the band, and if so, what have they told you?

Danie: Yes, met and spoke to them all. Noddy said it's just like looking in the mirror! Dave Hill has told us some songs we should throw into our set. Don Powell is a good friend, and Jim Lea and his brother, Frank, stay in touch. I was honoured to be asked to perform at Don and Jim's Q&A at Wolverhampton Art Gallery in August 2022. That was a memory I will always cherish.

What else would you class as your highlights along that five-year journey?

Danie: Meeting Noddy Holder outside Pret a Manger in Soho in 2021, dressed as his female counterpart, when he was promoting a Christmas sandwich in July, talking to him. He gave me a sandwich and I couldn't eat it cos I'm vegan, but I have it framed on my mantlepiece, like an award. It's a bit mouldy now!

Wendy: Being at that Q&A and watching Danie perform was a really proud moment. Spoiling it all with my kazoo playing is something that will always make me laugh! Chatting with Don and Jim in the green room afterwards and literally horsing around down the pub later with Don. There are too many brilliant gigs to name really, every one of them memorable! Supporting The Rezillos was a great experience as I am a bit of a fan of theirs. We are playing the Empress Ballroom at Rebellion this year too, which is total 'bucket list' stuff. There are just so many highlights.

Perhaps in the way Slade had to win over their critics here and there (Reading 1980 springs to mind), I guess you often have to overcome the doubters?
Danie: We do this entirely for the fans. That and the fun of it all. It's really a truly special feeling being onstage in front of hundreds of people who have all come together in one room to celebrate their love of Slade. Seeing men and women of all ages, screaming out those songs, and some even crying. Knowing that I've brought a special memory to people's lives, as a vessel of the Slade experience. We don't get critics at all really. We get the odd sexist comment or envious swipes, but that's expected. We can't make everyone as happy as we are.

Wendy: I agree it's really special. It's often about nostalgia for the fans, just capturing an essence of their youth through the songs, the atmosphere, the friends in the crowd. It's pretty emotional at times and there is a real sense of poignancy underneath the joyous craziness of it all. The doubters are few and far between – and very lonely and sad.

What's the dream for Slady from here? What happens next?
Danie: I'd really love to bring Slady to Europe, America and Australia. We're really in big demand. I'd also love us to record more singles. Maybe even an album. And I'd also like us to perform on TV, like, on *The One Show* at Christmas or something.

Wendy: What she said!

Have you got favourite songs from the Slade catalogue? And if so, for what reasons?
Danie: 'Nobody's Fool' is probably my ultimate favourite Slade song. I love that entire *Nobody's Fools* album. It's such a shame Slade didn't really crack America. It's a bit like Robbie Williams too. I really think Americans who are fans of Slade are really special people for 'getting' it all.

Wendy: I love playing 'Nobody's Fool' too, but also enjoy the riotous three-chord bangers – but then I also love the intricacies of 'Far Far Away', 'She Did It To Me' and 'Wonderin' Y', etc. Real goosebumps stuff! There is so much variety, you can never tire of it.

I WAS THERE: LES GLOVER, DON POWELL'S OCCASIONAL FLAMES

The 1971-72 era was a traumatic and difficult time for me, living with my two elderly aunties and up for adoption. I seemed to be suspended in a colourless world of general strikes, three-day weeks and power cuts that seemed to sap all the joy from the hapless eleven-year-old me. Life was black and white, newspapers were black and white, and our tiny, Bakelite TV was black and white. The black hole that had appeared in the middle of our council house living room in St Helens that once contained a fire was now a shrine to a strange lady with blue skin… and then came Slade!

Les Glover, right, here with bandmates Paul Cookson and Don Powell, was at Slade's final UK gig in 1983

Four colourful clowns from a strange place called Wolverhampton burst onto our newly-rented Rediffusion colour TV set and I was captivated. I traded in my braces and monkey boots for a bright yellow tank top, a pair of green and red platform shoes and a pair of the gaudiest loon trousers that you could ever imagine. My basin-cut hair was somehow transformed into a feather cut fit for a Glam rock king. And so, with a name change and my newly adopted family my life was complete. Oh Slade, Look Wot You Dun.

Slade weren't as cool as my older brother's heavier rock bands or as clever as my auntie's Fab Four but they were my band – loud, proud and colourful, tin-foil troubadours with TV appearances that always made you smile, beats that made you stomp, and songs you could sing along to at the top of your lungs, with misspelt titles that would distress even the most laid back of teachers.

Don was the coolest and powered the engine room, building the perfect beat; Jim was the jack of all trades and master of them all; Noddy had a voice that could strip wallpaper and set off car alarms and enough charm to silence them; and Dave was, well, Dave, a strutting metal peacock armed with his Super Yob guitar and riffs that could take you higher than his fringe. And when they appeared on *Top of the Pops*, singing, smiling and stomping were mandatory and the Slade storm raged and framed my black and white world with a rainbow.

By 1976, I'd moved onto other kinds of music and began my own musical career, but Slade were my first love, the band that coloured my world, lifted my mood and made my spirit soar at a time when I needed it most. Nearly 50 years later, there I am, sat in my own front room in Burtonwood, opposite Slade's engine room, Mr Donald George Powell, my grown-up children's pictures adorning the walls and Don regaling me with stories and tales of drunken nights, parties, performances, TV appearances, famous friends and failed marriages, and the contentment he's found in Hanne, and a family he always longed for. We discuss our third album of Christmas material and future Occasional Flames releases in between answering text and phone calls enquiring about his wellbeing and recent health issues, from Ric Lee (Ten Years After), Len Tuckey (Suzi Quatro), Andy Scott (Sweet, QSP) and Brian May (Queen) to name-drop just a few.

I ask Don if he's ever considered retirement and he says, 'No, I still love it, I love meeting the fans and chatting to them, asking how they're doing, and they ask about me. It's amazing really… Any chance of a cup of tea?'

PS. I got to see Slade live at the Royal Court Theatre in Liverpool on 18th December 1983, in what turned out to be the original band's last-ever full UK show. It was brilliant, a full-on assault of the senses. And I'm convinced that they, along with Judas Priest and Motörhead, were the main cause of my hearing problems in later years. I've seen them several times since, and although never as good as the original four, they can still make you sing, smile and stomp like the best of them.

I WAS THERE: GERED MANKOWITZ

I think there were over 40 (sessions). They were fun to be with, extremely creative, and it was always a very positive experience being with them. They were never moody or difficult, and they had a real sense of their identity. It was always a very enjoyable working relationship. We had fun. We were always giggling, and they were great piss-takers.

When we had the studio in Great Windmill Street (Soho), pretty much throughout the Seventies, they'd come several times a year. We'd have a big Christmas party there. I'd cook a turkey and a ton of sausages and we'd make a huge punch, famous for being an absolute killer punch. You had absolutely great sounds, and we invited people from all walks of life and we'd invite Slade and their roadies, particularly Swinn. They arrived one year (and) were almost the first there, and I'm at the door welcoming people, saying, 'Great to see you, go right through, there's food over there.' After about 20 minutes, I managed to escape the door, went inside, and the turkey had gone, the sausages had gone, and Slade and the roadies were just sitting around. 'Great grub!' They cleaned us out in 20 minutes!

The band didn't stop being good. I can understand anybody saying it was a mistake trying to crack America, but they really had to do it. Chas was very much of the management school where if you didn't make it in America, you hadn't really made it. And the interesting thing is that they were incredibly important influences to several American bands. You can get out of step very quickly, especially if you're an important part of a previous step – and they were, for the best part of a decade. It's very difficult when the mantle has been passed, to get back in. So that was a misstep, I guess.

I recall another great night with them (at The Trumpet in Bilston). I went to Wolverhampton with them to shoot some live stuff… We had such a great night. What struck me was that they were regulars and were truly treated as such, not as anything special. They loved that and were 100 per cent at home. Everybody loved them, nobody hassled them, it was a wonderful night. I'm not a big pub person, but I really loved that because the vibe was simply glorious, like being with a huge family.

I enjoyed their company from the outset, and I think they enjoyed mine. And it was the beginning of a long-lasting, very productive, lovely relationship. I mean, I loved them dearly, and consider them really good friends. I haven't seen Jimmy for years and years, but I've seen Nod, who sends me a shouty Christmas message and came to a couple of my openings at a gallery in Manchester. And I saw Dave and Don together when they were doing the rounds with (their version of) Slade at the Hall for Cornwall in Truro, having tea with them, which was great fun. And it was another incredible show, even though it's not the band it was. I also had a nice time hanging out with Don when we did the QSP session. My feelings towards them haven't changed. Nor has my sense of affection and admiration for them.

HE WAS THERE: GRAHAM 'SWINN' SWINNERTON

Swinn had the unenviable task of waking up each band member in their hotel rooms when it was time to move on.

Photo: www.donpowellofficial.com

Graham 'Swinn' Swinnerton, the legendary Slade roadie and tour manager, who died in 2015

Swinn was the first guy I met when I joined The Vendors. He was a great guy, funny, awkward, smart, well-read. My dad liked him a lot, which is a compliment. He was very much like a fifth member of the band. He wasn't one for self-pity – he got on with it. He was an excellent tour manager and mate, and he was one of us.

Swinn said to me when we last met, 'It took some guts to go out without Nod.' I appreciated that thought. **Dave Hill**

We were in the same class, went through together. I met him when we were eleven, at secondary modern school. Many years later, when Slade came off the road, he went on to tour-manage Saxon and a few American bands, and occasionally we'd bump into each other. That loyal thing between us never waned. We always had that. We were the best of mates.

Apparently (when he grew ill) he didn't want to see anybody, but I said to his wife, 'I don't care what he says, I'm going to see him.' And we had a laugh. It wasn't long after that. He was poorly. It was the worst thing I ever experienced when the doctor at the hospice said, 'Will you help me put him back to bed?' I never thought I'd be doing that. It was only about two days later that his wife called and said he'd gone. **Don Powell**

DAVID GRAHAM, SLADE IN ENGLAND

My father was in the Army. We had been in Singapore, Bahrain, Hong Kong and then Cyprus, and I came back in 1969 and we moved to Colchester in the middle of winter. I was 12 years old. I had a crew-cut haircut, like everybody I grew up with, and I stood out. People kept calling me a skinhead. I had no idea what they were talking about. But it was right slap-bang in the middle of the skinhead movement and somebody said, 'You should listen to this album. It's skinhead music. It's your music.' I bought it for, I think, 70p from Boots. It was *Play It Loud* and I was hooked. Not particularly because of the music, but because it meant I was accepted at school. When you're a new kid from an Army background, you want to be accepted.

I saw Day One of the recording of *Slade Alive!* when I was 14, having joined the fan club, and it's been a lifelong thing with me. I've seen just about every name band in the last 30 or 40 years and there's nobody better live than Slade.

In 1971 we found ourselves in Northern Ireland, living in an Army barracks when Slade really became huge. I'd sort of liked them and bought 'Get Down And Get With It' and a few other records with pocket money. You either liked Marc Bolan or Slade, and Marc was just a little too effeminate for me. Gary Glitter hadn't yet come along – he arrived in another six or nine months. The Sweet were around, and bands like Geordie came along, because every record company wanted to have their own Slade, so they were all looking for clones of Slade.

But there was just something about Slade. They weren't a teenybop band, although they were in all the teen mags, which didn't do them any favours in the long run. And they made some bizarre decisions over the years about appearing on children's television when they were desperately trying to create a market for themselves after the glory years, when they came back in '77. They were appearing on *Crackerjack* and things that were on at 4.30 in the afternoon. The people they wanted to buy their records wouldn't have seen them and the people watching those programmes had no interest in them. And this was in the pre-video days, so you either got to see them or you didn't.

When Slade were on their arse and nobody wanted to go and see them, we reckon there were 500 fans around the country that would turn up anywhere to go and see them. When Stu Rutter saw them in Blackburn, there were only 19 people in the audience. But they put on a fairly full show.

We always had an affinity with Slade. People would say, 'Slade? 'Merry Xmas!' I'm not interested.' Things changed. Music changed. We all changed. I've spent 35 years collecting all the video stuff of Slade just because I wanted it. I've got 170 videos on YouTube which I've created or made, a lot of them because there was no particular video footage of that track. And I run the website sladeinengland.co.uk.

I was a policeman and Slade thought that was strange. You'd get to know the band when you turned up at all these gigs. I could get backstage with a warrant card, and they'd say, 'Oh, the friendly policeman is here.' They were very, very approachable once you got to know them. Don and Dave are still very approachable, because they're still knocking around, doing the rounds on the oldies circuit in Germany and wherever. Noddy Holder and Jimmy Lea? Not so much. They were always a little bit aloof and a little bit wary of you until they got to know you, and then they were okay. They were fine. They were good blokes really. And I think it's their approachability that made them stand out for us. But people hated them. I could never get any of my friends to go and see them.

Nobody would go and see them between '74 and '77 when they came back from America. I saw them at Ipswich Gaumont in 1977. I hadn't seen them since 1974 and I was so excited to see them. I took a friend along who was a big Kiss fan and a big Boston fan. He said, 'I don't really want to go and see Slade.' He's now a lifelong fan. He'd never seen anything like it.

But you used to have ringing in your ears for a week afterwards. They were so loud. They were the loudest band I ever saw.

SLADE FAN CLUB
2 POSTAGE PAID SW DO SERIAL NO 5
MEMBERSHIP NO. 23/004760/5
D WHITE
8 LANGLEY RD
MERTON PARK
LONDON
SW19

MERRY XMAS EVERYBODY

MY FRIEND STAN

DIRECT FROM THE ORIGINATORS!
ORIGINAL
SKINNERS
24-inch
PARALLEL JEANS
£3.95
25p post
Heavy Blue DENIM or DRILL CLOTH in White, Navy or Black
Order with Confidence
STATE WAIST – Sizes 24" - 38"
'UNISEX'
GIRLS Order 1 size larger
IMMEDIATE DESPATCH SEND FOR LEAFLET SHOWING OUR OTHER FABULOUS GEAR "IN-GEAR" BY POST direct from
IN THINGS LTD. (Dept. N44) Grange Rd., Birkenhead, Cheshire.

THE BANGIN' MAN
SLADE

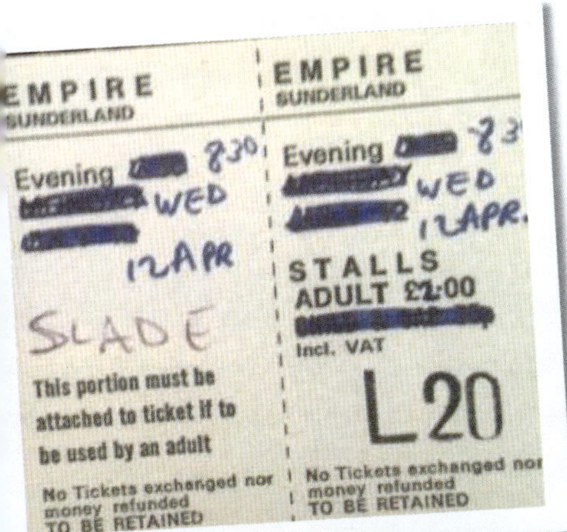

Photo: Paul Hughes

FEELING THE NOIZE...

I WAS THERE: OLEH BREZDEN

I saw them at the Detroit Masonic Temple. Must have been in the late 1970s, and Sweet opened. I was an import record buyer for record chain Peaches, and I was always influenced by the British rock scene. Both bands started with a bang, people rushing the stage. Slade played one encore.

I WAS THERE: MICK KELLY

It was, I guess, the Eighties. We hadn't seen them when they were really famous, so me and my wife went along. The place was called 'Romeo y Juliet' or some variant of that. Very big, with tables, a dancefloor and a small stage. They were very good. I enjoyed it, Dave Hill's guitar especially. Very professional and slick.

They played all the hits and more. One thing that sticks in my mind is that they used a smoke machine and something went awry. I think there should have been fans to blow the smoke around, but there weren't, and the smoke just built up on stage until the band were completely invisible – a wall of smoke illuminated by the lighting rig.

A good night, though, and fond (if patchy) memories.

I WAS THERE: PETER RAFFERTY

Slade were the first band I saw live. It was Freshers' Week in Manchester in 1970, and this was Slade before the hit singles. They were a totally different animal then, as evidenced by the fact that my main recollection was of a 20-minute version of 'Born To Be Wild'. After that I got the bug!

I WAS THERE: SHARON WARD

When I saw Slade, there was only Dave Hill and another original member, but they were still bloody great. They were doing their Christmas show along with Mud. My brother loves them and had seen them back in the Seventies, in London. My brother really enjoyed talking to Jim and helping put the equipment in their van.

My memories of hearing Slade for the first time were as a teenager, with my brother playing one of their albums. I instantly loved them.

AFTERWORD - BACK IN TOUCH WITH DON POWELL

MAY 2023, LEYLAND UK & SILKEBORG, DENMARK

Don Powell, as busy as ever in 2023

I WAS THERE: MALCOLM WYATT

In a twist on 'that song', it was the family waiting for Don to arrive when he talked to me via Zoom on a busy Whit weekend in Silkeborg, Denmark.

When would you say you first realised there was a following? Was that with The Vendors or The 'N Betweens when you realised people were coming back every week?
The vivid thing I remember was when it was myself, Johnny Howells and Mick Marson, playing youth clubs and birthday parties when we first got together. Only Mick was on the telephone, John coming back from somewhere, saying, 'We've got a booking at the town hall in Bilston and we're getting paid for it.' Getting paid? That was a total revelation for me! We got £6, so we got £1 each and could put the rest together and have chicken and chips that night from a place across the road from Johnny's house.

In those days, Mick and John would go through the same amp, I had my small kit, and we carried it round to the town hall, just around the corner. If we were playing a few miles away, you could take it on the bus – there'd be a luggage compartment under the stairs. Wonderful memories, when you think!

I recently discovered that on the day I was born in late October 1967, you were playing a pub called The Greenway in Baddeley Green, Stoke-on-Trent.
Baddeley Green! We used to do a lot of pub gigs in Stoke. We had a van by then, thought we were big time! We paid £90 for it, an Austin J2. We put a partition in, halfway through, so the equipment could go in the back and we could sit in the front. Stoke-on-Trent was about 30 minutes from us, and we'd feel like we were travelling to the other end of the world when we did that!

I recall you saying 'You Better Run' was a No.1 hit locally…
In Wolverhampton, yeah! We were big time then! John used to announce it as 'our No.1 record'. We kept going, thinking, 'We've done it now.' Our gig money went from £20 or £30 to £50. Incredible. We couldn't believe it.

When was the first time you experienced anything suggesting scenes of Slademania?
I think that was in Margate, a big ballroom right on the seafront. When we got there, there was a huge queue round the block. At first, we were thinking, 'Who else is on tonight?' We hadn't got a clue, and never thought of ourselves as anything like that. That was at the time of 'Get Down And Get With It' becoming a hit. We already had a great reputation for live work, before the hit records, but that really helped, especially that single.

In those days, it was considered a bit too rowdy for radio plays. But they had a lot of live sessions on Radio 1, and we'd always play 'Get Down And Get With It.' Until it went into the charts. I remember it being a nail-biting time. It was No.32 and you had to be in the Top 30 to get on *Top of the Pops*. We felt, 'Great, next week!' But the following week it was No.32 again! Nooo! The following week, luckily, it went to No.29 and we got on there.

It wasn't your first Top of the Pops *though.*
No, there was a song called 'The Shape Of Things To Come', by Barry

Mann and Cynthia Weil, apparently the theme tune for a film, only released in America. In those days they had a new release slot, and we got that. Unbelievable. That was in the main BBC studios in Shepherd's Bush, London. We'll always have fond memories of that, because they had a great canteen – we weren't earning much money, but you could get a great meal for just a few bob. We'd stuff our faces!

Gered Mankowitz told me how you Slade boys turned up early and more-or-less polished off the fresh-cooked turkey and sausages at one of his Christmas parties.
Yeah, free food! I saw Gered again a couple of years ago when I was working with Andy Scott and Suzi Quatro. He did the photographs. We've lots of memories with him, like when we became skinheads. He did all those early album covers, and was the photographer for Jimi Hendrix and in the early days did a lot with the Rolling Stones. His Christmas parties were fantastic. We were always first in! There was him and his partner, Red, who looked like a mad Viking with red hair, and they made these incredible big vats of punch. We'd go straight to the food and booze table!

I also talked to Bob Young and Ray Laidlaw regarding Status Quo and Lindisfarne's part in your Australian tour in early '73.
That was a great tour, about three weeks. That was the first time we properly got together with them, although our first UK tour was with Quo, when – would you believe it – the ticket price was 50p! We've been mates ever since, and that tour was mayhem – we ended up having police escorts on the plane. We were just kids really, fooling around, being silly. Great fun though.

The official line is that Slade never made it in America, but there must have been times where it felt like you were on the verge of success there.
Yes, when MTV started in the Eighties, and we got booked to do a tour with Ozzy Osbourne. But that got knocked on the head because Jim Lea went down with hepatitis. But we stayed over, Jim staying in his hotel room and being seen by a doctor every day while Nod, Dave and myself were doing promotion in LA, lots of radio interviews. 'Run Runaway' was the big record, going Top 20. We never went back though.

You were more of a studio outfit by then.
I suppose we were. Nod didn't particularly want to tour anymore.

Going back a little further, I wanted to touch on the wilderness years, after you returned from that huge spell in America in '77 and found yourself at rock bottom. The audience had largely deserted you, but there were those loyal fans who stuck by you and ultimately saw you through to that next big opportunity. I know it's complicated by the memory issues, but when you were on that chicken-in-a-basket circuit you must have recognised familiar faces out front.
I tell you what, it never deterred us. We were still giving them the same show. But we were down in the dumps, and it was hard to get gigs, so we started doing those particular kinds of clubs. We wanted to work, and it wasn't until the Reading Festival came up… I remember Nod calling me. We hadn't worked together for a couple of months, but he told me we'd been offered Reading Festival. We were killing ourselves laughing over the phone, but felt we'd got nothing to lose. We got our gear together, our equipment in the school room where we rehearsed in Wolverhampton – a classroom in a disused school.

The local vicar ran it, loaning classrooms out for bands to rehearse in. I think it was £4 or £5. We called him Holy Joe. He'd get his fiver, then he'd be up the pub on the corner, about 50 yards away. If you needed him to lock up, you'd find him in the pub! That's what we did when we were offered Reading. We just had a couple of rehearsals. We didn't really have any passes. We were walking through with the punters, everyone saying, 'What are you lot doing here?' We said, 'Well, we're playing tonight!' And it worked great for us, and as it was being recorded, we bought the tapes and released them.

At that stage, Dave Hill was looking at setting up a wedding car business, hiring out his gold Rolls-Royce, offering his services as a rock 'n' roll chauffeur, not so much 'Get Down And Get With It' as 'Get Me To The Church On Time'. How about you? You must have had your own doubts and fears.
I did. I was in no man's land. Me and Nod would see each other when he came to London, have a drink together. I was basically doing nothing. I'd helped a couple of guys out in the studio, did some drums for them. That was quite nice.

Was that hard for you, having so much time on your hands, at a time when you were – let's face it – hitting the bottle?
I was a bit over the top on the old falling down water. When I think back, I can't believe I'm still here. Unbelievable.'

It was the likes of the late Dave Kemp and all those loyal fans who kept you going until late August 1980, knowing full well Slade could still knock them dead every night.
It was wonderful. Those people were always there. I still had a place in Wolverhampton, and from North London I could get in my car and get on the M1 pretty quickly if going back. But when I lived in West Hampstead, I lived around the corner from Dave Kemp. We owe a lot to those guys. They stood by us through thick and thin.

Now into the second half of your seventies, appreciating your adopted home and loving family in Denmark but also getting back to the UK regularly for various projects, you clearly still got that buzz performing and reminiscing about Slade.
Oh, I love it. I've always said, soon as I stop enjoying it, I'm getting out. But I'm having a great time. I've been recording with those Danish musicians. Henrik, the keyboard player, approached me, and I thought it was great. I didn't know these guys in The Dreamers, but my wife Hanne did, saying they'd been in big bands around Denmark through the years. And it was great – like the old days, no machines. We went in and played as a band in the studio. I forgot what that was like! If anybody made a mistake, you stopped and started all over again. No messing around with computers.

Talking of mainland European links, any specific memories spring to mind of your time in Dortmund, Germany, with the band that would become Slade?
We were on £12, £13 a week each. I remember playing eight or so hours at night, going to the local railway station, where there was always a caravan where we could get chicken and chips. This was November and we stayed in this farmhouse, all in one room. I don't think I had a bath for a month. There was no hot water. But it didn't matter, we were just five kids having a great time.

Is that where the bond came from which saw you all through so much, as was the case with your Bahamas stay?
Definitely. I think that's what bands are missing today. Like you say, that bond, sharing bags of chips and things like that. Great memories.

It's clear there was always a close bond between the band and the fans, and those supporters pulled you through at key times. However strong a band you were, there were people out there who kept catching you live and being there for you.
We'd see that little group down the front at every gig, some even travelling to Europe if we had a gig there. An incredible mainstay, they were. We owe a lot to them. And we've always been a band that appreciated people who gave us help. We've never forgot it. I still speak to a lot of people who helped us along the way. It's been fantastic, I really appreciate it.

Photo: John Barker, Slade Are For Life, Not Just For Christmas

Don and Jim, off camera on a 2023 Don Powell Band videoshoot

SPECIAL THANKS TO

Geoff West; Stu & Diane Rutter; William Martin; Micky Spectrum; Maggie Bourne; Chris Hill; Phill Dann; Peter Davidson; Gary Willis; Steven Knight; Friz & Tina; Michael Mantelle; Robert Thorne; Sian Bundy; Les Glover; Kyle Eastwood; Ian Edmundson; Richard Ramage; Colin Kidd; Mark Cawdery; David Canevit; Martin Lewis; Alan Cockayne; Wendy John; Ian Petko-Bunney; Philip Bowden; Pete Keeley; Bill Thomson; Greg Simpson-Morgan; Bjørn Ertesvåg; Joe Murphy; Steven Mason; Steve Trusz; Francis Vandewalle; Tony Peach; Chris Harris; John Barker; Colin Foster; Kalle Homann; John Dalton; Colin McIntyre; Steven Wisner; Tod MacDonald; John Cullen; Mark Francis Tully; Niall Brannigan; Gavin Fletcher; Vidar Aas; Phil Barton; David Armstrong; Keith Hemingway; Terence Peppin; Ian McAdam; Ian McIver; Terry Wise; David Tinkham; Neil Partridge; Stephen F Durrans; Adrian Bowd; Mark Millicent; Mike Philpott; Stephen Merriman; Deborah Horton; Lynda McIntyre; Donna Jones; Ferg Ranson; Steve Cobbett; Nick Holme; Heather Blandford; Dan Weller; Gary Steward; Steven Claytonsmith; Tony Roach; Simon Kimmins; Carol Harwood; Michael Taylor; Alun Taylor; Doug Stafford; Steven Horne; Colin Ballard; Joachim Kornmayer; Steve & Kay Dix; Janet Beckett; Geir Arne Amundsen; Chris & Finn Coles; Peter Smith; Andrew Martin Smith; Paul Goverd; Jacqueline Kemp; Susan Kirk; Prentice James; Stephanie Henninger – Stevi; Teri Jean Henninger – TJ; David Barker; David Hughes; David Holdgate; Alun Perkins; Brian Wain; Andrew Bell; Martin Bell; Richard Bell; Darren Phillips; Peter Hawkins aka Knob Slade; John Parton; Stuart Wilson; Alan J Whitney, A F Mutch; John Briscoe; John Butler; Dawn Woolnough; Richard Gomersall; Dave Fearn; Tony Pye; Mark Pemberton; Clive Parker; Paul Smyth; Robert Fullone; Dave Avery; Dennis Burgin; Gary Abraham; Colin Grimshaw; Ray Webb; Michael Van Overstraeten; Steven Knight; Steve Edwards; Paul Claughton; Colin Fletcher; Rudolf Schubert; Keith Brunt; Gérard Goyer; Neil Lucas; Dave Slade Bennett; Roelof Bieze; Michael Taylor; Peter Baker; Frauke Braunschmidt; Andrew Socratous; Bjarne Fey; Nomis; Conor Milne; Isla Rose Milne; Emily Milne; Courteney Milne; Jessie Milne; John Milne; Dylan White; Harald Groesslinger; David Hughes; Kieran Flanagan.

SPENWOOD BOOKS

Spenwood Books is an independent publisher of music books. We're based in Manchester, UK and specialise in 'people's histories', telling the story of classic rock acts in the words of fans.

Check out our website at spenwoodbooks.com or drop us a line at iwasatthatgig@gmailcom.

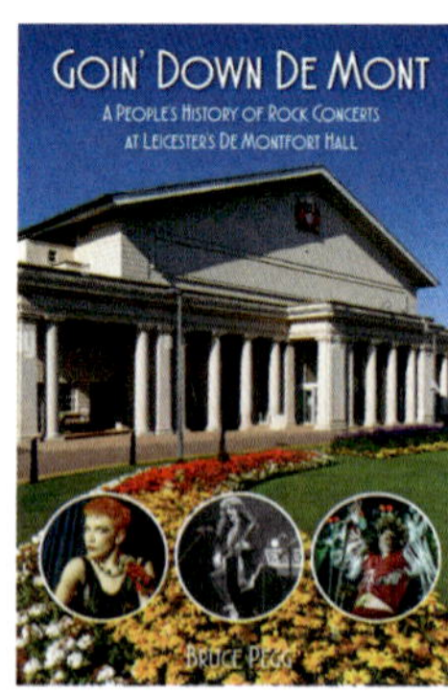

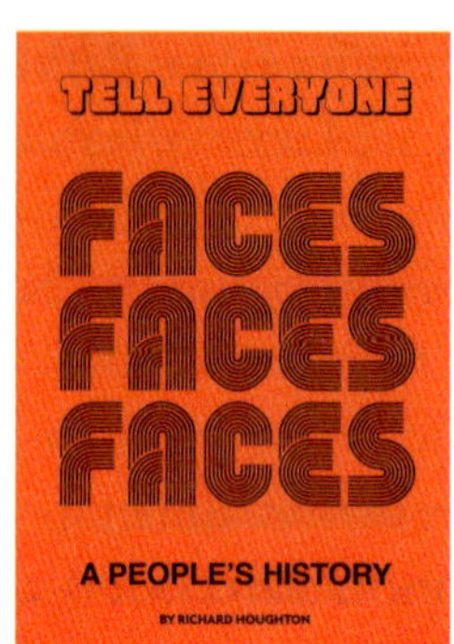

ODEON HAMMERSMITH
MEL BUSH presents
SLADE IN CONCERT plus SUPPORT
EVENING 8-0 p.m.
FRIDAY
MAY
17
CIRCLE
£1·00
2
BLOCK
3
SEAT
W57
No ticket exchanged nor money refunded
THIS PORTION TO BE RETAINED
FREE TRADE HALL, Peter St. Manchester
MEL BUSH presents
SLADE
IN CONCERT
SATURDAY, 7th MAY, 1977
at 7.30 p.m.
No Tickets Exchanged. No Money Refunded.
Official Programme Sold Only in the Hall.
STALLS
£2.00
including VAT
DD
7
RETAIN THIS PORTION
ABC Printers, Manchester
CITY HALL, Newcastle-upon-Tyne
M.C.P. presents—
SLADE plus Guests
Friday, 18th December 1981
Evenings 7-30
STALLS
£3.50
F
15
To be retained.
A. B. Cooper (Printers) Ltd. MANCHESTER
CAPITOL THEATRE, CARDIFF
EVENING 7-30 p.m.
MONDAY
APRIL
21
B
STALLS
£2·00
BLOCK B
I 4
NO TICKET EXCHANGED NOR MONEY REFUNDED
THIS PORTION TO BE RETAINED